D1289966

When in the winter of 1931–2 Britain first abandoned the gold standard and then free trade, two potent symbols of its nineteenth-century international economic predominance had gone within the space of little more than six months. Tim Rooth's comprehensive study in the political economy of protectionism examines the forces behind the abandonment of free trade and the way that Britain then used protection to bargain for trade advantages in the markets of her chief suppliers of food and raw materials. One result of the depression, greatly accentuated by the rise of protectionist barriers elsewhere in the world, was to heighten the importance of the British market, and particularly the dependence of primary producers, both within and outside the Empire, on Britain. The United Kingdom government, finding itself with enormously enhanced economic leverage, was therefore able to take advantage of this in a series of trade agreements both with the Commonwealth at Ottawa in 1932 and, comparatively neglected in previous studies, with the countries of Northern Europe and with Argentina. This book examines these, the World Economic and Monetary Conference of 1933, the trade dispute with Japan and the impact of Britain's trade treaty obligations on domestic agricultural protection. The symbiosis between economic policy and the deteriorating international political environment became all the more apparent in the negotiations with Germany and the USA in the late 1930s.

British protectionism and the international economy:
overseas commercial policy in the 1930s

LIBRARY
I.U.P.
Indiana, PA

382.30942
R6796

British protectionism and the international economy: overseas commercial policy in the 1930s

Tim Rooth

Principal Lecturer in the Department of Economics,
University of Portsmouth

CAMBRIDGE
UNIVERSITY PRESS

LIBRARY
I.U.P.
Indiana, PA.

Published by the Press Syndicate of the University of Cambridge
The Pitt Building, Trumpington Street, Cambridge CB2 1RP
40 West 20th Street, New York, NY 10011–4211, USA
10 Stamford Road, Oakleigh, Victoria 3166, Australia

© Cambridge University Press 1992

First published 1993

Printed in Great Britain at the University Press, Cambridge

A catalogue record for this book is available from the British Library

Library of Congress cataloguing in publication data

Rooth, Tim.
British Protectionism and the International
Economy: overseas commercial policy in the 1930s
    p.   cm.
Includes bibliographical references and index.
ISBN 0 521 41608 6
1. Great Britain – Commercial policy – History. 2. Protectionism –
Great Britain – History.   3. Great Britain – Foreign economic
relations. I. Title.
HF1533.R59 1993
382′.3′094109043 – dc20 92–8965 CIP

ISBN 0 521 41608 6 hardback

A00000546506A

UP

For my mother and the memory of my father

Contents

Preface

When two of the symbols of Britain's nineteenth-century economic hegemony, the gold standard and free trade, were abandoned in the winter of 1931–2, British external economic relations were revolutionised. One result of the new regime of protection and preferences was that access to the United Kingdom market, long determined by market forces alone, became subject to conscious regulation. One of the awful paradoxes of the 1930s was that in a decade scarred more than most by hunger and shortage, too many products sought too few outlets: selling them became a matter of privilege. As Britain entered into a series of trade agreements, the immense size of its market helped give government negotiators considerable leverage in their dealing with suppliers.

Historians have paid full attention to economic relations with the Empire, particularly the dominions. Sir Keith Hancock's classic study appeared in 1942, and since then Ian Drummond has made full use of official records to produce his authoritative surveys of imperial economic policy. Non-imperial relations have received much less attention, especially those with European suppliers. In this book I aim to make a contribution to filling this gap, and at the same time to take an overall view of British commercial policy in the 1930s, including the domestic implications of the treaty arrangements. It is a study of British policy, based mainly on UK official documents and seeing events primarily from London's perspective. To that extent it is perhaps more than usually open to re-interpretation, particularly from the records that have survived in other national archives. Incidentally, for reasons of style, I have used the terms Great Britain/ Britain and the UK interchangeably, and have also occasionally included Finland as part of Scandinavia.

It is a pleasure to acknowledge some of the many debts I have incurred in writing this book. I am one of many who have been inspired by John Saville, and he provided early encouragement and guidance. Robert Holland may be surprised to learn that it was he who first suggested this book. Colleagues at Portsmouth have provided support in many ways, and it may not be invidious to single out Cliff Gulvin for having borne more than his fair share. The process of research has been immensely aided by librarians and archivists. My debt to the Public Record Office will be evident from the footnotes. The library staff at the University of Portsmouth have also given highly valued assistance over the years, and I have benefited greatly from the help received when using sources at the Bank of England, Baring Brothers, the Modern Records Centre at the University of Warwick, the Bodleian Library, and the libraries of the London School of Economics, the Universities of Birmingham, Cambridge, and Newcastle, the House of Lords, Bradford City Archives and the Manchester Public Library. Cambridge University Press have proved easy publishers to work with. Anonymous readers have provided many useful suggestions, and Sheila McEnery has improved the clarity and consistency of the text.

I am also grateful for the assistance afforded by grants from the Social Science Research Council, the Nuffield Foundation, the Economic and Social Research Council and by the University of Portsmouth.

Some of the material in this book has appeared, mostly in a modified form, in other publications, and I am indebted to the editors of *The Agricultural History Review*, *The British Journal of Canadian Studies*, *The Economic History Review*, *The Journal of European Economic History*, and *The Scandinavian Economic History Review* for permission to draw on this writing.

I have obtained some pleasure from writing this book. I am not so confident that my family have. So my apologies, particularly to Iris, Geraldine and Bella, for absences and neglect, and my thanks for their forbearance; exasperation has rarely surfaced, and they have been immensely tolerant and supportive.

Tables

Introduction

On 21 September 1931 the United Kingdom abandoned the gold standard. On 1 March 1932 when the Import Duties Act came into effect, Britain had finally adopted full protection. Thus within less than six months two of the great symbols of Britain's leadership of the nineteenth-century international economy, the gold standard and free trade, had gone. Moreover, the Import Duties Act signified more than simple protection. By temporarily exempting Empire products from the new duties, and by including a bargaining clause, the construction of regional or imperial trading blocs was envisaged.

This accords with a view of how a once dominant economic power behaves in retreat. Robert Gilpin writes of Great Britain

As the periphery advances, as it frees itself from dependence on the core and the terms of investment shift to its advantage, the core retreats into protectionism or some form of preference system. It throws up barriers both to the export of capital and to the import of foreign goods. It favors preferential commercial arrangements.[1]

Robert Skidelsky argues of the emerging economic pluralism before the First World War that the spread of industrialisation created a paradox because it increased global interdependence at the same time as new democratic and nationalist forces were displaying growing intolerance of the *Pax Britannica*. In the face of such a threat to the stability of the international system, adjustments had to be made: either authority had to be raised to a new level, perhaps with international institutions, or interdependence had to be reduced to the level of existing international authority.[2] Ultimately with 'the disintegration of the wider system in the interwar years, there was an increasing tendency to see the economic future in terms of blocs'.[3] Stephen Krasner portrays the years between the wars

---

[1] Robert Gilpin, *American Power and the Multinationals: the political economy of foreign investment* (New York, 1975), 66.

[2] Robert J. Skidelsky, 'Retreat from leadership: the evolution of British economic foreign policy, 1870–1939', in B. M. Rowland (ed.), *Balance of Power or Hegemony?: the interwar monetary system* (New York, 1976), 164.   [3] *Ibid.*, 178.

as an interregnum between British nineteenth and American twentieth-century leadership of the international economy. Since in his view it is a hegemonic distribution of power that encourages an open trading system, the transitional period between the eras of British and American predominance saw the closure of the system.[4]

An open world economic system had been in Britain's interests in the mid-nineteenth century. It had enabled its industrialists to capitalise on Britain's technical and industrial leadership, and, of crucial importance to those familiar with the ideas of Malthus and Ricardo, it gave access to low cost foodstuffs and raw materials. The opening up of the international economy was in considerable measure a result of British action, including its unilateral adoption of free trade from the 1840s. The UK, as a potentially dominant state, had symbolic, economic and military capabilities to entice or compel less powerful countries to join the system.[5] By 1870 Britain's position at the apex of the international economy was unchallenged. The era of free trade was reaching its zenith, although with the United States standing conspicuously outside the movement. Britain had harnessed and was continuing to harness the productive resources of the regions of recent settlement to meet the burgeoning needs for foodstuffs and raw materials. In return, and as part of the process, it supplied manufactured goods and long-term investment. Capital exports were a vital component in the weaponry of an ascendant economic power seeking to shape, police and stabilise the international system. But they may also have played the paradoxical role of undermining Britain's pre-eminent international position. By nurturing its overseas competitors, Britain's capital exports may have contributed to its own demise. Skidelsky suggests that UK overseas investment diffused industrialisation and shifted the capacity to innovate from Britain to other countries.[6]

It is doubtful, however, whether British funds played such a direct role in financing industrialisation overseas. Sometimes, it is true, British entrepreneurs established textile or iron-works in Europe, especially in the first half of the nineteenth century, and some of these investments had an impact out of all proportion to their size. But for the most part British funds did not make an important direct contribution to the indus-

---

[4] Stephen D. Krasner, 'State power and the structure of international trade', *World Politics*, 28 (1976), 317–47. For similar views, see Robert Gilpin, *The Political Economy of International Relations* (Princeton, 1987), and Robert W. Cox, *Production, Power and World Order: social forces in the making of history* (New York 1987).

[5] Krasner, 'State power', 335–7; Gilpin, *American power*, 79–85; Skidelsky, 'Retreat from leadership', 154–8.

[6] Skidelsky, 'Retreat from leadership', 163. In similar vein Gilpin writes that though 'foreign investment is not the primary cause of the shift in the locus of industrial power from core to periphery, it both accentuates this tendency and tends to abort any effort to invigorate the core's industrial base'. *American power*, 77.

trialisation of its overseas rivals. If the industrial development of Western Europe or the United States had depended on British finance, it would have been long delayed – only a small proportion of these countries' total investment was supplied by the UK, and a minute fraction was channelled to industrial enterprises. Where British funds did supply a greater proportion of total investment needs, as in Canada, it has been argued that the net effect may well have discouraged industrialisation.[7] For many primary producing countries, borrowing from abroad served only to lock them more firmly into the international economy, and did little or nothing to stimulate diversification of their economies.

Instead, the connection between Britain's overseas lending and the industrial growth of its rivals was an indirect one. British funds contributed to their development in two major ways. The first of these lay in the boost they gave to primary production, sometimes through investment in land and mines, but principally through the construction of railways, port facilities and urban infrastructure. This helped ensure plentiful and cheap supplies for rivals as well as itself. The maintenance of free trade by the UK was an integral part of the growth-inducing process. Access to the British market enabled borrowing countries to service their debts, and it provided West European countries with the sterling to buy food and raw materials. The second vital contribution was the reinvestment of Britain's current account surplus. Counter-cyclical investment meant that the international system as a whole was never short of sterling. Charles Kindleberger lists this, together with the maintenance of an open market for 'distress' goods at times of overproduction, and the fulfilment of a lender of last resort function (discounting in a crisis) as the three major ways in which the UK stabilised the international economy before 1914.[8] Whether the gold standard also contributed to stability may long remain a matter of debate. If it did so, it was powerfully supplemented by other factors, and was confined to the industrial powers; for the periphery the gold standard mechanism was almost certainly a destabilising agent.[9]

[7] The increase in the money supply from imported capital is likely to be inflationary, even when in a country such as pre-1914 Canada a fairly sophisticated banking system provides some offset. A. K. Cairncross, *Home and Foreign Investment 1870–1913* (Cambridge, 1953), ch. 3. The corollary to this is that inflation is likely to be greatest in 'non-traded' and 'domestic' goods, as opposed to internationally traded goods. Therefore import substitution may be checked when capital imports are high because domestic capital is diverted into the non-international sectors. A. R. Hall, 'Capital imports and the composition of investment in a borrowing country', in A. R. Hall (ed.), *The Export of Capital from Britain 1870–1914* (1968), 143–52.

[8] C. P. Kindleberger, *The World in Depression, 1929–1939* (1973), 293–8. He added some more functions in the paperback edition and in subsequent work.

[9] A. G. Ford, *The Gold Standard 1880–1914: Britain and Argentina* (Oxford, 1962), where the gold standard mechanism is seen as reinforcing expansionary and contractionary movements in the Argentine economy.

In the course of the nineteenth century the UK shaped the international economy to its own particular needs. Britain also helped keep the system relatively free of crisis, and thereby further facilitated its integration and growth. Ultimately Britain contributed to its own demise as the pre-eminent power. In part this may have occurred because the international economy acted as an agent in the transfer of technology and in the transmission of industrialisation. Perhaps overseas investment fatally weakened the domestic economy. Certainly the scale of international investment was unprecedented, and in relation to national income dwarfed the foreign investments of the USA in the twentieth century.[10] An institutional bias in the London capital market might have deprived British industry of funds and have inhibited necessary structural change.[11] If so, evidence nonetheless suggests that overseas investment yielded higher returns than home investment, even when allowing for their greater risk.[12] Perhaps the City missed the more profitable ventures in Britain, but otherwise, judged by the criterion of private returns, the market acted rationally and overseas investment may have postponed a decline in the rate of profit. From the perspective of maintaining British power the problems were not merely the domestic costs of heavy overseas lending but the fact that the social return on these investments was shared by potential rivals.

Whatever the mechanism, British industrial hegemony was seriously challenged during the last quarter of the nineteenth century. UK steel output was exceeded by that of the USA in 1890 and by Germany in 1893. Britain's share of world exports in manufactures declined from 40·7 per cent in 1890 to 29·9 per cent in 1913.[13] In the half-century before 1914 imports, both in terms of value and volume, were growing faster than

---

[10] United States of America Department of Commerce, *Survey of Current Business* August 1982. By 1981 the stock of US private long-term international investments stood at $290·3 billion, approximately 9·9 per cent of gnp, a ratio which fell later in the decade. Britain's overseas assets stock of about £4 billion in 1913 was probably about 160 per cent of gnp. Even allowing for the scaling down of British overseas investments suggested by D. C. M. Platt, 'British portfolio investment overseas before 1870: some doubts', *Economic History Review*, 2nd ser., 33 (1980), 1–16, the discrepancy remains enormous.

[11] J. Saville 'Some retarding factors in the British economy before 1914', *Yorkshire Bulletin of Economic and Social Research*, 13 (1961), 51–60; W. P. Kennedy, *Industrial Structure, Capital Markets and the Origins of British Economic Decline* (Cambridge, 1987).

[12] M. Edelstein 'Realised rates of return on U.K. Home and Overseas portfolio investment in the age of high imperialism', *Explorations in Economic History*, 13 (1976), 283–329. But see Sidney Pollard, 'Capital exports, 1870–1914: harmful or beneficial?' *Economic History Review*, 2nd. ser., 37 (1985), 489–514 for a critique of these results as well as a wide-ranging survey of the debate.

[13] S. B. Saul 'The export economy 1870–1914', *Yorkshire Bulletin of Economic and Social Research*, 17 (1965), Special Number *Studies in the British Economy, 1870–1914*, ed. J. Saville, 12.

exports.[14] By the 1880s there was widespread concern in industry about foreign competition, and particularly about German rivalry. E. E. Williams, *Made in Germany* (1896), reflected and fed a growing awareness of the conditions faced by British producers. Anxiety was all the greater because wages appeared to be eating into profits.[15]

The problems faced by British entrepreneurs were greatly aggravated by the revival of protectionism among the larger European states after 1878, and by higher American tariffs from 1890. Industrial protection in the more sophisticated North American and West European markets was high and often aimed specifically at British exports. Roderick Floud has suggested that two courses of action were open to British businessmen: to develop new products, or to find new markets.[16] Again, British entrepreneurs acted rationally by taking both courses. They concentrated on higher quality exports to the industrial countries of Western Europe and the USA, and for the older products they sought new and bigger markets among the semi-industrial and primary producing countries of the southern hemisphere. The second response, however, was the predominant one.

The return to protection in the late nineteenth century meant that the European countries were in some measure detaching themselves from an international economy dominated by Britain who now lacked the power and resources to prevent them doing so.[17] A close assessment of the interest of the state at this time might have suggested that since Britain's hegemony was now threatened, Britain should leave the system.[18] One answer for the UK was to move to greater self-sufficiency, or to seek closer ties with the Empire and client states, thus perpetuating its dominance within a more restricted sphere. The main thrust of the Fair Trade movement of the 1880s was towards protection. In the early years of this century Joseph Chamberlain revitalised the movement and gave it a clear and explicitly imperial dimension. A formidable campaign came close to success. It probably failed because it embodied too many contradictions as well as threatening strongly entrenched interests. Not the least of its difficulties

---

[14] M. Kirby, *The Decline of British Power Since 1870* (1981), 2.

[15] J. Saville, 'Review article: the development of British industry and foreign competition 1875–1914', *Business History*, 12 (1970), 62.

[16] R. C. Floud, 'Britain 1860–1914: a survey', in R. C. Floud and D. McCloskey (eds.), *The Economic History of Britain since 1700*, II, *1860 to the 1970s* (Cambridge, 1981), 20.

[17] The process of detachment should not be exaggerated however – the multilateral economy evolved a new degree of refinement in the twenty years or so before 1914. S. B. Saul, *Studies in British Overseas Trade 1870–1914* (Liverpool, 1960), ch. 3.

[18] Krasner, 'State power', 341. He argues that vested interests and inertia delayed such a change. The response will be delayed until a cataclysmic event (war, famine or severe depression), forces a reassessment.

was having to create new forms of conceptualising the economy.[19] The vision of maintaining an old complementarity between Britain and the Empire was probably already false: economic nationalism was apparent in the dominions, certainly in Canada and Australia, and it was unlikely they would have been prepared to sacrifice their secondary industries. It is also questionable whether protection and preference would really have helped solve Britain's economic problen ~. Apart from iron and steel, import penetration was not a serious threat, and even in the steel industry many of the imports were of semi-manufactures which other sectors of the industry processed further. The outstanding problem was of competition in overseas markets, and the imperial solution hardly helped here. Even in the peak year of 1902 the Empire absorbed only 38·5 per cent of UK exports.[20] Not only were tariffs likely to raise costs and jeopardise exports to non-Empire markets, but they also carried with them the danger of retaliation, particularly if Europeans had greater difficulty in earning in Britain the sterling they needed for their imports. Here lay the fundamental problem of the imperial solution – it cut across Britain's global interests. This was most apparent in Britain's role as world shipper, and in the City of London's role as world banker and financier: the 'gentlemanly capitalists' were hostile to any policy that by restricting access to the British import market would have impaired their role by threatening the servicing and redemption of overseas debt.[21]

In effect Britain continued at the centre of the international economy, playing the part of stabiliser even while its predominance faded. The UK could still perform this stabilising function because it managed to avoid any external economic crisis. But despite signs of external strength the domestic economy was weak in the early years of the twentieth century. Gross domestic product per man-year grew at only 0·5 per cent a year between 1899 and 1913[22] and industrial productivity at a lower rate still. This was not only a slower growth rate than in late Victorian times, but was comfortably exceeded by Britain's competitors. Testimony to poor economic conditions is that by the early years of the twentieth century Britain alone among the countries of North-west Europe experienced substantial emigration. The UK merchandise trade balance had widened until 1904. During the next ten years it narrowed. Partly this was because

[19] Jim Tomlinson, *Problems of British Economic Policy, 1870–1945* (1981), ch. 3.

[20] F. Crouzet, 'Trade and Empire: the British experience from the establishment of free trade until the First World War', in B. M. Ratcliffe (ed.), *Great Britain and Her World, 1750–1914: Essays in Honour of W. O. Henderson* (Manchester, 1975), 221.

[21] P. J. Cain and A. G. Hopkins, 'Gentlemanly capitalism and British expansion overseas, 11: new imperialism, 1850–1945', *Economic History Review*, 2nd ser., 40 (1987), 1–26.

[22] R. C. O. Matthews, C. H. Feinstein and J. C. Odling-Smee, *British Economic Growth 1856–1973* (Oxford, 1982), 31.

of the sluggishness of the domestic economy; but exports received a stimulus from the rising incomes of the primary producers and from a great burst of overseas investment. The current account was helped by the growth of income from services: shipping receipts, especially high with rising freight rates and expanded world trade, were supplemented by income from investments that grew to around £200 million annually on the eve of the First World War. Britain's long-term creditor position was immensely strong and confidence in the pound remained high. A crisis at the centre was avoided and the British market remained open.

The cost was not immediately apparent. With hindsight it is clearer: failing to make much headway in the markets for newer and more sophisticated products in Western Europe and North America, Britain came to depend more heavily on the less industrial countries as an outlet for its manufactures. Capital exports had accentuated this process, giving the economy a curiously lopsided appearance. Before the war, textiles, iron and steel and coal accounted for 70 per cent of British exports.[23] The UK was supplying 70 per cent of world cotton textile exports, 80 per cent of coal, and had a virtual monopoly of world exports of ships. This dependence on a narrow range of export products was dangerous. Business decision-making had in many ways been rational in its own terms. It had meant exploiting Britain's comparative advantage in skill or labour-intensive technologies: shipbuilding exemplifies this. But what was rational, judged by immediate private returns, did not always accord with broader conceptions of social or national interest, all the more so when viewed in longer perspective. This is true of the slow progress of new production techniques, particularly those involving a deepening in capital, the structural rigidity of the economy reflected in the commodity composition of exports, and in heavy overseas investment, none of which necessarily met broader national interests, especially in the long term. In retrospect the dangers were apparent enough. Like any export economy with a narrow base, Britain was vulnerable to unfavourable shifts in demand, to the development of substitutes and to the emergence of new sources of supply. Above all, the ability to remain competitive in the supply of these products was to be crucial to its future prosperity. Before 1914 there were intimations of failing competitiveness and of unfavourable trends in world demand and supply conditions, but these were either muted or were masked by the overall expansiveness of the international economy. However, the war and the 1920s saw an acceleration in the pace of developments that undermined the internal stability and external balance of the UK economy. By the end of the 1920s the British economy no longer

---

[23] H. W. Richardson, 'Overcommitment in Britain before 1930', *Oxford Economic Papers*, 17 (1965), 240.

possessed the resilience to withstand an international crisis. Ultimately the pressures generated by the slump forced Britain off the gold standard and delivered the final blow to free trade. With their abandonment, Britain relinquished its pretensions to global economic leadership, seeking instead regional and imperial trading and monetary arrangements within the framework of a protectionist regime.

1 Britain's international economic position in the 1920s

Although industrial predominance had been ceded to the United States and Germany before 1914, Britain had remained the world's premier trader, shipper and financier, adhering not only to free trade, but by maintaining a strong balance of payments position, having no difficulty in continuing to operate the gold standard. A great burst of overseas investment, together with rising food and raw material prices, had stimulated exports, increasing Britain's dependence on the primary producing countries. There had not been, however, at least from the 1880s, any notable increase in relative dependence on the formal empire, whether measured by exports, imports or investment.

A growing proportion of UK output had been exported before 1914, especially in the last decade and a half before the war.[1] In effect, instead of meeting the challenge posed by the growing strength of its industrial competitors by developing newer lines of commodities, Britain had deflected it by finding new markets for the old products, and pumping up demand in those markets by the export of capital. By the 1920s this option was no longer available, and Britain paid the price for the earlier choice. Curiously enough, the growth record of the 1920s, as some economic historians have stressed, was quite respectable. It certainly marked an acceleration over the years 1899 to 1913. Between 1920 and 1929 industrial production grew at a rate of 2·8 per cent a year and industrial productivity by 3·8 per cent. Between 1924 and 1929 gdp increased annually by 3·1 per cent if measured by income, total factor productivity contributing 1·7 per cent of this.[2] There was also some structural change in favour of the newer and higher growth sectors of the economy, and a measure of managerial innovation may have paved the way for more effective control of large business units.[3] This is one side of the picture. The other is the appalling

[1] The export–output ratio in manufacturing industry rose from 114 in 1899 to 132 in 1913 (1929 = 100). R. C. O. Matthews, C. H. Feinstein and J. C. Odling-Smee, *British Economic Growth 1856–1973* (Oxford, 1982), 429, 433 and 436.   [2] *Ibid.*, 609.

[3] D. H. Aldcroft, 'Economic progress in Britain in the 1920s' in D. H. Aldcroft and H. W. Richardson (eds.), *The British Economy 1870–1939* (1969), 227–9. Leslie Hannah, 'Managerial innovation and the rise of the large-scale company in interwar Britain',

export record and the resulting high levels of unemployment concentrated in the old staples of cotton, shipbuilding and coal. Unemployment never dropped below a million after 1920, in every year at least 10 per cent of the insured workforce being without jobs. By the end of the 1920s Britain's international economic position had become very vulnerable, and with it adherence to the great symbols of pre-war status, the gold standard and free trade, was threatened. In addition, and in some respects a symptom of its weakness, Britain's economic reliance on the Empire had grown.

British exports

When in 1929 British exports reached their highest level between the wars they were still nearly a fifth below the volume of 1913.[4] This had little to do with the sluggishness of world demand – indeed according to Alfred Maizels's figures world exports of manufactures increased by 37·5 per cent between 1913 and 1929 – but was largely because of a dramatic fall in the UK's share of world trade. In 1913 Britain had accounted for 30·2 per cent of world manufactured exports, but by 1929 was responsible for only 20·4 per cent (in 1913 prices).[5]

These losses have often been attributed, at least in part, to an unfavourable composition of exports and to a peculiarly heavy dependence on the markets of primary producers. Britain was over-committed to exports of the wrong commodities and to the wrong places. Taking first the geographical distribution of exports, D. H. Aldcroft states that the concentration of overseas sales on the market of low income primary producers tended to damp down the growth of exports. Over two-thirds of all British exports went to primary producing countries: the incomes of these countries were depressed, especially in the 1930s, while the UK was easily the principal loser from the process of import-substitution in the semi-industrial countries.[6] Similarly, S. B. Saul has suggested that the

Economic History Review, 2nd ser., 27 (1974), 252–70. But see also N. Buxton, 'The role of the "New" industries in Britain during the 1930s: a reinterpretation', *Business History Review*, 49 (1975); G. von Tunzlemann, 'Structural change and leading sectors in British manufacturing, 1907–68', in C. P. Kindleberger and G. di Tella (eds.), *Economics in the Long View: Essays in Honour of W. W. Rostow* (1982), vol. 3; S. Broadberry, 'Unemployment in interwar Britain: a disequilibrium approach', *Oxford Economic Papers*, 35 (1983) and B. Alford, 'New industries for old? British industries between the wars', in R. Floud and D. McCloskey, *The Economic History of Britain since 1700*, II, *1860–1970s* (Cambridge, 1981).

[4] London and Cambridge Economic Services, *The British Economy Key Statistics 1900–1970* (1972), 14.
[5] A. Maizels, *Industrial Growth and World Trade* (Cambridge, 1963), Table A4, 5 and 6.
[6] D. H. Aldcroft, *The Inter-War Economy: Britain, 1919–1939* (1970), 247.

Table 1.1. *Percentage shares in world exports of manufactures,*
1913

	UK	Germany	France	USA
To industrial countries	19·2	28·5	15·5	16·5
To semi-industrial countries	55·9	15·1	6·0	9·5
To rest of world	29·2	32·4	11·2	9·5

Source: A. Maizels, *Growth and Trade* (Cambridge, 1970), Table A4.

geographical structure of trade, which had been favourable before the First
World War, was to operate increasingly to Britain's disadvantage
afterwards. This was because of the tendency for exports of manufactures
to non-industrial countries, and eventually between the industrial countries
themselves, to grow faster than those to semi-industrial countries such as
India, South Africa, Australia and New Zealand where Britain had, for
historical reasons, considerable competitive advantages.[7] Maizels also
argues that in the markets of the semi-industrial countries Britain was the
main victim from import-substitution and points out that between 1913
and 1959 this effect was considerably greater in the semi-industrial than in
the industrial economies.[8]

Much depends on the period being discussed. Between 1913 and 1929,
world exports of manufactures to industrial countries rose by 74 per cent,
to semi-industrial countries by 83 per cent and to the rest of the world by
99 per cent.[9] Table 1.1 shows that Britain's competitive position was
weakest in the markets growing least strongly, and was strongest in the
semi-industrial countries which increased their imports at the same pace as
total world trade in manufactures. Whatever may have happened after
1929, during the years between 1913 and 1929 Britain did not stand to lose
from the market distribution of its exports.

While Britain was served quite well by the geographical spread of its
exports, at least up until 1929, the commodity structure of its exports might
nonetheless have accounted for part of its declining share of world trade.
The antiquated composition of European exports plays an important part
in I. Svennilson's analysis of the need for a transformation of the European
economies between the wars.[10] A classification of exports into those which

---

[7] S. B. Saul, 'The export economy 1870–1914', *Yorkshire Bulletin of Economic and Social
Research*, 17 (1965), Special number, *Studies in the British Economy, 1870–1914*, ed. J.
Saville, 12.   [8] Maizels, *Growth and Trade*, 151.
[9] *Ibid.*, Tables A5, A7, A9, A11.
[10] I. Svennilson, *Growth and Stagnation in the European Economy* (Geneva, 1954).

Table 1.2. *1913 percentage share of trade in manufactures grouped by rates of growth, 1913–1929*

	Expanding	Stable	Declining
UK	14	18	67
USA	33	20	47
France	18	19	63
Germany	28	29	42
Belgium	13	34	53
Japan	3	10	87

Source: H. Tyszynski, 'World trade in manufactured commodities 1899–1950', *Manchester School of Economic and Social Studies*, 19 (1951). Calculated from Tables 2 and 7.

accounted for an expanding, stable or declining share of world trade in manufactures reveals the positions shown in Table 1.2.

Only Japan appears to have had a poorer commodity structure of trade than the UK. However, this can only act as a crude measure of trade structure because some commodities within the expanding group were growing faster than others, and some in the declining group were doing worse than others.

A more accurate impression of the UK's position at the outset of the period can be obtained by measuring its share of world trade in each commodity group in 1913 and then assuming that these shares had been retained in 1929. The difference between the hypothetical percentage share for 1929 and the actual percentage share for 1913 will therefore reflect the gain or loss through changes in the structure of world trade. Calculations from Tyszynski's figures of world trade in manufactures show that if the UK had retained shares of world trade in each of the commodity groups, it would have had 28·3 per cent of world trade in 1929, only 1·6 per cent less than in 1913.[11] Since Britain's actual share, on Tyszynski's figure, was 23·6 per cent, it appears that the major cause of declining share was not trade structure but competitive weakness. This is substantiated by R. E. Baldwin's analysis.[12] Using a different classification system, he calculated that between 1900 and 1928 the UK's trade structure was positively helpful, and that export losses were due exclusively to competitive failings. Maizels has estimated that between 1913 and 1929, the UK lost only $10 million of exports because of commodity and area patterns of trade, while

[11] H. Tyszynski, 'World trade in manufactured commodities, 1899–1950', *Manchester School of Economic and Social Studies*, 19 (1951), 278–9.

[12] R. E. Baldwin, 'The commodity composition of trade: selected industrial countries, 1900–1954', *Review of Economics and Statistics*, 40 (1958).

$860 million were lost as the result of falling shares in individual markets.[13] Svennilson, although concerned to stress Europe's poor export structure, nevertheless tends to confirm the picture of competitiveness as the decisive element in world trade. He does point out, however, that a breakdown of trade into smaller commodity groups (he uses only six commodity groups for manufactures) might lead to trade composition being credited with a bigger role in explaining world market shares.[14]

This can be illustrated by the example of transport equipment. Tyszynski's fairly fine classification allows a distinction to be made between railways, ships etc. (which he terms 'old means of transport'), and cars, aircraft etc. ('modern means of transport'). In Svennilson's and Baldwin's classification 'old' and 'modern' transport are lumped together as one category. The UK was a major supplier of the older means of transport before the First World War and a relatively minor supplier of new transport equipment. One suspects that an even more rigorous classification, although impossible to carry out, might reveal that the UK was a better supplier of coal-fired ships and a rather poorer competitor in oil-fired and diesel vessels, the type for which world demand in the 1920s was relatively high. So even within the classification used by Tyszynski, the structural position is not given its full weight.

An attempt is made below to assess the role of structural factors in the loss of market shares in some dominion markets. Nineteen commodity groups are used.[15] Several interesting points emerge from this analysis. First, taking the full period 1913–29, structural changes in the composition of imports account for a major part of the UK's reduced share in four of the dominion markets. So, contrary to the usual result in this type of analysis, structural elements were more important than 'competitive' factors in four of the five dominions examined. The exception was India where it emerges clearly that structural factors up to 1929 accounted for only the most minimal of losses when compared to the massive 'competitive' loss.

Secondly, these calculations suggest that it was only after 1924 that structural factors became an important threat to British exports. Before 1924 losses in the southern dominions were small, the Indian structure was

[13] Maizels, *Growth and Trade*, 200. At 1913 prices.
[14] Svennilson, *Growth and Stagnation*, 194.
[15] Alcoholic beverages; coal; iron and steel – pigs, billets, blooms and ingots; iron and steel-bars, rods, plates etc; iron and steel – other (including hardware); agricultural implements and machinery; electrical machinery and apparatus; other machinery; motor cars etc. and parts; other metals and manufactures thereof; yarn and thread (including wool tops); cotton piece goods; woollen piece goods; other piece goods; other textiles (including apparel); earthenware (including bricks), glass and glassware; wood and timber and manufactures thereof; paper newsprint; leather and manufactures thereof.

Table 1.3. *Market shares held by UK of selected commodities in dominion markets, 1913–1929 (percentages)*

	Actual shares		Hypothetical shares
	1913	1929	1929
Canada	23·9	15·8	17·7
Australia	57·2	44·8	49·0
New Zealand	69·9	46·0	55·0
South Africa	68·3	43·9	55·6
India (by sea)	79·1	54·1	76·5

Changes due to

	Structural factors	Competitive factors	Total change
Canada	−6·2	−1·9	−8·1
Australia	−8·2	−4·2	−12·4
New Zealand	−14·9	−9·0	−23·9
South Africa	−12·7	−11·7	−24·4
India (by sea)	−2·6	−22·4	−25·0

1913–1924

	Actual shares		Hypothetical shares
	1913	1924	1924
Canada	23·9	27·1	29·2
Australia	57·2	54·4	55·4
New Zealand	69·9	58·4	68·1
South Africa	68·3	61·3	65·3
India (by sea)	79·1	69·2	78·9

Changes due to

	Structural factors	Competitive factors	Total change
Canada	+5·3	−2·1	+3·2
Australia	−1·8	−1·0	−2·8
New Zealand	−1·8	−9·7	−11·5
South Africa	−3·0	−4·0	−7·0
India (by sea)	−0·2	−9·7	−9·9

Table 1.3. (*cont.*)

1924–1929			Hypothetical
	Actual shares		shares
	1924	1929	1929
Canada	27·1	15·8	17·5
Australia	54·4	44·8	49·4
New Zealand	58·4	46·0	45·4
South Africa	61·3	43·9	49·7
India (by sea)	69·2	54·1	66·5
Changes due to			
	Structural factors	Competitive factors	Total change
Canada	−9·6	−1·7	−11·3
Australia	−5·0	−4·6	−9·6
New Zealand	−13·0	+0·6	−12·4
South Africa	−11·6	−5·8	−17·4
India (by sea)	−2·7	−12·4	−15·1

Source: Calculated from Parliamentary Papers, *Statistical Abstract for the British Empire* (Various years).

virtually neutral, and there was a favourable shift in Canadian imports. Indeed, if cars are excluded from the calculations, the UK would have made structural gains in New Zealand and Australia.

'Competitive' losses were far more severe, certainly in the cases of India and New Zealand. In view of the dislocation of supplies caused by the war this is not surprising, and UK exporters had to fight their way back into these markets after 1918. In the southern dominions, British businessmen, aided by preferential tariffs, were able to deal with Japanese competition fairly easily. The United States proved more difficult to dislodge, but again, aided by preferences and also by the depreciated pound, British exporters made some headway against American competition. If the war had stimulated non-European competition, it had also eliminated Germany as a supplier, and postwar ill-feeling was responsible for an embargo being maintained against German goods by Australia and New Zealand until August 1922 and September 1923 respectively.[16] Germany had supplied 11·4 per cent of the Australian market in 1913, and rather more in items competitive with the UK. By 1923/4, the figure was about 1 per cent. In New Zealand Germany had been a less important competitor, and after the war the UK had not only to meet United States and Japanese competition,

[16] Committee on Industry and Trade, *Survey of Overseas Markets* (1925), 360–1 and 371–6.

Table 1.4. *Shares in world trade by UK, 1913–1929*

	1913	1929	Change
Iron and steel	36·5	25·1	−10·5
Non-ferrous metals	10·4	13·9	+3·5
Chemicals	21·8	18·8	−3·0
Non-metalliferous materials	16·9	16·4	−0·5
Miscellaneous materials	10·6	10·4	−0·2
Industrial equipment (non-electrical)	28·1	20·8	−7·3
Electrical goods	23·3	21·3	−2·0
Agricultural equipment	21·9	7·7	−14·2
Railways, ships etc.	48·2	45·9	−2·3
Motor-cars, aircrafts etc.	17·1	11·7	−5·4
Spirits and tobacco	30·5	38·3	+7·8
Textiles	44·6	36·0	−8·6
Apparel	25·7	20·3	−5·4
Metal manufactures nes[a]	24·0	16·9	−7·1
Books, films, cameras, etc.	17·0	23·6	+6·6
Finished goods nes	22·3	23·8	+1·5
Non-classified	20·7	33·8	+13·1
Total	29·9	23·6	−6·3

Source: Tyszynski, 'World trade in manufactured commodities', 278 and 279.
[a] nes = not elsewhere specified.

but also Australian (steel and wire products, glass bottles, paints) and Canadian competition (cars, wire and photographic supplies).

Britain suffered very substantial losses in market shares between 1924 and 1929, and in at least three cases (New Zealand, South Africa and Canada) shifts in the pattern of import demand were of major importance. The competitive position varied enormously – from a minor gain in New Zealand, a fairly trivial loss in Canada to a major decline in India. It is significant that the losses in India were not restricted to textiles; competitive losses were made in practically every commodity group, including the important iron, steel and machinery markets.

The analysis confirms the view, denied by the calculations of Tyszynski, Baldwin and Maizels, that Britain had become over-committed to selling the wrong commodities and was too dependent on those for which world demand was growing only slowly. This result may reflect the greater number of commodities analysed, but the sample of countries is of course a small one, and, with the exception of India, where structural shifts between 1913 and 1929 were muted, all the countries conform to the 'region of recent settlement' type. Nor, of course, was the structure of demand independent of price levels, so the high price of British products may itself have contributed to the slow growth of demand. Moreover, lack of competitiveness accounted for substantial losses, particularly in India and South Africa where preferences were very small. This is underlined by Table 1.4 which shows that on a world scale Britain suffered losses in most groups of commodities.

Case studies of some of the more important products reveal more of the factors accounting for the decline.

Iron and steel

Britain's share of the world market in iron and steel fell from 25·6 per cent in 1913 to 25·1 per cent in 1929 according to Tyszynski's figures. If exports are measured simply by tonnage, the UK was overhauled in the 1920s by Belgium/Luxembourg, France and Germany (by 1929 reverting to its pre-war dominance).[17] Part of the reason for British problems in iron and steel exports does seem to have been in their market distribution, and the UK was badly hit by the development of the steel industry in the dominions. Maizels points to the decline of imports into Oceania, and Svennilson cites the concentration of British exports on 'stagnating British Commonwealth markets' as part of the explanation for the decline in the British share of world steel exports.[18] In all non-European countries, world output (excluding the USA and USSR) rose from 1·2 million tons in 1913 to 9·6 million tons in 1936–7.[19] Galvanised sheets capacity in India, Australia, Canada and Japan, tinplate production in India, and rail production in India and Australia were only some of the examples. The 'rest of Europe' – i.e., excluding the four main producers – an area where Britain was traditionally weak, developed its capacity far less in this period. The industry, devoid of the major innovations that had spurred its growth in the late nineteenth century, expanded less rapidly in the inter-war period, but the use of autarkic policies created problems for the European industry as a whole, and, as Steven Tolliday argues, '[i]n the face of such a situation Britain could not regain its previous position in world steel trade whatever its competitive performance'.[20]

But British losses were not simply a result of the development of local steel capacity. The UK was also failing to retain its share of imports in

[17] D. L. Burn, *The Economic History of Steelmaking 1867–1939: a study in competition* (1940), 394.
[18] Maizels, *Growth and Trade*, 245 and 246; Svennilson, *Growth and Stagnation*, 138.
[19] Committee on Industry and Trade, *Survey of Metal Industries* (1928), 65, 67, 71, 107 and 109. British exports and employment may have been affected by this process, but British capital, by financing such developments, obtained at least some offset. See H. Hughes, *The Australian Iron and Steel Industry, 1848–1962* (Melbourne, 1964), 85, 102 and 106.
[20] Steven Tolliday, *Business, Banking and Politics: The Case of British Steel, 1918–1939* (Cambridge, Mass., 1987), 18–19.

many of these markets, notably in the biggest of them all, India, where Belgium was proving a formidable competitor. Setbacks were also experienced in Argentina, Brazil, Japan and Egypt. On the other hand gains were made in the share of Australian imports held by the UK, imperial preference being cited as a factor.[21]

Underlying these losses was a notable lack of competitiveness. By the late 1920s labour productivity was substantially lower than in Germany and Belgium, and fuel consumption much higher. Part of the problem arose from the high capitalisation costs incurred in the postwar boom, a substantial amount in fixed interest debt.[22] Yet, as Svennilson argues, this was not uniquely a British problem, and in the case of Sweden, where firms also became highly indebted, they were partly taken over by the banks which then enforced rationalisation.[23] British firms, many of them with high reserves from the war and postwar boom, were able to survive through much of the 1920s without coming under bank control. Yet profits were too low for new capital to be attracted into the industry. The industry did not escape the general British trend of the 1920s towards greater concentration, and indeed there was some increase in bank intervention. But there was nothing to match the rationalisation of West European industry. Plants remained small, poorly sited, and unintegrated by European and American standards, and techniques, particularly in blast furnaces, were well behind best practice elsewhere. Belgian and French producers had the advantages of a fresh start after the war, much of the rebuilding being subsidised by government grants, and French and Belgian prices, reflecting higher productivity and probably depreciated currencies, were much lower than British. Only German domestic prices matched the British, and German steel exporters had the advantage of differential pricing, subsidising their exports by higher domestic charges.[24] For some products, British prices were not so uncompetitive. A marked trend in the 1920s was for British producers to import semi-manufactured steel and work up finished products such as plates, sheets, rails and tubes.[25] When open-hearth steel was specified, the gap between British and Continental prices was smaller than when the open-hearth product had to compete against Thomas steel.[26] But there can be no doubt that Britain's reduced share in world steel exports reflected not simply an unfavourable market dependence but a failure to compete.

[21] Burn, *Steelmaking*, 397 and Balfour Committee, *Survey of Metal Industries*, 66.
[22] Burn, *Steelmaking*, 417 and 434, and J. Vaizey, *The History of British Steel* (1974), 12–13.
[23] Svennilson, *Growth and Stagnation*, 133.
[24] Burn, *Steelmaking*, 427–8; Svennilson, *Growth and Stagnation*, 128–9.
[25] *Survey of Metal Industries*, 51–4.   [26] Burn, *Steelmaking*, 429–30.

Capital goods

Turning to the broad category of capital goods, the UK would appear to have been in a position of strength before the First World War. Although no longer dominating world exports of capital goods as it had done at the turn of the century, with 31·1 per cent of the markets Britain was still just ahead of Germany as the principal supplier.[27] The concentration of capital goods exports to the smaller industrial countries and semi-industrial countries where Britain was traditionally strong helped to account for this position. Moreover, capital goods were an expanding sector of world trade. It is true that superficially Britain appeared to be at a disadvantage in the composition of capital goods exports because railway vehicles, ships, power generators and textile machinery were in the relatively declining categories, but Maizels calculates that the UK actually made a marginal gain in changes in world trade in capital goods between 1913 and 1937.[28]

The geographical pattern of trade does not appear to have been particularly unkind to British exports, although not as favourable as to capital goods from the USA. As mentioned above, capital goods exports went mainly to the smaller industrial and the semi-industrial countries, and the UK dominated the imports of India and the southern dominions. The overwhelming explanation for Britain's declining share of world exports of capital goods lay in competitive failure.

The main exception to this was electrical machinery, and here, at least until the mid-1920s, the UK was able to capitalise on Germany's war-induced decline as a competitor. This was true to a limited extent in Europe, and more especially in the dominions, particularly South Africa.[29] But yet again the major beneficiary in practically every market was the USA, and it is noticeable that in India, New Zealand and South Africa the UK made large relative losses between 1924 and 1929.[30]

For non-electrical machinery the UK share of world exports was slipping even before 1925–6, and this despite the position of Germany. Once more the USA gained most from Germany's decline. In some spheres such as railway equipment, the UK maintained its share of world trade, although the volume of exports fell. The UK was a highly efficient supplier of custom built locomotives, although no doubt helped in Latin America by British ownership of railways, particularly in Argentina. Britain remained the predominant supplier of textile machinery, although there was increasing competition. There was a big absolute and relative decline in British exports of agricultural machinery. Sales to Europe, and above all

[27] Maizels, *Growth and Trade*, 276.   [28] *Ibid.*, 275 and 282.
[29] *Survey of Metal Industries*, 337–45.
[30] Parliamentary Papers, *Statistical Abstract of the British Empire.*

to Russia, collapsed, although the USA continued to supply large quantities of agricultural machinery to the Soviet Union. The huge domestic sales of the USA probably gave it an advantage, and it dominated the world market in harvesting machinery, most of which was mass produced.[31] The Balfour Report noted that up to the mid-1920s the USA had increased its share of all machinery imports into Europe, the dominions, Central and South America and the Far East.[32]

Textiles

The industry most vulnerable to world market conditions was textiles, and particularly the enormous cotton weaving section. Sales, probably freakishly high in 1913,[33] fell drastically during and after the war. The cause of low postwar sales was a combination of import substitution and foreign competition, principally though not exclusively from Japan.

Yarn exports were fairly well maintained, despite a smaller world market.[34] The UK was unusually dependent on European outlets, and as these proved highly resilient during the 1920s they provided an offset to the UK's competitive losses in India and elsewhere, with the net result that the British share of world trade in cotton yarns probably increased.[35] India was the principal loser from the development of spindleage in China, an important market before the war.

The greatest misfortunes were in the piece-goods sector, where the volume of British exports fell by over 40 per cent between 1910–13 and 1927–9, and continued to decline afterwards. Industry overseas had developed rapidly during the war, and in a number of countries expansion was maintained during the 1920s. There were enormous gains in the capacity of India, Japan, China and Brazil. From a British perspective, the most disastrous of these was the growth of the Indian industry. Such was the extraordinary dominance of India as an outlet for Lancashire's piece-goods that at least one-third of the decline in British exports of cotton was attributable to the collapse of the Indian market alone.[36] The greater part of this decline was the result of the growth of Indian production, encouraged by higher tariffs, especially after the 1919 Fiscal Autonomy

[31] *Survey of Metal Industries*, 167.   [32] *Ibid.*, 209–13.
[33] S. B. Saul, *Studies in British Overseas Trade, 1870–1914* (Liverpool, 1960), 190.
[34] Committee on Industry and Trade, *Survey of Textile Industries* (1928), 69. 'Exports of all the countries for which comparable figures are given...averaged 287,500 metric tons in 1910–13 and 200,700 metric tons in 1924–6, a loss of 30%.' In 1927 UK exports of yarn were about 8 per cent below the 1910–13 level, although they slipped in 1928 and 1929.
[35] *Ibid.*, 71. In 1910–13, British yarn represented 48 per cent in value of world exports of yarn, while they represented 51 per cent in 1924–6.
[36] L. G. Sandberg, *Lancashire in Decline: A Study in Entrepreneurship, Technology and International Trade* (Columbus, 1974), 184.

Convention had given India a virtually free hand over import duties. Although there is some evidence that Lancashire did not think the tariff that important, at least in the early 1920s, an informed observer, Henry Clay, later commented: 'When our Government granted fiscal autonomy to India, as personally I think they were bound to do, they put permanently out of employment about one quarter of the operatives in Lancashire.'[37] Clearly there were adverse movements and developments in the structure of world trade that were beyond Lancashire's control. Moreover, it is difficult to believe that very much could have been done to counter competition from low cost countries. The industry has been criticised for the slow adoption of ring-spinning and of automatic looms, and for its excessive adherence to specialised spinning and weaving sheds.[38] It is true that the industry demonstrated increasing uncompetitiveness in the 1920s. Over-capitalisation, particularly from the short, sharp postwar boom, was one factor, and whatever may have been the rationality of sticking to the 'stubborn mule' before 1913, later technical developments gave a pronounced premium to ring-spinning as well as enhancing the advantage of the automatic loom, neither very widespread in the Lancashire of the 1920s. But as Gary Saxonhouse and Gavin Wright observe, the cotton industry in New England, 'the birthplace of both ring-spinning and integrated mills, experienced a collapse which was if anything even more thorough-going'.[39] Clearly technical progressivism was not enough, and any industry in a developed economy was going to find enormous difficulty in competing against determined import substitution and against low wage and efficient competitors. The Japanese industry was making huge strides in productivity, and wages were low.[40]

Losses were made world-wide – in the Far East, the Near East, East and South Africa, Canada and Latin America. Japanese competition was

---

[37] Commenting on a paper by A. R. Burnett-Hurst, 'Lancashire and the Indian market', *Journal of the Royal Statistical Society*, pt. 3 (1932).

[38] W. Lazonick, 'The cotton industry', in B. Elbaum and W. Lazonick (eds.), *The Decline of the British Economy* (Oxford, 1986).

[39] G. R. Saxonhouse and G. Wright, 'New evidence on the stubborn English mule and the cotton industry, 1878–1920', *Economic History Review*, 2nd ser. 37 (1984), 507–19.

[40] There were tremendous advances in labour productivity in the Japanese cotton industry in the later 1920s. The weaving sections experienced rising productivity earlier in the decade and then continued in the later 1920s and the 1930s. By contrast, the spinning sectors only showed much progress from 1926. See G. C. Allen, *A Short Economic History of Japan* (3rd edn 1972), 120. According to figures in G. E. Hubbard, *Eastern Industrialisation and Its Effect on the West* (1935), 119 and 120, daily output per female worker in the spinning mills rose from 18·13 lb in 1925 to 22·44 lb in 1929; the equivalent annual output in the weaving factories was 25,083 and 44,967 yards. Gary Saxonhouse, 'Productivity change and labour absorption in Japanese cotton spinning, 1891–1935', *Quarterly Journal of Economics*, 91 (1977), points to efficiency improvements of such a type that between 1922 and 1935 a substantial increase in output was accompanied by a decline in employment.

Table 1.5. *Unit values of exports of manufactures from the main industrial countries and from their competitors (in terms of $US), 1913–1929* 1899 = 100

Exporting countries	1913	1929
France		
1 Exports	112	143
2 Exports from competing countries	115	162
1 as a percentage of 2	97	88
Germany		
1 Exports	108	147
2 Exports from competing countries	113	163
1 as a percentage of 2	96	90
United Kingdom		
1 Exports	125	189
2 Exports from competing countries	111	149
1 as a percentage of 2	113	127
Other Western Europe		
1 Exports	100	126
2 Exports from competing countries	117	165
1 as a percentage of 2	85	76
United States		
1 Exports	112	134
2 Exports from competing countries	109	134
1 as a percentage of 2	103	100
Japan		
1 Exports	111	160
2 Exports from competing countries	122	187
1 as a percentage of 2	91	86

Source: Maizels, *Growth and Trade*, 205.

particularly sharp, especially for lower grade textiles. It certainly aggravated Lancashire's position in India where exporters found themselves with a declining share of a sharply contracting import market, and it accounted for the greater part of British losses in China and in Turkey.[41] There were other competitors too, and the United States made inroads into Canadian and Latin American markets, and Italy and to a lesser extent France into Egypt and North Africa. On the other hand, the UK held on to the sales of high quality cotton goods. In high income markets, for example Australia and New Zealand, the UK's pre-war share was

[41] *Survey of Textile Industries*, 74 and 112; Svennilson, *Growth and Stagnation*, 296–8 and Sandberg, *Lancashire in Decline*.

maintained, although no doubt helped by tariff preferences. Sales volumes to Europe increased, and even where tariffs were high, as in the USA and Brazil, Britain's share of reduced imports was maintained by dint of virtually monopolising the highest quality goods. In contrast to Brazil, tariffs were low in Argentina and the UK lost its share of the market because of fierce competition in lower quality sectors.[42] Technical conservatism and uncompetitiveness certainly accelerated Lancashire's decline, but world trends were operating against the industry and it paid the price for excessive dependence on one major market, so that even on the eve of the depression cotton had all the hallmarks of a depressed industry.

Woollen textile exports were affected by some of the same features as cotton textiles, although the decline was a good deal less dramatic and damaging. World markets for woollen products had been sluggish for a generation or more before the First World War, and by the mid-1920s international trade in tops, yarns and piece-goods, despite the addition of national frontiers, was generally smaller than it had been on the eve of the war. The Balfour Committee concluded that by the middle of the 1920s the UK had probably held its share of the tops market but lost its share of the declining markets in yarn.[43] The position for woollen and worsted manufactures was less certain. International trade was probably smaller than before the war, and the committee thought that the UK may have lost its share if calculated by weight, although in value terms this share had been maintained. The main problem for the industry was the decline of the European market. As with cotton, British woollen exports increased their share in Australia, and lost in India, South Africa and Argentina, but, unlike cotton, made gains in the Far East, notably in Japan.

Conclusions

The earlier analysis of the structural and competitive factors in Britain's declining share of world trade suggested that at least for the dominions structural factors may account for a larger part of the loss than has generally been thought. Yet even these calculations make it quite clear that a major part of the shortfall was the result of competitive failings. Contemporary accounts echo, but more loudly, the concern of late-nineteenth-century consular reports about marketing techniques, inadequate stocks, and, more persistently in the 1920s, about packaging. It is difficult to assess the responsibility of failures in marketing for Britain's competitive position. But in aggregate they were probably unimportant when compared with prices.

[42] *Survey of Textile Industries*, 56, 75 and 119–21.   [43] *Ibid.*, 190, 191, and 221–28.

Maizels has compiled a table of the unit values of exports of manufactures from the main industrial countries and from their competitors (Table 1.5).

The deterioration in Britain's position, even from 1913, was very marked and in stark contrast to the experience of competitors. Calculations by John Redmond of the real exchange rate suggest that by some measures, using retail prices, sterling may have been between 20 and 25 per cent overvalued in 1925–6, although the gap narrowed towards the end of the decade.[44] Estimates of price elasticity of demand vary considerably: Maizels calculates one for British exports of − 1·40, Harberger one of at least − 1·35, and probably near or above − 2, while Zelder estimates that elasticities for United States and British exports might have been of the order of − 3·0.[45] Moggridge, having reviewed the literature, plumps for an export elasticity of demand of − 1·5, although stating that this is conservative.[46] On the basis of such an estimate, a relative deterioration of Britain's competitive position of over 12 per cent between 1913 and 1929 might therefore account for exports being nearly one-fifth below the volume they would otherwise have obtained – and this, if anything, is likely to be an underestimate.

To summarise, the geographical distribution of UK exports was not in itself a problem: the least dynamic markets were those of the industrial countries themselves. On the other hand, although Britain was selling to markets which otherwise were expanding, the products being sold may well have been the wrong kind – this was certainly true of sales to the dominions. But uncompetitiveness, above all price uncompetitiveness, which had been compounded by the overvaluation of sterling, was the major cause of trade losses.

Balance of payments and the gold standard

The failure of British exports to recover to anything like their pre-war level was a major and underlying source of weakness in the balance of payments. This in turn meant that maintaining the value of sterling once the gold standard had been restored in 1925 became immensely difficult.

The choice of parity in 1925 undoubtedly aggravated the problems of UK exporters. There is some evidence that the return to gold was seen as

---

[44] J. Redmond, 'The sterling overvaluation of 1925: a multilateral approach, *Economic History Review*, 2nd ser., 37 (1984), 520–32.

[45] Maizels, *Growth and Trade*, 211–16; A. C. Harberger, 'Some evidence on the international price mechanism', *Journal of Political Economy*, 65 (1957), 521; R. E. Zelder, 'Estimates of elasticities of demand for exports of the United Kingdom and the United States, 1921–1938', *Manchester School of Economic and Social Studies*, 26 (1958).

[46] D. Moggridge, *British Monetary Policy, 1924–31. The Norman Conquest of $4·86* (Cambridge, 1972), 245.

a way of solving unemployment, concentrated as it was in the export industries: British exports would only recover when the international economy was functioning smoothly again, and a precondition for this was international financial stability associated with a fully operational gold standard. Probably the City had other issues uppermost in its mind, the chief of these being restoration of London's position as the world financial centre. There was a clear defensive motivation behind the authorities' decision to return to gold in 1925, and, the Cunliffe Report notwithstanding, the decision does mark a shift in policy from the early 1920s. The general adoption of the gold-exchange standard centred on London with European currencies linked to sterling would have enabled Britain to economise on its slender gold reserves, to run balance of payments deficits and may well have facilitated trade with other countries in the system.[47] The Americans, aware of Britain's motives, opposed the scheme, advocating instead a full gold standard. By early 1925 it was evident that Britain's objectives had not been achieved. In Europe only relatively minor economic powers such as Austria, Hungary and Danzig were tied to the British pound. Moreover, at least two dominions, South Africa and Australia, were likely to break with sterling and link with gold.[48] Adoption of the gold standard was therefore in large measure forced by the need to meet the challenge of the United States. Indicative of Britain's reduced power is that American help in the form of stand-by credits and low discount rates was necessary.[49]

The choice of the pre-war parity of £3 17s 10½d per ounce of gold or $4·866 to the pound, was a major source of weakness in the international financial system of the late 1920s. It probably made it not only more difficult for the southern dominions to export, but also contributed to the depression in the Scandinavian countries.[50] Moggridge makes a rough estimate that the British balance of payments was worsened by £80 million as a result of the 11 per cent appreciation of sterling between 1924 and 1925.[51]

[47] Frank C. Costigliola, 'Anglo-American financial rivalry in the 1920s', *Journal of Economic History*, 37 (1977), 911–34. The remainder of this paragraph draws on Costigliola's article.
[48] *Ibid.*, pp. 923–4 and L. S. Pressnell, '1925: the burden of sterling', *Economic History Review*, 2nd ser. 31 (1978), 80–1.
[49] Elmer R. Wicker, 'Federal reserve monetary policy, 1922–1933: a re-interpretation', *Journal of Political Economy*, 73 (1965), 334–5. The credits were not used.
[50] Pressnell, '1925', 84; R. A. Lester, 'The gold parity depression in Norway and Denmark, 1925–1928', *Journal of Political Economy*, 45 (1937), 433–65, and S. N. Broadberry, 'The North European depression of the 1920s', *Scandinavian Economic History Review*, 32 (1984), 159–67.
[51] Moggridge, *British Monetary Policy*, 246–9; see also N. H. Dimsdale, 'British monetary policy and the exchange rate, 1920–38', in W. A. Eltis and P. J. N. Sinclair (eds.), *The Money Supply and the Exchange Rate* (Oxford, 1981).

British prices had become badly out of line with American in the second half of 1919,[52] and subsequently, despite the severe deflation of the early 1920s, this gap was never closed. The gamble that American prices would rise, so sparing Britain the pain of adjustment that the 1925 parity otherwise implied, failed. After 1926 employers were nervous of pressing for wage reductions and the authorities nervous of forcing deflation. Accordingly interest rates were not raised to the levels necessary to ensure a strong pound.

As suggested above, the fundamental problem for sterling was the decline of exports. The overall trade volume position was startling. While export volume was at only 75·8 per cent of the 1913 level by 1924, retained imports had increased by 9 per cent. Only a 25 per cent improvement in the terms of trade prevented the British external accounts going completely awry in the 1920s. Of course the improved terms of trade partly reflected the high export prices which were themselves responsible for the small export volume, but import prices do seem to have been relatively lower for the rest of industrial Europe than they had been in 1913.[53]

The net trade deficit in 1924 was £214 million. In subsequent years it tended to worsen. In 1924 net invisible income was £272 million, giving a current account surplus of £58 million. In the later 1920s net income from invisibles rose (largely because of higher interest, dividends etc. on overseas assets), providing an offset to the worsening trade deficit and yielding altogether a net current account surplus averaging £86 million between 1927 and 1929. Despite the role of invisible earnings and of the terms of trade, probably the most important factor in keeping the current account solvent in the 1920s was the low level of economic activity in the UK. Depressed exports and sluggish activity in the export industries provided their own corrective in the external accounts – raw material imports never recovered their pre-war volume, although, significantly, manufactured imports by 1929 were 20 per cent above their 1913 level.[54]

The surplus on current account, however, was too small to allow uncontrolled overseas lending, and to the extent that the inadequate surplus was partly the consequence of the rate of exchange chosen in 1925, this reflects a failure to achieve the implicit objectives of the architects of that decision, the restoration of the City of London's pre-war international position. Controls, after the repeal of the relevant war-time legislation in

[52] J. A. Dowie, '1919–1920 is in need of attention', *Economic History Review*, 2nd ser., 28 (1975), 447.

[53] C. P. Kindleberger, *The Terms of Trade: A European Case Study* (Cambridge, Mass. 1956), 95. Kindleberger's calculations are for the rest of industrial Europe minus Germany.

[54] W. S. Schlote, *British Overseas Trade from 1700 to the 1930s*, translated by W. O. Henderson and W. H. Chaloner (Oxford, 1952), Table 13.

November 1919, were indirect, an example of the monetary authorities using 'moral suasion'.[55] The motive behind controls until 1924 was principally the desire of the Treasury and the Bank of England to fund the war-swollen national debt and to reassert a measure of discipline over the money markets. The early controls were on foreign short and medium-term lending; long-term loans, mainly because they were not seen as likely to clash with government requirements, were seen as less of a problem. In February 1922 the foreign embargo was effectively reduced to loans of less than ten years. Two years later the embargo was removed, and this represents the end of control dictated by the competing needs of government. The dominant concern now became the exchanges, and in November 1924, with the monetary authorities anxious to secure an appreciation of sterling prior to the gold standard return, controls were reintroduced. The new parity was in need of defence, however, and in mid-1925, despite opposition from Leopold Amery, even the dominions were being asked to restrain their demands. There was a drop in dominion borrowing in response to this call, but there was no recorded attempt to block such loans after 1925, although of course colonial lending could be controlled more easily.[56] In general, foreign borrowing was not regulated between 1925 and 1928, although by this time New York, with low interest rates and falling issuing costs, was a very attractive alternative to London. Pressures on the reserves and severe disturbances in international financial markets led to the reintroduction of controls in 1929 and their intermittent retention afterwards. In general the authorities appeared reluctant to restrict foreign lending, partly out of a belief in the value of overseas lending, and partly because of opposition from the City, which was annoyed at having to forgo the profits of issuing and trading in such securities. But there seems to have been a recognition that controls were not totally effective because British funds could participate in foreign issues abroad, whether in Europe or New York. New issues are not therefore a completely accurate guide to the distribution of British overseas investment in the 1920s, but nonetheless suggest strongly the dominance of imperial lending. Between 1923 and 1929, new issues for the Empire, both government and company, were made for £497 million while foreign issues were worth £280 million.[57] Restriction on foreign government borrowing, together with the preference created by the Colonial Stock Act of 1900

---

[55] John Atkin, 'Official regulation of British overseas investment 1914–1931', *Economic History Review*, 2nd ser., 23 (1970), 324–35. The following two paragraphs are based on Atkin's article and on Moggridge, *British Monetary Policy*, 199–219.

[56] Moggridge, *British Monetary Policy*, 213. The dominions were annoyed, and the British government became afraid they would turn to New York for loans, thus jeopardising UK exports – see Costigliola, 'Anglo-American financial rivalry', 927.

[57] Figures by Atkin, quoted in Moggridge. *British Monetary Policy*, 204.

(which made imperial government stock eligible for trustee status) were important factors in this change in the pattern of British overseas investment. Together with the liquidation of dollar holdings during the war, this shift helped to bring about a situation where, by the eve of the depression, holdings of investments in the Empire are thought to have exceeded non-imperial holdings, in contrast to the pre-war position.[58]

Capital controls or not, Britain was lending long-term substantially more than the current account surplus warranted, and financing the difference by short-term borrowing. The precise amounts are not known, but by December 1929 sterling balances were already considerably larger than £275 million while reserves were only £146 million.[59] London's illiquid position was all the more dangerous because confidence in sterling was weaker than before the war, and because some of the reserves were held reluctantly by the French.[60] Britain's illiquidity was, however, only one part of an increasingly precarious external economic position. The pattern of settlements was another.

In 1910 Britain had depended on running balance of payments surpluses on current account with India, the rest of Asia and Australia in order to finance deficits with North America and the rest of Europe.[61] By 1924 there were indications of a dollar problem in the British balance of payments (see Table 1.6). The trade balance with North and South America had worsened very considerably. Moreover, with the sale of dollar investments during the war, with war debts and the shifting of a number of financial services to New York, the decline of the pre-war invisibles surplus created a potential problem in the structure of multilateral payments.[62] To some extent, as Table 1.6 indicates, Britain was successful in reducing the American trade deficit in the later 1920s. The Indian surplus, so critical to the British balance of payments before 1914, had also declined, aggravating the problem. But the buoyancy of the US economy, with its huge imports of raw materials and tropical foodstuffs, together with heavy overseas lending, helped postpone a crisis. The United Kingdom's traditional strength as a supplier of industrial products to the tropics remained long enough to enable it to earn trade surpluses which tapped the dollar

---

[58] Royal Institute of International Affairs, *The Problem of International Investment* (1937), 142 and 144. The figures for the percentage of British overseas investment invested in the Empire are 47 per cent in 1913 and 59 per cent in 1930.

[59] I. M. Drummond, 'Britain and the world economy 1900–1945', in Floud and McCloskey (eds.), *Economic History of Britain*, vol. 2.

[60] See, for example, Judith L. Kooker, 'French financial diplomacy: the interwar years', in B. M. Rowland (ed.), *Balance of Power or Hegemony?: The Interwar Monetary System* (New York, 1976). Most of the rundown in French-held sterling assets prior to 1931 was by private holders.   [61] Saul, *Studies in British Overseas Trade*, 57–9.

[62] *Ibid.*, 34.

Table 1.6. *Bilateral trade balances, 1913, 1924 and 1928* (£m)

Area	Balance		
	1913	1924	1928
N. and NE Europe	−35·8	−65·1	−88·7
W. Europe	−16·9	−29·0	−54·8
Central and SE Europe	−21·2	+22·1	+4·5
S. Europe and N. Africa	+6·1	+0·6	−2·2
Turkey and Middle East	−8·5	−22·0	−20·3
Rest of Africa	+19·8	+7·8	+9·7
Asia	+35·7	+31·5	+30·2
USA	−82·2	−162·6	−119·6
British N. America	−3·2	−35·2	−20·9
West Indies	+0·2	−12·4	−14·3
Central and S. America	−17·2	−61·2	−49·5
Australia and New Zealand	−8·7	−18·7	−23·6

Source: B. R. Mitchell and P. Deane, *Abstract of British Historical Statistics* (Cambridge, 1962), Overseas Trade 12.

surpluses of these regions.[63] The stability of the system, however, was dependent on the willingness and ability of the USA to continue importing and lending abroad. The dramatic decline in American foreign investment from 1928 and the subsequent slump in imports threatened Britain's position in at least two indirect ways. First, if the primary producers could not earn or borrow dollars, the UK's ability to finance its American deficits from current earnings would be impaired. Secondly, those primary producing countries that kept their reserves in London were likely to be forced to liquidate them. The Australian position, for example, was already weak by the late 1920s; sterling balances had to be bolstered by very heavy borrowing in 1927–8, and were run down in 1929.[64] Britain's links with the primary producing countries, as trader, banker and financier, were a major source of weakness to it in the financial and economic crisis that set in from 1929.

Britain's trade dependence on the Empire

The adoption of free trade by Britain in the middle of the nineteenth century signalled that the industrialists and bankers felt strong enough to dispense with the props of Empire preferences and to assert their

[63] League of Nations, *Network of World Trade* (Geneva, 1942), 57–64 and 73–89.
[64] Pressnell, '1925', 81–2.

dominance on a world stage. This global role had been maintained into the twentieth century, so that on the eve of the First World War by far the greater part of British trade was conducted with non-imperial countries and the greater part of overseas investments were placed outside the Empire.

In the 1920s Britain came to depend more heavily on the Empire, and to that extent the decade marks some retreat from the world-wide position held earlier. Greater reliance on the Empire reflected weaknesses in the metropolitan centre. As discussed above, this is evident in the shift in the pattern of overseas investment which stemmed partly from capital controls that from 1925 were themselves a product of the difficulties with sterling, but also from the greater competitive strength of Wall Street.[65] Another symptom of the problems of the British economy, unemployment, was an influential and perhaps decisive consideration in the implementation of two imperial schemes in the 1920s.

One of these was colonial aid. There was some provision for this in the Trade Facilities Act of 1921, but the main measure was the Colonial Development Act of 1929. The initiative for the first measure is directly traceable to a Cabinet Committee on Unemployment, appointed in September 1920,[66] and in his study of the Colonial Development Act, G. C. Abbott concludes that far from being a specific objective of the Act, colonial development was envisaged rather as a means by which to achieve the more immediate objectives of reducing unemployment at home and of stimulating British exports.[67] Unemployment was also a major cause of the commitment of money to settlement schemes aimed at boosting emigration. I. M. Drummond, in discussing the Empire Settlement Act of 1922 and the '£34 million Agreement' with Australia, and having explained the role of the Australians and of Leopold Amery in these projects, concludes that

nevertheless the ideology of Empire settlement, and the Australian pressure, would probably not have yielded an Act if the British Government had not been worried about unemployment, which at critical points advanced the Cause. Much of Amery's support came from Ministers who were departmentally concerned with the unemployment problem.[68]

---

[65] In effect the Colonial Stock Act gave Empire borrowers a preference in the British capital market.

[66] E. A. Brett, *Colonialism and Underdevelopment in East Africa: the politics of economic change 1919–1939* (1973), 124–7.

[67] G. C. Abbott, 'A re-examination of the 1929 colonial development act', *Economic History Review*, 2nd ser., 24 (1971), 71. This conclusion is supported by D. Meredith, 'The British government and colonial economic policy, 1919–1939', *Economic History Review*, 2nd ser., 28 (1975), 485–7 and 498 in an article otherwise somewhat critical of Abbott.

[68] I. M. Drummond, *British Economic Policy and the Empire, 1919–1939* (1972), 43–4. W. R. Garside, *British Unemployment, 1919–1939: A study in public policy* (Cambridge, 1990), ch. 7, in a useful discussion both of settlement and colonial development schemes,

Table 1.7. *Percentage share of the Empire in British trade*

	Imports	Exports
1860–9	26·2	30·1
1870–9	22·1	29·1
1880–9	23·1	34·7
1890–9	22·2	33·7
1900–9	22·1	34·8
1910–13	24·2	35·8

Source: S. B. Saul, 'The export economy 1870–1914', *Yorkshire Bulletin of Economic and Social Research*, 17 (1965), Special number, *Studies in the British Economy 1870–1914*, J. Saville (ed).

Perhaps even more significant was the growing reliance of Britain on the Empire as an outlet for exports. As indicated in Table 1.7 there had been no discernible trend in this direction before the war in the decades since the 1880s.[69] By contrast, during the postwar years, the share of the Empire in British domestic exports had reached 43·1 per cent in 1927 although it then declined to 1931, when it was only 38·8 per cent,[70] reflecting the earlier impact of the depression on primary producers.

Even in the case of cotton goods, where so much is blamed on the devastating collapse of the Indian market, and where substantial losses were made in East Africa, the West Indies and Malaya, the decline in the share of the Empire was marginal.[71] Elsewhere increased dependence on the Empire was experienced for a wide range of products as Table 1.8 below makes clear. The Balfour Report cited a large number of instances – agricultural machinery, road tractors, boilers, machine tools, prime movers, sewing machines, textile machinery, cars and parts, cycles, cutlery and most iron and steel products.[72]

It is significant that dependence on the Empire was high for some of the newer and more expansive products in world trade. (Even before the war, international cartels such as the International Rail Makers' Association had influenced the distribution of exports in such a way that British sales were concentrated on Empire markets, and cartels were of course an

emphasises that the relief of UK unemployment was uppermost in the minds of British politicians.

[69] Although the view that dependence was increasing is still expressed occasionally. See M. de Cecco, *Money and Empire: The International Gold Standard, 1890–1914* (Oxford, 1974), ch. 2.   [70] Schlote, *British Overseas Trade*, Table 20b.

[71] K. Evans, 'The development of the overseas trade of the British Empire with particular reference to the period 1870–1939', M.A. Thesis, University of Manchester (1956), 492. In 1913, 51·7 per cent, in 1929, 50·0 per cent.

[72] *Survey of Metal Industries*, 62–8, 165, 174, 178, 181, 188, 192–3, 195, 235, 254–5.

Table 1.8. *Percentage share of British exports to Empire by commodity groups, 1913, 1925 and 1929*

	1913	1925	1929
Textile manufactures	43·9	39·5	42·2
Iron and steel goods	48·2	53·1	51·4
Machinery	32·5	46·7	43·5
Motor vehicles	67·4	77·0	81·2
Railway carriages	58·4	50·7	43·8
Locomotives	58·6	74·7	69·5
Hardware and cutlery	57·2	72·6	64·2
Electrical goods	61·6	55·3	56·5
Steamships	20·6	34·8	52·3
Paper-wares	62·0	73·4	72·8
Pottery and porcelain	41·9	48·5	50·8
Tobacco products	44·5	75·1	71·9
Coal	3·7	6·1	5·8

Source: K. Evans, 'The development of the overseas trade of the British Empire with particular reference to the period 1870–1939' (MA Thesis, University of Manchester, 1956), Table III D. 492.

Table 1.9. *Percentage of total imports of merchandise into British dominions and protectorates supplied by UK, 1913 and 1924–1929*

1913	1924	1925	1926	1927	1928	1929
44·3	42·0	39·2	36·2	36·0	35·3	34·1

Source: Parliamentary Papers, *Statistical Abstract for the British Empire, 1929.*

influence on market distribution between the wars as well.) This is noticeable for capital goods exports as a whole, but especially for electrical engineering products, and, even more so, for motor vehicles. Nonetheless, it appears that the newer industries leaned more heavily on the crutch of imperial preferences and other institutional distortions in the Empire to offset their competitive weaknesses in the rest of the world; the newer products were less capable of withstanding open competition than the nineteenth-century staples.

Britain's greater reliance on the Empire was thus in part a result of failing competitiveness, a consequence of an inability to compete effectively in non-Empire markets. But, as discussed above, Britain was certainly not fire-proof in the Empire, and its weaknesses were underlined by a very

Table 1.10. *Percentage share of UK in exports of selected dominions, 1913, 1927 and 1929*

	1913	1927	1929
Canada	49·9	33·8	24·7
Australia	45·5	36·9	38·1
New Zealand	83·4	77·0	74·4
South Africa	80·4	52·3	49·5
India (by sea)	23·5	24·4	21·4

Source: Parliamentary Papers, *Statistical Abstract for the British Empire, 1929.*

marked tendency for imperial customers to draw a decreasing proportion of their supplies from the UK (see Table 1.9).

Not only did the Empire countries draw a smaller ratio of their imports from Britain, but they became less dependent on Britain as an outlet for their exports. This can be shown by an examination of the proportion of exports that went from the self-governing dominions and India to the UK (see Table 1.10). All five countries by 1929 were selling a smaller proportion of their exports to the UK than in 1913, although in the case of India the reduction was small. The Canadian and South African diversifications were most pronounced, while Australian dependence on the UK declined more gradually and had actually started to increase again before the depression.

Although the dominions were less dependent on the UK as an outlet for their exports, Britain was in fact drawing a higher proportion of its imports from the Empire than before the war.[73] W. Schlote points out that before 1913, apart from a few years in the 1860s, 25 per cent was the maximum proportion of UK imports drawn from the Empire.[74] After 1913 the proportion was never less than 25 per cent, averaging 28 per cent in 1919–26, and 27 per cent during the years 1927–9. Viewed from the perspective of trade, Britain was more reliant on the Empire in the 1920s while the Empire was increasingly looking beyond the UK for sales and supplies.

Conclusion

The failure of British exports to regain their pre-war volume not only contributed to high and apparently intractable unemployment, but by undermining the current account surplus it jeopardised maintenance of the

[73] Maizels, *Growth and Trade*, 277.   [74] Schlote, *British Overseas Trade*, 88.

gold standard, certainly at the old parity. By the late 1920s London's external position had become increasingly illiquid, and the whole multi-lateral payments system had come to depend on the continuance of high levels of imports and of foreign lending by the USA.

Weaknesses in the UK economy and in competitiveness were reflected in some withdrawal from a global economic role. This manifested itself less in policy than in increased economic dependence on the Empire. Capital exports in the 1920s went largely to Empire countries. Nothing so serves to highlight the failing competitiveness of British exporters as their growing reliance on imperial markets at the very same time that dramatic losses of share were being experienced. However, from the perspective of the dominions, the 1920s were a decade of growing economic independence from Britain. Imports were increasingly drawn from sources other than the UK and other sales outlets were also found.

The onset of the depression in 1929 brought intense pressure on sterling, and finally precipitated the abandonment of free trade.

2 The political economy of protectionism, 1919–1932

After nearly eighty years of free trade, the return to protectionism by Great Britain in 1931–2 was a dramatic event in its economic history. Interpretations of this policy reversal vary widely. For some authors it was an inevitable if perhaps belated consequence of relative economic decline. As mentioned earlier, Stephen Krasner argues that since free trade suits the strong, Britain's loss of international economic hegemony in the late nineteenth or early twentieth century demanded a change in the commercial policy regime. This does not mean the depression was insignificant in the decision. Quite the reverse, for 'systems are initiated and ended, not as state-power theory would predict, by close assessments of the interests of the state at every given moment, but by external events – usually cataclysmic ones',[1] and Krasner argues that the slump provided the spur necessary to bring about a return to protection that objective assessment would long have seen as the appropriate policy regime for a second-class economic power. This longer-term perspective is consistent with the views of Forrest Capie, who has emphasised the build-up of protectionist pressures in Britain before the slump, particularly from the steel industry.[2]

A radically different perspective is provided by Barry Eichengreen in his study *Sterling and the Tariff, 1929–32*.[3] Relying heavily on the records of the Treasury and the Economic Advisory Council, Eichengreen produces a lucid study of economic thought and policy advice in the early stages of the slump. As a result he sees the tariff as a response to the immediate pressures generated by the depression, and particularly to the deterioration in the balance of payments. If there was a predominant objective in adopting protection, it was not to create jobs, but, on the contrary, to secure the exchange rate and avoid hyperinflation, even if this carried with it the risk of higher unemployment. In this view, the floating of sterling

---

[1] Stephen D. Krasner, 'State power and the structure of international trade', *World Politics*, 28 (1976), 317–48.

[2] Forrest Capie, 'The pressure for tariff protection in Britain, 1917–31' *Journal of European Economic History*, 9 (1980), 431–47.

[3] B. J. Eichengreen, *Sterling and the Tariff, 1929–32*, Princeton Studies in International Finance, no. 48, Sept. 1981, 7–14.

following the abandonment of the gold standard in September 1931, far from promising to rectify the current account deficit on the balance of payments, carried the risk of an uncontrolled depreciation on the pound that might replicate in Britain the German experience of 1923. In Eichengreen's opinion, if one looks for an underlying motivation, it was that 'the authorities' fears and their distrust of the effects of a floating exchange rate formed the basis of their decision to impose the General Tariff'.[4]

The interpretation of Samuel Beer provides a striking contrast to Eichengreen's conclusion. Having summarised the work of a committee of the Conservative Research Department, chaired by Philip Cunliffe-Lister, Beer points out that by early 1931 this had produced a complete tariff scheme ready to be rushed through parliament when required. He concludes:

To be sure, when the National Government embarked on framing the Import Duties bill a Cabinet committee was formally charged with drafting the measure. The principal function of this 'make-believe inquiry', however, was to arrange temporary concessions intended to retain certain Liberal support, particularly that of Walter Runciman, a wavering free trader who was President of the Board of Trade. In fact that basis of the tariff legislation of the National Government ... was provided by the detailed proposals of the Cunliffe-Lister committee. Few British Governments have taken office equipped with such thorough and programmatic preparation for a major innovation in public policy. For a party often identified with *ad hoc* empiricism – not to say 'muddling through' – in its decision-making, the Conservatives in this instance showed a remarkable degree of systematic foresight.[5]

This chapter aims to answer two questions. First, to what extent was the return to protection the consequence of the longer-term pressures associated with the decline of the British economy and to what extent was it the product of the depression of the 1930s? Secondly, if a pre-eminent objective in introducing protection can be identified, was it to stimulate employment, or was it to control the level of sterling and of prices?

The First World War and the early 1920s

By 1925 British policy appeared committed to the restoration of the pre-war international economic order, including virtually free trade. Economic liberalism had survived two challenges. The first had been the war-induced enthusiasm for protection and greater imperial unity, a movement that spawned several organisations, often instigated by Dudley Docker.[6]

---

[4] *Ibid.*, 38.   [5] Samuel H. Beer, *Modern British Politics* (3rd edn 1982), 288.
[6] R. P. T. Davenport-Hines, *Dudley Docker. The Life and Times of a Trade Warrior* (Cambridge, 1984).

Docker's ideas and those of his associates can be seen as a response to the international challenge faced by British industry. His aims stretched well beyond mere protectionism to encompass the reorganisation and rationalisation of industry in vast trusts, the harnessing of financial resources to productive power, aggressive marketing overseas and an overhaul of the machinery of government. Greater imperial unity, especially closer economic integration, was an essential part of the programme. The harnessing of the Empire's economic power for war spurred enormous enthusiasm for the view that the Empire 'must remain mobilised if it was to dominate the peace'.[7] However, following the allied victory in November 1918 the protectionist/imperialist cause lost momentum. The suddenness and completeness of Germany's collapse in 1918 dissolved the fears of those who had envisaged bitter commercial rivalry after the war,[8] and the boom of 1919–20, a last spasm of the pre-war industrial order, encouraged the scrapping of wartime controls as part of a search for 'normalcy'.

The protectionists had to be content with a modest legacy from the war. One part of this was the McKenna duties, involving a 33·3 per cent *ad valorem* tariff on gramophones, clocks, watches, cinematograph film and certain types of motor vehicle, which had been introduced in 1915 to save foreign exchange and shipping space; they survived the peace and in the 1919 Finance Act had an imperial preference element added to them. Another result of the war had been the first piece of unambiguously protectionist inspired legislation, the Safeguarding of Industries Act of 1921. The origin of this had been the discovery that Britain was dependent on Germany for certain vital supplies, to remedy which the Act gave protection for five years to a number of 'key' industries producing scientific instruments, selected chemicals and electrical products. Commonwealth products were exempt.

The second challenge to the liberal international economic order came in Baldwin's surprise call for protection in 1923. There were several motives behind Baldwin's apparently sudden switch in policy.[9] One was inspired by the need to maintain party unity: by opting for protection, Baldwin might have pre-empted a similar call by Lloyd George which if made could have detached Austen Chamberlain, Lord Birkenhead and other restive coalitionists from the Conservative Party. But high and apparently

[7] W. K. Hancock, *Survey of British Commonwealth Affairs*, II, *Problems of Economic Policy 1918–1939* (Oxford, 1942), pt. I, 95.   [8] Davenport-Hines, *Docker*, 132.
[9] Keith Middlemas and John Barnes, *Baldwin, A Biography* (1969); John Ramsden, *A History of the Conservative Party: the age of Balfour and Baldwin 1902–1940* (1978); K. W. D. Rolfe, 'Tories, tariffs, and elections: the West Midlands and English politics 1918–1935' (Cambridge Ph.D. 1974), and Maurice Cowling, *The Impact of Labour, 1920–1924: the beginning of modern British politics* (Cambridge, 1971).

intractable unemployment also worried Baldwin, all the more so since Conservative inaction could benefit the increasingly powerful Labour Party. Moreover, an international solution to British unemployment looked increasingly improbable because the Franco-Belgian occupation of the Ruhr in January threatened the chances of European economic recovery in the foreseeable future. In these circumstances an active development of the home market and closer imperial integration appeared to Baldwin all the more urgent.

The return to power late in 1924 of a chastened Baldwin symbolised a victory of sorts for the internationalist option. It was not that the other two major parties had campaigned for anything different – quite the contrary – but that the Tories turned their backs on the protectionist policies offered the year before. Nothing reflected this internationalism more clearly than the decision to return to the gold standard. While this may be seen as predominantly an attempt by the City of London to regain its pre-war international ascendancy, the case for returning at the pre-war parity of $4.86 to the pound sterling could muster a measure of plausibility as an employment policy on the grounds that the revival of production, employment and profits in the old export-based staples stood no chance until the international economy had been restored: only with exchange rate stability and the appropriate instruments for securing balance of payments adjustment (i.e. the gold standard) would confidence revive, investment and trade flourish and the export industries regain their pre-war prosperity. Industry, half-convinced, gave grudging acquiescence. As for tariffs, the surprising appointment of Winston Churchill, a free trader, as Chancellor of the Exchequer helped keep the government to its election promises: as Chancellor he was in a powerful position to frustrate protectionist moves made by colleagues.

It is true that the protectionists had to be mollified to some extent, notably in the reinstatement of the McKenna duties which had been scrapped by the Labour government in 1924, and by a series of small extensions to Safeguarding tariffs. Essentially, however, the Baldwin administration stuck to its 1924 election pledge not to introduce a full protectionist regime. At first the task of Churchill and Baldwin in warding off protectionist claims was made much easier by the conflict in business opinion over tariffs that still existed in mid-decade. There was no ambiguity about the City of London's views, prominent City figures issuing a free trade manifesto in 1925. Industrial views were another matter. The structure of industry was shifting slowly towards newer sectors that were much more heavily dependent on domestic and imperial markets than the cosmopolitan nineteenth-century staples. The British and Allied Manufacturers' Association, having pointed out in evidence to the Balfour

Committee on Industrial Efficiency that two-thirds of electrical machinery exports were sold in the dominions, stated that the best thing the Committee 'could do for us would be to get a protectionist tariff'.[10] The manufacturers of fine chemicals in the UK contended that the industry was dependent on the continuance of the Safeguarding Act, and when Lord Melchett had formed Imperial Chemical Industries in 1926, the choice of name had been a deliberate statement of policy.[11] Car and truck production was protected by the McKenna duties, and the bulk of overseas shipments was sold in the dominions. Both Austin and Morris were involved in the campaign for protection. While leaders of some of the new industries, such as the motorcycle firms and the cable makers, were confident of their ability to compete in world markets, these were the exceptions, most of the growth sectors favouring protection.[12] Yet these were still only a small part of the industrial scene, the newer industries on the basis of von Tunzlemann's classification accounting for 13 per cent of manufacturing employment in 1924 and 15 per cent by 1930.[13] The staples may have been shrinking in relative importance, but they nonetheless continued to dominate industrial output and employment.

Important sectors of the textile industry favoured protection by 1925. The hosiery manufacturers, heavily dependent on dominion markets and worried by increasing import penetration of the domestic market, favoured tariffs and imperial preference. The carpet producers, overwhelmingly reliant on Empire markets and also concerned about increasing imports, were with one or two exceptions of the opinion 'that most of the difficulties which confront the industry of their country at the present time, and which form the subject of the Committee's enquiry, would disappear if a moderate general tariff were placed on all manufactured imports'.[14] The greater part of employment in the textile industries was concentrated in the woollen and worsted mills, and, more important still, in cottons. Although the woollen and worsted industry had a long association with the protectionist movement, stretching back well before the war, the industry was divided on the issue in the early 1920s, possibly reflecting a slackening in import competition: spokesmen for the West Riding Chambers of Commerce

---

[10] BT 55/123, Balfour Committee on Industry and Trade, evidence 27 May 1925.

[11] W. J. Reader, 'Imperial Chemical Industries and the state, 1926–1945', in B. Supple (ed.), *Essays in British Business History* (Oxford, 1977), 227.

[12] BT 55/122 and 123, Evidence of British Cycle and Motor Cycle Manufacturers' and Traders' Union Ltd. and Cable Makers' Association.

[13] G. N. von Tunzlemann, 'Structural change and leading sectors in British manufacturing, 1907–68', in *Economics in the Long View*, III, ed. C. P. Kindleberger and G. di Tella (1982).

[14] BT 55/122, Balfour Committee, evidence of National Federation of Hosiery Manufacturers' Association, 428, and BT 55/123, Balfour Committee, evidence of Carpet Manufacturers' Association, 757.

were specifically instructed not to give an opinion about tariffs to the Balfour Committee in 1925.[15] There were no such divisions in Lancashire in the middle of the decade, both the Cotton Spinners' and Manufacturers' Association and the Federation of Calico Printers stating emphatically their opposition to tariffs.[16]

Even the steel industry, which gave the government more trouble about tariffs than any other sector, was fairly muted in its demands until after 1925. The 1923 Ruhr crisis had obscured the competitive strength of the continental European industry. Moreover, there was considerable division in the industry with important parts of the downstream sectors benefiting from cheap steel and wary of the effects of tariffs on their input costs.[17] This was particularly true of the re-rollers who in 1924 having set up the British Steel Re-Rollers Association specifically to counter tariffs, formed an active lobby able to exploit the broad political problems raised by the tariff issue, and as a recent historian of the industry observes, were able to exert a degree of influence well beyond their economic weight.[18] The shipbuilders were also opposed. Another important consumer of steel was the engineering industry, 12 to 15 per cent of the selling value of whose products was accounted for by steel.[19] Reflecting trends affecting much of British industry, by the early 1920s engineering had become more dependent on the home market. Whereas pre-war over half the value of machinery output had been exported, by 1923 and 1924 nearly three-quarters of sales were made within Britain. The proportion of exports shipped to the dominions rose from 34 per cent in 1913 to 53 per cent in 1923. D. A. Bremner, Secretary of the Engineers' Association, emphasised in evidence to the Balfour Committee that although the impact of foreign competition on the industry was out of all proportion to its size, it was only one of a range of problems affecting the industry. He personally favoured a tariff, but the Association, much as it had been in earlier years, was divided.[20]

Protection was a taboo subject for the Federation of British Industries. In the first years the Dudley Docker group, seeking a radical restructuring of British industry, finance and overseas marketing, had been in the ascendant. As FBI membership grew, so the influence of Dudley Docker and his associates was diluted. Docker's biographer records that he had anticipated this, but not the strength of opposition to his policies.[21] Lancashire opinion was particularly hostile to schemes involving tariff

[15] *Ibid.*, evidence of West Riding Chambers of Commerce, 813–17.
[16] BT 55/122 and 123, 494 and 642.   [17] Capie, 'Pressure for tariff protection', 435.
[18] Steven Tolliday, *Business, Banking and Politics: The Case of British Steel, 1918–1939* (1987), 294–8.
[19] D. A. Bremner, Director of British Engineers' Association, 12 Jan. 1928, *Bulletin* of the BEA.   [20] BT 55/122, 565.   [21] Davenport-Hines, *Docker*, ch. 6.

protection, and in 1919, following the rejection of merger terms with the British Empire Producers Organisation that might have committed the FBI to policies of imperialist protection, Docker ceased playing an active part in the organisation's policy-making. The FBI was especially weak in the textile districts of the West Riding, and these, it was argued, would not join a protectionist organisation.[22] Between 1921 and 1926 the numerical and financial strength of Manchester in the Federation overhauled that of Birmingham.[23] The organisation was caught in a dilemma because as membership became more representative of industry, particularly English industry, the diversity of views this reflected made it difficult for the FBI to speak with clarity or authority. As the protectionist issue came increasingly to the fore at the end of the decade, the impotence of the FBI led to it being by-passed and its future threatened.[24]

Failure of the international option

In the late 1920s the world economy boomed: between 1925 and 1929 world manufacturing production expanded by more than a quarter, world trade by 19 per cent.[25] This did not entirely by-pass the British economy. Total industrial production increased by 9 per cent, the amount of electricity generated rose sharply, the number of vehicles on the roads increased by 45 per cent, the tonnage of new shipping commenced doubled between 1925 and 1929 and even the steel industry, so vocal in its demands for protection, increased output from 7·4 to 9·6 million tons.[26] Total agricultural output also rose, despite the misfortunes of cereal producers. Gross company profits grew from £450 million in 1925 to £499 million in 1929.

That is one side of the picture. There were also major weaknesses, particularly in overseas markets. The re-emergence of Germany as an exporter, and sharp competition from France and Belgium, both aided by undervalued currencies, made life difficult for exporters. As detailed in the previous chapter, British exporters suffered a dramatic retreat in many markets after 1925. Despite the overall expansion of world trade, British exports in 1929 had still not regained the values of 1925 and in volume

[22] Federation of British Industries (FBI)/200/F1/1/1, Grand Council minutes, 15 Oct. 1919.
[23] FBI/200/F3/S1/7/18.
[24] R. F. Holland, 'The Federation of British Industries and the international economy, 1929–39', Economic History Review, 2nd. ser., 34 (1981), 287–300. Robert W. D. Boyce, Capitalism at the Crossroads, 1919–1932. A study in politics, economics and international relations (Cambridge, 1987), 123.
[25] W. A. Lewis, Economic Survey, 1919–1939 (1949), 38.
[26] London and Cambridge Economic Services, The British Economy Key Statistics 1900–1970 (1972). Statistics quoted in the remainder of this paragraph are also drawn from this source.

terms were well below 1913 levels. In the cotton industry employment declined as did the number of spindles and looms. Reacting to the fall in world grain prices, the amount of arable land and the output of corn contracted. Although total employment expanded by nearly 1 million, the number out of work stayed obstinately above the million mark, around 10 per cent of the workforce. The Industrial Transference Scheme of 1928, aimed to assist the movement of unemployed workers, was tacit admission of the failure of the restored gold standard to cure unemployment in the export industries.

Demands for protection and for imperialist policies gained fresh momentum from 1925. In July the National Union of Manufacturers held a lunch for 250 businessmen in the Queen's Hotel, Birmingham to launch a campaign for extended Safeguarding.[27] In the same year the Empire Industries Association took over from the British Commonwealth Union, an organisation which had lost both its rationale and, through embezzlement by its secretary, some of its funds.[28] Launched as the Empire Industries Association for the Extension of British Preference and the Safeguarding of Home Industries, with Leopold Amery and Neville Chamberlain active behind the scenes, it aimed both to lobby MPs and government as well as to educate the public.[29] A massive programme of public meetings was launched in the year or so from 1926 and more than a thousand meetings were addressed by speakers from the association, including a special series in the Midlands and Manchester; each Sunday in summer meetings were held in nine London parks.[30]

The pacemakers in the protectionist movement were from the political right wing. The EIA was dominated by the right, although it professed to be non-political. But there was support for protection from Labour MPs. In early 1925 unease in the trade union movement was created by two well-publicised events, the establishment of an office in Glasgow by the Hugo Stinnes syndicate to promote the sale of Ruhr coal, and the placing of a contract in Hamburg for five 10,000 ton diesel-powered ships.[31] Some feared that living standards and working conditions in Britain, including the hard won 8-hour day, might be undermined by sweated foreign labour. Although efforts were concentrated on international action to deal with the sweating problem, a number of people were quite prepared to see import controls as a solution. The protected industries also created a constituency of workers with an interest in the prolongation of the legislation. Arthur Pugh's Iron and Steel Trades Confederation had clear protectionist inclinations. There was a distinct commonwealth grouping in the Labour

[27] Boyce, *Capitalism*, 110.   [28] Davenport-Hines, *Docker*, 190–1.
[29] Empire Industries Association (EIA)/221/1/2/1/and Hannon Papers, minute books.
[30] EIA/221/1/2/2.   [31] Boyce, *Capitalism*, 86.

Party, and in June 1925 nineteen MPs voted with the Conservatives on a clause in the Finance Bill to extend imperial preference on dried fruits.[32] Early in 1926 four Labour members, Dr Leslie Haden-Guest, Robert Young, Frank Hodges and Major A. G. Church, were in active but secret negotiations with the Empire Industries Association (they used Sir Hugo Hirst's GEC offices rather than those of the Association!).[33] But although the committee of the EIA resigned to accommodate the Labour men, and amendments to the constitution were considered, the negotiations were eventually broken off, Haden-Guest explaining that there was insufficient support.

In the last years before the depression growing scepticism about free trade and mounting pressure for protection increasingly affected the great staple industries.

Agriculture had never taken happily to free trade, and this was particularly true of the specialist cereal growers who had borne the main brunt of foreign competition in the late nineteenth century. The retreat from cereal growing had been reversed during the First World War, and in 1919–20 a policy had been formulated to support domestic output through a system of price guarantees. These had been precipitantly withdrawn in 1921 following a price collapse, leaving farmers with reduced incomes and a pronounced sense of grievance.[34] By the late 1920s weakening world cereal prices were bearing heavily on the arable farming districts with 200,000 acres of land a year going out of grain production. In 1927 the National Farmers Union launched a campaign calling on county branches to pressure local MPs for some form of help.[35]

While agricultural assistance might have to cross the politically formidable barriers against food taxes, manufacturing industry could in principle be assisted by Safeguarding legislation. In practice this proved difficult, the criteria laid down proving too great an obstacle for the majority of applicants, so that of the forty-nine applications lodged between 1925 and 1929 (several more were headed off by the Board of Trade from applying), only nine were successful. They were most commonly ruled out on the grounds that the industries were not of substantial importance.[36] Yet at the same time industries could be too important, as the steel industry knew well. In the summer of 1925 an application was made to the Board of Trade for duties on pig-iron, wrought iron, heavy steel products and wire. With the industry working

[32] Partha Sarathi Gupta, *Imperialism and the British Labour Movement 1914–1964* (1975), 65.   [33] EIA/221/1/2/1 and Hannon Papers, minute books.
[34] Alan Webber, 'Cereals production and policy 1921–39: the background to the international trade agreements policy of the 1930s', The City University, Centre for Banking and International Finance, Discussion Papers, no. 59.
[35] Boyce, *Capitalism*, 122–3.   [36] BT 55/101, OSI 193.

well below capacity and unemployment high, a potentially powerful case existed. However, opponents of a steel tariff argued that the answer to the industry's problems lay in reorganisation and amalgamation: protection would merely postpone the necessary rationalisation of the industry. The tariff proponents of the industry insisted that the key to lower costs lay in full capacity operation. Sir William Larke, President of the National Federation of Iron and Steel Manufacturers argued that rationalisation, by transferring production from the small mills to the large would make only a minimal difference, whereas shutting out 2 million tons of imports would lower costs by 10 shillings per ton, or approximately 10 per cent. The government referred the application to a Committee of Civil Research rather than use the Safeguarding procedures.[37] It was clear that the case would not be settled on its intrinsic merits or demerits; the industry was simply too large, too central, to be granted a tariff that would open the floodgates to protection and make a nonsense of electoral pledges. The clear division of opinion in the industry in 1925 made the task of warding off claims much easier for the government. Steven Tolliday notes, however, that much of the opposition to tariffs within the steel industry disappeared in 1925–6.[38] The North-East coast steel makers virtually all came over to protectionism between 1924–5, and even GKN, the country's largest importer of semi-finished steel and an opponent of protection in 1925, shifted its position during the next three years. Of crucial importance to the erosion of free trade views in the industry was the realisation after the events of 1926 that workers were not going to be forced easily into accepting lower wages. By the late 1920s opposition to protection had all but disappeared among major firms in the industry. The engineering industries also abandoned their equivocation of 1925, in early 1928 the Secretary of the British Engineers' Association writing to Sir William Larke of the NFISM that his organisation was 'sympathetic towards the safeguarding of Iron and Steel as a contributing means of assisting the Iron and Steel industry to improve its economic efficiency and thereby preserve in a state of robust vitality that great basic industry...'[39]

There was weakening allegiance to free trade in the textile industries later in the 1920s, with the woollen industry all but securing a tariff in 1929. Between 1923 and 1928 imports of woollens had doubled and unemployment in the industry rose about 25 per cent. Growing anxiety about the industry's future was reflected in support for tariffs. The woollen and

---

[37] CAB 24/175 CP 48 (25), Position of the Iron and Steel Industry, minutes of 15th meeting of the Committee of Civil Research, 19 Nov. 1925.   [38] Tolliday, *British Steel*.

[39] Bremner to Larke, 13 Mar. 1928. At Larke's request copies of the letter were sent to the Prime Minister and President of the Board of Trade. British Engineers' Association (BEA) 267/1/1/3.

worsted industry had been refused duties in 1926, but having convinced the committee that there were grounds for concern, it bombarded the President of the Board of Trade with complaints that its situation was deteriorating.[40] In September 1928 the Leeds Chamber of Commerce, which previously had refused to discuss protection because it was a 'political matter', voted for an extension of Safeguarding duties.[41] Union support was defeated in January 1928 by Philip Snowden and other West Riding Labour MPs, but in the autumn delegates to the National Association of Unions in the Textile Trades joined with employers in a Safeguarding application.[42] The Board relented at the end of 1928, appointing a committee which recommended duties, technically only for womens' dress goods, although in effect it was recognised they would have to cover a wide range of woollen and worsted imports.[43] Very significantly the Cabinet accepted this recommendation, although Baldwin was able to persuade it to delay implementing the tariff until after the forthcoming election.[44]

Until late in the decade Lancashire stayed largely proof against the protectionist proclivities of the rest of the textile industry, although by 1928 there were signs of apostasy. In September J. J. Butler, the FBI's Secretary in Manchester, reported moves to support Safeguarding in the Manchester Chamber of Commerce, and early in 1929, when a protectionist motion was withdrawn because of the impending election, its MP sponsor, Robert Waddington, expressed surprise at the amount of support he had received.[45]

The impact of the slump

It is the steady erosion of support for free trade in the late 1920s that helps explain the speed with which it collapsed once it was subject to the main force of the world slump following the Wall Street crash in the autumn of 1929. As early as January 1930 there were debates in the Europe and United States section of the Manchester Chamber of Commerce where opposition was expressed to Britain signing an international tariff truce, and concern was voiced about Britain's lack of retaliatory powers.[46] In March the same section passed a resolution by 10 votes to 3 in favour of

[40] CAB 24/178 CP96 (26) and CAB 24/187 CP161 (27), memoranda by Cunliffe-Lister, 5 Mar. 1926 and 23 May 1927.
[41] M. W. Beresford, *The Leeds Chamber of Commerce* (Leeds, 1951), 163.
[42] Boyce, *Capitalism*, 124.
[43] CAB 24/203 CP137 (29), memorandum by Cunliffe-Lister, 2 May 1929.
[44] CAB 23/60 21 (29) 4, 9 May 1929.
[45] FBI/200/F/3/D1/6/121, Butler to Nugent, 27 Sept. 1928 and Manchester Chamber of Commerce (M)/8/5/5, meetings of the Board of Directors, 18 Feb., 11 Mar. and 8 Apr. 1929.   [46] M/8/5/8, Board of Directors, 15 and 24 Jan. 1930.

UK tariffs.[47] More conclusively, in May the Chamber held a referendum in which 1,736 members voted in favour of some form of tariff with only 607 opposed. In June the Bradford Chamber of Commerce voted nearly 7 to 1 in favour of protection, the Leeds Chamber by 497 to 37 and in October another textile chamber, Kidderminster, by 28 to 2.[48] When, in July, the British Engineers' Association polled their membership, 96 per cent of respondents favoured protection.[49]

The shift in Lancashire opinion registered by the vote in May was surprising enough, but the renunciation of free trade by the City of London a few weeks later was even more dramatic. Following a meeting at Hambros Bank on 2 July, a protectionist resolution was passed urging an open market in Britain for Empire goods with a tariff on foreign imports. In 1926 a Bankers' Manifesto had called for free trade. Now:

Bitter experience has taught Great Britain that the hopes expressed four years ago in a plea for the removal of the restrictions upon European trade have failed to be realised. The restrictions have been materially increased, and the sale of surplus foreign products in the British market has steadily grown.[50]

The list of signatories was short but weighty: among the twenty-three who signed were directors of merchant bankers Morgan Grenfell, Baring Brothers and Hambros, Sir George May of the Prudential, chairmen of the main clearing banks and directors of the Bank of England. Eighteen of the twenty-three were bankers. It was, wrote Amery to Baldwin, 'the biggest leg up we have been given since 1903'.[51] When eventually in September a counter-resolution was published in support of continued free trade, it drew 114 signatories, but as a Bank of England memorandum noted, only 17 were bankers. It might have added that although it included the names of Sir Charles Addis and Lord Bradbury, it was not as prestigious a group as the July signatories. Conversions to protection had meanwhile continued, including such influential city figures as Grenfell, Schuster, Holland-Martin and Lewis of the National Provincial Bank.[52] While the Bank memorandum asserted, perhaps disingenuously, that there was 'no documentary evidence of a sweeping change of view',[53] this conflicted with press reports that the call for tariffs represented not a sudden shift of

[47] M/8/5/7, Board of Directors, 23 June 1930.
[48] Bradford Chamber of Commerce 71 D80/1/27, Council, 24 June 1930 and 71 D80/1/28.
[49] BEA 267/1/1/3, Report by Bremner to meeting of Council.
[50] *The Times* 10 July 1930.
[51] Amery to Baldwin, 4 May 1930, Baldwin Mss. Quoted by John Barnes and David Nicholson (eds.), *The Empire at Bay. The Leo Amery Diaries 1929–45* (London, 1988), 28.
[52] Philip Williamson, 'Financiers, the gold standard and British politics, 1925–31', in John Turner (ed.), *Businessmen and Politics. Studies of business activity in British politics, 1900–1945* (London, 1984).   [53] Bank of England, G/19/1, note of 3 Sept. 1930.

opinion but a movement that had been apparent in the City for some time.[54]

Harmony in the views of City and industry may have reflected the closer links that had been formed in the 1920s. Banks and large industrial firms had begun to exchange directors. The close involvement of banks in the postwar boom had led several of them into a precarious dependence on the fortunes of declining industries, notably in the case of some Lancashire based banks, including William Deacons, the District Bank and the Manchester and County. Midland and Barclays through the Union Bank were involved reluctantly in a rescue scheme.[55] On only a slightly smaller scale, the banks were similarly involved in the steel industry, Midland, Lloyds and National Provincial all being closely concerned. This did not immediately propel the banks towards protection. Indeed it was rationalisation, often advocated as an alternative to tariffs, that was seen as the route to the survival of companies, although the commercial banks possessed neither the inclination, the expertise, nor even perhaps the commercial leverage to encourage such a process.[56] Debts, however, drew the Bank of England and Barclays into company reconstruction and rationalisation, notably with Armstrong Whitworth and Beardmore. The reduced foreign business handled in London by the merchant banks in the 1920s was also impelling a move, albeit a reluctant one, towards domestic industry. The links between closer involvement with industry and the shift in City opinion are not easy to establish, but it seems plausible that greater knowledge of industry led to greater sensitivity to the problems faced by industry and the solutions it advocated.

By the autumn of 1930 the FBI, increasingly concerned that it might otherwise become marginalised as the voice of industry, had joined the protectionist bandwagon. When in the summer it had decided to poll its membership on protection, of the 72 per cent of constituencies that recorded a vote, 96 per cent favoured some form of tariff, with no single grouping within the Federation showing a majority in favour of free trade.[57] The FBI joined the Empire Economic Union, the Empire Industries Association, the National Council of Industry and Commerce and the National Union of Manufacturers in a Coordinating Committee on Fiscal Policy that was set up to launch a protectionist propaganda campaign. Morris subscribed £5,000 specifically for campaigning. Efforts were concentrated on obtaining working-class support for protection, the National Council of Industry emphasising that employers should not try to reduce wages at the very time that workers were being persuaded to vote

---

[54] *The Times*, 10 July 1930.
[55] Bank of England, SMT 2/240, Textiles, meetings 24 July and 5 Dec. 1928.
[56] Tolliday, *British Steel*, 178.   [57] FBI/200/F/1/1/74, Fiscal Enquiry Committee.

for a tariff.[58] The FBI arranged for prominent industrialists to address lunch-time meetings; the EIA, which now had the ability to arrange 2,500 meetings a year, concentrated much of its activity in Lancashire, and by June 1931, the coordinating committee reported that more than a million leaflets and 30,000 posters had been distributed.[59]

The politics of the tariff, 1929–1930

There may have been a growing consensus in the business world in 1930 about the need for protection and imperial preference, but from June 1929 it was met by a government that at the outset was profoundly opposed to tariffs.

The advent of a Labour government appeared to have settled the protectionist issue for the time being. Although a market economy and free trade might have appeared difficult to reconcile with socialism, Labour had no plans for the immediate supersession of capitalism. The government also had to depend on Liberals' votes in parliament, and the Liberals, if united on little else, at least agreed on the benefits of free trade: Sir John Simon, later to lead the protectionist wing of the party, was in 1928 attacking Safeguarding tariffs.[60] Even without their dependence on the Liberals, Labour's concern about the price of food, together with a more acute sense of internationalism than the Conservatives, ensured the sanctity of economic liberalism, at least while the pale prosperity of the late 1920s continued. Ramsay MacDonald's position as Prime Minister reinforced the internationalism of Foreign Secretary Arthur Henderson, and key economic portfolios went to free traders Philip Snowden at the Treasury and Willie Graham at the Board of Trade. The free trade stance of the new government was immediately apparent when in June Graham recommended an announcement that Safeguarding duties would not be renewed and key industry duties would stay in force only until the statutory periods expired in 1936. Apparently meeting with no opposition in Cabinet, the statement was strengthened on Snowden's insistence to suggest that duties might be abolished earlier.[61]

The onset of the depression, however, brought the government under protectionist pressure from several directions. In 1930 the major impetus stemmed from the problems and demands of specific industries, notably agriculture and steel, from the Imperial Conference held in London during

[58] EIA/221/1/2/1, 20 Nov. 1930.
[59] FBI/200/F/1/1/74, Coordinating Committee on Fiscal Policy, 8 Feb., 19 June 1931.
[60] D. Abel, *A History of British Tariffs, 1923–1942* (1945), 46–7.
[61] CAB 24/204 CP 156 (29), 19 June 1929; CAB 23/61 25 (29) 3 and 26 (29) 2, Meetings of 26, 28 June 1929.

the autumn, and more generally as a possible solution to mounting unemployment.

As early as January 1930, MacDonald, in conversation with J. H. Thomas, was contemplating the end of free trade, and by February he was actively canvassing a form of levy-subsidy for cereals.[62] This drew a sharp reply from Snowden, who wrote:

I was staggered by the suggestion you make of a registration fee for imported wheat, barley and oats. You do not change a food tax by calling it a registration fee instead of an import duty. I could imagine nothing that would be more disastrous at this moment for us to be associated with anything which had an implication of food taxation.[63]

Grain prices were falling sharply: wheat had touched 9s 7d a quarter in January, but by March was fetching only 8s 3d, well below the levels of the previous year.[64] At the beginning of March, 20–35,000 farmers and farm workers gathered in Cambridge to demand 'immediate attention to the plight of the ploughland'. This was one of many such meetings that helped convince Noel Buxton, the Agriculture Minister, that the government needed to take action. With Baldwin promising help for grain farmers, the government investigated various schemes for countervailing duties, quotas and import boards, but Snowden was able to persuade the Cabinet to postpone any decision until later in the year when an Imperial Conference was due to be held in London.[65] Demands from the steel industry continued unabated. More unexpectedly, a further source of pressure on free trade opinion in government was the shift in expert opinion. Keynes's private policy advice had started to move towards a revenue tariff as early as February 1930.[66] In May, Hubert Henderson, secretary to the Economic Advisory Council, produced a 'bombshell' suggestion of a revenue tariff to finance industrial rationalisation. In October the Committee of Economists (a sub-committee of the EAC) produced a report on the causes of the depression and remedies for it. A majority, Keynes, Henderson and Josiah Stamp, recommended protection, arguing in favour of a tariff on four principal grounds:

(1) that import saving would, on balance, increase employment, probably quite substantially;
(2) that it was doubtful whether the country would find it possible to expand or even to retain a favourable balance of trade by means of a

[62] T. Jones, *Whitehall Diary: Volume II, 1926/1930*, ed. K. Middlemas (1969), 235, and D. Marquand, *Ramsay MacDonald* (1977), 558. The conversation took place on 14 Jan. 1930.
[63] PRO/69, 4 Pt. 2 (MacDonald Papers), Snowden to MacDonald, 24 Feb. 1930.
[64] *The Times*, 15 Jan. 1931.   [65] Marquand, *MacDonald*, 558.
[66] I. M. Drummond, *Imperial Economic Policy 1917–1939* (1974), 149.

cut in money costs without a restriction of imports. A favourable
balance might help with overseas investment;

(3) that in the present circumstances a tariff might have a favourable effect
on the terms of trade;

(4) and that '[w]e consider that the development of inter-Imperial
preferences may become a wise economic policy for this country'.[67]

These arguments, together with budgetary considerations and the likely
favourable effect on business confidence, led the majority to advocate both
a revenue tariff and a Safeguarding duty for the steel industry. They also
suggested an examination of the feasibility of substituting home production for imports. Underlying the economists' call for protection was the
belief that tariffs would create jobs. In this analysis, a major cause of
unemployment was undue rigidity of money wages. In the early 1920s,
when wartime-negotiated sliding scale agreements were still in force,
money wages and prices had fallen very much in line. Subsequently,
indexation had slipped from favour, and by the late 1920s money wages
were exhibiting considerable inflexibility at a time of falling prices. Since
money wages could only be squeezed further by costly and disruptive
industrial struggles, an alternative was to raise price levels by the use of
tariffs on the assumption that money wages would fail to keep pace, real
wages would fall and profits be raised. Output, employment and investment
would be stimulated.[68] Keynes did not favour devaluation, which might
well have had the same effect on wages and prices, because it would
undermine London's status as an international banking centre, and might
start a series of competitive devaluations and financial crises. A tariff could
therefore help solve unemployment without jeopardising the gold standard.

The economists were far from unanimous. A. C. Pigou signed the report
but dissented from the tariff recommendation. Lionel Robbins refused to
sign, objecting both to the conclusions and to Keynes's attempts to force
a unanimous report on the committee.[69] Instead, he wrote his own report,
most of it a vigorous attack on the tariff recommendation of the majority.
In general, the most vocal academic criticism of protectionism came from
Robbins and his colleagues at the London School of Economics. Robbins
was especially critical of Keynes's arguments. He stated that there was no
evidence that wages were inflexible in an upward direction; moreover, a
tariff was likely to stimulate import-competing industries where the
unemployment problem was less pronounced, and it would frustrate the
recovery of the export industries where unemployment was high and

[67] CAB 24/213 CP 234 (30), 5 July 1930.
[68] Eichengreen, *Sterling and the Tariff*, 7–14.
[69] J. Harris, *William Beveridge: a biography* (Oxford, 1977), 317.

money wages already low. This argument found an echo in a book written by a group of economists from the London School of Economics: *Tariffs: The Case Examined*, which was edited by William Beveridge, and included contributions from Robbins, Frederick Benham and John Hicks. Part of the case against Keynes and Stamp was that unemployment was concentrated with particular severity in the export industries – the exporter was concerned with the level of money wages, and it was of no advantage to him if the real wages of his workers fell.[70]

The book was a direct response to the EAC committee's report of October 1930, although it was not published until a year later. For the most part it was a restatement of the liberal case for the power of the market, if unhindered, to secure economic adjustment and maximisation of welfare. It certainly did not stem the protectionist movement, and perhaps lost impact through some ambivalence of purpose.[71] The book had originally been planned as a popular refutation of common fallacies, but in the midst of preparation it was decided to challenge the more sophisticated views of Keynes and Stamp. The authors were not in full agreement, and privately Beveridge was even prepared to contemplate a plan of preferential arrangements between Britain and the primary producing countries.[72]

The EAC committee's report was referred to a Trade Policy Committee of the Cabinet, safely under the chairmanship of Snowden, which not surprisingly came to the view that 'it was a disappointing document', lacking certainty in its conclusion, and containing 'no practical proposition to which immediate effect could be given'.[73] But when at a second meeting Snowden attempted to dismiss the report, he was challenged by Vernon Hartshorn, the Privy Seal, who argued for consideration of the steel industry. There seems little doubt that the report on the industry had considerable influence,[74] and even Graham was suggesting that the circumstances of the controversy over iron and steel had changed in that steel users would not put up the same fight for free trade as in the past. However, Snowden's committee agreed not to pursue the tariff question for the present because, repeating an argument heard throughout the debate of the 1920s, they were 'unanimous in thinking that re-organisation of the industry was an essential preliminary to any further step'.[75]

While the economists' advice in October was confidential, the convening of the Imperial Conference in London in the same month placed much

---

[70] W. H. Beveridge (ed.), *Tariffs: The Case Examined* (1931), 72.
[71] Harris, *Beveridge*, 317–18.   [72] *Ibid.*, 319.
[73] CAB 27/435 T.P.C. (30), 1st meeting, 1 Dec. 1930.
[74] Tom Jones said that it had 'shaken the free trade faith of several of its readers, including Hankey'. Jones, *Whitehall Diary*, 263. Bevin, G. D. H. Cole and Keynes favoured a tariff and nationalisation. CAB 58/2 E.A.C. 12th meeting, 12 Mar. 1931.
[75] CAB 27/435 T.P.C. (30), 2nd meeting, 2 Dec. 1930.

more public pressure on the government to respond to the demands of the dominions, particularly Canada, for greater imperial preferences.

Domestic demands were also building up. Beaverbrook's Empire Free Trade campaign was at its height, and other sections of the press were stressing the opportunities that the conference provided for strengthening imperial economic links. Snowden, in his autobiography, expressed his sympathy for Thomas: 'the Tory press had been flattering him, declaring that here was an opportunity for him to show that he was a great Imperial Statesman'.[76] Thomas probably had his own convictions. The Conservative Party, as discussed below, was moving rapidly in the direction of clear and explicit support for imperial preference. Perhaps more surprisingly, the TUC was edging towards a policy of intra-imperial development.[77] In June 1930 a report of the TUC economic committee, looking at future world economic relationships, dismissed both isolation and world economic unity as impracticable, and went on to examine the relative advantages for Britain of membership of a European bloc, an Anglo-US bloc and a British Commonwealth bloc. Significantly, the first two having been dismissed because of competing economic interests and because the United States showed little enthusiasm for such a venture, the report advocated consolidation of the constituent parts of the British Commonwealth.[78] This was a tentative step in the same direction as many industrialists and financiers were moving. In September the TUC and FBI sent the Prime Minister a joint letter and memorandum in which, on the eve of the conference, they expressed their joint desire 'to place upon record the paramount importance which they attach to all possible steps being taken to increase inter-Commonwealth trade', and that the opportunity should not be missed to place the economic life of the Commonwealth on a 'sound and enduring basis'.[79] The report and joint letters stopped short of explicit advocacy of imperial preference, and instead placed emphasis on the creation of machinery and of a secretariat for Commonwealth cooperation.

There is little evidence of the government coming under pressure from its own backbenchers or from the labour movement as a whole. Nonetheless opinion was shifting. David Marquand states that the parliamentary party's position was unclear, and that traditionally the movement had seen tariffs, especially on food, 'as evil devices to lower working-class living standards'.[80] The Conservatives' soundings, however, suggested 70 per

[76] Philip, Viscount Snowden, *An Autobiography*, II, *1919–34* (1934), 871.
[77] This is traced in A. Bullock, *The Life and Times of Ernest Bevin*, I, *Trade Union Leader, 1881–1940* (1960), 440–7.
[78] A copy of the report is filed in CAB 24/215 as an appendix to CP 304 (30).
[79] CAB 24/215 CP 317 (30), 24 Sept. 1930.   [80] Marquand, *MacDonald*, 556.

cent of Labour MPs would support Safeguarding,[81] and *The Times* reported that although a considerable section of Labour MPs remained orthodox free traders, a growing number were willing to examine the question 'impartially'.[82] Most of the running on tariffs had been made by the political right, many Conservatives seeing protection and imperial preference as a panacea for Britain's economic problems. The more sceptical, pragmatic position of the left was represented by Ernest Bevin. By 1930 he had come to favour tariffs for the steel industry, and to the TUC Conference that year he reported

I have never accepted, as a Socialist, that an inflexible Free Trade attitude is synonomous with Socialism ... I do not believe that tariffs can solve our problem of unemployment at the present moment. On the other hand, I cannot reconcile the real operation of Free Trade with the organisation of industry under public ownership.[83]

The TUC economic committee's report in 1930 had contained a sentence stating that 'In particular circumstances where it is desirable to help a specific trade, a tariff may be justifiable ...'. An attempt in Council to delete the sentence was defeated by 17 votes to 5.[84]

Opinions in the labour movement were changing, but not so decisively as to create concerted pressure on the government. The one occasion when the administration did face a major challenge from within was over the memorandum circulated by Oswald Mosley, Chancellor of the Duchy of Lancaster. Although protection was not specified in the memorandum, it was developed by Mosley shortly after its circulation. Central features of Mosley's plan were an overhaul of the government administration of unemployment and higher public expenditure. An integral part of his conception, as he later explained to the House of Commons in his resignation speech, was development of the home market and rejection of the 'dangerous illusion' that there was hope of recovery through exports. Because the nation 'must to some extent be insulated from the electric shocks of present world conditions', he advocated protection through the agency of an import control board.[85] There was widespread support for Mosley's proposals within the parliamentary party and probably more so within the movement as a whole. Only because he was manoeuvred into making a direct challenge to the government, turning the issue into a test of loyalty, was he defeated so decisively in the parliamentary group. His subsequent defeat at the party conference in October was narrow, and did not prevent him being re-elected to the executive.

[81] Boyce, *Capitalism*, 264.   [82] *The Times*, 5 July 1930.
[83] Cited by Bullock, *Bevin*, 443.
[84] Skidelsky, *Politicians and the Slump: The Labour Government of 1929–1931* (1967), 259.
[85] *Hansard* (Commons), vol. 239, no. 148, 28 May 1930, cols. 1357–9.

But for the presence of Snowden, the Labour government would almost certainly have introduced protectionist measures in 1930. MacDonald, worried by pressures from the grain farmers, and lacking any clear alternative ideas about how to deal with unemployment, favoured tariffs. But he was unwilling to take on Snowden or to muster sufficient support for his position in the Cabinet. Marquand argues that his failure to give a firm lead or to make his views prevail were among the most fatal failures of his career.[86] He had sustained support only from Thomas, by now a somewhat discredited figure, and from Hartshorn and Addison. But clearly he could have mustered much wider backing. One indicator of the shift in Cabinet opinion were the discussions surrounding ratification of a tariff truce Britain had initiated at the League of Nations. In March 1930, Britain had been one of eleven countries to sign a convention ruling out tariff increases before April 1931. It needed ratification by November 1930. The truce was strongly opposed by a wide cross-section of British industry, even the FBI joining the chorus of disapproval.[87] Whilst early in the year Graham had had no difficulty in obtaining the support of his colleagues, by June the mood had changed sufficiently for the Cabinet to decide that ratification should be postponed.[88] In July the Cabinet, without Snowden present, had decided not to ratify.[89] Thomas reportedly told a Conservative MP that the Cabinet had discussed tariffs and that all were in favour apart from Snowden and Graham.[90] Graham does not seem to have been adamantly opposed, but Snowden most emphatically was. Snowden's persistent opposition to tariffs may have reflected intellectual rigidity, but he was well aware of the economists' desire to use them as a way of reducing real wages. He played a vital part in the defence of free trade. He and Graham were able to secure a reversal of the Cabinet's July decision on tariff ratification. Not only in the tariff truce debate, but in his sceptical presence at the imperial conference, in warding off protectionist demands from the steel industry and agriculture, and in stifling the economists' apostasy, Snowden throughout 1930 blocked demands for protection. MacDonald wanted Snowden to go, and in October Snowden threatened to do so.[91] MacDonald, however, was too weak to take the opportunity.

While Snowden helped the government resist tariffs in 1930, the Conservatives in opposition embraced them. Baldwin as Prime Minister had played an important part in keeping the Conservative government to its election pledges of 1924. In doing so he had certainly disappointed the keener protectionists in the party who had banked on the government

[86] Marquand, *MacDonald*, 564.
[87] FBI/200/F/1/1/2, Grand Council minutes, 12 March 1930.
[88] CAB 24/214 CP 285 (30), 30 July 1930 and Marquand, *MacDonald*, 561.
[89] CAB 23/64 49 (30), 6 Aug. 1930.   [90] Boyce, *Capitalism*, 264.   [91] *Ibid.* 274–5.

finding greater scope for extending tariffs under the Safeguarding procedures. For a leader who had gambled on protection in 1923, and who might be judged favourably predisposed to it, he proved surprisingly resistant to the vast pressures that built up in 1930 to adopt tariffs as party policy, this resistance all but costing him leadership of the party.[92]

The loss of the 1929 contest meant that Baldwin had led his party to defeat in two out of three elections. He was also more vulnerable because the election had cut large swathes through the more moderate members from the midlands and northern constituencies while leaving the diehard elements of the southern constituencies, potentially hostile to Baldwin, virtually untouched. In formulating policy in the wake of defeat, Baldwin was concerned above all to preserve party unity as well as to see that the policies adopted were not electoral liabilities. Protection was likely to split the party, and any suggestion of imposing tariffs on foodstuffs might well be fatal for the party's electoral prospects, particularly its chances of regaining seats in the north and midlands.

Baldwin's position as party leader remained comparatively secure in late 1929, although there was some restlessness after the lacklustre campaign of the summer as well as over his uninspiring performance as leader of the opposition, a role for which by temperament he was peculiarly unsuited. From early 1930, however, Baldwin came under attack. That he retained the leadership owed much to the tactical errors of his opponents, especially the blundering, ill-timed moves of the press barons. Baldwin was able to use these open challenges to his authority to win the party's affirmation of his position. Yet in the process he had to move some way to appease his opponents.

By late in 1929 it was evident that Beaverbrook's Empire Crusade campaign, launched in July, was finding a ready response in the south. Empire Free Trade would have been a non-starter in Joseph Chamberlain's day, let alone a generation later and in the face of the mounting protection the dominions were giving their secondary industry as the depression deepened. By the same token, although it was by no means clear how agricultural protection combined with free entry for Empire produce would in fact help UK agriculture, the campaign nonetheless had great appeal. Collapsing wheat prices helped its reception in the rural areas. This put pressure on Baldwin to act before being stampeded by the constituencies. In a speech at the Coliseum on 5 February 1930, he pledged a future Conservative government to extend Safeguarding duties to steel and

---

[92] The following three paragraphs rely heavily on Middlemas and Barnes, *Baldwin*, ch. 10; Ramsden, *History of the Conservative Party*, ch. 8; Stuart Ball, *Baldwin and the Conservative Party: the Crisis of 1929–31* (New Haven, London, 1988), and Barnes and Nicholson, *Amery Diaries*.

textiles. A year earlier this would have been a dramatic move, but as Amery commented 'opinion has moved so fast in our party that a speech which would have been rapturously welcomed a year ago is now felt to be inadequate'.[93] It certainly promised nothing for agriculture, prompting Beaverbrook's crusade committee to pass a resolution the same day that although Baldwin had made a step in the right direction he had not gone far enough on foodstuffs and raw materials. On 18 February, Beaverbrook, with Lord Rothermere's support, transformed the Empire Crusade into the United Empire Party to campaign for protection and closer imperial integration. While the Empire Crusade had been an attempt to win the Conservative Party round for the policy, the new party was a direct challenge, threatening to run candidates in fifty Conservative seats. Baldwin responded quickly, instigating a meeting with Beaverbrook at which he agreed to hold a national referendum on food taxes. This was announced by Baldwin the next day, 4 March, in a speech at the Hotel Cecil. The pledge appeared to patch up differences, staying Beaverbrook's hand as well as drawing at least public support from figures as diametrically opposed on the issue as Amery and Churchill.[94] Beaverbrook and Baldwin, however, each interpreted the agreement differently. While Baldwin thought the food tax issue had been shelved for the time-being, Beaverbrook believed the Tories were now committed to agricultural protection, a belief probably encouraged by private assurances from Neville Chamberlain that the referendum idea would be buried as soon as possible. Baldwin proved to have bought very little time. The strength of Conservative backbench opinion was shown after Lord Salisbury had written to *The Times* suggesting British industry needed something more immediate than tariffs and imperial economic integration.[95] When Page Croft threatened to hold a meeting of the EIA which could call upon 187 Tory MPs, Salisbury was forced to write again in 'clarification' of his earlier letter.[96] Rothermere rejected the Hotel Cecil statement, facing Beaverbrook with the choice of a split in the United Empire Party or moving to the attack again. Beaverbrook was beginning to doubt the genuineness of Baldwin's commitment to the referendum, complaining that he 'used it as a shield instead of a sword'.[97] The continued assault of the press lords probably helped fuel growing dissatisfaction with Baldwin's leadership, especially in London and the south-east where their papers, including the London evening press, found their principal readership. It was the southern constituencies that were the most restive. By July 1930 disaffection was widespread, by September it had reached unprecedented levels. Maladroit

[93] Diary, 5 Feb. 1930, Barnes and Nicholson, *Amery Diaries*.
[94] *The Times*, 6, 7 March 1930.   [95] *Ibid.*, 25 Mar. 1930.   [96] *Ibid.*, 8 Apr. 1930.
[97] Beaverbrook to Hoare, 15 May 1930, quoted Barnes and Nicholson, *Amery Diaries*, 24.

moves by Beaverbrook and Rothermere, apparent attempts to dictate terms to a future Conservative government, open challenges to Baldwin's authority, forced the party to rally to its leader. To take some of the steam from the movement and with an eye to the forthcoming imperial conference, Chamberlain announced much more aggressive proposals in what he called his 'unauthorised programme', particularly in a speech of 20 September when he demanded a free hand to negotiate with the dominions to make the best bargain possible whether it included a food tax or not. Baldwin's survival as leader probably rested on his acceptance of such a programme when he returned from his annual stay in France. He was helped by clear indications of growing support for protection in the country as a whole. If there had been any doubt about views in the south, they had been dispelled by the shift in City opinion and by Beaverbrook's vigorous campaign. It was the north that worried Baldwin. The crumbling of free trade support during the winter of 1929–30 has been indicated above, and mounting unemployment reinforced this. It was the sharp deterioration of the economy after years of difficult conditions that weakened adherence to free trade, not Beaverbrook's campaign, which had little discernible influence in the north. By September the protectionist views of the southern constituencies were finding support from those in the north, with Lord Derby himself, 'King of Lancashire' and long the leader of the anti-protectionist group in the Tory party, having decided in June to back the tariff campaign. This turnabout Amery ascribed to the change of opinion in Lancashire.[98] Baldwin was therefore both relieved of the earlier constraints he had felt and at the same time compelled to act for his political survival. On 7 October the Business Committee, an inner shadow cabinet, adopted a full protectionist programme with Churchill alone dissenting. The opportunity to make this public came in the wake of the government's rejection of Bennett's reciprocal preference offer at the imperial conference. Chamberlain seized the opportunity to draft an open letter, ostensibly written by Baldwin to him, which outlined the change in Conservative policy.[99] The Conservatives intended to bring in an emergency tariff on manufactured goods 'which would preserve the home market while the necessary investigations and negotiations with other countries, incidental to the preparation of a more scientific scheme, were pursued'. Baldwin stated that he had 'already promised to guarantee the price of home-grown wheat used for breadmaking; to stop the dumping of foreign bounty-fed oats; to put a tax on foreign malting barley; and to see

[98] *Ibid.*, 23 June 1930.
[99] *The Times*, 16 Oct. 1930. The letter was in fact drafted by Chamberlain and approved by the Shadow Cabinet, Churchill dissenting. K. G. Feiling, *The Life of Neville Chamberlain* (1946), 181.

to it that a large proportion of the supplies of meat and wheat to the Defence Forces shall be home products'. In addition, he asserted that the whole country had been shocked by the intensive dumping of foreign fruit and vegetables which had destroyed markets before smallholders were in a position to dispose of their crops, and therefore agriculture must be protected from such disturbances. Agriculture must be seen in the framework of imperial policy, and in this context Baldwin now withdrew his idea of a referendum, substituting the idea of a single electoral mandate for protection.

Chamberlain used the recently established Conservative Research Department to draft tariff proposals as well as to recommend ways of implementing legislation both quickly and lastingly. The Research Department had already been working on imperial trade policy. A committee to plan the future shape of agriculture was established, and in early December a group under Sir Philip Cunliffe-Lister's chairmanship, including Amery, Sir Basil Blackett, George Lloyd and Herbert Williams was established to investigate duties on manufacturers.[100] Chamberlain wanted to capitalise on the current disillusionment with free trade to build a permanent tariff structure. The committee met twenty-five times in the first six months of 1931 before producing a bulky report in July. It recommended a wideranging three-decker tariff with rates of 10, $16\frac{2}{3}$ and $33\frac{1}{3}$ per cent, together with scope for imperial preferences.

The committee concentrated on devising parliamentary procedures that would allow protectionism to be legislated with the minimum of fuss and the maximum of speed.[101] There would first be an emergency tariff before the introduction of a more 'scientific' Tariff Act embodying permanent legislation, a method that would avoid using the framework of a Finance Bill which would have involved annual debates on the tariff schedules. A 'scientific' tariff, a common inter-war conception, was to be arrived at through a Tariff Advisory Committee under a legally qualified chairman. The idea had been floated by the 1923 Tariff Advisory Committee which had drawn its inspiration from the Australian model. As Baldwin expressed it, he was not going to be responsible for making the country a profiteer's paradise or parliament a 'crooks' corner', and, echoing Lord Bradbury's remarks on the gold standard six years earlier, he was going to make the tariff 'knave-proof', taking it 'as far from politics as you can'.[102]

The committee had been anxious to avoid being seen as simply responding to pressure from industry. Yet the committee included prominent industrialists, carried out extensive informal consultations with other industrial leaders, and for years there had been a fusion of

---

[100] Conservative Research Department (CRD)/1/2/11, Report of the Tariff Committee of the CRD.   [101] *Ibid.*   [102] CRD/1/2/13.

involvement between politicians and businessmen through such groupings as the Empire Industries Association, and, more recently, Amery's Empire Economic Union. It is therefore not surprising that when later the FBI produced a memorandum on tariffs, Cunliffe-Lister could comment, 'the whole thing is in substance an adoption of our original "Research" proposal'.[103]

The fall of the Labour government

By the end of 1930 the government was faced by a Tory opposition clamouring for protection. Yet almost at the same moment that the Conservatives finally took the plunge on tariffs the preoccupation of the party's economic policy began to centre on the budgetary position of the government and the need for 'Economy'. The debate about tariffs changed in 1931, and although protectionist demands remained strong, the greatest pressure for the remainder of the life of the second Labour government stemmed from the budget deficit and the financial crisis.

The problems of revenue had been foreshadowed in discussions during the summer of 1930. Thomas had argued that to rule out tariffs would, in effect, declare that the only source of revenue from which prospective deficits could be remedied was direct taxation.[104] When in the late summer MacDonald had canvassed Cabinet Ministers about their views on tariffs, he suggested that the budgetary position would be so weak the next year that the choice would be between a heavy increase in direct tax and a revenue tariff.[105]

In March 1931 the *New Statesman* published an article by Keynes advocating a revenue tariff.[106] He argued for expansionary policies, but suggested that unless accompanied by other measures there would be dangerous effects on the trade balance, the budget and confidence. Ultimately the expansion would generate revenue for the budget and confidence would be regained, but in the interim there was a problem. This was best met by a wideranging revenue tariff with one or two flat rates and with rebates on imported materials entering exports. The tariff would relieve the pressing problem of the budget, restore business confidence and provide a margin to finance the extra imports generated by expansion as well as providing finance for overseas loans. He concluded, presciently, 'if Free Traders reject these counsels of expediency, the certain result will be

---

[103] T 172/1768. Sir Philip Cunliffe-Lister to N. Chamberlain, 15 Jan. 1932. Amery makes the same observation in L. S. Amery, *My Political Life*, III, *The Unforgiving Years 1929–1940* (1955), 20. [104] CAB 23/65 50 (30), 2 Sept. 1930.
[105] Snowden, *Autobiography*, 923.
[106] *New Statesman and Nation*, 7 Mar. 1931. Reprinted in J. M. Keynes, *Essays in Persuasion* (1951), 271–80.

to break the present Government and to substitute for it, in the confusion of a Crisis of Confidence, a Cabinet pledged to a full protectionist programme'. Five days later Keynes returned to his theme in a meeting of the Economic Advisory Council, stressing 'that the dangers of doing nothing were so great that the country might easily be faced with a crisis of confidence [and that] what was needed, above all, was that the Government should secure their Budgetary position and do so quickly. This could only be done by a Revenue Tariff.'[107] His fellow member of the EIC, Josiah Stamp, stated that he felt the case for a tariff was much stronger now than six months ago when the economists' report was written. There was a lengthy discussion of the steel industry, and the meeting, under Mac-Donald's chairmanship, ended inconclusively.

Despite the prospect of a fiscal deficit in 1931–2, Snowden in his budget of 27 April rejected increases in direct taxation, and dismissed the revenue tariff as a device for 'relieving the well-to-do at the expense of the poor'.[108] While Snowden stayed in office the free trade policy of the government was secure; when ill-health and the need to strengthen Labour in the House of Lords threatened his tenure, the prospect of Thomas as his successor 'was enough to make Snowden cling to office with redoubled vigour'.[109]

Thomas suffered another setback in June. The Cabinet committee preparing for Ottawa recommended to the Cabinet that Britain should offer a quota for dominion wheat milled in the UK. After opposition from Snowden, and a threat of resignation from A. V. Alexander (First Lord of the Admiralty), to prevent a split the Cabinet rejected the quota and 'disposed ... of any proposal increasing the price of food, *under whatever alias*'.[110]

The issue of the revenue tariff arose in its most acute form during the financial crisis of the late summer. Yet even though a revenue tariff must have seemed an obvious answer to the government's needs, the Labour administration's commitment to free trade remained intact through the last desperate days of office. A tariff to provide revenue and help towards balancing the budget was one of the measures suggested to MacDonald by

[107] CAB 58/2 E.A.C. 12th meeting, 12 Mar. 1931.
[108] Cited in Skidelsky, *Politicians*, 340. W. H. Janeway, 'The economic policy of the second Labour Government, 1929–31' (Ph.D. thesis, University of Cambridge, 1971), 221–5, reports Treasury advice to Snowden that if tariffs were to have been introduced to parliament in April, a decision in principle would have been needed months in advance. Despite repeated requests from his colleagues, Snowden rejected any pre-Budget consultation.
[109] Skidelsky, *Politicians*, 361. Skidelsky quotes B. Webb's diaries and a conversation between her and Ethel Snowden. Snowden himself thought Graham the only person fitted to take over his office.
[110] S. Webb to B. Webb, 4 June 1931, quoted in Gupta, *Imperialism*, 159 and Skidelsky, *Politicians*, 362. Emphasis in original.

Harvey and Peacock of the Bank of England.[111] Apparently it was considered by the Economy Committee set up to examine the May Report, but was outvoted four to one.[112] When in the full Cabinet of 19 August Arthur Henderson raised the question of a tariff, fifteen members voted for a revenue tariff on manufactured goods, with some willing to support its extension to foodstuffs and raw materials.[113] In Cabinet next evening reports were made on meetings with Conservative and Liberal leaders. The Conservatives made no reference to a revenue tariff, concentrating their advice on bigger savings in unemployment insurance, but the Liberals were strongly opposed to one.[114] Later that evening a General Committee of the TUC delegation met members of the Economy Committee. The General Committee had spent a major part of their meeting earlier in the day discussing the crisis, and although a majority were probably sympathetic to a tariff, at least as an alternative to reductions in the standard of living, they felt that Congress decisions in the past precluded the General Council from advocating such a measure.[115] They proposed to submit a resolution to Congress on the subject. The issue was finally dismissed in the Cabinet of 21 August. The minute states that:

In the course of discussion it was represented that since the last discussion of this question by the Cabinet the situation had completely altered by reason of the rejection by the Liberal Party of any such expedient and by the acceptance in principle of the suspension of the Sinking Fund which it was claimed rendered recourse to a Revenue Tariff unnecessary. There was considerable support for the view that the Revenue Tariff should be excluded from the proposals, if, and only if, no further economies were made in regard to Unemployment Insurance. In reply to the Chancellor of the Exchequer, who expressed the strongest possible objections

[111] MacDonald's diary, 11 Aug. 1931, cited by Marquand, *MacDonald*, 615.
[112] CAB 27/454. The committee, consisting of MacDonald, Snowden, Arthur Henderson, Thomas and Graham, did not circulate any minutes or conclusions of meetings. Skidelsky, *Politicians*, 397, quoting a memorandum by Graham in the Lansbury papers, records the vote, with only Thomas in favour of a tariff, although the committee thought a tariff preferable to a cut in benefit (also by four votes to one – Snowden the minority). See also R. Bassett, *1931, Political Crisis* (1958), 71. MacDonald's diary records only the one vote, with four in favour of a tax and Snowden against. Marquand, *MacDonald*, 616. It is evident that Graham's opposition to tariffs had weakened.
[113] Bassett, *1931*, 76–7. The minority, according to B. Webb's diary, cited in Bassett, were Snowden, Benn, Parmoor, Alexander and Passfield himself. MacDonald's diary, as reported by Marquand, *MacDonald*, 618, records five voting for a tax on all imports and ten for a duty on manufactured goods only (this must mean another ten supported its application to manufactured goods alone).
[114] CAB 23/67, Meeting of 20 Aug. 1931. N. Chamberlain was anxious to establish a National Government, and, although possibly seeing the economy measures as necessary, certainly saw cutting the dole as a way to split the Labour Party irrevocably. See Middlemas and Barnes, *Baldwin*, 623–5 (Baldwin was still in France). His diary suggests that he did think budget cuts necessary to restore foreign confidence, but that he had plans for tariffs later. N. Chamberlain's diary, 22 Aug. 1931. Neville Chamberlain Papers (N.C.) 2/22.   [115] Bassett, *1931*, 98.

to the Government being committed in any way to the principle of a Revenue Tariff, the Prime Minister stated that it would be clearly understood that no decision of any kind had been reached on the subject of a Revenue Tariff.[116]

In principle a revenue tariff might have formed an effective part of a package of government economy measures because it would have operated on two related aspects of the problem. By raising revenue it would have contributed to closing the budgetary gap, and by cutting back imports it would have brought about an immediate improvement in the balance of payments, and moreover, have done so without the time-lag associated with orthodox deflationary measures. In reality it would have been an ineffective measure. Even without Snowden's resignation (and it is doubtful whether by this time the government or sterling could have survived that),[117] the revenue tariff would not have been successful in restoring confidence in the pound unless it was accompanied by precisely those economy measures that the Cabinet could not agree anyway. While in its early stages the crisis was seen as essentially a reflection of the German situation, by late in August it was seen as much more directly a British crisis.[118] All members of the Cabinet were committed to preserving the pound, and to balancing the budget as the only way of securing that objective.[119] Once this had been decided, the Cabinet had to please the holders of sterling. This meant not merely balancing the budget, but doing so in the particular way that impressed the bankers. There may not have been a banker's ramp in that the financial community was deliberately engineering the downfall of the government,[120] but there was in the sense that the Cabinet had to do what the City wanted if the Bank of England was to recommend Paris and New York to provide further loans. And the central issue here was the willingness of the government to cut unemployment pay – it was this that became the test of the Labour government's resolve. So a tariff, which would almost certainly not have obtained support from the Liberals, would have been useless unless accompanied by cuts in unemployment benefit.

The fall of the Labour government paved the way for a National government which took little more than six months to build the skeletal

---

[116] CAB 23/67, meeting of 21 Aug. 1931.

[117] R. S. Sayers, *The Bank of England 1891–1944*, II (Cambridge, 1976), 398, states that the American bankers from whom the British government was trying to secure a credit would accept the view of the Bank of England, the Chancellor and the Opposition parties as to what constituted an adequate programme.   [118] *Ibid.*, 402.

[119] No alternative objectives or methods seem to have been discussed. The focus of the split became the extent to which the budget would be balanced and the means of doing so.

[120] Philip Williamson, 'A Bankers' Ramp? Financiers and the British political crisis of August 1931', *English Historical Review*, 99 (1984); Boyce, *Capitalism*, ch. 11 and Diane B. Kunz, *The Battle for Britain's Gold Standard in 1931* (London, 1987).

structure of Britain's protectionist system, and just over a year to flesh it out, finally precipitating the resignation of the remaining free traders from the government.

The National government

There was no overt move to protection in the brief life of the first National government. Instead the Conservatives jockeyed for position, attempting to commit the government to tariffs in its election platform in October. MacDonald, anxious to preserve some substance to the 'National' label of the government, and to prevent the Conservatives from forcing out the Samuelite Liberals, managed to block a joint protectionist manifesto, substituting the curious arrangement whereby the government would 'go to the country on a general policy on which the Cabinet was unanimous, leaving discretion to the various Parties to deal with the control of imports and tariffs on their own lines'.[121] As a result the Tories advocated protection while MacDonald and other candidates attempted to play the issue down.

The sweeping victory of the National government, with 556 out of 615 seats, left it in an unassailable position after the election. The realities of power were clear: if necessary, the Conservatives could have governed perfectly well by themselves. Tom Jones judged that 'here is a Parliamentary Dictatorship and the Tory wolves will howl for high tariffs and will give S[tanley] B[aldwin] hell'.[122] MacDonald, obviously anxious to prevent a split in the Cabinet, tried to preserve a reasonable balance in the distribution of posts between parties and protectionist predilections. He wanted Neville Chamberlain as Minister of Health with Cunliffe-Lister at the Board of Trade, but Baldwin insisted Chamberlain should go to the Treasury.[123] At Snowden's suggestion (he was later to regret it), to avoid having protectionists in two key economic posts, Walter Runciman, the Liberal, became President of the Board of Trade, and Cunliffe-Lister became Colonial Secretary.[124] MacDonald was able to exclude the hardline protectionist Amery from office altogether.

With the Cabinet formed, the 'Great Policy' was implemented at exceptional speed. On 10 November Chamberlain and Runciman were asked to investigate a recent reported rise in imports.[125] They produced a

---

[121] Quoted in Marquand, *MacDonald*, 666.
[122] Jones, *Whitehall Diary*, II, 20, quoted by Barnes and Nicholson, *Amery Diaries*.
[123] Marquand, *MacDonald*, 703.
[124] Snowden, *Autobiography*, 999. In view of Runciman's later role in the controversy, Snowden commented 'I hope that the Recording Angel has kept no note of my responsibility for Mr. Runciman's appointment to this office!'
[125] CAB 23/69 CAB 74 (31), 10 Nov. 1931.

memorandum the next day, and on somewhat fragmentary evidence showed that although imports in October 1931 were not significantly higher than the year before, there had been a considerable increase in the first few days of November.[126] On this slender basis, and the fear that the rise might continue, they asked for a Bill enabling the government to impose duties of up to 100 per cent *ad valorem* on any type of manufactured good being imported in abnormal quantities. On the 12th the Cabinet approved the preparation of a Bill, which was to expire after a year.[127]

Pressure from members of agricultural constituencies ensured that another part of Conservative policy was implemented at speed.[128] Duties were applied to various imported fruits, vegetables and horticultural products. Proposals were presented to parliament so rapidly that they did not have Cabinet approval.[129] 'Luxury' foodstuffs were less controversial than the great staples, but *The Economist*, condemning as derisory the argument used in supporting the 'greengrocery bill' that it was needed for the stability of the pound, saw the measure as 'an attempt to insert the thin edge of a food tax wedge'.[130] The free traders in the Cabinet were curiously muted, Snowden later arguing that they did not oppose the measures because they were temporary.[131] Chamberlain recorded that 'Snowden growled but almost inaudibly and the Samuelites offered no objection... But as for me, I laff and laff.'[132]

The vehicle for the implementation of the permanent tariff was a Balance of Trade committee. It needed some careful manoeuvring by Chamberlain.[133] MacDonald clearly wanted to avoid such a potentially divisive issue, yet faced by the necessity for action he was outwitted by Chamberlain. According to Chamberlain's record of events, MacDonald planned to establish two small committees, one to ascertain the facts, and a second committee to deal with any political ramifications that might arise out of the recommendations of the first. The fact-finding committee was to consist of Chamberlain, Snowden, Runciman and Hilton Young, a group bound to disagree on policy. The second, comprising MacDonald, Baldwin, Samuel and Simon, was designed to avoid too contentious a

---

[126] The import surge may well have occurred because tariffs, especially on manufactures, were widely anticipated. Capie, 'Pressure for tariff protection', 446–7.

[127] CAB 24/224 CP 274 (31), 11 Nov. 1931; CAB 23/69 CAB 76 (31), 12 Nov. 1931.

[128] One hundred and fifty members of the Conservative Agricultural Committee met on 17 Nov. and decided to press for a clear statement of agricultural policy and the programme that session on various aspects of import policy, including that dealing with the 'dumping of luxury imports'. A deputation from the Committee later went to see MacDonald, and one from various agricultural organisations also saw Gilmour (Minister of Agriculture) that day. *The Times*, 18 Nov. 1931.   [129] CAB 24/224 CP 299 (31).

[130] *The Economist*, 113, 5 Dec. 1931, 1057–8.   [131] Snowden, *Autobiography*, 1004–5.

[132] Iain Macleod, *Neville Chamberlain* (1961), 155.

[133] Twelve page memorandum, concluded 30 Jan. 1932, outlines the events. NC 8/18/1.

programme. Chamberlain managed to transform the first committee into a much larger group that would obviate the need for the second committee. Runciman and Chamberlain played the key roles. The central contribution of Runciman helped to ensure that tariffs, behind which lay a multiplicity of motives and conflicting objectives, would be structured and used for bargaining in international trade. The price Chamberlain had to accept for securing protection was that it was more modest in the first place than he and the protectionists would have liked. The Conservative Research Department's three-decker emergency tariff structure was unacceptable to Runciman. Instead, he suggested a wide 10 per cent revenue tariff. Chamberlain, reluctantly accepting this, was able to take advantage of Runciman's interest in trade bargaining to suggest a surtax on certain goods, of use in trade negotiations.

The fact that the protectionists hoped to use the trade deficit as the excuse for tariffs created difficulty after the devaluation of sterling. Either measure might have rectified the trade imbalance. Both together seemed excessive. To complicate matters further, Samuel thought that capital movements had a great bearing on the overall balance of payments and should be taken into account. Chamberlain, chairman of the committee, drafted a memorandum (on a wet Christmas Day) which was highly tendentious.[134] He argued that capital movements were irrelevant and that financing a current account deficit by running down assets meant living off capital: the real point was that exports had to be increased or imports reduced. Since little could be done in export expansion, it was in import reduction that the scope for action lay.

The whole question of adjustment should have been transformed by the suspension of the gold standard in September and the subsequent depreciation of sterling. Keynes had withdrawn his support for a tariff, and urged the currency question as the dominant issue.[135] Beveridge had argued in the *News Chronicle* of 22 September that tariffs and the suspension of the gold standard were mutually exclusive policies.[136] Later in June 1932, a second edition of *Tariffs: The Case Examined*, had a chapter added by Frederick Benham, examining the balance of payments arguments in the light of the departure from the gold standard. Here he stated flatly of the floating exchange 'that it *is* a solution, and a complete solution, of the problem of restoring equilibrium, is beyond dispute'.[137] Meanwhile the Treasury had provided a battery of arguments why the external value of the pound should be prevented from falling excessively. These included the harmful effects on investment account, the serious inflationary potential of

---

[134] T 172/1768, handwritten draft, 25 Dec. 1931.   [135] *The Times*, 28 Sept. 1931.
[136] Quoted in Abel, *Tariffs*, 79–80.
[137] W. H. Beveridge (ed.), *Tariffs. The Case Examined* (2nd edn 1932), 253.

excessive depreciation and the need for sterling stability if London's international financial status was to be maintained or enhanced.[138] A memorandum by Sir Richard Hopkins, later circulated to the committee as one of Chamberlain's, also argued strongly against letting market forces dictate the value of the pound.[139] Certainly the Treasury did not want sterling to appreciate too far because of the harm to exports: 'we *know* from bitter experience (tho on no account could we afford to say so openly now) that they *cannot* stand an exchange value of \$4.86' (emphasis in original). The lower range (\$3.80–4.10 was Hopkins' view in December) was still a matter of debate. Treasury views were in fact undergoing some modification, and by early in 1932 the tendency was to consider the optimum rate of exchange to be around \$3.40.[140] It is doubtful whether the Treasury really thought the commercial policy of the government an important influence on the exchange rate. They were much more concerned with short-term balances still in London and with speculation; the main thrust of policy was in managing affairs so that despite the ending of the gold standard, inflation could be avoided.[141] Paradoxically, official thinking favoured modest inflation as a way of reducing real wages and restoring profitability, thus echoing the arguments of the economists; a low rate for the pound would contribute to this price adjustment, as well as assisting exports.[142] The emphasis was on *controlled* inflation.

Samuel's request that economists be consulted by the committee was rejected by Chamberlain, although Samuel was permitted to canvass their opinions privately.[143] The committee concluded that the current account was likely to reach a deficit of £90 to £120 million in 1931 and to worsen in 1932 in the absence of remedial action. A revenue tariff was calculated to reduce this by £34 million, with various assumptions about lower, preferential rates for dominion produce and free entry for some colonial produce. Certain exemptions for staple foodstuffs (not dairy products) and the principal raw materials were suggested. Depreciation of sterling was assumed to help exports, boosting them by £106 million, it was calculated.[144] Obviously the report had the support of Runciman, as well as that of his Liberal colleague, Sir John Simon, and of Labour's J. H. Thomas. This was what Chamberlain had aimed to secure because MacDonald, by

---

[138] T 172/1768. The memorandum is not dated, but probably Dec. 1931.
[139] *Ibid.*, 15 Dec. 1931.
[140] This discussion is traced in Susan Howson, *Domestic Monetary Management in Britain, 1919–1938* (Cambridge 1975), 82–6 and 173–80.
[141] Various memoranda in T 175/57 (Hopkins Papers).   [142] *Ibid.*
[143] T 172/1768. Samuel to Chamberlain and Chamberlain to Samuel, 17 Dec. 1931.
[144] CAB 27/476. Committee on the Balance of Trade. Report 19 Jan. 1932. The committee consisted of N. Chamberlain (Chairman), Samuel, Simon, Thomas, Cunliffe-Lister, Hilton Young, Runciman, Snowden and Gilmour.

accepting it, was less likely to appear simply as a tool of the Tories and the government a façade for unadulterated Conservatism.

Nonetheless, the scale of opposition to the report was far greater than Chamberlain and Runciman had anticipated in December.[145] They had assumed Samuel could be accommodated and had even had hopes of gaining acceptance from Snowden. In the event both strongly disagreed with the report, and wrote dissenting memoranda.[146] Samuel reported his consultations with a number of economists and pointed to technical errors in the calculations (i.e. that while the depreciation of sterling was assumed to lead to higher prices of imports, no allowance was made for a consequential reduction in volume) and Snowden seized upon the confusion of thought in introducing a Revenue tariff in order to curtail imports.

The first battle was fought in Cabinet on 21 January 1932. Unusually full minutes exist of the discussion, and the debate reveals the pre-determined position of most Cabinet members.[147] There was argument over the cost of living and the effects of currency depreciation. The use of the tariff as a bargaining instrument was advocated by several proponents. Baldwin, Ormsby-Gore, Londonderry and Thomas stressed the necessity for a British tariff to bring about a general reduction in world tariff levels, but apart from Chamberlain, who appeared to see it as a way of obtaining a 'private entrance for ourselves' into other markets, nobody indicated whether the object was the pursuit of special privileges for British exports or a multilateral reduction in protection. Several speakers, including Chamberlain, Hilton Young and Runciman, summoned the spectre of the German mark in laying stress on the inflationary dangers of a depreciating currency. The most repeated argument in favour of protection pointed to the underlying political realities of the Cabinet's situation. If the Cabinet failed to initiate protectionist legislation, the House of Commons would see to it that they were replaced by a Cabinet that would. Hoare and Hailsham circumspectly referred to 'political difficulties', Ormsby-Gore and Eyres-Monsell were more direct, and Baldwin 'would regret (the National government's) collapse as keenly as that of a Conservative Government'.

Protection may have preserved the position of the Cabinet from Conservative backbenchers, but it exposed it to the resignations of Snowden and the Liberals Samuel, Sinclair and Maclean. The Conservatives, reversing their earlier stance, were by this time anxious to keep the

---

[145] NC 8/18/1, memorandum, 30 Jan. 1932 and Walter Runciman Papers (WR) 245, Runciman to MacDonald, 21 Dec. 1931.
[146] CAB 27/467. These memoranda were circulated as CP 31 (32) and CP 32 (32), 18 and 19 Jan. 1932 respectively.   [147] CAB 23/70 CAB 5 (32), 21 Jan. 1932.

Samuelite Liberals in the government, some of them hoping one day to effect a merger between the Liberals and themselves.[148] The acceptance of Hailsham's suggestion that the dissenting ministers be allowed to voice their opposition to government policy postponed the resignations. Although Amery predicted '[t]he whole world would rock with laughter at the fatuity of the proposal and that it would break down before the week was out',[149] in fact it endured until the autumn. The continued presence in the Cabinet of the free trade group may well have moderated the scale of protection when the details of the programme were settled. It was not the only factor. Runciman was opposed to food taxes, as was Thomas.[150] MacDonald also appears to have been strongly opposed to them, writing to Runciman that it would be suicidal to think of taxing food essentials: 'No greater calamity to the country could happen than that by our handling of affairs we encourage the marshalling of a real class movement supported by the better minded skilled artisans'.[151] Among the Conservatives in the Cabinet, even the protectionist Cunliffe-Lister had been doubtful about food duties.[152] But the continued presence of the tariff dissidents probably helped make the Cabinet more nervous of accepting proposals from the Minister of Agriculture.

The principles of industrial protection were agreed readily – a 10 per cent tariff on finished and semi-manufactured products not already charged under other acts, while raw materials would be duty free. The Import Duties Advisory Committee would make recommendations on higher selective duties, and could therefore develop a 'scientific' tariff. Over agriculture there was conflict, as there was to be for the remainder of the decade, between the Ministry of Agriculture and a coalition of other interests. The Agricultural Policy Committee of the Cabinet reported on 16 January, its protectionist stance immediately apparent.[153] The committee argued for parity of treatment with industry, either by the introduction of a low wide-ranging tariff or by selective but higher duties. The Minister, Sir John Gilmour, was under heavy pressure from the agricultural constituencies but found the Cabinet unsympathetic. On two occasions he either had to apologise for statements to the Cabinet or to go away and redraft a proposed public statement that was considered too protectionist in language.[154] At least he must have been prepared for the successive defeats

---

[148] Marquand, *MacDonald*, 713.
[149] Amery diary, 22 Jan. 1932, Barnes and Nicholson, *Amery Diaries*.
[150] NC 8/81/1, memorandum, 30 Jan. 1932, for Runciman's statement to Chamberlain.
[151] WR 245, MacDonald to Runciman, 28 Dec. 1931.
[152] NC 2/22. Diary, 8 Dec. 1929.
[153] CAB 27/465, Agricultural Policy Committee Report, 16 Jan. 1932.
[154] CAB 23/69 CAB 81 (31) 25 Nov. 1931 discussing a memorandum of 23 Nov. 1931 and CAB/23/70 CAB 11 (32) 3 Feb. 1932, discussing a memorandum of 27 Jan. 1932.

he was to endure over imperial preference and free entry before and during the Ottawa Conference.

Conclusion

Ian Drummond has argued that if the government desired to use tariffs to combat unemployment, it was in fact using measures designed to do precisely the reverse once sterling had been floated. Tariffs, by causing the exchange rate to appreciate, would reduce national output and employment.[155] As pointed out above, the view that the government was primarily concerned with tackling unemployment is contested by Eichengreen. The politicians, he suggests, 'supported the imposition of the General Tariff in order to guard against the dangers of hyperinflation and unbounded exchange-rate depreciation, and they made this choice knowing that the tariff might exacerbate the problem of domestic unemployment'.[156] Eichengreen has performed a valuable service in drawing attention to the apparent concern of the government about the balance of payments. The mere name, 'The Balance of Trade Committee', the report of which formed the basis for the Cabinet discussion, suggests this. The experience of Germany in 1923 was a dreadful example of the results of uncontrolled exchange depreciation. Moreover, Treasury officials provided arguments for the Chancellor, and were opposed to market forces dictating the value of the pound. But to present their concern as the primary motive for tariffs is to ignore the domestic political environment in which the government operated. The Conservatives dominated the National government. The party was led by men who believed in protection, and it had been committed to a protectionist policy since the autumn of 1930. Conservative backbenchers were overwhelmingly, unrelentingly, protectionist. Similarly, industry and the City of London had advocated tariffs and imperial preference since 1930, and the deepening depression did nothing to weaken their advocacy. What constrained the Conservatives was the need to introduce the 'Great Policy' within the confines of a National government that included several prominent free traders in the Cabinet, and to do so in the wake of a devaluation which undermined a major prop in the protectionist case. It was impossible to introduce tariffs, part of the Conservative creed, simply as the realisation of principle of the victorious party – if protection was to be legislated, it had to be shown that there were urgent and pragmatic grounds for it. Hence, the 'make-believe inquiry', in Beer's phrase, carried out by the Balance of Trade Committee, was nothing more than a necessary vehicle

[155] Drummond, *Imperial Economic Policy*, 179.   [156] Eichengreen, *Sterling*, 38.

for the General Tariff, not an indication of the primary motive for its introduction.

The issue was taken up in the parliamentary debates on the Import Duties Bill. Chamberlain, in introducing the Bill, placed emphasis on the balance of trade motive, but went on to list seven principal objectives of the proposed legislation.[157] This gave opponents of the Bill opportunity to deride the contradictory and mutually conflicting purposes of protection, imperial preference, reciprocal trade bargaining and revenue raising.[158] But few were in doubt that the prime objective was protection. Chamberlain himself let this slip in the much-quoted conclusion to his speech when he referred to the privilege he had of setting the seal on work which his father had begun.[159] Amery was in no doubt when he congratulated Chamberlain on 'the triumph of the cause in which he and I have long been fellow workers'.[160] Perhaps the clearest statement, if not the most eloquent, came from Attlee:

> If we had a favourable trade balance, if we had been on the pound sterling, if trade had been looking up all around us, in a House of Commons constituted as it is, we should have had full tariff proposals introduced. It is sheer hypocrisy to suggest anything else.[161]

The tariff did not arise simply out of the conditions of the slump. It was the result of longer-term forces associated with Britain's economic decline which had created a protectionist constituency by the early years of the twentieth century. Although internationalism appeared to have triumphed when the decision was made in 1925 to return to the gold standard, this proved a pyrrhic victory, the costs of an overvalued exchange rate helping to erode support for free trade. While it was the onset of the depression that gave the final decisive thrust to protectionism, the speed and completeness with which the remaining free trade support collapsed in 1930 can only be understood in the context of growing disillusion with trade liberalism in the late 1920s.

---

[157] *Hansard* (Commons), vol. 261, no. 30, 4 Feb. 1932, col. 287.
[158] For example, Sinclair, *Hansard* (Commons), vol. 261, no. 38, 16 Feb. 1932, col. 1504.
[159] *Hansard* (Commons), vol. 261, no. 30, 4 Feb. 1932, col. 296.   [160] *Ibid.*, col. 305.
[161] *Ibid.*, col. 304.

3 Imperial preference and the Ottawa Conference

Almost invariably demands for protection had been accompanied by calls for closer imperial integration. For some this was vital for the maintenance of Britain's world standing: political, diplomatic and even military status was enhanced by Britain's position at the head of a united commonwealth. Each move to greater autonomy for the self-governing dominions shaded London's authority. Although in 1931 the Statute of Westminster only gave formal expression to a reality that had been clear for some years, it nonetheless could be regarded as a climax to the process of political independence for the white dominions. Writing at the beginning of 1932, Sir Robert Vansittart, head of the Foreign Office, had suggested:

one reason for our loss of weight since 1926 has been that the 'foreigner' – we must be insular for a minute – has been secretly anticipating the gradual dissolution of the Empire, and some of the Commonwealth delegations have not at times exactly discouraged the idea. It is therefore essential that this hand should be played with the greatest possible measure of unity among the Commonwealth representatives... it is impossible to separate ourselves from, or to go against the Dominions at this crisis...[1]

Imperial unity might be buttressed by closer ties, particularly in economic relations. Chamberlain later described the Ottawa agreements as 'an attempt to bring the Empire together again and to supplement and support the common sentiment by bringing more material interests into line with it'.[2]

For some advocates, closer commercial links with the Empire were vital if Britain was to succeed in a new economic era dominated by mass production. The United States provided both the model and the threat. A procession of visitors had returned from America profoundly impressed by the scale and organisation of production – it was this that solved the paradox of high wages, comparative industrial peace and all too evident international competitiveness. If Britain was to meet the challenge,

[1] Quoted in Robert Holland, *Britain and the Commonwealth Alliance, 1918–1939* (1981), 127.
[2] W. K. Hancock, *Survey of British Commonwealth Affairs*, II, pt. 1 (Oxford, 1942), 233.

industry must be rationalised, old or small-scale plant scrapped and production concentrated in the large units which could afford not only the costly research and development an increasingly technological age dictated, but could organise output on the scale required to compete internationally.[3] Mass production demanded mass markets. Not for the last time in British experience, political and business opinion was bewitched by the notion that access to vast markets was a prerequisite for economic regeneration. American strength was often uncritically assumed to depend on possession of an internal market of 120 million consumers. The answer for Britain was both to protect her domestic markets and to tap those of the Empire. What, Lord Melchett asked, were the alternatives? He answered his question:

The one a Customs Union with the United States of America, which would result in our ultimately becoming a mere subsidiary unit, the other a Customs Union with Europe, which would involve our permanent association with peoples of a lower standard than our own, and in the end an almost inevitable degradation of our own standard.[4]

Melchett was writing before the depression began really to bite, but even then he expressed anxiety that the tendency of United States productive powers to outstrip domestic consumption might presage an onslaught on world markets to maintain the momentum of expansion. As the depression worsened, fears of American dumping intensified.[5]

Britain, it was argued, was failing to harness the resources of the Empire or to exploit potential markets there. Sir Robert Horne compared American experience in Puerto Rico with that of Britain and Jamaica. Shortly after becoming a US possession, Puerto Rico in 1901 had exports of £1.7 million, of which 65 per cent went to the US, and imports of £1.8 million of which the US supplied 75 per cent. By 1928 exports had climbed to £20 million, 94 per cent destined for the USA, and imports to £19 million, 86 per cent supplied by the US. By contrast, Jamaica's trade had grown sluggishly while Britain's share of it had declined. At the beginning of the century exports and imports both had been approximately £1.9 million with the UK purchasing one-fifth of exports and supplying half of Jamaica's imports; by 1928 exports had increased only to £4.75 million, 18 per cent destined for Britain, and imports to £6.0 million, a mere 28 per cent of which were supplied by Britain.[6]

---

[3] Leslie Hannah, *The Rise of the Corporate Economy* (1976), esp. ch. 3, and C. S. Maier, 'Between Taylorism and technocracy: European ideologies and the vision of industrial productivity in the 1920s', *Contemporary History*, 5 (1970), 27–61.

[4] Lord Melchett, *Imperial Economic Unity* (1930), 20.

[5] John Barnes and David Nicholson (eds.), *The Empire at Bay. The Leo Amery Diaries 1929–45* (1988).

[6] Speech in Edinburgh, 10 March 1930, *The Times*, 11 Mar., 1930.

In a microcosm Jamaica symbolised Britain's predicament. There had been a clear divergence in intra-imperial trade trends during the 1920s which serve to highlight British economic weakness. As outlined in chapter 1, the UK came to lean more heavily on Empire markets at the very time that the rest of the Empire was drawing a decreasing proportion of its supplies from the metropolitan centre.

Even during the twenties this all gave cogency to those who wanted closer imperial integration. Protection and development of the Empire went hand in hand. The depression added force to the campaign. Although the imperial element benefited from the slipstream of the protectionist campaign it also possessed its own momentum, gaining impetus from the dominions' desperate search for markets as the world economic crisis deepened. But once Britain had introduced full-scale protection it was as good as inevitable that it would include imperial preferences. For years the dominions, with the exceptions of Newfoundland and India, had granted Britain preference in their markets and received little in return. Free trade had provided either the excuse for lack of action by Britain or the obstacle in the way of full reciprocity. Imperial relations would have been seriously jeopardised if Britain did not reciprocate now the opportunity existed. Economic self-interest blended with high imperial sentiment. Assistance for the hard-pressed dominions' exports would help to ensure external solvency and the maintenance of debt service. Trade bargaining might also reverse some of the tariff increases in the dominions, and secure wider preferential margins for British exports. Moreover, London's chances of securing advantages for UK exports should have been enhanced by trends in the British import trade from the late 1920s.

Although Empire countries had been successful in increasing their share of British imports in the early twenties, by the end of the decade the dominions were experiencing growing competition in the market for livestock products from Argentina and northern Europe. The onset of the depression led not only to an intensification of competition but made the rivalry all the more bitter because, in contrast to the 1920s, the dominions came to depend even more heavily on sales to the UK.

The struggle for the British market gave added importance to protection and preferences. Market forces alone were no longer to determine the source of imports. Instead the government now had the power to regulate access to the market at the very time that Britain's predominance as a world importer was being reasserted. This greatly enhanced Britain's negotiating strength; it was no longer impotent to extract favourable terms from other countries for its exports.[7] These trade trends, and of course

---

[7] One case study of Britain's difficulties in the 1920s is by Roger Gravil, 'Anglo-United States trade rivalry in Argentina and the D'Abernon mission of 1929' in D. P. Rock (ed.),

protection, were central to the aims, conduct and outcome of the Ottawa Conference.

Competition in the British food import market in the 1920s

In contrast to exports, the volume of British imports was higher in 1929 than it had been in 1913, although the rate of growth had slowed (see Table 3.1). This deceleration was part of a world trend, although somewhat more marked in the UK than elsewhere, so that by 1929 Britain absorbed 14.9 per cent of world imports as opposed to 15.8 per cent in 1913.[8]

While between the 1870s and 1914 the Empire had never supplied as much as 25 per cent of UK imports, between 1919 and 1926 it supplied 28 per cent, and in 1927–9 averaged 27 per cent. There was also a slight tendency for the dominions to take a larger share of total Empire supplies.[9]

Can these increases in the Empire's share of British imports be attributed to changes in the commodity composition of imports? There were substantial changes in the pattern of imports. Not surprisingly, the greatest increase occurred in fuel, mainly as a result of the need for petroleum. The volume of imported manufactures also rose, reflecting the combined problems of British industrial costs and an overvalued exchange rate from 1925. Neither of these changes was likely to be of much benefit to the Empire.

More important were the fortunes of food and raw material imports. The volume of food imports increased, in large measure because British incomes were more buoyant than domestic agricultural production. The sluggish recovery of industrial production helped to account for a continuation of the long-run tendency for raw material imports to decline as a proportion of total imports.[10] Raw material imports, excluding fuel, actually fell in volume, 1913–29, while industrial production rose slightly, so other forces were working to reduce the imported material content of industrial production. There were some dramatic changes in the composition of imported raw materials, notably the decline of raw cotton and the rise of paper-making materials and, associated with the expanding motor and electrical industries, petroleum and non-ferrous metals. The

Argentina in the Twentieth Century (1975). See also the comment by Robert Skidelsky on the failure of J. H. Thomas's trip to Canada in 1929: 'He could hardly have accomplished anything more, especially since he did not carry imperial preference, the one thing that would have interested the Canadians, in his traveller's bag.' R. Skidelsky, *Politicians and the Slump: The Labour Government of 1929–1931* (1967), 138–9.

[8] A. Maddison, 'Growth and fluctuations in the world economy, 1870–1960', *Banca Nazionale del Lavoro Quarterly Review*, 15 (1962), 161.

[9] W. Schlote, *British Overseas Trade from 1700 to the 1930s*, translated by W. O. Henderson and W. H. Chaloner (Oxford, 1952), Table 13.   [10] *Ibid.*, 55–7.

Table 3.1. *Rate of change in the volume of imports into the United Kingdom (annual compound rates)*

	%
1870–90	3·2
1890–1913	2·1
1913–25	1·1

Source: A. Maddison, 'Growth and fluctuations in the world economy, 1870–1960', *Banca Nazionale del Lavoro Quarterly Review*, 15 (1962), 127–95.

position of the Empire as a supplier of primary imports into the UK is outlined in Table 3.2.

A structural analysis, calculating the gains or losses likely to accrue to the Empire from changes in composition of the imports listed above, and treating the difference between the hypothetical and actual shares as a 'competitive' loss or gain, reveals the results shown in Table 3.3. The calculations suggest that the composition of UK imports moved unfavourably from the Empire's perspective, but that gains made by the Empire suppliers in individual commodity groups were sufficiently great to more than offset the structural shift. These changes had all occurred by 1924, a similar analysis of the sub-period 1924–9 revealing no net structural change for the Empire, but instead a small 'competitive' loss. The gains and losses in individual commodity groups can be seen in Table 3.2.

Although the dominions were successful in diversifying the geographical spread of their export trade in the 1920s, the UK remained an outlet of supreme importance to them, especially those in the southern hemisphere, so that trends in the British market were of vital concern to the dominions even in a period of expansion. The overall foreign share of imports had declined, of course. Wartime losers included Russia and Germany, although both were recovering their position in the later 1920s, especially Germany. One of the most notable declines was suffered by the USA, Britain's premier supplier. In the late 1920s Belgium, France and the Netherlands were all experiencing declining exports and a decreasing share of UK imports despite the highly competitive exchange rates of the former two countries. But, significantly, and for the dominions ominously, the major gains made by foreign countries were by Argentina and the Scandinavian nations, particularly Denmark. Of importance for later developments, these advances were concentrated in the products in which they and the dominions were competing suppliers, especially in meat and dairy products. It is worthwhile analysing the position in more detail.

Meat had become by 1929 Britain's most valuable single imported

Table 3.2. *UK imports of food and raw materials from the Empire, and percentage of total imports of each commodity from the Empire, 1913, 1924 and 1929 (£000s)*

	1913	%	1924	%	1929	%
Grain and milling	29,747	35·2	53,164	43·3	32,774	33·3
Meat and poultry	13,926	24·7	27,018	25·4	23,095	20·4
Butter, cheese, eggs	10,321	25·4	36,697	44·9	38,325	4·25
Fruit, fresh and dried	1,576	11·4	7,740	20·6	9,640	24·6
Sugar	931	4·0	7,677	17·5	9,656	41·1
Tea	12,033	87·3	34,995	86·5	32,262	85·9
Alcoholic beverages	490	8·3	6,985	45·3	6,232	46·6
Tobacco, raw and manufactured	115	1·4	1,250	7·2	1,878	10·2
Ores, concentrates and scrap metal	3,653	18·3	4,701	19·8	5,563	23·7
Wood, timber and manufactures thereof	5,992	13·9	6,906	10·3	4,944	7·3
Paper and newsprint	459	31·3	1,229	38·4	3,376	71·1
Seeds and nuts for expressing oil	8,474	53·3	15,006	49·4	10,569	48·6
Petroleum, crude and refined	827	7·6	2,239	5·4	1,718	3·9
Hides, skins etc.	8,020	53·2	9,939	46·7	11,319	55·4
Leather and manufactures	3,799	26·6	4,776	27·2	5,625	30·6
Rubber	12,443	56·8	7,347	76·3	13,915	80·5
Total	112,806	29·1	227,669	33·5	210,891	32·4

Source: British Parliamentary Papers, *Statistical Abstract for the British Empire* (various years).

Table 3.3. *Selected UK imports from the Empire: percentage changes 1913 and 1929*

1913	Actual share	29·1
1929	Actual share	32·4
1929	Hypothetical share	27·8
1913–29	Change due to structural movements	−1·3
1913–29	Change due to 'competitive' factors	+4·6
1913–29	Net change	+3·3

Source: Calculated from British Parliamentary Papers, *Statistical Abstract for the British Empire* (various years).

commodity, and was to be the source of more contention at Ottawa and subsequently than any other product. Looking first at sheepmeat, the New Zealanders had expanded their share of the market by the 1920s, and were especially well placed in the fast increasing trade in lamb. The major change in share was the decline of Australian shipments (wool prices were a major determinant of supplies), and the rise of Argentina.[11] The market continued to expand in the 1920s, with the shares of the three main suppliers remaining fairly constant.

Argentina was the principal beef exporter. Empire countries, mainly Australia and New Zealand, which had supplied 17·2 per cent of UK imports in 1909–13, accounted for only 9·5 per cent by 1929.[12] The chief reason for this was the switch in imports from frozen to chilled beef. Argentina was the main supplier of chilled beef, and the southern dominions were at this time unable to compete.[13] Although Australia and New Zealand managed to increase their participation in the frozen beef trade, this was a growing share in a sharply contracting market.

The major competition to the Empire as suppliers of UK imports of pigmeat and dairy products came from the Scandinavian and Baltic countries. In broad terms, the experience of the imperial suppliers was somewhat similar for both bacon and butter: huge increases in supplies and market share were achieved between 1913 and the early 1920s, only to be followed by a relative retreat to the end of the decade.

Canada accounted for 16·2 per cent of the value of British bacon imports in 1925, but only 2·4 per cent four years later. This decline was attributed to the indifference of Canadian farmers to pig production at times when cereal growing was more profitable, to falling prices in the UK market in the later 1920s as European supplies increased, and to the rise of domestic consumption in Canada.[14] The major changes among foreign suppliers were the decline of the USA, and the rise of the Netherlands and of the Scandinavian and Baltic countries. The Baltic states (including Poland) increased their shipments from £899,000 in 1924 (2·4 per cent of imports) to £3·9 million by 1929 (9·0 per cent of imports). By 1929 Denmark accounted for 62 per cent of UK bacon imports.[15]

Australia and New Zealand made spectacular advances in the UK butter

---

[11] Imperial Economic Committee, *Mutton and Lamb Survey* (1935), 151–2, and United Kingdom *Annual Statement of Trade, 1922*. In 1913 New Zealand supplied 42·3 per cent of UK imports of frozen mutton and lamb, Australia 32 per cent and Argentina 19·5 per cent. All figures refer to volume.

[12] Imperial Economic Committee, *Cattle and Beef Survey* (1934), 188. The figures refer to volume. [13] This is discussed more fully in chs. 2 and 6.

[14] CAB 32/104, O (B) (32) 36, Briefs for Ministers by Inter-departmental Preparatory Committee.

[15] Earlier Danish supplies were: 1913 – £8·9 m. (50·9 per cent); 1924 – £20·3 m. (54·3 per cent); 1926 – £21·7 m. (50·8 per cent); 1928 – £25·3 m. (62·7 per cent).

market between 1913 and 1925, increasing their supplies nearly threefold and their share of imports from 20·5 per cent to 51 per cent of total tonnage. Australian shipments, however, were particularly vulnerable to drought, and fell sharply in 1926 and 1927.[16] Argentina became progressively less important as an exporter, but, as with bacon, the Scandinavian (excluding Danish) and Baltic producers made considerable advances in the later 1920s.[17] Denmark, the principal exporter of butter to the UK, was supplying less in 1925 than before the war, but thereafter the volume of its butter shipments increased and by 1929 it accounted for 34 per cent of UK imports.

The depression and British imports

The onset of the depression modified or reversed a number of these trends. Of outstanding importance, it transformed the relationship of the dominions to the UK, substituting a strong centripetal movement in trade for the disintegrative tendencies of the 1920s. The British share of world imports increased from 14·9 per cent in 1929 to 17·0 per cent in 1931,[18] a consequence of the relatively less severe impact of the world depression on UK demand and of the maintenance of virtual free trade until late 1931. For certain primary products, especially meat and butter, Britain's dominance as a world importer became even more pronounced (see Table 3.4).

In the case of beef, the early 1920s saw a substantial rise on pre-war levels of world trade. A taste for refrigerated meat acquired during the period of wartime shortage, together with the depletion of European cattle stocks, led to the emergence of Continental Europe as a major importer in the postwar period.[19] This position was reversed in the later 1920s when the restoration of cattle stocks in Europe led to restrictions being placed on beef imports into Germany in 1927, and into France and Belgium in the following year. With a fall in British consumption, and, apart from a temporary increase in US imports, no compensating increases elsewhere, world trade in beef began a slide that lasted until 1936. The plight of beef exporters is underlined by the growing relative dominance of the UK as a world importer of beef despite the fall in the actual volume of British imports. The UK accounted for 64·4 per cent of the beef and veal taken by

[16] Imperial Economic Committee, *Dairy Produce Supplies* (1933), 60.
[17] In 1925 Finland, Estonia, Latvia, Lithuania, Sweden, Norway and Poland supplied 302,000 cwts (5·2 per cent of imports); by 1929 shipments had reached 761,000 cwts, and accounted for 11·9 per cent of imports.
[18] Maddison, 'Growth and Fluctuations', 183–4.
[19] Weddel's considered that on the Continent the war 'did the work of 20 years of peaceful penetration'. *Weddel's Review of the Frozen Meat Trade* (1920), 24.

Table 3.4. *Proportion of world imports of selected livestock products taken by UK*

	1924–8	1929–33	1934
Mutton and lamb	93·9	94·5	96·6
Pigmeat	78·1	81·3	88·1
Beef and veal	64·1x	75·2	81·8 (1933)
Butter	n.a.	68·9	80·8

Sources: International Institute of Agriculture, *World Trade in Agricultural Products* (Rome, 1940), 194, 199, 560, 564, 447. Imperial Economic Committee, *Cattle and Beef Survey* (1934), 333 (x 1925–28).

the main importing countries in 1927, but 70 per cent of the tonnage by 1930 and, after further restrictions by other European countries in the early 1930s, 81·6 per cent in 1932.[20]

Britain also occupied a commanding position as a world importer of mutton and lamb in the 1920s, and this was reinforced by the cut-back of imports into France in 1931 (earlier tariffs had been eroded by the exchange depreciation of suppliers, and so were supplemented by quotas and a surtax on imports), and into Germany, where stringent veterinary regulations in 1931 eliminated the trade.[21] In contrast to beef, however British sheepmeat imports increased during the 1920s, reaching their peak volume in 1931.

The pattern was repeated for the international trade in pigmeat. It was evident as early as 1927 that Continental markets were becoming more restricted, and as the UK's imports continued to expand during the depression, so its dominance became even more striking.[22]

The proportion of world exports of butter taken by the UK rose from just over 60 per cent in 1928–30 to 75 per cent in 1930 and over 80 per cent in 1932. The story is the familiar one of British imports rising rapidly during the depression while in other parts of the world import restrictions were introduced or tightened. Germany, the second largest importer, implemented higher duties in 1931 and quotas in 1932 which were made harsher in 1933. Other European importers, having increased imports in 1931, imposed a battery of quotas and higher duties between 1931 and 1933.[23]

[20] Imperial Economic Committee, *Cattle and Beef Survey* (1934), 338.
[21] Imperial Economic Committee, *Mutton and Lamb Survey* (1935), 182–3, and 216.
[22] International Institute of Agriculture, *World Trade in Agricultural Products, Its Growth, Its Crisis and the New Trade Policies* (Rome, 1940), 195.
[23] Imperial Economic Committee, *Dairy Produce Supplies 1933* (1934), 66, 69, 73, 75, 76.

Table 3.5. *Percentage of selected countries' total exports destined for UK, 1928–1933*

	1928	1929	1930	1931	1932	1933
Australia	37·9	38·1	53·0	50·7	53·1	55·7
New Zealand	72·1	73·7	80·1	88·0	87·8	86·1
South Africa[a]	55·2	65·8	69·4	77·4	82·3	77·8
Canada	31·5	25·2	27·4	30·2	38·9	39·3
Denmark	55·5	56·4	58·8	61·1	64·1	64·5
Estonia	34·8	38·1	32·3	36·6	36·7	37·1
Finland	35·3	38·0	38·9	44·7	46·8	45·8
Latvia	27·0	27·4	28·4	25·4	30·8	42·5
Lithuania	20·4	17·4	19·5	33·1	41·4	44·7
Norway	26·4	27·0	25·3	28·1	25·7	20·6
Poland and Danzig	9·0	10·3	12·1	16·9	16·7	20·1
Sweden	25·0	24·8	25·5	26·7	25·6	26·6
Argentina	28·7	32·2	36·5	39·0	36·1	36·5

[a] Excluding specie.
Source: League of Nations, *International Trade Statistics* (Geneva various years).

Among other products in which the UK absorbed a growing proportion of world imports during the depression, although not to such a dominant extent, were wheat, maize and wool.[24] The obvious corollary to this was that a number of countries, including the dominions, came to depend much more heavily on the British market, as Table 3.5 shows. Of the primary producers included in the table, there were few exceptions to this pattern: only Estonia, Norway and Sweden, the latter two mainly exporters of forest products, escaped from noticeably greater reliance on the UK market. This further intensification of the rivalry for the British market meant that by the summer of 1932 the outcome of the Ottawa Conference was of vital importance to many countries.

The Ottawa Conference

Preparation

The Ottawa Conference had been planned even before the formation of the National government, and in a sense was merely a continuation of the Imperial Conference of 1930. That meeting had postponed discussions of trade matters, deciding to carry them over to a specifically economic

[24] International Institute of Agriculture, *World Trade in Agricultural Products*, 447, 560, 564.

conference to be held in Ottawa the following year. In fact it was not possible to meet until 1932.

It would have been difficult to avoid holding the conference, but that does not mean that all the participants had high expectations of it. The South African premier was apparently not keen, and did not feel that South Africa would benefit much.[25] The great bulk of preference accorded to South Africa under the Import Duties Act only affected very small areas of the country, and they tended to be those areas where the government was politically weak. N. C. Havenga, the South African Finance Minister, told the Canadians that if Britain could not offer anything for wool, maize and meat, the negotiations were pointless.[26] Even in New Zealand the attitude was cool. The UK Trade Commissioner indicated the mood prevailing in New Zealand: 'What is the use of going to Ottawa? Everyone here assumes that the UK is so benevolent that having offered the 10 per cent it is permanent and there is no need to offer anything in return.'[27]

In Australia the official attitude was more forthcoming and preliminary discussions with Britain made some advance before the conference. In Canada, as host, it might have been expected that attitudes towards the conference would have been positive, but R. B. Bennett was slow to prepare for the event either in general plans or in preliminary discussions with Britain. The UK High Commissioner wrote of the anxiety felt in Canada about the lack of preparedness for the conference, attributing this to Bennett's distrust of his own ministers and reluctance to delegate.[28] Canadian officials complained that with twelve days left before the conference several matters still needed ministerial authority, including the appointment of the Canadian delegation and a decision on those parts of the Commonwealth with which Canada was going to negotiate an agreement![29]

What could the UK expect from Ottawa? Nobody had serious expectations of creating a free trade area. Such ideas had had a ring of fantasy about them even at the beginning of the century. By the 1930s most

---

[25] FO 371/16405, British representative in South Africa (Cosier) to Thomas, reporting interview with South African Prime Minister, 26 Jan. 1932. and DO 35/238/8831/E/67. Meeting of South African and UK officials, 7 July 1932.

[26] I. M. Drummond, *Imperial Economic Policy, 1917–1939* (1974), 189.

[27] Quoted in F. Capie, *Ottawa. An Aspect of Imperial Commercial Policy*, Warwick University Discussion Paper no. 41 (1974), 10.

[28] FO 371/16406, Sir W. Clark to Sir E. Harding, 17 Mar. 1932.

[29] Drummond, *Imperial Economic Policy*, 216–18. But lack of Canadian preparation worried UK officials before Ottawa, and the Public Archives show their anxieties to have been well-founded. The major problem was in obtaining ministerial decisions. A study of the administrative lessons to be learned from the conference also concluded that effectiveness would have been far greater if members of the Cabinet Committee had made a detailed study of the data prepared for them. NAC, RG25, vol. 1589, F159-U.

dominions were firmly committed to industrial development, especially Australia and Canada. Protection had been rising sharply before the conference, partly because of the exigencies of the crisis, partly because of the protectionist leanings of governments in power at the time. This is undoubtedly true of Bennett's Canadian administration of 1930–5. Bennett, in a vigorous election campaign in 1930, had pledged a future in which Canadians would no longer be 'hewers of wood and drawers of water', also promising to use tariffs 'to blast a way into markets that have been closed'.[30] Duties had been raised sharply, and as the conference gathered Ottawa was alive with industrial pressure groups including the Canadian Manufacturers' Association which held its 1932 annual meeting in the capital.[31] The Australian Labour government of 1929–31 was probably more sympathetic to manufacturing than the United Australian government which succeeded it, but even this was dependent on the support of manufacturers, and the manufacturers wanted protection. Indeed, after Ottawa

the manufacturers planted themselves on the Government doorsteps with a big stick and have stayed there ever since. There is no doubt that this strong and wealthy influence coupled with the furious opposition of the Scullin party and the 'Age' newspaper, have made the Government increasingly nervous of (reducing tariffs).[32]

In South Africa, following an election-winning pact between the Nationalist and Labour parties, tariffs had been raised in 1925 as part of a deliberate attempt to accelerate industrial development, mainly to provide more jobs for whites, to help solve the 'poor white problem'.[33] In New Zealand customs revenue as a proportion of the total value of imports had risen at the end of the 1920s although this was due mainly to a rise in the proportion of foreign (and more highly taxed) imports, and to a decline in lower duty UK imports, rather than to increased protection.[34] A more positive policy of industrial development awaited disillusionment with Ottawa and, in 1935, the advent of a Labour government. In India, virtual tariff autonomy since 1919 had been associated with substantial industrial advance, much of it at the expense of British cotton textiles and steel. In what one writer has described as the geriatric years of the Raj, industrialisation and fiscal autonomy were intimately bound up with the

[30] Quoted by J. H. Thompson and A. Seager, *Canada 1922–1939: Decades of Discord* (Toronto, 1985), 202.   [31] NAC, RG20, vol. 1423, F7-1.

[32] DO 35/280/9279 A/169, E. T. Crutchley (UK Representative in Australia) to E. G. Machtig, 27 June 1933.

[33] See D. Hobart Houghton and Jenifer Dagut, *Source Material on the South African Economy 1860–1970*, III (Cape Town, 1973).

[34] M. F. Lloyd Prichard, *An Economic History of New Zealand* (Auckland, 1970), 303.

nationalist movement.[35] Moreover, dominion governments, their revenues undermined by the depression, were struggling to balance budgets, and even with the relatively sophisticated tax structure of Canada and Australia, customs receipts were an important element in budgetary revenue. Concessions to Britain would therefore probably have to be counter-balanced by raising duties on foreign imports; to the extent these duties were effective in shutting out imports, government receipts would obviously suffer.

Well aware of all this, those people most closely in touch with conditions were pessimistic about a major expansion of British exports. The Federation of British Industries, while advocating an extension of intra-imperial trade, had recognised that the dominions were going to industrialise, but hoped at least that they would equip themselves with British capital goods.[36] British trade officials tended to be cool about prospects. A senior officer in the Department of Overseas Trade reported:

We do not feel it is necessary to over-estimate the immediate effect of Empire preference on the course of world trade. The national trend of development may be impeded here and stimulated there, but any large change is likely to come slowly and to remain conditioned by broad consideration of economic ability.[37]

Such an assessment reflected both the unlikelihood of dramatic concessions by the dominions to Britain at Ottawa as well as the considerable limitations on what Britain itself could offer the dominions.

Britain had already made a major concession to the dominions when the decision had been made to include preferences in the Import Duties Act, and not to extend new duties to Empire products. This had not been a foregone conclusion. During the previous winter various Cabinet committees had either assumed or recommended preferences for imperial produce but not necessarily free entry.[38] The Cabinet had still been considering duties in February 1932, but consultation with Bennett led to a change of mind when he said that 'it would be no use to hold a Conference at all' if duties were applied to dominion produce.[39] Bennett himself suggested the

---

[35] B. R. Tomlinson, 'Britain and the Indian currency crisis, 1930–2', *Economic History Review*, 2nd. ser., 32 (1979), 99.

[36] CAB 24/215 CP 304, (Enclosure) FBI report of Preparatory Committee for Imperial Conference of 1930, Feb. 1930. Although inter-imperial trade increasingly figured in FBI discussions in the 1920s, there was scepticism about its possibilities because it felt that economic nationalism was as firmly rooted in the dominions as elsewhere. R. F. Holland, 'The Federation of British Industries and the international economy, 1929–39', *Economic History Review*, 2nd. ser., 34 (1981), 291.

[37] FO 371/16405, J. Picton Bagge to F. Ashton Gwatkin, 23 Mar. 1932.

[38] CAB 24/225 (Ottawa Committee), CP 324(31), 15 Dec. 1931; CAB 27/467 (Balance of Trade Committee), 18 Jan. 1932; CAB 27/465, Agricultural Policy Committee Report, 16 Jan. 1932.   [39] CAB 23/70 CAB 11(32), 3 Feb. 1932.

solution: the dominions would have free entry but only until 15 November, its continuance thereafter being conditional on Britain obtaining satisfactory agreements at Ottawa. On the other hand, produce from the Colonial empire not already subject to duty obtained unconditional free entry under the Imports Duties Act. While Britain took the attitude that the dominions would have to pay for these privileges by offering something extra at Ottawa over and above their existing preferences, nonetheless the scope for concessions by the United Kingdom was limited.

There were three major obstacles standing in the way of useful trade diversion to the dominions. One important restriction on what could be offered was the assumption that it was worthless to give concessions on products which the Empire produced more of than it consumed. Preferences, it was argued then and has been argued since, would merely divert dominion supplies to the UK, displacing foreign supplies which in turn would replace dominion supplies in other world markets. World production, consumption and prices, as well as British prices, would remain unchanged. Since wool and wheat were two such products, and of outstanding importance to the dominions, the useful scope of preferences was correspondingly reduced. Dominion tactics were therefore centred on persuading Britain to introduce new tariffs, raise existing ones or restrict foreign imports by quotas on as many other products as possible. This, however, conflicted with British interests in two ways: having taxed a number of foreign foodstuffs in the tariff legislation of February, London was reluctant to go further because of the likely impact on foreign suppliers and on consumer prices. These twin concerns were frequently reflected in the preparatory discussions on individual products.

The Foreign Office argued that more alarm would be expressed in Denmark and the Baltic states about imperial preference for butter than about the tariff itself. Recent trade drives in Argentina and Denmark were likely to be nullified if their exports were discriminated against.[40] These views were echoed by an inter-departmental committee which also warned about the cost to consumers of raising duties.[41]

One of the most controversial products in the negotiations, and one on which they almost foundered, was meat. The Australians especially had made it clear that they expected concessions on meat, and British officials and ministers were aware that a satisfactory agreement with Australia hinged on this.[42] New Zealand, and to a lesser extent South Africa, were also interested. The British response reflected confusion and division. At

[40] FO 371/16405, Note for Dominions Office.
[41] CAB 32/104 0 (B)(32), Brief for Ministers 4 June 1932.
[42] CAB 32/104 0 (B)(32) 22, General Report on possible preferences to be accorded by UK to Australia.

the technical level the preparatory documents show uncertainty about the state of the meat markets and the likely impact of tariffs. While one report suggested that the burden would be passed on to producers, and therefore would be at the same time harmful to the Argentine and useless to the dominions,[43] another suggested that prices would rise because of the difficulty of substituting Empire supplies for foreign.[44] Yet other reports suggested that market forces would shortly lead to higher mutton and lamb prices anyway – tariffs might have no influence on them, but would be blamed nonetheless. Moreover, to tax frozen meat while leaving chilled beef untouched would be represented as discriminating against the food of the poor.[45] Quotas too were rejected by an inter-departmental committee, although the Ministry of Agriculture representative dissented[46] Thomas and Runciman warned that a good treaty with Argentina would be prejudiced by meat restrictions but went on to argue that 'the question of the price of meat to the home consumer is perhaps the over-riding consideration', even suggesting that price rises might bring the whole policy of imperial economic cooperation into disrepute.[47]

Britain's ability to concede much of further value to the dominions at Ottawa, beyond confirming existing preferences, was therefore constrained by several factors. Important products such as wheat and wool were virtually ruled out because it was not thought the dominions would benefit from preferences. Higher preferential duties on other products would weaken Britain's subsequent treaty-making capacity. They might also have exposed the government to accusations that it was raising the cost of living. Here the continued presence of a small but determined free trade phalanx in the Cabinet restricted the freedom of manoeuvre of the negotiators. At the same time, as will be argued below, it meant that agricultural protection at home had not yet advanced far and did not feature as the serious blockage to negotiations that it might well otherwise have done.

The conference

The conference was held in Ottawa between 21 July and 20 August 1932. Not only was it a protracted business, it was also exceptionally well attended, the British delegation alone consisting of seven Cabinet ministers together with scores of advisers, officials and secretarial staff. This mainly reflected the importance attached to the proceedings as well as the sheer

[43] CAB 27/473. Cabinet Committee on Proposed Economic Conference at Ottawa. Second Report of Inter-departmental Preparatory Committee, Dec. 1931.
[44] FO 371/16406, Inter-departmental meeting, 13 Mar. 1931.
[45] CAB 27/474 0 (B)(32) 35.
[46] CAB 32/104 0 (B)(32) 126, Inter-departmental Preparatory Committee (Dissenting note, 6 July 1932).   [47] CAB 27/474, 7 June 1932.

volume of work involved in negotiating a series of bilateral treaties as well as that generated by various sub-committees. But the size and leadership of the team had also been dictated by the need to prevent J. H. Thomas, as Secretary of State for the Dominions, heading the delegation. In the view of some prominent Conservatives this would have been a disaster. Amery found it 'perfectly appalling that a man of Thomas's outlook should be allowed to represent this country at the most critical conference there has ever been…[h]is lack of tact as well as of knowledge is incredible'.[48] Bennett, it seemed, was still smarting from Thomas's description of his offer at the 1930 conference of reciprocal concessions as 'humbug'.[49] After Thomas, probably well lubricated, had had a furious late night row in February with the Canadian High Commissioner, G. H. Ferguson, pressure had been put on a reluctant Baldwin to go to Ottawa. As Lord President of the Council and an ex-premier he could take precedence over Thomas to head the delegation. He agreed on condition that he would not be involved in detailed negotiations but would have a largely ceremonial role. The brunt of the work fell on Chamberlain and Hailsham, the latter being taken to the verge of collapse; but at least if the negotiations were to have failed, the die-hards at home would know it was not for lack of commitment.[50]

Australia was represented by Stanley Bruce, ex-premier but by 1932 Resident Minister in London, and by Trade Minister Henry Gullett, New Zealand by Prime Minister J. G. Coates and G. W. Forbes. Bennett both hosted the conference and headed the Canadian delegation.

The Ottawa summer was cooler than usual but tempers frayed anyway. By the end of the conference the chief Canadian and British delegates held each other in low esteem. Bennett had a poor opinion of most of the British ministers, finding even Chamberlain 'a very great disappointment'. It was a personal estimate that was returned with interest: Chamberlain ascribed 'most of our difficulties [to] the personality of Bennett'.[51] He was described as 'blustering, sobbing', and British delegates quoted with approval a Canadian Liberal's characterisation of Bennett as combining 'the manners of a Chicago policeman and the temperament of a Hollywood film star'. Personality may have played its part, but much of the friction was generated by the circumstances – the slump, the collapse of primary prices and the massive obstacles in the way of offering mutual trade-inducing concessions.

[48] Barnes and Nicholson, *Amery Diaries*, 29 Feb. and 4 May 1932.
[49] Marguerite Dupree (ed.), *Lancashire and Whitehall. The Diary of Sir Raymond Streat*, I, *1931–39* (Manchester, 1987), 168.
[50] D. Dilks, *Three Visitors to Canada: Baldwin, Chamberlain and Churchill*, Canada House Lecture Series, 28 (1985) 23.
[51] Baldwin to T. Jones, 15 Aug. 1932, *A Diary with Letters 1931–1950* (1954), 49.

The Ottawa conference was an *economic* conference and not concerned with trade alone. If there had been the will and imagination almost certainly more could have been achieved for prosperity on the monetary side than was possible through the trade agreements.[52] Certainly Amery thought so, spending much of his time in Ottawa proselytising his views about tightening the financial links of empire, expanding the monetary base including the use of silver, so as to achieve a concerted rise in prices.[53] The UK Treasury, determined to avoid becoming enmeshed in schemes that would have involved the participation of the dominions in the management of sterling, was able to block any initiatives. Since the other committees achieved little of substance, the real work of the conference was done in a series of mainly bilateral discussions that concentrated on trade.

The UK sought easier access to the dominion markets by reducing the tariffs that were protecting secondary industries, by encouraging the dominions to abolish emergency fiscal duties and to amend various protectionist customs practices. Wider preferential margins would discourage foreign competition. The scope for reducing dominion protection was, as indicated above, very limited. The poverty of immediate prospects was brought home to ministers in a meeting at the start of the conference. On 23 July British ministers discussed with the Trade Commissioners the prospects with each of the dominions. The official minutes give little hint of the sense of gloom pervading the discussions, but Chamberlain's diary entry is stark enough: 'the result was very startling as it appeared that the value of the increased trade to be expected from the concessions would amount to something very small'.[54] Instead there emerged the idea of 'getting a progressive decrease of duties over a period of years so as gradually to break down the excessive protection of the home production'. This was encapsulated in the domestic competitor principle: the dominions were to adjust their tariffs so that where they had efficient industries the protection afforded them would only offset Britain's lower costs. British industries would therefore compete on level terms as though they were domestic firms. Tariff Boards would adjudicate the precise degree of protection necessary. The UK also asked the dominions for immediate reductions in preferential rates of duty, and for the increase and guaranteeing of preferential margins.

The Australians readily accepted the domestic competitor clause, promised to protect only industries reasonably assured of success, to get their Tariff Board to review all protective duties, and not to introduce new

[52] Drummond, *Imperial Economic Policy*, 282–3.
[53] Barnes and Nicholson, *Amery Diaries*, ch. 4.
[54] N. Chamberlain diary, 23 July 1932. NC 2/17.

protective duties or raise existing ones without reference to the Board. Perhaps because of these guarantees the UK government was satisfied with an agreement which did not fix tariffs but merely established preferential margins, and even here made specified exceptions where margins could be reduced. Wrenching an agreement from the Canadians was a prolonged and fraught affair. Bennett was reluctant to accept the domestic competition principle, agreeing only after considerable British pressure, and only then, Drummond suggests, because the idea was unenforceable unless Bennett wished to enforce it. The immediate tariff changes led to 132 reductions in the preferential rate and increases in the intermediate or general rates on 83 items. The Canadians, though, were bound to maximum preferential rates and minimum margins of preference, a tighter agreement than that between the UK and Australia. The South Africans refused to countenance a Tariff Board and conceded little in the way of lower tariffs or higher preferences. New Zealand accepted the domestic competition clause and agreed to examine all protective duties, reducing them as soon as possible and protecting only industries with good prospects. Despite the fact that New Zealand already gave substantial preferences, Britain was able to secure guarantees that margins would be maintained and some preferential rates reduced. India already had a Tariff Board, but, importantly, accepted the *principle* of imperial preference, and introduced preferential margins of 10 and $7\frac{1}{2}$ per cent on selected products. Nonetheless, on the products that really mattered for Britain, cottons and steel, cottons were the subject of an investigation by the Tariff Board, and steel duties were bound by existing legislation for another two years.

Other important concessions secured were confidential assurances from Canada that British products would be excluded from arbitrary customs valuations, and promises to consider sympathetically the possibility of reducing and ultimately abolishing the exchange dumping valuations levied on sterling.[55] South Africa, on the other hand, refused to make any promises to modify similar exchange dumping duties. The Australian category of deferred duties was a potent source of irritation to British exporters. Low rates were charged on specific products not made in Australia, but once production was started much higher rates were enforced. The Australians promised they would not raise rates of duty on these items. Britain also obtained assurances from Australia, Canada and New Zealand that the supplementary fiscal surchages known as primage duties would be removed as soon as practicable, an undertaking like the

[55] The UK Trade Commissioner in Canada had thought that the removal of these practices in customs administration, including arbitrary valuation, would be of greater value to British trade with Canada than a large number of tariff preferences without removal of these practices. F. W. Field to E. T. F. Crowe, 20 Jan. 1932, FO 371/16405.

Canadian promises on exchange dumping duties which would be dependent on goodwill and the 'Ottawa spirit'.[56]

What price did Britain pay for these benefits? The first bargaining point had been the conditional grant of preferences for dominion produce under the Import Duties Act; ostensibly the dominions were to pay for them by meeting British requests at Ottawa. When, en route to Canada, Thomas had asked Amery whether he thought the Canadians would offer enough to justify Britain keeping on the 10 per cent preference, Amery had suggested Thomas land at Rimouski and find a boat home without going to Ottawa. Mere continuance of preferences beyond 15 November would not in itself achieve dramatic concessions from the dominions, and it had, of course, been anticipated that more would have to be given. The most important of these changes, particularly as they affected later negotiations, are summarised below.

Wheat and Flour. A duty of 2 shillings per quarter on foreign wheat was reluctantly imposed after heavy pressure from Canada.[57] Neither the Canadians nor the Australians thought the preference would bring them any benefit, Bennett stressing that he wanted it for political purposes.[58] As if to underline the uselessness of the duty, Britain could withdraw it if Empire wheat prices rose above the world level. On Britain's side, there was no protectionist motive behind the duty. Wheat growers already had encouragement from deficiency payments introduced earlier in the year under the Wheat Act, and it was simply Canadian importunity that induced the concession. The duty applied also to flour; at first it was assumed that there would be no preference on Empire flour on the grounds that it would penalise the UK millers using dutied grain. However, in the tense, last ditch negotiations, free entry for imperial flour was agreed.

Timber and the Russian Clause. The Australians and Canadians were worried that Russian dumping of grain and timber would destroy their markets for these products. They really wanted exclusion of Russian products from the UK, a move which would also have found some favour in Britain. But the British government was reluctant to take such an extreme step, largely because it would have jeopardised a useful export market as well as some sizeable export credits.

Canadian timber requests eventually settled around the Russian clause. Canada supplied only about 5 per cent of British imports of sawn timber. Higher duties would at first be ineffective, British officials thought, because

---

[56] The above two paragraphs are based largely on Drummond, *Imperial Economic Policy*, 219–251.

[57] The Canadians threatened to withdraw their offers if the British team did not agree to this duty. CAB 32, 102, 49th meeting 13 Aug. 1932.

[58] CAB 32/102, 47th meeting 12 Aug. 1932.

they would be absorbed by producers, and therefore would be of little help to Canada, and in particular to British Columbia where the collapse of the American lumber market was being felt most. High freight charges and the unsuitability of timber preparations for the British market would have needed vast preferences, a report suggested, and went on to point out the importance of timber to Northern Europe and to the impending negotiations.[59] Bennett, who had asked for higher duties on foreign timber, accepted British arguments about the impact on Scandinavian supplies, overruled a more pressing colleague and eventually settled for a Soviet anti-dumping clause.[60]

Early agreement was reached on the general desirability of a clause about Russian competition. The British negotiators were not willing to go as far as complete exclusion of Russian products but did agree to take action if Soviet supplies destroyed the value of the British market for the dominions.[61]

Meat. The main drama at Ottawa centred on the question of meat duties and quotas. It was heightened because of the failure of the British to decide on policy beforehand, a failure which resulted from divisions within the British Cabinet and delegation. The negotiations between Australia and the UK very nearly foundered on the issue, and the eventual outcome later created major difficulties between Britain and the chief suppliers of meat.

At first sight it appears strange that Australia was particularly interested in meat anyway. Table 3.6 makes it clear that while sheepmeat was obviously important to New Zealand, Australia's dependence on meat exports was slight. The explanation for the Australian government's insistence on meat concessions lies in its view that preferences for wheat and wool, the major exports, were useless and that it had therefore better look for help with butter, meat and fruits.[62] South Africa, which had even smaller interests in meat exports, also wanted preferences so that the Boer farmers who provided support for the ruling National Party might benefit.[63]

British Ministers knew that meat was going to figure prominently in the

[59] CAB 32/104 0 (B)(32) 85, Inter-departmental Preparatory Committee, 2 July 1932.

[60] CAB 32/102, 49th 51st and 68th meetings 13, 15, and 18 Aug. 1932.

[61] The clause, No. 21 of the agreements with Australia and Canada, was as follows: 'This agreement is made on the express conditions that, if either government is satisfied that any preferences are likely to be frustrated in whole or in part by reason of the creation or maintenance directly or indirectly of prices for such class of commodities through state action on the part of any foreign country, that government hereby declares that it will exercise the powers which it now has or will hereafter take to prohibit the entry from such foreign country directly or indirectly of such commodities into its country for such time as may be necessary to make effective and to maintain the preferences hereby granted by it.'

[62] CAB 32/101, 27th meeting 3 Aug. 1932.

[63] CAB 32/101, 33rd meeting 5 Aug. 1932.

Table 3.6. *Percentage value of beef, veal, mutton and lamb to total exports, 1931–1934*

	Beef and Veal (%)	Mutton and Lamb (%)
Australia	2·0	3·2
New Zealand	1·9	21·0

Source: Imperial Economic Committee, *Meat. A Summary of Figures of Production and Trade* (1936), 20, 29.

negotiations, but as outlined above, took no decisions about policy before they left for Ottawa. En route there was another discussion when a paper circulated by Gilmour was considered.[64] This argued that action was necessary, not so much to placate the dominions but more to protect British farmers, especially sheep rearers. Duties were not thought useful: they would be absorbed by suppliers, and therefore be worthless both as a protectionist device and as aid to the dominions. The minister argued that quotas on mutton and lamb imports, on the other hand, would help British farmers by raising prices and would also provide some scope for substituting dominion for foreign supplies. Probably it was the emphasis on protecting domestic agriculture that led to the dismissal of the report's recommendations, although as already mentioned, an inter-departmental committee had already argued against quotas. Yet there was agreement among the British team that primary prices were too low, and that supply regulation was the way to raise them. The southern dominions were repeatedly told that it was the huge expansion of their shipments of mutton and lamb that had driven prices down. If supplies were curtailed, prices would recover. The Australasians were vehemently opposed to this as a solution to their problems. It cut across assumptions about the sanctity of expanding production, and was not a message they were anxious to take back to their rural electorates. Moreover, they argued that if cut-backs of mutton and lamb did succeed in raising prices, demand would be switched to South American beef.[65] The meat market must be viewed as a whole, and not in its component parts, so it was pointless to take action on mutton and lamb without also restricting foreign beef supplies. What the southern dominions really wanted was a duty on foreign meat and free entry for dominion supplies. British assent to Canadian requests for a wheat duty, far from being regarded as a concession to Australia, served to make

[64] CAB 32/105 0 (B)(32) 138, 6 July 1932.
[65] CAB 32/101, 31st and 35th meetings 4 and 5 Aug. 1932.

Bruce's position infinitely worse if nothing was conceded on meat.[66] By the same token, it also made it harder for the British to agree to take any action on meat. The issue exposed the divisions in the British delegation. Having reluctantly agreed to a wheat duty, Runciman and Thomas were stiffened in their opposition to meat duties,[67] and even Cunliffe-Lister preferred a restriction scheme to a tariff.[68] One cause of the opposition of Thomas and Runciman was that they thought the immediate benefits Britain was likely to get from Ottawa were too small.[69] Price rises at home would be hard to defend,[70] and Runciman in particular was very concerned about the impact of meat restrictions on Argentina:

He drew a distinction between the Argentine and other foreign countries. Our interests in the Argentine were of enormous importance and value and he felt that the adoption of the policy proposed must destroy any real chance of making a satisfactory commercial agreement with one of our most important foreign customers.[71]

These disagreements amongst the British delegation must have confused the Australians. As late as 13 August, when Chamberlain was discussing meat duties with the Australians, they were told the matter was still under active consideration.[72] Yet apparently later the same day Baldwin informed Bruce that meat duties were out of the question.[73] A furious Bruce had to be talked by Baldwin into staying at Ottawa. Duties on mutton and lamb imports, Baldwin argued, might endanger the National government at a time when problems in Ireland and India had to be confronted. Bruce reported to Prime Minister Lyons:

The whole tenor of his conversation with me was to make an appeal to Australia not to wreck the National Government, with an implication behind it that if we persisted in our attitude we would imperil the possibility of the Conference being a success, with disastrous results to the British Empire and probably to the whole world. I said very little at that interview beyond pointing out that it seemed to me hardly fair to try and throw the whole responsibility on my shoulders when in fact the critical situation which had arisen was due to the fact that the British Government had not made their position clear in the beginning.[74]

---

[66] CAB 32/102, 45th meeting 11 Aug. 1932.
[67] Runciman had stated in the House of Commons that he was against the taxation of wheat and meat. *Hansard* (Commons), vol. 261, no. 34, 10 Feb. 1932, col. 905.
[68] N. Chamberlain diary, 11, 13 Aug. 1932. NC 2/17.
[69] CAB 32/102, 49th meeting 13 Aug. 1932.
[70] N. Chamberlain diary, 11 Aug. 1932. NC 2/17.
[71] CAB 32/102, 45th meeting 11 Aug. 1932.
[72] N. Chamberlain diary, 13 Aug. 1932 and CAB 32/102, 49th meeting 13 Aug. 1932.
[73] C. Edwards, *Bruce of Melbourne* (1965), 209–10.
[74] S. M. Bruce to J. A. Lyons, 23 Aug. 1932, cited in K. Tsokhas, *Markets, Money and Empire. The political economy of the Australian wool industry* (Melbourne, 1990), 94.

Two days later, at the next meeting of British and Australian ministers, the Australian offers to Britain were withdrawn.[75] The British delegation remained divided: Runciman and Thomas threatened resignation if a meat duty was imposed, and Chamberlain threatened resignation if the conference broke down because a meat duty was refused.[76] Thomas later changed his mind, reporting to MacDonald that he was prepared to accept a meat duty. From London, MacDonald pointed out the difficulties of such a duty, including five likely resignations, but did not specifically overrule it. Within two days, by 17 August, both the Australian and New Zealand delegations had accepted quantitative restrictions in principle,[77] although the details were not settled without further drama, the Australians insisting on controls being placed on foreign chilled beet and on bigger reductions on other foreign meats. The eventual agreement was that foreign sheepmeat and frozen beef would be cut back in stages so that by mid-1934 they would be at 65 per cent of their July 1931 to June 1932 level (the 'Ottawa Year'). Foreign chilled beef was to be restricted to the Ottawa Year level. No duties would be placed on Empire supplies for five years, and Britain pledged not to impose quantitative restrictions on them before July 1934. In turn, Australia and New Zealand agreed to limit their shipments during 1933. These arrangements were to be an enormous source of friction during the next few years and, together with the Argentine agreements of 1933, a powerful restraint on Britain's freedom of action in managing its own agricultural crisis.

Bacon. It had not been expected that bacon would feature much in the Ottawa negotiations. The only imperial supplier of any importance, apart from the Irish Free State, was Canada, and although Canadian shipments had been considerable up until the mid-1920s, they had since fallen so sharply that by 1931 Canada was furnishing less than 0·5 per cent of UK imports. Concessions were not regarded as practicable because of the home consumer and Denmark.[78] However, the Canadians pressed for duties and for unimpeded entry for their supplies. Because of incipient British plans to develop domestic bacon production, using quantitative regulations of imports, the request for unimpeded entry was not unimportant. Duties were opposed successfully, the Canadians instead being offered in principle an expanding share of the British market. This was acceptable to Bennett,[79] but he wanted a specific and tangible expression of the principle. The British delegation first conceded 2 million cwts and then,

[75] CAB 32/102, 54th meeting 15 Aug. 1932.
[76] N. Chamberlain diary, 15 Aug. 1932.
[77] CAB 32/102, 60th and 61st meetings 17 Aug. 1932.
[78] CAB 32/104 0 (B)(32) 36, Brief for Ministers, 7 June 1932.
[79] CAB 32/102, 49th meeting 13 Aug. 1932.

at a very tense phase of the negotiations with Canada, offered $2\frac{1}{2}$ million cwts, overriding the hesitations of the Minister of Agriculture.[80] Since this was fifty times the amount Canada had shipped in 1931 it was widely reported that the figure was the result of clerical error; the documents make clear it was not. As with other meats, these arrangements were later to create difficulties in formulating trade and agricultural policy.

Dairy produce and eggs. Australasian butter production, and small supplies from Canada, clashed largely with competition from northern Europe. British production supplied less than 10 per cent of the market and was declining. The Ottawa Preparatory Committee had decided that this was one of the products where preferences could be increased, although a later document warned of the cost to domestic consumers and the value of the British market to Denmark and other northern European producers.[81] Although the butter proposals formulated by the New Zealanders on behalf of the interested dominions were, according to a British adviser, 'simply fantastic – 2d a lb plus a quota which will at once reduce foreign supplies by 40% and thereafter to nothing...', requests for extra duties were readily conceded and quotas on foreign supplies were refused.[82] Importantly, free entry for dominion produce was given for three years. Similar terms were granted for cheese, of greater relevance to Canada.

Egg production was of less value to the dominions but more important in Britain itself.[83] Extra duties were granted, specific rather than *ad valorem*, and again the dominions were given free entry for three years, overruling suggestions from Gilmour that Empire suppliers should be subject to a preferential duty.[84]

Other products. New or higher duties were also conceded on foreign apples, pears, canned fruits, dried fruits, honey and flat maize. Seasonal duties were introduced for peaches, nectarines, plums, grapes, oranges and grapefruit. Britain also pledged itself not to reduce existing duties on a range of products from ostrich feathers and wattle bark through to fresh fish, marine shell, canned salmon, zinc and lead. Existing margins of preference on tobacco and tea, amongst other products, were also guaranteed, together with free entry for Indian iron and steel.[85]

---

[80] CAB 32/102, 67th and 68th meetings 18 and 19 Aug. 1932.
[81] CAB 32/104 0 (B)(32) 60, Brief for Minister, 4 June 1932.
[82] DO 121/61, G. Whiskard to Sir E. J. Harding, 29 July 1932 and CAB 32/101, 27th, 31st and 33rd meetings 3, 4, 5 Aug. 1932.
[83] CAB 32/104 0 (B)(32) 60, Brief for Ministers. 4 June 1932.
[84] CAB 32/102, 47th meeting 12 Aug. 1932 and CAB 32/105 0 (B)(32) 167, for M.A.F. suggestion 11 Aug. 1932.
[85] Drummond, *Imperial Economic Policy*, 270–2.

Ottawa: Conclusions

Hard bargaining was the rule at Ottawa, and imperial spirit was at a premium. Amery suggested that the conditional preference clause of the Import Duties Act had 'struck a false, bargaining note at the very outset', and that it had been sustained throughout the conference.[86] Certainly in retrospect it is difficult to imagine a conference at Ottawa in 1932 in which mutual advantages were freely given with little regard to reciprocity. As it was, the bargaining was intense and the conference twice nearly broke up. The benefits for Britain were limited, as was realised at the conference, and as will be further discussed in chapter 9. Why was more not achieved? Britain possessed enormous potential bargaining power through its position as the world's greatest importer. The dominions were critically dependent on the British market for their exports and for any semblance of economic prosperity. Although dominion markets were clearly of great importance to Britain it was not as dependent on them as they on the UK market. It is true that heavy UK investments in the Empire had to be considered as well, but the results at Ottawa do not reflect the disparity of bargaining strength. Were tactics at fault?

It might be argued that the granting of conditional preferences prior to the conference, the decision not to discriminate between the Commonwealth countries but to extend concessions uniformly to all, and the fact that the dominions were being met collectively rather than singly, served to limit the ability of the negotiators to maximise concessions for UK interests. Yet in at least two of these matters Britain had little choice. The conference had been agreed in 1930 and in some respects was a continuation of the Imperial Conference of 1930. Moreover, to have negotiated separately would have created great practical difficulties when discussing issues affecting more than one dominion. Discriminating between countries of the Commonwealth, offering concessions to one and refusing the same to others would have been impossible – within the British market imperial produce, except for that of the Irish Free State, entered on identical terms. While Britain did perhaps have greater choice on the matter of conditional free entry, it is almost certain that if it had not been granted the dominions would have been angered, and it is difficult to believe that significantly more would have been offered to Britain without it.

In the particular case of Australia it is possible that the UK failed to use full bargaining leverage. The Australians were very anxious to convert their external debts to lower rates of interest. A measure of this concern

[86] Amery to Runciman, 16 Aug. 1932. W.R. 256.

was that Bruce went to London as Resident Minister specifically to arrange the conversion of Australian debts.[87] They hoped to get support from the Treasury and the Bank of England. R. W. Dalton, Britain's Trade Commissioner in Australia, argued that the UK could have obtained much better terms from Australia if they had used the threat to withhold support from the debt conversion operation.[88] Although Runciman mentioned the issue at Ottawa to other members of the British delegation, he apparently got no support, presumably because the use of such tactics would have been inconsistent with British policy.[89]

Certainly some British advisers blamed poor tactics and weak leadership for the UK's failure to win better terms. Geoffrey Whiskard, the Dominions Office representative at the conference, was particularly scathing about the British delegation. He was frustrated with his own minister, Thomas, who carried little weight with his colleagues, but the dissatisfaction was apparently more widespread: 'We officials are all in despair', he reported on 16 August, '[n]one of our masters has the backbone of a louse.' Later, returning home, and in a more relaxed and reflective mood after two days at sea, he lamented the size of the British delegation and the lack of influence of the officials. There were too many ministers:

It was because they themselves were 7 and we were legion that we advisers were so little consulted – never, in my experience, have Ministers used their advisers so little, or disregarded so wholly such advice as they did receive. Three Ministers, with say 6 advisers, would have formed a compact team which might have produced very much better results than have in fact emerged. Also it would be desirable, if such an occasion ever occurs again, to have something faintly resembling a policy before we start. As it was we had all the materials (far more plentiful, accurate, and carefully prepared than any other delegation) for formulating a policy, but made very little use of them – and in the end Bennett and Bruce made up our minds for us.[90]

Perhaps Amery would have drawn wry amusement from Whiskard's picture of powerless civil servants. In his view the problem at Ottawa had been that far from possessing too little influence the British advisers had held too much sway over their masters. They were prejudiced against the

---

[87] Edwards, *Bruce*, 212. According to R. M. Kottman, *Reciprocity and the North Atlantic Triangle, 1932–1938* (Ithaca, 1968) 24, Bennett was the spokesman in the main clashes with the UK delegates because Bruce was inhibited by his need to arrange a conversion loan later in the year. British delegates would have been surprised to learn that Bruce was in any way inhibited at Ottawa. For an interesting account of the loan conversion negotiations, see Neville Cain and Sean Glynn, 'Imperial relations under strain: the British-Australian debt contretemps of 1933', *Australian Economic History Review*, 25 (1985), 39–58.
[88] DO 35/281/9279/A/287.   [89] CAB 32/102, 49th meeting 13 Aug. 1932.
[90] DO 121/61, Whiskard to Harding, 16, 22 Aug. 1932.

whole policy of imperial preference and 'certainly did their best to wreck this Conference'.[91] There is no suggestion in Whiskard's correspondence that he felt the British delegates were failing to push their advantages hard enough to secure better terms for UK exports, but much more a sense that they were conceding too much.

The real inhibitions on Britain's achieving spectacular results at Ottawa arose not from poor tactics but from broader considerations of circumstance and policy. One important factor here was that Britain needed some sort of agreement at Ottawa: for Thomas, failure would be a fatal blow to imperial interests. While he was 'determined to get real concessions in return for any advantages which we might be able to offer...he felt bound to keep in mind that, ultimately, the over-riding consideration must be the maintenance of imperial unity'.[92] This worried Ramsay MacDonald who, long before Ottawa, had written 'our danger will be that we will become so afraid of a breakdown that we will allow the Dominions to play with us...'[93] Britain needed agreements at Ottawa, and could not really contemplate applying trade sanctions against any of the major dominions. This both restricted the pressure that could be applied by the British negotiators while at the same time forcing them to concede more than most of them would have liked, notably in the case of the meat arrangements.

It has been implied that the needs of British agriculture limited the value of what Britain could offer the dominions.[94] While considerations of British agriculture lingered in the background, they never appear to have been of decisive importance at Ottawa. They never led to refusals of dominion requests that jeopardised any negotiations or provided a serious obstacle to a satisfactory agreement. The UK had ambitions for its pig producers which might have stood in the way of Canada, and indeed a Canadian proposal that it should have equal competitive footing was rejected.[95] But Canada was offered an absurdly generous quota, the Minister of Agriculture being overruled on a break clause, and Bennett was satisfied. UK egg producers provided a major share of home consumption, and a foreign tariff schedule, graduated according to size of egg, was developed with the idea of protecting British egg producers. The dominions, however, were allowed duty free and unrestricted entry, although with a warning that Britain might need duties later. Again, attempts by the Minister of Agriculture to insert preferential duties on

[91] Barnes and Nicholson, *Amery Diaries*, 24 Aug. 1932. See also 13, 17 Aug.

[92] CAB 27 473 OC (31), Cabinet Committee on Proposed Economic Conference at Ottawa. 16 Nov. 1931.   [93] MacDonald to Runciman 28 Dec. 1931. WR 245.

[94] Drummond writes that the 'emerging agrarian protectionism of the U.K. was as much a part of the Conference fabric as the established industrial protectionism of India and the Dominions', *Imperial Economic Policy*, 254.

[95] CAB 32/102, 54th meeting 15 Aug. 1932.

Empire supplies were rejected.[96] The dominions were also allowed free and unrestricted entry for their dairy produce, requests for price raising quotas being refused.[97]

In the case of meat quotas, the needs of Britain's livestock farmers may have figured in the eventual outcome of quota restrictions on foreign supplies. But these restrictions came as the result of Australian pressure and the refusal of the UK delegates to agree to a meat duty, not because of British insistence. They were a concession, a move to allow the substitution of Empire supplies for foreign meat, and an attempt at the same time to stop a decline in prices that was certainly alarming the Ministry of Agriculture. They were not primarily an impediment to commonwealth supplies, although the southern dominions were notably unenthusiastic about the temporary halt to the growth of their own shipments. Arrangements made for Britain's wheat growers – the deficiency payment system – might have exercised a check on an important market, but this occurred well before the conference, and does not appear to have worried the dominions. Instead, a duty on foreign supplies was instituted to meet Canadian wishes, and it is significant that the duty would have been withdrawn if imperial prices rose above the world level, for this would have affected the domestic consumer. Certainly British farmers had no direct say in proceedings, and in the view of one recent historian, 'had to watch from a distance as their industry was offered as a bargaining "chip"'.[98]

The price to the British consumer was a much greater obstacle to granting dominion wishes than worries about domestic agriculture. Concern about the home consumer played a part in meeting only half-way the requests for higher duties on eggs and dairy products, and it was central in the refusal of meat duties, and, much less important, a tariff on bacon. It may even have been partly responsible for the rejection of Canadian demands for a higher duty on foreign timber. Yet even in the case of the cost of living, the attitude of much of the British delegation was conditioned by the form of the advantage offered, not the real effect. Chamberlain and Hailsham, and perhaps Baldwin and Cunliffe-Lister, would have conceded a duty on meat. Some of the delegation, notably Chamberlain, wanted to raise prices anyway, believing it essential for world recovery. But the way in which it was done was vitally important. Food taxes were political

[96] CAB 32/102, 47th meeting 12 Aug. 1932.

[97] Although it would be wrong to look for too much internal logic or consistency in the Ottawa arrangements, it does appear likely that Britain may have refused butter quotas because butter was not important to her own producers, and emphasised restrictions on meat because of home producers' interests. But the cut back of foreign supplies was the result of dominion insistence.

[98] A. F. Cooper, *British Agricultural Policy, 1912–1936. A study in Conservative politics* (Manchester, 1989), 155.

dynamite, unpopular with the electorate and certain to divide the Cabinet. Quotas and supply restrictions were surer ways of raising prices and, at the same time, less familiar and politically less dangerous.

Generally the dominions were prepared to accept arguments based on the protection of domestic agriculture. At least they said they were, and were they not protecting their own industries anyway? But what raised the temperature at Ottawa were attempts to shield foreign supplies from dominion demands. Foreign supplies had been squeezed before Ottawa and generally foreign countries seemed to accept that Ottawa was going to increase the pressure further. Yet Britain did not go to Ottawa with a one-eyed imperial commitment. Throughout the conference preparations and the conference itself, the British government maintained an awareness of world interests and of the need to keep something in reserve for future trade negotiations. Frank Ashton Gwatkin, head of the Foreign Office Economic Section, felt that foreign affairs had been an issue throughout the conference, and at crucial times a dominant one, and yet the Foreign Office, apart from two officials sent as observers, had been unrepresented.[99] However, this probably did not have a serious impact on decisions. Runciman kept a close watch on foreign interests, notably those of Argentina. It is impossible to assess the relative weight of the consumer and the foreigner in restricting the concessions that were made to the dominions. A number of products escaped new or higher duties because some of the delegation were keen to avoid the protectionist tag – but the likely adverse effect on Denmark and North European producers was also important.

It was the interests of British consumers and the wish to avoid destroying the market for foreign suppliers that stood in the way of meeting dominion aspirations, not the needs of British farmers. UK agricultural protection only became of major importance in imperial relations in the years after Ottawa. Apart from these vitally important constraints, however, and the need to maintain the unity of the Empire, the factors most preventing dramatic gains for Britain arose from the context in which the conference was occurring. The depression was the catalyst which brought Britain and other commonwealth countries together at Ottawa. It also made dominion governments extremely reluctant to sacrifice budget revenue or employment in secondary industry. Perhaps more dramatic inroads into imperial protectionist systems might have been made if cooperative elite groups with political power existed. But in the dominions, certainly in Canada, Australia and New Zealand, the political system was too broadly representative, and in the former two countries the range of economic

---

[99] FO 371/16409, Ashton Gwatkin to Wellesley, 19 Aug. 1932.

interest too wide, to permit of any clear sacrifice of secondary industry in exchange for higher primary product sales, and in India the development of secondary industry was linked both symbolically and financially to the nationalist cause. Britain therefore obtained increased preferential margins, modest immediate concessions in the form of reduced tariff rates, together with some guarantees limiting future protection. The dominions obtained privileges against foreign competition, and, most importantly, guarantees of free entry that were to be of immense value to them in the next few years as British agricultural policy underwent a transformation.

4   The Scandinavian negotiations: formulation of policy

With the Ottawa conference concluded, attention was switched to negotiating with non-imperial suppliers. British trade was widely dispersed geographically: much of the tension at Ottawa had been generated by the UK's determination not to concede too much to dominion suppliers, and to leave a reserve of bargaining leverage for the later negotiations. The Ottawa conference, which had been carried out in a glare of publicity with widespread press coverage, had provided a forum for political drama. In contrast, the subsequent trade negotiations, at least from the British perspective, were muted affairs, more a matter of mundane administration than of high politics. While at Ottawa Britain had been represented by seven Cabinet Ministers who engaged in concentrated discussions for more than four weeks, the later trade talks were carried out from the British side largely by officials with only occasional participation by the Secretary of the Department of Overseas Trade, John Colville, or, even more rarely by the President of the Board of Trade, Walter Runciman. References were made to Cabinet and Cabinet Committee, but except for the resolution of a clash between domestic agricultural interests and the prospects for good treaties, this were merely for formal approval of the start of the negotiations and of the agreements themselves. There was debate in parliament where vent was given to the unease or scorn of both imperialists and free traders, but generally the negotiations were undertaken quietly, with little publicity and no great political controversy.

The choice of negotiating partners

While much of British industry had been enthusiastic about making the imperial agreements, it was distinctly less so when it came to treaty making outside the Commonwealth. The Federation of British Industries was worried that protection, so recently won, would be whittled away in the course of negotiations. A memorandum from the FBI, in July 1932 argued that:

negotiations during the immediate future would inevitably take place under conditions unfavourable to this country, as our home tariff policy is not yet sufficiently settled, nor is its classification sufficiently detailed or its rates sufficiently graded to make it a safe basis for negotiations with countries with well-established and highly detailed tariffs. At the moment we have very wisely satisfied ourselves with a very simple form of tariff. During the course of the next two years, as investigations into conditions affecting various industries proceed, this old-fashioned tariff with its large flat rate groups will presumably have to be subdivided, graded and re-classified. To be engaged in treaty negotiations before this process is completed would obviously place our negotiators at a grave disadvantage which might easily produce very unsatisfactory treaties. At present in negotiations with a country with a modern detailed tariff, our opponents would know the value of what they were offering and asking with a fair degree of precision, and, owing to the detailed character of their tariff classification and the careful grading of their rates, could adjust their offers with considerable nicety.[1]

The memorandum went on to argue that the crude UK tariff would make it very hard for British negotiators to assess the costs of any offer they made, and that the conventionalisation[2] of large portions of the tariff would seriously embarrass the Import Duties Advisory Committee (IDAC) in its work of tariff construction.[3] The course of action recommended by the Federation was to develop the UK tariff, making the protection of the home market the overriding objective, and to avoid treaty negotiations as far as possible.

This was ruled out by Whitehall. The government had committed itself in parliament to trade negotiations; if the policy was delayed for two years it would give little time for the benefits to become apparent before the next election, and, anyway, Germany was contesting duties placed on its goods, claiming rights of consultation under the Anglo-German Commercial Treaty of 1924. If the UK did not negotiate with Germany fairly shortly, there would be a risk of retaliation.[4]

Negotiations were to go ahead. But quite apart from any other considerations there were obvious limitations on the physical ability of the Board of Trade to carry out negotiations with more than a very few countries at the same time. Why should Argentina and the Scandinavians have had priority?

Clearly, as Table 4.1 shows, the eventual choice of countries was not in the main a reflection of their relative importance to the UK's export trade.

[1] BT 11/87, memorandum from FBI July 1932.
[2] 'Conventionalisation' or 'consolidation' meant that free entry would be assured, or, in the case of duties, that the existing rate would be guaranteed as the maximum.
[3] BT 11/87, memorandum from FBI July 1932.
[4] BT 11/87, minute by Hill, 28 July 1932. Almost certainly Germany had retaliated already by cutting imports of coal from the UK. This is discussed in ch. 5 below.

Table 4.1. *UK exports to selected foreign countries, 1932*

Country	£000s	% of exports to foreign countries
France	18,446	9·3
USA	15,091	7·6
Germany	14,575	7·3
Netherlands	12,106	6·1
Argentina	10,660	5·3
Denmark	9,853	4·9
Soviet Union	9,223	4·6
Belgium	8,678	4·4
Italy	8,639	4·3
Sweden	6,885	3·5
Norway	5,802	2·9
Spain	5,224	2·6

Source: UK, *Annual Statement of Trade, 1932* (1933).

Walter Runciman spelled out to the Cabinet the reasoning behind his policy.[5] The decision partly reflected the anxiety of Argentina and the Scandinavians about their exports to the UK and the pressure applied by them to enter early negotiations. Argentina was considered the most promising of the non-European countries because of the size of its purchases, its close financial and commercial ties with the UK and its desire to negotiate. The United States, despite being the largest non-European foreign market, was excluded because the government 'would not be likely to consider any substantial reductions of their autonomous tariff whatever inducements were offered in exchange'.[6] Of the European countries, the Scandinavians had not only pressed for trade negotiations, but these were likely to reach a successful conclusion more rapidly than those with France or Germany which 'would inevitably prove difficult and protracted'. Nevertheless, Runciman argued, negotiations with Germany and France would have to be carried out fairly soon because France had placed a discriminatory surtax on UK goods, and Germany, as mentioned above, wanted discussions over mutual grievances. The political need for early results from the trade negotiations was therefore one important factor in the choice of countries. The irony lay in the Ottawa agreements, which as Runciman pointed out would have hampered Britain hardly at all in negotiations with industrial countries but would 'limit substantially the

[5] CAB 27/489 CFC (32), Memorandum by President of the Board of Trade, 22 Oct. 1932.
[6] *Ibid.*

scope of the concessions we can make to countries such as the Scandinavian countries and Argentina'.[7] Here the attitude of British industry was of outstanding importance. The dearly prized protection it had won was not to be hazarded in serious negotiations with industrial countries. It would have been extraordinarily difficult for the government to secure the concurrence of industry in any major reduction in the British tariff on industrial products; the modest concessions on steel and paper resulting from the Scandinavian negotiations were to cause furore enough as it was. The vulnerability of Argentina and the North-west European countries, resulting from their dependence on the UK market, was obviously a major factor in the decision – their vulnerability and their anxiety made them appear relatively easy pickings.

British leverage: opportunities and constraints

But just how strong was Britain's negotiating position? In common with many primary producers, the Scandinavian countries, especially Denmark, were in a poor bargaining position because their resources were less mobile than those of industrial countries; this reinforced the weakness of any small country negotiating with a larger trading partner.[8] Certainly it was greatly aided by Scandinavia's reliance on the British market. The Danes carried this to extreme lengths, and in Europe only the Irish Free State was more dependent on the UK as an export outlet. Danish exports were dominated by four products, bacon, butter, cattle and eggs, and all except cattle went in large quantities to the UK; 70 per cent of Danish bacon production was consumed in Britain, and a very high proportion of butter and egg output was exported. In total, 62 per cent of Danish exports went to the UK in 1930. A smaller but nonetheless considerable degree of dependence was exhibited by Sweden and Norway, each of which sent about a quarter of their exports to Britain in 1930.[9]

Another condition enhancing the attractiveness of Scandinavia for bargaining purposes was the heavy balance of trade surplus it had with Britain. The precise amounts tended to be a fruitful source of dispute, hinging on whose trade statistics were being used, and in turn reflecting whether country of production, consignment or payment was used. On British figures, Denmark had in 1930 exported more than five times as

[7] CAB 24/233 CP 336 (32).
[8] A. O. Hirschman, *National Power and the Structure of Foreign Trade* (Berkeley and Los Angeles, 1945), 28.
[9] CAB 27/489 CFC (32) 10, Trade Negotiations with Denmark, memorandum by Runciman, 30 Nov. 1932.

much as it had imported from the UK,[10] the Swedes had exported roughly twice as much as they had imported, and only in the case of Norway in 1930 had Britain had a surplus, and that was reckoned to be an exceptional year because of unusually large Norwegian purchases of British-built ships.[11] What was both a source of irritation and of hope to the British side was that Denmark and Sweden found their major export outlets in the UK while Germany was far and away the biggest supplier of their imports. Only in the case of Norway was Britain the major supplier of imports as well as the most valuable market.

Scandinavian awareness of their exposed position on these scores is shown by the measures taken in 1931 and 1932 to boost purchases of British products. In Denmark the 'Buy British' movement had started early. In 1930, after Germany had restricted Danish products, there had been an attempt to boycott German goods, an attempt frowned upon by the authorities. But organisations such as the British Import Union, an aggressive, self-interested group engaged in importing British goods, and the Dano-British Association, a more prestigious but less energetic body, were set up and campaigned for British imports.[12] Various organisations were active in the rural areas, and there seems little doubt that there was genuine support for 'Buying British' amongst anxious farmers.[13] A British Exhibition was launched in the autumn of 1932 in Copenhagen with a great fanfare of publicity and a visit by the Prince of Wales.[14] Huge numbers of visitors were reported. The state's influence can be seen in greater coal purchases from Britain, and also in arms expenditure where, in 1931 for example, Denmark bought over ten times more arms from the UK than from any other country.[15] Further examples of state purchases could be given, but of greater significance and major importance for the rest of the decade was the introduction in early 1932 of exchange control and a system of import licensing in Denmark. The Danish Minister of Commerce informed the British Minister in Copenhagen that the main reason the control was being introduced was that 'it would be the best plan, without touching treaties etc., whereby a real change in the direction of attaining equipoise in the trade between Denmark and Great Britain could be

[10] *Ibid.*
[11] CAB 27/489 CFC(32) 7 and 8, negotiations with Sweden, and negotiations with Norway, memoranda by Runciman, 3, 22 Nov. 1932.
[12] FO 371/16281, Sir T. Hohler to Sir R. Vansittart, 13 Sept. 1932.
[13] Various reports and despatches mention this e.g. FO 371/16281, Hohler to Sir J. Simon, 11 June 1932.
[14] As Colville pointed out, it must have been 'almost without parallel that there should be an exhibition in a foreign country entirely of British goods and paid for by that foreign country'. *Hansard* (Commons), vol. 227, no. 83, col. 1667, 10 May 1933.
[15] CAB 24/229 CP 107(32), Anglo-Danish Commercial Relations. Memorandum by Colville, 18 Mar. 1932.

brought about'.[16] While this was probably not the main motive – the main motive was the defence of the krone – it was nonetheless an important consideration and it certainly created a powerful instrument for controlling the direction of imports. It is difficult to disentangle the relative strength of these measures from a number of other factors, notably the depreciation of sterling, but exports from Britain to Denmark rose from a 1931 low of £8·7 million to £9·9 million in 1932, and did this in the face of declining aggregate imports into Denmark. There was nothing to match this in Norway or Sweden, neither in the extent of a 'Buy British' movement nor in terms of bigger exports, yet in both these countries the dramatic decline in British coal exports was reversed in 1932 in preparation for the negotiations.

There was one further factor which, if it did not positively aid Britain's negotiating hand, then at least did not weaken it. This was the comparatively low level of British investments in Scandinavia. While in the case of Argentina and all of the dominions, British investments had been something of a hostage, this barely applied in the Scandinavian countries.

In at least two respects then, Britain's negotiating position was a strong one. The British market was an outlet of outstanding and critical importance for the Scandinavians, above all for Denmark, and they were far more dependent on the UK than the UK was on them. The balance of trade was also very favourable to Denmark and Sweden. Generally these factors were enough more or less to guarantee favourable agreements to the UK, agreements which would give a good prospect of increasing its share in the import markets of Scandinavia. But Britain was far from being able to dictate terms. There were a number of limitations on its bargaining position. While, on the one hand, in view of Ottawa and of its own agricultural interests, the UK had very little of positive value to offer the Scandinavians, on the other hand, there were a number of constraints which both limited the scope of the concessions that might be realistically sought and also shaped the formulation of requests.

It was clear that London, having given first pickings in the British market to the dominions, had less enticing offers to make in the second round of negotiations with the main foreign suppliers. There was no question of the Scandinavians buying access on the same terms as the dominions – the hostility of the Empire countries to the 'Black Pacts', as the agreements with foreign suppliers later came to be known, and notably those with Argentina and Denmark, was witness to the impossibility of any such idea. The dominions had their Ottawa clauses to protect them anyway. Although, as discussed in chapter 3, the British negotiating team

[16] FO 371/1628, Hohler to Simon, 23 Feb. 1932.

Table 4.2. *The impact of the Import Duties Act and Ottawa Agreements on tariff incidence on Scandinavian imports into the UK (1930 imports)*

	Denmark	Sweden	Norway
% of imports taxed in 1930	0·1	2·2	0·6
% of imports subject to *new* duties, 1932, before Ottawa	48·2	64·0	67·3
% subject to 10% duties	46·7	36·7	47·2
% subject to 11% duties or above	1·5	27·3	20·1
% of imports subject to *new* duties, 1932, after Ottawa	48·2	64·0	67·3
% subject to 10% duties	5·9	26·4	46·4
% subject to 11% duties or above	42·3	37·6	20·9

Source: The Economist, 'Ottawa Supplement', 22 Oct. 1932, 6.

at Ottawa had been careful to leave a margin for subsequent tariff bargaining with other countries, Scandinavian trade had been subject to higher duties (see Table 4.2). Denmark had been worst affected by Ottawa, and some Danish agricultural spokesmen were so annoyed at the preferential system that they were reluctant to negotiate a treaty with Britain and had to be persuaded by their government to drop their opposition.[17]

A much greater threat to Scandinavian exports, and particularly to Danish trade, lay in the ambitions of the Ministry of Agriculture for restoring British agriculture. These had not acted as a major impediment to negotiations at Ottawa, but the rising pressures for agricultural protectionism were to form a central part of the trade discussions with foreign countries.[18] Again it was Denmark, with a much heavier reliance on agricultural exports than Sweden or Norway, that was to suffer most, and in particular from the bacon proposals. Frank Ashton Gwatkin, head of the Economic Section of the Foreign Office, was so pessimistic about the unfavourable effects of the scheme on the bacon supplying countries that he thought the UK could hardly expect to obtain any advantage from the negotiations.[19] More accurately, *The Economist* suggested that 'though there is presumably room for a "deal" with Denmark in the operation of

---

[17] Susan Seymour, 'Anglo-Danish relations and Germany: 1933–45' (Ph.D. thesis, University of London, 1979), 27. [18] See above, pp. 80–100 and ch. 5.
[19] FO 371/16294, memorandum, 27 Oct. 1932.

the vicious system of import quotas for bacon, the British line of approach in this direction seems likely to resemble blackmail rather than bribery'.[20] Nonetheless, British agricultural policy was to reduce the scope and attractiveness of the concessions that could be made to Scandinavia.

The UK, then, could offer little in the way of positive inducements in its market for foreign suppliers. The Scandinavians were going to have to accept third place in the British market after the needs of domestic producers and then Empire suppliers had first been met. Far from holding out the prospects of security or advantage, the negotiations were to determine the extent and pace of their retreat. There were other constraints which at the same time restricted what the UK might achieve and also helped determine the precise form of British requests. Leaving aside questions of national prestige which might stop a country from signing agreements that were too patently a capitulation to greater negotiating strength, Britain could not make demands which might seriously weaken the economy of the agreement country. UK exports depended heavily on the purchasing power and foreign exchange position of the trading partner: this in turn hinged on access on the British market and therefore, among other factors, on British agricultural and trade policy. But the use of bargaining leverage to sell too much to agreement countries might ultimately rebound to the disadvantage of British exports. Although the balance of trade surplus these countries had with Britain gave it a negotiating advantage, the elimination of the surplus would clearly have caused the Scandinavians severe economic problems. Denmark in particular was deficient in natural resources, and both Danish agriculture and manufacturing industry were to a large extent processors of imported materials. Access to raw materials, including feeding stuffs, was therefore essential to the viability of the Danish economy, and for this Denmark needed to be able to import from other areas and to maintain a surplus on trade with the UK. To squeeze the Danes or Swedes too hard, or to insist on strict bilateral balancing, was likely to cripple their economies and therefore their capacity to purchase British goods.

Again with special reference to Denmark, a further and related inhibition on UK negotiators was the position of the krone. The Bank of England was very keen that exchange rates should be stabilised, and had made available to Denmark a drawing credit of £1 million in June 1932 to help the krone.[21] It seems probable that the Bank advised the Danes to restrict imports; certainly a senior Bank official told the Department of Overseas trade that 'Denmark can still...only afford to import necessities and frequent approaches to the Danish authorities on behalf of United

[20] *The Economist*, 21 Jan. 1933, 109.
[21] T 160/920/12659/08/2, minute by S. D. Waley, 2 June 1932.

Kingdom exporters of non-essentials were to be deprecated. Similarly exhibits at the Danish Exhibition should be confined to essentials.'[22] Conflict between the Bank of England's priority of exchange rate stability and the government's concern with pushing exports was to re-emerge during the next two years.

However much these broader considerations may have set the parameters of British pressure, there were a number of other policy decisions and circumstances which ensured that for the most part Britain had to operate well within them. Bargaining power and the negotiating position was shaped by factors such as the decision to keep the most-favoured-nation clause (mfn) as the basis of the agreements, by the degree of protection, the strength of local industry and the often dominant position of other exporters.

One of the key policy decisions had concerned the retention of the mfn clause. The government was under heavy pressure from industry and its own backbenchers to drop the clause. The Manchester Chamber of Commerce and the National Association of Chambers campaigned actively for a modification of policy. Raymond Streat, Secretary of the Manchester Chamber, recorded that the

officials are so thronged it is perhaps unfair to criticise. But I regret to find their minds all closed to any suggestion that the most favoured nation clause may no longer be the desirable 'sheet anchor' of British policy which it has been for so long...[t]he fact remains that whether consciously or otherwise these men are forming a policy of international commercial relationships which will be the basis of England's foreign trade for, shall we say, the next decade or two.[23]

Concessions had to be generalised, so 'what Sweden gives to us, she must give to twenty or thirty other countries'.[24] The FBI argued that the unconditional mfn clause stood in the way of effective trade treaties and the liberalisation of international trade.[25] While to depart from mfn treaties was hazardous, adherence to the principle was preventing countries from making concessions to others because these concessions would become universalised. This, to the Board of Trade, was a complete fallacy. In the Board's view the dominant motive behind the erection of trade barriers and the chief obstacle to their removal lay in the protection of domestic production.[26] The Federation's attitude was a widely held one, however, and the issue was to remain a subject of controversy during the next two years. Repeatedly, when industrialists were consulted about their

[22] FO 371/16282, record of conversation between Mr Rodd of Bank of England and Minister of Department of Overseas Trade. 23 June 1932.
[23] M. Dupree (ed.), *Lancashire and Whitehall: the diary of Sir E. Raymond Streat*, I, *1931–39* (Manchester, 1987), 194, 13 Nov. 1932.   [24] *Ibid.*, 198, 5 Dec. 1932.
[25] BT 11/87, memorandum from FBI, July 1932.
[26] *Ibid.*, minute by Hill, 28 July 1932.

requirements in the trade negotiations, they wanted preferences. This was most noticeably so with Argentina: a number of industrialists thought that without preferences a treaty would be virtually useless, and a special committee set up by the FBI to examine treaty prospects 'was unanimously of the definite opinion that adjustments of the Argentine tariff by way either of reduction or specialisation of duties within a general scheme of most-favoured-nation treatments would not meet the requirements of the present situation'.[27] The clause had been an important agent in the liberalisation of international trade in the third quarter of the nineteenth century, and at the core of the UK's policy since the winding down of the imperial trade system. In the new trade era, did it not make sense for Britain to abandon the principle so as to be free to capitalise on the value of its markets and to secure special privileges for exports? It was quite possible that the decision would be made for it anyway. Britain had long enjoyed preferential treatment for exports to most of the dominions. Now that it had reciprocated, had not a flagrant breach of the mfn clause occurred? Certainly it was thought in London that a successful legal challenge in the international courts might compel the government to choose between mfn and imperial preference. In that case the UK would have chosen imperial preference, the Board of Trade agreeing to this 'despite their unswerving fidelity to mfn treatment'.[28] Ideas of second preference groups were floated. Apparently Runciman had thought Denmark might be placed in such a group, but after Britain's Minister in Copenhagen had mentioned this to the Danes, the Board of Trade suggested he should avoid any further such references.[29] There had been occasional discussion of abandonment of mfn in Scandinavia, but it seems it would have been contemplated without enthusiasm. Apparently Danish experts felt that Denmark would be compelled to denounce the mfn principle if Britain did so, but would only have done it with the greatest reluctance.[30] The Commercial Secretary reported that he did not think such a course would be practical politics in Denmark as only the Conservatives favoured it, although apparently the Danes, later in 1933, did consider giving Britain preferential treatment before deciding it would be too inimical to their trade with Germany.[31] At one time too, the Swedes had assumed that a new treaty would be needed because the existing Anglo-Swedish treaty contained the mfn clause.[32]

[27] BT 11/143, Sir Guy Locock (Director-General of the FBI) to Runciman, 11 Oct. 1932.
[28] FO 371/16417, minute by R. Dunbar, 13 July 1932.
[29] FO 371/16281, Hohler to Simon, 23 Feb. 1932, and Board of Trade to Foreign Office, 6 Apr. 1932.   [30] The Times, 1 Sept. 1932.
[31] BT 11/119, H. Cassells to J. Picton-Bagge, 15 Nov. 1932 and information given by Col. Colville to sub-committee of the Conservative Research Department. Runciman Papers, Box 269.   [32] BT 11/124, Meeting with Swedish Minister, 18 Oct. 1932.

But the Board of Trade was resolute in its opposition to a voluntary departure from mfn. Hill minuted that 'the risk of disaster to our export trade by a wholesale denunciation of these instruments must be very serious'.[33] Britain's trade was far too diversified to benefit from abandonment of mfn; the danger of discrimination against British trade was enormous.[34] Britain had more than forty treaties, some of which, including those with Argentina and Denmark, had no provision for termination, and the Board of Trade looked with some horror at the prospect of renegotiating these agreements. On top of all this, it was really Britain's partners in the trade negotiations which would have to denounce *their* treaties and mfn rights. There was no guarantee they would be prepared to do this, subjecting themselves to trade upheaval as well as the prospect of thraldom to the UK. The sophisticated course for Britain was to hold on to the preferences in the Empire and to maintain the very tangible benefits of unconditional mfn rights for its goods in other countries. In the trade negotiations there was to be scope for circumventing some of the restrictions of the mfn clause anyway. And in the Board of Trade it was recognised that Britain was enjoying the best of both worlds with Empire preference and mfn.[35]

While this important decision may have been to the overall advantage of Britain's trade, it seriously limited the whole scope and possibilities of the trade agreements. Britain's bargaining power was reduced because it was unable to discriminate between supplying countries, to offer one country markedly more favourable treatment of its bacon, for example, than that of another bacon supplier. Naturally there could be some minor juggling of the figures of the choice of base years when quotas were being allocated, but the opportunity to offer big inducements to countries through positive discrimination in their favour had been lost. The decision also meant that the UK's power to gain valuable preferential concessions for exports was enormously curtailed. Not only was British industry disappointed, but officials were doubtful of the prospects. Cassells wrote that '[i]n these circumstances, I do not see how we can hope to increase our trade very much by securing tariff concessions or by conventionalising free entry', and writing from Oslo the Commercial Secretary also thought that the decision 'renders most tariff concessions from Norway more valuable to our competitors than ourselves'.[36]

With the decision to retain mfn clauses as the basis of the treaties, the most obvious device for securing trade diversion had been rejected. Nor

---

[33] BT 11/87, 28 July 1932.   [34] *Ibid.*, note by Jenkins, July 1932.
[35] BT 11/234, note on most-favoured-nation treatment nd.
[36] BT 11/119, Cassells to Picton-Bagge, 15 Nov. 1932 and T 160/13090/03/2, C. L. Paus to Crowe, 12 Jan. 1933.

was there much scope for trade creation. The Scandinavians were low tariff countries. Although Danish tariffs had been raised in October 1932, this had been mainly for revenue raising.[37] Swedish duties were low, and except for some luxury duties there had been few important changes in the duties since before the war; in 1930, 47 per cent of imports were duty free while duties on taxed imports averaged only 18 per cent *ad valorem*; the Manchester Chamber of Commerce reported that the Swedish tariff on cotton textiles was one of the lowest in Europe.[38] Norwegian tariffs were also generally modest, although, when protective, for example on textiles and footwear, they were high.[39]

Substantial gains therefore were not generally to be achieved by making inroads into high tariff structures. Nor could it be readily assumed that British industry would gain at the expense of local industries, protected or not. Swedish industry, in particular, was often highly competitive. According to the Sheffield Chamber of Commerce, the Swedes produced all classes of steel and tools and were efficient. They were also efficient producers of electrical machinery.[40] But even where there was little local industry, these moderate or non-existent tariffs left British industry with little interest in the negotiations. Repeatedly, industries reported to the Board of Trade or the organisation handling the initial consultative procedures that there was no point in doing anything: in the Danish market the boot and shoe industry was satisfied, paints and colours exporters wanted no changes, the radio gramophone manufacturers could live with $7\frac{1}{2}$ per cent tariffs, photographic producers felt that duties were moderate or at least not outrageous, the road tar exporters wanted free entry conventionalised while the earthenware and glass producers wanted the present duties conventionalised. The response to the Board of Trade enquiries was thin, the Associated Chambers of Commerce describing the replies of the trades as 'meagre and not very helpful'.[41] For Sweden much the same picture emerged: duties on sewing cotton were only 2 per cent. Dunlop, the British Chemical Manufacturers' Association and the Association of British Chemical Manufacturers all considered that they had little to complain of and that their position was satisfactory.[42]

For many important products though, the real limitation on their prospects was the power of competitors, particularly German competitors. Unless preferences were to be given, action was useless. At best, tariff reductions might work largely or exclusively to the benefit of other

---

[37] BT 11/119.
[38] BT 11/124. Views of Manchester Chamber of Commerce on Swedish Tariff 12 Oct. 1932. The Swedish tariff on cotton goods was, on 1930 values, about 16 per cent on piece goods and 5 per cent on yarns.   [39] BT 11/127.   [40] BT 11/124.
[41] BT 11/119, nd. They excepted textiles from this generalisation.   [42] BT 11/124.

Table 4.3. *Principal UK exports to Scandinavian countries,*
1930–1932 (£000s)

	1930	1931	1932
Denmark			
Coal	1,422	1,121	1,399
Coke	750	753	700
Cotton	1,001	883	1,048
Machinery and parts	359	306	314
Iron and steel	915	715	674
Petroleum	566	247	370
Motor vehicles and parts	402	513	447
Woollens and worsteds	935	860	1,108
Total exports	10,249	8,657	9,853
Norway			
Coal	877	436	550
Coke	342	378	333
Cotton	784	627	770
Iron and steel	662	434	444
Ships and boats (new)	6,265	2,667	185
Woollens and worsteds	444	406	528
Total exports	12,931	7,559	5,802
Sweden			
Coal	1,371	797	927
Coke	413	377	243
Cotton	1,149	1,074	1,019
Machinery and parts	587	439	302
Iron and steel	467	366	341
Woollens and worsteds	913	807	819
Total exports	10,068	7,744	6,885

Source: UK *Annual Statement of Trade 1932* (1933).

countries' exporters. At worst, trade might be lost because of diversion of demand away from British staples or because local industry, which British semi-manufactures might be serving, would be harmed by competition from third countries. For some products the arguments were straightforward: lower duties on glue in Sweden would simply benefit competitors; in Denmark duties on bicycles were protecting a local assembly industry, any liberalisation of the tariff being likely to assist German exporters; nor could the UK compete in the machine tool market.[43] More complex and less predictable were the possible consequences of adjustments in the textile

[43] *Ibid.*, and BT 11/119.

tariff schedules. Textiles were among the chief British exports to the Nordic countries (see Table 4.3). One of the principles that Lancashire wished to see established was that artificial silk (rayon) should be taxed at a much lower rate than real silk, and both the cotton and wool textile industries also wished to secure adjustments in the tariff schedules for mixed fabrics that included silk (real or artificial). It was also feared that lower duties on wool and worsted products were also thought likely to benefit European competitors rather than British producers. For example, in Sweden, where specific duties weighed heavily on cheaper cloths, Yorkshire wanted the introduction of a 'stop' of 20 or 25 per cent whereby the tariff charged would be the specific rate or the 'stop' percentage, whichever was least. The intention was to give British producers a chance of competing against the lower quality ranges of Swedish output – but the fear was that German or Czechoslovak competitors would benefit, possibly to the detriment of fine woollens.[44]

These were the most important factors which acted both to curb Britain's bargaining power and at the same time to shape the tariff desiderata. There were some other, generally less important, influences which reduced the scope for concessions or helped to determine British tariff requests, these including cartel arrangements, local manufacture by British firms and the contribution made by customs duties to total budget revenue. British American Tobacco, for example, had more interests as shareholders in a Danish tobacco company than as exporters.[45] Cartels sometimes limited the value of potential tariff concessions. The chemical industry was rife with agreements, so much so that parts of the industry unaffected by agreements failed to obtain orders because of the assumption in Sweden that enquiries need only be addressed to Germany. The Swedish market for aniline dyes and sodium sulphate was allocated to competitors, and the prospects for Pilkington Glass were also affected by international arrangements.

Overall then, the ability to win much in the way of tariff concessions was very limited. Once it was decided to keep the mfn clause, the capacity to wrest much from low tariff countries in the face of strong, mainly German, competition was seriously jeopardised. In view of the British general tariff rate of 10 per cent, it seemed unreasonable, to the Board of Trade anyway, to press for reductions in Scandinavian tariffs below that level. Another, more important, consideration was that it was of little use to demand lower tariffs on products where Britain was a minority supplier because the benefits would accrue to the opposition. When the strength of local industry, or the determination to protect it, are also taken into account,

---

[44] BT 11/124, minute, 27 Mar. 1933.   [45] BT 11/119.

plus fiscal needs and generally less important considerations such as cartels, then the true scale of the limitations is apparent.

British objectives

Consequently British tariff requests were modest. Reductions were wanted mainly on textiles, especially cotton and woollen piece goods. Great emphasis was put on these requests, and some tariff manipulation was thought useful. For example, Streat suggested that tariff reductions on cloth of a width of 36 inches, as opposed to 27 inches, might give the UK an advantage.[46] But this still left the question of which types of cotton cloths really to push. Duty reductions on bleached or coloured woven would be of little benefit to the UK, and Lancashire wished to see increased shipments of dyed and printed cloths to Sweden, even if at the cost of unbleached exports, because the manufacture of finished fabrics involved greater employment.[47] Emphasis was also placed on cars, where it was hoped that by tariff manipulation smaller British models would secure at least some effective preference over American competition; lower duties were looked for on motor cycles and parts, of which Britain was an efficient supplier, and gramophones and records in Norway and Sweden. Conventionalisation of duties was sought on a wide range of products, and guarantees of continued free entry for coal and coke and a combination of products, often raw materials, which varied from country to country. It has to be emphasised just how extraordinarily modest these demands for tariff reductions were, covering only 10·6 per cent and 9·7 per cent of Swedish and Norwegian imports from Britain in 1930, although at 17·7 per cent of Denmark's 1931 imports from Britain, the desiderata were a little more ambitious.

Therefore, what Britain sought on tariffs was essentially the stabilisation of duties, a guarantee that during the currency of the agreement duties would not be raised. Once the decision had been made to keep the mfn clause as a basis of the agreements, Britain was clearly powerless to achieve very much with the Scandinavians through tariff changes. Tangible and immediate benefits, which were necessary for political reasons if nothing else, would have to be gained in other ways which made nonsense of mfn principles. This is an important part of the reason why coal came to dominate the trade negotiations between Britain and the Scandinavians. Of course the choice reflected other factors, including the intensity of the crisis affecting the industry. The market problems of the British coal

---

[46] BT 11/124, memorandum by Streat on meeting with Board of Trade, 2 Dec. 1932.
[47] *Ibid.*, Supplementary memorandum for Board of Trade by Manchester Chamber of Commerce Special Committee on Sweden, 15 Dec. 1932.

Table 4.4. *Imports of coal into Denmark, Norway and Sweden* ('000 metric tons)

	Total imports	Imports from UK	% of total	Imports from Poland
Denmark				
1913	3,152	2,931	93·0	—
1925	3,125	2,766	88·5	108
1931	3,663	1,595	43·5	1,315
Norway[a]				
1913	2,246	2,228	99·2	—
1925	1,803	1,778	98·6	—
1931	1,719	665	38·7	985
Sweden				
1913	4,879	4,655	95·4	—
1925	3,663	2,869	78·3	109
1931	4,535	1,069	23·6	2,638

[a] Norwegian total coal imports exclude those from Spitzbergen. The 1931 figures were provisional.
Source: FO 371/17319. Memorandum Respecting Trade Agreements.

industry in the later 1920s had been almost exclusively the failure of exports. The depression, however, weakened the home market and further aggravated the export problem. Unemployment was extremely severe, particularly in those sectors of the mining industry that depended heavily on exports; perhaps 30 per cent of coalminers in north-east England were unemployed by July 1931.[48] The decline of coal exports also affected other industries, notably shipping: in the early 1920s while coal accounted for less than 10 per cent of the value of British exports, it accounted for more than 80 per cent of the volume. Little had been achieved for the coal industry at Ottawa apart from a few minor concessions from Canada, so in the Scandinavian negotiations lay a chance to compensate.

The preoccupation with coal made sense in other respects too. It was the major export. Even in 1930 it still headed the list of British exports to Denmark and Sweden and, in an unusual year, came second only to ships in exports to Norway. A very important motive, however, stemmed from the huge losses which had been made to Polish competition in the North European coal markets since 1925. The reversal had been spectacular, and in all cases represented the loss of a virtual monopoly position.

Polish competition had become more intense following the restoration of Germany's tariff autonomy in 1925. Through the peace treaties Poland

[48] W. R. Garside, 'The north-eastern-coalfield and the export trade, 1919–1939', *Durham University Journal*, 83 (1969), 74–89.

had gained from Germany the major part of the Silesian coalfields; the transitional arrangements allowed for the output to be sold in Germany, expected at the time to be desperately short of coal.[49] When in 1925 the Germans refused to allow some 5,000,000 tons a month of Polish coal to flow into Germany, the closure of the market forced the Poles to seek alternative export outlets. Initial inroads into Scandinavian markets in 1925 paved the way for an enormous expansion during the British coal strike of the following year. The Scandinavians, once acquainted with Polish coal, liked it, and despite some revival in the later 1920s, British coal was again on the retreat from 1929. By far and away the most important factor in the continued displacement of British coal was price, especially in Norway and Sweden.[50] Polish production costs were low. In 1928 costs of production in Poland were the equivalent of 7s 10d per ton, compared with Northumberland costs of just under 12s and Durham costs of over 13s per ton. The differences partly reflected the lower Polish wage rates, but equipment and organisation also impressed British visitors.[51] The syndication of the Polish coal industry, like that in Germany, enabled it to charge higher prices for home consumption than for exports. Low freight rates helped, too. Rail construction linking the Upper Silesian coalfields to the newly developed port of Gdynia and the establishment of a national merchant navy made Poland a formidable competitor in the Baltic.[52] But the British coal mission to Scandinavia in 1930 found that Polish coal was selling well not only because it was cheaper, but because it tended to arrive in better condition, well screened and sorted, cleaner, with the calorific value guaranteed and, if the cargoes were below specification, compensation was given. UK negotiators looked for a return to 1924 shares in these markets, an ambition that in the light of British coal's disadvantages could not possibly have been realised through unfettered or 'fair' competition. Purchasing agreements for coal had to be made, and these were the most important items in the British demands.

Only in the case of Denmark did Britain go substantially further in extending the principle of special purchases to other products. In this instance the UK wanted Danish agreement to guarantee purchases of iron and steel together with a number of smaller items which were used, one way or another, in helping to supply the British market. The items involved were jute wrappers used in packaging bacon sides, cattle-feed, and salt, which was used in bacon curing, tanning and butter preparation. Cattle-

[49] J. M. Keynes, *The Economic Consequences of the Peace* (1919), 74–89.

[50] POWE 16/184. Report of the British Coal Delegation to Sweden, Norway and Denmark. 13–25 Sept. 1930. Part VII. Summary of the Report.

[51] For example, Archer, a British coalowner, on a visit to Poland in July, 1928. POWE 16/181.   [52] POWE 16/184. Delegates Report, n. 50 above.

feed was an important Danish import, of which only a tiny proportion came from the UK.[53]

Scandinavian objectives

The major products of interest to the Scandinavians are shown in Table 4.5. The great scale of Danish exports to the British market is apparent from the figures, and the Danes took the main weight of the negotiations about agricultural products.

Bacon. Obviously at the forefront of Danish concern was the need for as much security for their bacon exports as they could obtain. Bacon dominated Denmark's agricultural production, the greatest part of bacon output was exported, and to all intents and purposes there was no other market than that of the United Kingdom. Sweden too was interested in securing some guarantees for bacon exports.[54] Although nothing like as important as timber, it is worth recording that Swedish bacon exports to Britain of £2·4 million had comfortably exceeded British coal and coke exports to Sweden in 1930. The threat from imperial suppliers was fairly muted. The political dispute between the UK and the Irish Free State entailed heavy penalties against Irish exports. Canada had been made some extravagant promises, but there were doubts about the ability of the Canadians to mount a serious challenge to the Danes and to fulfil their quota.

The main threat to the position of North European producers lay in the ambitions of the Minister of Agriculture for British bacon. In sorry contrast to the superb organisation of the Scandinavians the UK industry was chaotic: a report to the Committee on Trade Policy at the end of 1930 had spelt out the problems in terms of the quality and costs of the raw material, and the production and marketing of the bacon itself.[55] Domestic producers supplied only about 10 per cent of British consumption. Nonetheless a Reorganisation Commission for Pigs and Pig Products (the Lane–Fox Commission) reported on the industry in the autumn of 1932 and made proposals that posed a serious threat to foreign suppliers. Agreed minimum contract prices were to be established for sales between a Pigs Marketing Board and a Bacon Marketing Board. To bolster prices, total supplies to the market were to be cut back from the 1931 level of 13·3 million cwts to the average supply for 1925–30 of 10·67 million cwts. Within the reduced total it was proposed that domestic supplies would

[53] In 1931, Danish imports had been 87 million kroner, of which the UK supplied only 5 million kroner. BT 11/119, minute, 31 Oct. 1932.

[54] Table 4.5 shows Sweden as a very minor supplier when contrasted with Denmark. Even so, in 1931 Swedish bacon exports to the UK were ten times the Canadian total.

[55] CAB 27/435 APC(30) 3, Note by the Lord Privy Seal, 10 Dec. 1930.

Table 4.5. *Principal UK retained imports from Scandinavian countries, 1930–1932* (£000s)

	1930	1931	1932
Denmark			
Bacon	27,399	22,200	20,782
Butter	17,042	15,595	13,401
Eggs in shell	4,697	4,405	2,965
Fish	1,051	916	668
Machinery	447	316	126
Total	55,796	46,212	40,294
Norway			
Wood Pulp	2,439	1,651	1,843
Paper and cardboard	1,995	1,195	1,391
Wood and timber and manufactures thereof	1,918	1,154	899
Fish	1,616	1,454	1,386
Aluminium	878	455	266
Iron Ore	657	188	163
Manufactures of iron and steel	269	238	156
Total	11,577	8,308	8,047
Sweden			
Wood and timber	5,546	3,635	3,656
Wood pulp	3,832	2,694	1,971
Bacon	2,403	1,688	1,096
Butter	1,952	1,269	892
Packing and wrapping paper	1,652	1,779	1,305
Wood and timber manufactures	1,264	1,010	653
Steel	920	762	600
Other paper	706	674	495
Total	22,227	17,067	13,239

Source: UK *Annual Statement of Trade 1932* (1933).

increase by stages – but to make matters worse for foreign suppliers, the Canadians would have to be accommodated within the total as well, and this up to a level of $2\frac{1}{2}$ million cwts if they could produce it. On all counts it was the Europeans who would bear the cost in the form of sharply curtailed quotas. Initial optimism that Denmark had escaped relatively lightly was followed by a more alarmist assessment of the magnitude of the cuts, and press reaction showed considerable bitterness.[56] Yet Denmark and Sweden had no choice but to accept the cuts; any bargaining would

[56] FO 371/16294, Hohler to Simon and Birch to Simon, 1 Nov. 1932.

Table 4.6. *Imports of bacon into the United Kingdom – selected suppliers, 1913, 1928, 1931, 1932* ('000 cwts)

	1913	1928	1931	1932
Canada	244	307	50	182
Irish Free State	(na)	555	297	200
Denmark	2,355	5,376	7,339	7,670
Netherlands	186	1,061	1,000	976
Poland	(na)	118	1,077	1,135
Lithuania	(na)	2	362	512
Sweden	62	441	577	424
Estonia	(na)	41	64	82
Finland	(na)	—	35	38
Latvia	(na)	145	31	19
USA	1,803	538	189	64
Argentina	(na)	49	50	39
Total	4,859	8,853	11,134	11,391

Source: UK *Annual Statement of Trade* (various years).

centre on the base years for quotas, flexibility here being limited by mfn, rights of suppliers, and, an important consideration, Denmark and Sweden wanted a guarantee of free entry for bacon during the currency of the agreement.

Butter and eggs. The other product of outstanding importance to Denmark was butter. The greater part of production was exported, and a high and increasing percentage of exports went to the United Kingdom market. As Table 4.5 shows, Sweden was also interested, although to only a minor extent. Britain was by far the world's greatest importer. Domestic production accounted for about 10 per cent of consumption, and was mainly a sideline to the liquid milk trade. Consumption had risen, boosted in large part by falling prices, from 15·6 pounds per capita in the mid-1920s to 21·8 pounds by 1932. Moreover, the UK's dominance as an importer was magnified by the restrictions widely applied in Europe in 1931–2. Following Britain's abandonment of the gold standard, its principal suppliers had also depreciated their currencies, leading to an expansion in their exports to the gold standard countries. In 1931 and 1932, a series of tariff increases and quota schemes were introduced in Europe, most importantly in Germany but also in France, Belgium, Switzerland and Italy.[57] Accordingly Britain, which had accounted for a little over 60 per cent of world imports in 1928–30, increased its share to three-quarters by

[57] Imperial Economic Committee, *Dairy Produce Supplies in 1933* (1934), 12 and 69–76.

Table 4.7. *Imports of butter into the United Kingdom – selected suppliers 1913, 1928, 1931, 1932* ('000 cwts)

	1913	1928	1931	1932
New Zealand	252	1,222	1,926	2,140
Australia	594	873	1,558	1,795
Irish Free State		559	381	315
Denmark	1,707	2,016	2,466	2,584
Russia	751	336	404	323
Sweden	332	176	212	176
Latvia		50	39	113
Netherlands	153	129	96	47
Finland		199	254	217
Lithuania		1	40	68
Estonia		78	125	83
Norway	20		13	15
Poland		29	33	3
Argentina	73	366	374	391
Total	4,139	6,113	8,060	8,364

Source: UK *Annual Statement of Trade* (various years).

1932.[58] Denmark was still the world's largest exporter of butter in 1931, but its position was being challenged by the southern dominions, which had greatly expanded exports during the war and had also sharply increased their efficiency as suppliers in the 1920s.[59] The Baltic states, modelling their industry on that of Denmark, had also emerged inside a decade as important suppliers. At Ottawa a duty of 10 per cent had been raised to 15s per cwt, roughly equivalent to a 50 per cent hike at prevailing prices. There was no prospect of the Danes securing a reduction since they would have needed the agreement of the dominions.[60] It was pointed out that the substitution of specific for *ad valorem* duties might help the typically high quality Danish suppliers, at least against other European exporters. In fact the Danes do not appear to have been too worried about the duty, instead concentrating on obtaining guarantees that they would not be hampered by quantitative restrictions as well.[61] The third great Danish contribution to the British breakfast table was eggs. As with bacon

---

[58] *Ibid.*, 66.   [59] *Ibid.*, 58.

[60] BT 11/119. They did ask about this in preliminary discussions. Meeting at Danish Foreign Office 25 Sept. 1932.

[61] FO 371/16297. Preliminary list of Danish desiderata, 8 Dec. 1932. According to the memoranda, and perhaps assured by Colville's remarks in September that he had not heard of any scheme for quantitative restriction of butter, Denmark presumed that the present duty would not be combined with a quota system. This was optimistic.

and butter, Denmark was the most important supplier of British imports with, in this case, very substantial but declining supplies coming from the Irish Free State. However, British poultry keepers were expanding production rapidly, and by the early 1930s were supplying over half of consumers' needs.[62] Tariffs had been introduced in 1932 and then modified at Ottawa with a sliding scale of duties, graded according to weight, of 1s, 1s 3d and 1s 6d per great hundred. These measures had contributed to a marked decline of imports in 1932 and had also given a greater margin for dominion supplies, particularly Australian. The Danes, specialising in medium sized eggs, felt that the duties discriminated particularly against their supplies and encouraged their European competitors.[63] Yet again the imperial agreements precluded adjustments, so the Scandinavians (Norway and Sweden both had some interest in egg exports) requested conventionalisation of duties and a pledge that no quantitative restrictions would be imposed.[64]

Fish. In the division of Scandinavian labour in the negotiations, Norway, although having major interests in wood and wood products, handled the discussions on fish. The requests made in the preliminary list of desiderata show either genuine ignorance or a crude bargaining technique. The initial requests were that fish, cod liver oil and whale oil, all subject to 10 per cent duties, should be admitted duty free, and the higher duties on lobsters and prawns should be cut to 10 per cent.[65] The obstacles in the way of the Norwegian requests lay in Britain's Ottawa commitments and in the worsening plight of British trawlermen. Canada had been promised that the 10 per cent duty on white fish, herrings and canned fish would not be reduced, and the agreement with Newfoundland which had not entered into force would stand in the way of lower duties on dried or salted codfish. Prawn and lobster duties could be lowered to 10 per cent if necessary.[66] The growing crisis in the British fishing industry, which was to feature prominently in the negotiations in the New Year, was foreshadowed by an application to the Import Duties Advisory Board (IDAC) for higher duties. This was rejected at the time, although with a proviso that it could be reconsidered early the following year.[67]

Wood and timber. The Swedish team took chief responsibility in the negotiations about timber and timber products, coordinating their requests with the Norwegians. They wanted conventionalisation of free entry for newsprint, woodpulp and pit-props and of the 10 per cent duty on wood,

---

[62] *Dairy Produce Supplies in 1933* (1934), 31.

[63] FO 371/16281. Memorandum for Prince of Wales on Anglo-Danish Trade, 20 Sept. 1932.

[64] BT 11/162. The Negotiations with Denmark, Norway and Sweden Agricultural Products Summary, 31 Jan. 1933.   [65] BT 11/128, Norwegian desiderata, 1 Dec. 1932.

[66] BT 11/134, memorandum by Hoskins, 20 Jan. 1933.

[67] FO 371/16295 (CP 403(32)), 29 Nov. 1932.

a duty fixed in the agreement between Britain and Canada.[68] The position on manufactured woods was more complicated because of the variety of categories and duties involved, but broadly they wanted a combination of duty reductions and conventionalisations.[69] A general line of argument, apart from pointing out inconsistencies in the structure of the British tariff, centred on the economics of processing wood near where it was grown. Planed wood could be sold in Britain for practically the same price as sawn timber because of the economies of on-site processing, and the savings of freights (23 per cent of wood was wasted in the process of it being planed). The same argument applied to box-boards, although more forcibly because the waste in this case was 30 per cent of volume.

The problems about paper were more vexed. Obviously some of the large producers of pulp favoured the manufacture of paper in Britain from their exports,[70] but both Sweden and Norway were highly critical of the increased duties on paper which had resulted from an IDAC report, and reductions of these duties formed an important part of their objectives.[71] While the British woodworking industry had been long established, the renaissance of the paper industry was a more recent phenomenon. The contention of the Swedes and Norwegians was that the temporary nature of the Safeguarding Duties had not offered sufficient long-term protection to encourage the expansion of the industry in the United Kingdom.[72] The Import Duties Act, on the other hand, offered just such assurance, and new machinery was being installed. Duties of 10 per cent were bearable, but 25 per cent, they contended, would kill Scandinavian exports. In both Norway and Sweden, domestic consumption was tiny and export dependence high, with Swedish consumption of kraft and greaseproof paper accounting for only about 6 per cent of output. Britain bought approximately 54 per cent of greaseproof paper produced in Sweden and about one-third of kraft and of Mg sulphite production. In bargaining, both countries stressed that high value added by each man employed would mean few jobs being created in Britain if production was transferred. Although neither country sold much of its newsprint in the United Kingdom, both wanted conventionalisation of free entry. The British

[68] BT 11/128 and BT 11/132 for preliminary Norwegian and Swedish desiderata, 1 Dec. and 21 Nov. 1932.
[69] FO 371/16296, Anglo-Swedish Tariff Negotiations: Agreed Summary of timber requests, received in Foreign Office 7 Dec. 1932.
[70] BT 11/132, note on Swedish proposals, prepared by HM Commercial Counsellor, Stockholm, 12 Nov. 1932.
[71] BT 11/128, Anglo-Norwegian Trade Negotiations, meeting 15 Nov. 1932 and BT 11/132, Anglo-Swedish Trade Negotiations, meeting 7 Dec. 1932.
[72] FO 371/16297, Anglo-Swedish Tariff Negotiations Agreed Summary of Swedish requests on paper, drawn up after discussions with the Board of Trade, 12 Dec. 1932. The Norwegian requests followed very similar lines.

industry, despite being well established – the output of one firm, Lloyds, exceeded the entire Swedish output – as well as profitable, had applied to IDAC for protective duties. The Scandinavians also wanted tariff reductions on various types of board and packing material and for writing paper and tissues.

Steel. This was a major area of conflict between Swedish and British industrialists. Along with paper, the Swedes placed more importance on this than any other request and Sir Henry Fountain thought that it was only on steel that Britain had anything substantial to offer them.[73] There had been anger in Sweden over the IDAC recommendation that the new steel duties should be continued for two years before being next reviewed, and not three months as before. Coming on top of the duty increase on wrapping papers and the impending restrictions on bacon, the Swedes were so incensed about the steel duties that they even doubted whether it was worth coming, accusing Britain of raising the price during negotiations. Public opinion and individual members of the Swedish government felt that negotiations were now useless and that discussions might as well be postponed for two years.[74] If this was a serious threat, calmer counsels evidently prevailed, but the Scandinavians were determined that something should be achieved for their special steels. The steel exported to Britain was of high quality and tended to be expensive, and partly for this reason Sweden wanted the duty to be levied on a specific as opposed to *ad valorem* basis which they felt discriminated against them.[75] The Swedes claimed that their steels did not generally compete with United Kingdom production, and indeed often acted as a raw material for the British industry. Duties of $33\frac{1}{3}$ per cent, they contended, failed in their main objective of checking imports of cheap continental steel, but succeeded in almost entirely shutting out high quality steels. Even during the preparatory stages of the negotiations it was clear that the British steel industry was worried about Swedish competition and was dubious of the Swedish claim that they were competing only against other importers, not British production. The industry suggested that, on the contrary, Swedish steel did compete largely with British industry, the only exception being the very specialised categories of steel manufactured from pig-iron which had been wholly smelted with charcoal. Ungenerously, the industry said it would not object to duties on this being lowered to 10 per cent provided that this applied only to ingots which could be further manufactured in Sheffield.[76]

[73] BT 11/124, note by Fountain, 1 Oct. 1932.
[74] BT 11/124, note on meeting between Swedish Minister and Runciman, 27 Oct. 1932, and Kerr to Simon, 23 Oct. 1932.
[75] BT 11/132, Swedish memorandum on iron and steel.   [76] BT 11/124.

Steel was the industrial product to which the Swedes attached real importance in the negotiations but the greater sophistication of the Swedish economic structure was reflected in the relatively wide range of other industrial products that featured in their demands. There were only a handful of industrial items in the Danish and Norwegian lists. Swedish steel apart, the Scandinavian objectives centred on the food products of bacon, butter, eggs and fish and on the output of the forest industries.

None of the discussions were to prove simple or frictionless. With good reason Whitehall regarded the Danish as the most promising of the Scandinavian negotiations. On the eve of the talks, the British Minister to Denmark wrote that 'we have of course entirely the whip hand of the Danes', although we should not use it.[77] Colville agreed, but 'circumstances may arise in which it will be extremely difficult to refrain from showing them just the handle of the whip'.[78] Despite his earlier pessimism over the impact of Ottawa and of the bacon proposals, Ashton Gwatkin was able to record that the Danish were 'the most hopeful of our present negotiations'.[79] Nonetheless, Scandinavian requests entailed concessions by the UK that took time to resolve. British protectionism was still on the march, policy was still evolving, and nowhere more so than in the sphere of agriculture. This was one of the reasons why the talks, which started in early December, were not concluded by the end of the year as had at first been hoped. In fact they were not to be completed until April 1933.

---

[77] FO 371/16296, Hohler to Colville, 29 Nov. 1932.
[78] *Ibid.*, Colville to Hohler, 1 Dec. 1932.
[79] *Ibid.*, minute by Ashton Gwatkin, 7 Dec. 1932.

5 Completion of the first phase of negotiations: Scandinavia, Germany and Argentina

Scandinavia

Britain's bargaining power had already been strong when the preliminary negotiations were held in late 1932. The predominance of the British market for livestock products had been accentuated by a host of protectionist measures in continental Europe. In Scandinavia it was German action that was most damaging. By 1931 the bias within German agricultural protection towards arable farming was as evident as ever, grain tariffs at a rate of 180 to 200 per cent having successfully isolated German prices from the world level. By contrast, the duties on butter and pig products were modest, and the ability of the government to act was limited by tariff agreements with Denmark and the Netherlands. Chancellor Brüning, anyhow, was unwilling to agree to the proposals of his Agriculture Minister, Schiele, for higher duties. The hostile reaction of the peasantry caused the government to change its mind and introduce a quota system for butter imports.[1] German import restrictions had been biting before, but in 1932 German popularity in Scandinavia began to sink further. The announcement by Germany in July that the trade agreement with Sweden would be terminated when it expired in February 1933 was met there with relative equanimity.[2] By the autumn, however, the new British Minister to Sweden, Sir Archibald Clark Kerr, was reporting a different mood,[3] a mood also being noted in the German press. Germany was becoming increasingly unpopular in Sweden because of the renunciation of the trade treaty. This was aggravated by a number of other grievances: new currency restrictions, higher butter duties, import quotas together with the inability of German manufacturers to fulfil long-term contracts for the purchase of Swedish iron-ore, and losses incurred by

---

[1] J. E. Farquharson, *The Plough and the Swastika: The NSDAP and agriculture in Germany 1928–45* (1976), 30.
[2] FO 371/16347, N. H. H. Charles (British Chargé d'Affaires in Stockholm) to Sir John Simon, 7 July 1932.   [3] *Ibid.*, Clark Kerr to Simon, 11 Oct. 1932.

126

Sweden on loans to Germany.[4] A two week visit by the Prince of Wales and the Duke of York in early October, Clark Kerr reported, acted as a 'timely stimulant to the growing inclination in Sweden to turn to Great Britain'.[5]

All this was happening before the negotiations between Britain and the Scandinavians started. But the process was given a sharp stimulus by further German measures during the recess of the negotiations. Agricultural pressure groups were probably the decisive influence on policy. Intense agricultural opposition to the Schleicher Cabinet, divided on agricultural protection, played an important part in its downfall in January 1933. It is little surprise, then, that Hitler's administration, warmly welcomed by farm interests, should feel it needed to act, particularly at a time when it was only beginning to consolidate its power. The government moved quickly to raise protection on livestock and livestock products, and started to implement a more complete 'Fats Plan'. The major objective was to provide assistance to livestock farmers, although the pressure of foreign exchange shortage and the desire for self-sufficiency were also influential. Hitler, however, was keenly aware of the political risks involved in higher prices and possible food shortages.[6] Since the measures were designed principally to assist German livestock producers, it was inevitable that tighter import controls would hit just those countries in northern Europe with which Britain was in the process of negotiation.

In its international context German action was extraordinarily ill-timed. Butter imports, controlled by quota, had been tending to decline, and in the first quarter of 1933, at under 200,000 cwts, they were far below previous levels, and well below the level reached later in the year.[7] In January, negotiations between Germany and Sweden for a new treaty broke down because the Germans refused to give an assurance that new duties would not be prohibitive.[8] Although there was no German–Norwegian trade treaty, Norway did have most-favoured-nation rights and therefore stood to lose through the ending of the German treaties with Sweden and Yugoslavia. Rates of duty on wrapping paper, granite kerbstones and lobsters were all considered prohibitive, new duties on fish and eggs were thought likely, and when the new 'Fats Plan' was

---

[4] *Ibid.*, Clark Kerr to Simon, 19 Oct. 1932, enclosing copy of article from *Svenska Dagbladet*, summary of *Kohnische Zeitung*.

[5] *Ibid.*, Clark Kerr to Simon, 15 Oct. 1932.

[6] Farquharson, *The Plough and the Swastika*, 51. Based on archival material, Farquharson's study gives a different emphasis to that of K. Brandt, 'German agricultural policy – some selected lessons', *Journal of Farm Economics*, 19 (1937).

[7] Imperial Economic Committee, *Dairy Produce Supplies in 1933*, (1934), 71. For the rest of 1933 they were above the corresponding levels of 1932. In the first quarter of 1932 butter imports had been just over 400,000 cwts.

[8] FO 371/17279, Sir H. Rumbold (British Ambassador in Berlin) to Simon, 19 Jan. 1933.

introduced, whale oil was included in the scheme as well.[9] In Sweden, German restrictions on timber caused a further hardening of opinion against Germany. The Danes suffered too, the extent and scale of new duties announced on 9 February, particularly on cattle and lard, catching them unprepared. According to some estimates, these were likely to reduce German–Danish trade by as much as 80 per cent.[10]

The extent of the rift between Sweden and Germany, given their close cultural and political ties, caused surprise to Foreign Office officials. For the area as a whole, Laurence Collier of the Foreign Office minuted '[t]he Germans are... presenting us with unparalleled opportunities in Scandinavia'.[11]

British protectionism and Scandinavia

German action was creating a vacuum for British trade and influence, and from a British perspective doing so at a peculiarly opportune moment. Yet German agrarian protectionism had its counterpart in Britain, a pale imitation perhaps, but one that nonetheless threatened Britain's ability to capitalise on the situation. Agricultural organisations, which were mobilising more effectively, were able to point to the growing wall of industrial tariffs. In Walter Elliot they also had a vigorous new Minister of Agriculture. The clash between the interests of domestic agriculture and those of the export industries, desiring low costs and easy access to markets overseas, was to become an enduring feature of economic policy making for the rest of the decade. In the winter of 1932–3, British agricultural protectionism was one of the outstanding obstacles to exploiting the openings in Scandinavia that German policy was creating. Elliot had even attempted to delay the negotiations from starting in the first place. Arguing that Runciman's proposed concessions were almost wholly agricultural, he pointed to the size and purchasing power of the farming community, the central role of livestock within it, and the need to determine the main lines of agricultural policy before moving on to negotiations with foreign suppliers.[12] Nonetheless, a few days later he accepted the impossibility of cancelling negotiations that were already underway with the Argentine and in an advanced stage of preparation with Scandinavia.[13] The committee decided that inter-departmental discussions should be held, and that the

---

[9] FO 371/17724, Sir Charles Wingfield, (British Minister in Oslo) to Department of Overseas Trade, 20 Jan. 1933, 11 Feb. 1933, and Wingfield to Simon, 14 Feb., 27 Mar. 1933.

[10] FO 371/17201, Sir Thomas Hohler (British Minister in Copenhagen) to Simon, 10 Feb. 1933.

[11] FO 371/17279, various minutes between Feb. and May 1933. Collier minute, 10 Feb. 1933.

[12] CAB 27/489 CFC (32) 2, memorandum, 21 Oct. 1932.

[13] *Ibid.*, CFC (32), 1st meeting, 24 Oct. 1932.

committee would meet again in a week. In fact, it was not to reconvene until February.

The starting point for discussions was the response to be made to the Scandinavian requests for agricultural concessions. Essentially the Ministry of Agriculture and Fisheries was attempting to keep as much freedom of manoeuvre as possible, and at the same time to provide space for the expansion of home agriculture. In the early 1930s, however, any future expansion depended first on staving off collapse, so this meant keeping in reserve the necessary defensive instruments. The Ministry wanted clauses included in the Scandinavian agreements that would allow imports to be controlled quantitatively.[14] In a question-begging phrase, the Ministry stated that it wished to adjust supplies from all sources to the demand situation in the United Kingdom market. In detail, it wanted practically all the Scandinavian requests refused. There was some measure of agreement at the Board of Trade; the Board was generally reluctant to make concessions to countries on products of which they were minor suppliers since Britain was likely to lose a bargaining counter in later negotiations. The real differences between the departments were, first, the refusal of the Ministry to guarantee free entry of bacon and ham and the existing duties on canned pork products and cream, and, secondly, of greater difficulty, the refusal of the Ministry to have its hands tied over quotas for butter, eggs and cream.[15] Board of Trade representatives pressed strongly the great disadvantages of attempting to restrict bacon imports by both quotas and duties – agreement with Denmark would be difficult or impossible.[16] The inter-departmental meetings were inconclusive on the major dispute, so decisions had to be made by Ministers with the outstanding issues referred to the Committee on Commercial Negotiations with Foreign Countries. The Minister of Agriculture quickly conceded the right to impose duties on chilled or frozen beef and bacon, items of central importance to the negotiations with Argentina and Denmark.[17] The need for a 'crash' quota proved more difficult to decide. Elliot was not prepared to agree to a formula which would allow dairy quotas only if there was a 'disastrous fall in prices' *and* the dominions voluntarily agreed to a corresponding restriction of imports. The price fall, he argued, had already been disastrous, so the phrase might be open to a charge of disingenuousness. The committee shelved the problem by referring it to the consideration of meetings between the UK and dominion representatives; the

---

[14] BT 11/162, Secretary, Ministry of Agriculture and Fisheries to Secretary, Board of Trade, 11 Jan. 1933.   [15] BT 11/162, minute by T. St. Quintin Hill, 20 Jan. 1933.

[16] FO 371/17212, minute by F. Ashton Gwatkin, 6 Feb. 1933 on meetings of 1, 2 Feb. 1933. The Board of Trade papers contain the minutes of just the one meeting of 1 Feb. 1933.

[17] CAB 27/489 CFC (32), 2nd meeting, 8 Feb. 1933.

continual growth of shipments from Australia and New Zealand was threatening a crisis in the butter markets, and these discussions were aimed at restricting dominion butter supplies so as to avert it. The issue threaded through the negotiations with Denmark. As for the beef quota, the actual extent of the restrictions on the Argentine proved contentious enough, leading to a further clash between Runciman and Elliot in March.

The other major area of food policy bearing on the Scandinavian negotiations was fish. Runciman had warned of the need for sacrifices here. However, as with the markets for meat and for dairy products, the Ministry of Agriculture foresaw impending disaster for the fishing industry too, and this coloured attitudes towards the Scandinavian requests. In November 1932, the Ministry was concerned largely with preventing the concession of low duties,[18] which for the important category of fresh white fish they defined as anything less than 20 to 25 per cent. By January the Ministry was thinking beyond duties to a range of other lines of action, including quota restrictions.[19] In the next two months these ideas were developed further. The essential problem was the ubiquitous one of increasing supplies and falling prices. Prices had fallen from an average figure in the late 1920s of about 25s per cwt to approximately 18s per cwt in 1932, a level the Ministry claimed was unremunerative.[20] It contended that increasing landings, especially of foreign takings, were threatening a grave crisis within a year. As with other products, the Minister was doubtful of the efficacy of a tariff: currency depreciation and the willingness of foreign producers to bear the duty tended to nullify it. Action, unless by very high tariffs, should be concentrated on quotas, and should be directed towards the less marketable types of fish. Because British trawlers supplied the bulk of landings, measures would have to be taken to restrict their supplies as well. It was suggested that net meshes should be enlarged to prevent the landing of small fish, a growing practice in which the UK fleets were the worst offenders. The other action proposed on less marketable fish was to end summer landings from the more distant fishing grounds such as Murmansk and Bear Island. To preclude the danger that Germany would divert Murmansk fish to its home markets and provide the United Kingdom from other grounds, quotas would have to be imposed. The Ministry suggested cutting back foreign supplies by about 25 per cent from the 2 million cwt level. If these proposals could be agreed, then the Ministry was prepared to concede practically all the Scandinavians had requested.

Refinement of these ideas led to a proposal that direct landings and imports from Norway, Denmark and Iceland should be reduced by 10 per

[18] BT 11/134, inter-departmental meeting, 24 Nov. 1932.
[19] BT 11/162, Secretary, Ministry of Agriculture to Secretary, Board of Trade 11 Jan. 1933.
[20] BT 11/134, memorandum by Ministry of Agriculture, 3 Mar. 1933.

cent. To prevent German vessels from evading the restriction on landings from Bear Island by diverting other supplies, a quota of 100 per cent was imposed on these other landings. The eventual proposals were far milder in their impact on foreign supplies than the original suggestion of the Ministry of Agriculture.[21] The overall cut-back on foreign supplies was about 200,000 cwts, approximately 10 per cent of foreign landings. Quotas were to be allocated to foreign suppliers on the basis of total maximum landings of white fish of 1·8 million cwts, and similar arrangements were to be made for herrings. The Ministry, armed with these quantitative assurances, was then content to bind the 10 per cent duties on most types of fish, and also to reduce the duty on prawns to 30 per cent. These arrangements were put to the Scandinavians, although with a warning that if agreement could not be made with supplying countries, the United Kingdom reserved the right to introduce tariffs.[22] Nothing appears to have been said about the treatment of British trawlers in the disputed waters around the Norwegian coast, although the Ministry had hoped that some assurances that the recent harassment would end might be obtained during negotiations.[23]

The other major area of contention affecting the negotiations had been steel, with the British industry opposed to concessions on Swedish products. As mentioned earlier, in the autumn of 1932 the Swedes had been angered over the IDAC decision to maintain the steel duties in force for another two years. Together with the bacon proposals and wrapping paper duties, the decision had gone some way to sour the otherwise improving relations between Britain and Sweden. Great importance was laid on concessions on steel: the essence of the Swedish demand was for the substitution of specific for *ad valorem* duties which, the Swedes contended, were discriminatory and even virtually prohibitive on their expensive, high quality steels. Although British officials were apparently impressed with the Swedish case,[24] there were legislative complications in switching from one basis of tariff to the other. More difficult still was the attitude of the iron and steel industry. Although this was prepared to concede duty free

---

[21] *Ibid.*, United Kingdom Fish Policy. Draft proposals, 23 Mar. 1933.

[22] *Ibid.*, minute by Hill, 29 Mar. 1933.

[23] The Norwegians claimed a 4 mile limit, often measured from outlying rocks and islands. Britain insisted on a 3 mile limit. Negotiations in 1925 failed, but until 1932 there was little trouble – British trawlers stayed outside the 4 mile zones and the Norwegians did not molest them. From 1932 the Norwegians became much more aggressive: there were frequent arrests of vessels several miles outside the former limits, and skippers of British trawlers entering Norwegian ports often found themselves prosecuted for a variety of alleged offences. The tacit arrangements of 1925–32 were revived in early 1934 after implied threats of a British gunboat being sent to the area.

[24] BT 11/132, Anglo-Swedish Tariff Negotiations, note on meeting with Dr A. Wahlberg, 21 Nov. 1932.

entry for selected charcoal-smelted products, its general line of argument was that Swedish competition was too severe, particularly in the high grade products such as alloy steels, a speciality of Sheffield employing far more labour per ton than the cheaper steels.[25]

In accepting these viewpoints, the Board of Trade failed to anticipate the hostility of the Swedes to the very limited concessions proposed. The Swedes felt they had been badly treated. They replied that the spirit of the negotiations as a whole would be governed by British intentions on iron and steel, and they were reluctant to reconvene the negotiations until they had a firmer statement of those intentions.[26] There followed a rapid reassessment in the Board of Trade. Good progress had been made in the negotiations with Sweden prior to Christmas, and it was argued that this had been in large part because the Swedish team had thought that the question was one of how to meet them on their steel requests, not whether to meet them at all.[27] While the negotiations might lead to an agreement, 'it was also extremely important from the point of view of tariff policy here that the first foreign negotiation, and probably the easiest, should not break down or fizzle out into something very unimportant'.[28] The Foreign Office feared that the opportunities that Germany's action had presented to Britain would be thrown away, 'either through excessive demands by the Ministry of Agriculture here or through undue deference to sectional interests among our manufacturers'.[29] Proposals were worked out suggesting two-tiered duties of $33\frac{1}{3}$ per cent on cheaper steels and 15 per cent on the more expensive grades. The range was much more extensive than the steelmakers had been prepared to contemplate in January, and included not just ingot blooms and billets, but more highly manufactured steels. Various ferro-alloys would be admitted duty free, as would a range of products made from pig-iron smelted wholly with charcoal.[30] After a meeting between Runciman and the steel manufacturers, a more modest set of proposals eventually emerged.[31] The range of products on which concessions were proposed remained much the same, but instead of a reduction from $33\frac{1}{3}$ per cent to 15 per cent, 25 per cent was suggested. Even

---

[25] *Ibid.*, meeting between British iron and steel industry representatives and Board of Trade officials, 11 Jan. 1933.

[26] *Ibid.*, W. J. Glenny (Commercial Secretary in Stockholm), to Hill and telegram from Clark Kerr, 8 Feb. 1933, both outlining Swedish reaction.

[27] *Ibid.*, minute by A. Kilroy, 14 Feb. 1933.   [28] *Ibid.*

[29] *Ibid.*, Sir Robert Vansittart to Runciman, 14 Feb. 1933.

[30] *Ibid.*, note by L. Browett for President, 15 Feb. 1933. An example of the type of formula proposed is that for forgings and castings: not exceeding £24 per ton, the duty would be 33·3 per cent; exceeding £24 per ton, 15 per cent would be charged but with a minimum duty of £8.

[31] *Ibid.*, the meeting between Runciman, Colville and steel representatives took place on 1 Mar. 1933, and there was a further meeting with officials on 10 Mar. 1933.

then the industry reserved the right to make representations against lower duties. Ultimately the Board decided to offer the Swedes a tariff of 25 per cent, but go to 20 per cent if necessary. Emphasis would be placed on the number of items being transferred to the free list.

One further issue of importance to the negotiations was resolved before their resumption. Early in 1932 the Danes had wanted to borrow £2 million in London to finance the construction of a major bridge, the Storstrom, which was to connect Zeeland and Falster. Financial interests used influence on Runciman to persuade the Bank of England to lift the foreign loan embargo. The Treasury refused to intervene, partly on grounds that it was the City authorities' decision, partly because the balance of payments was too weak.[32] Representations from the steel industry, likely to obtain the contract if the money was raised in London, left the Bank of England unmoved.[33] The argument was reiterated that foreign loans should be banned while sterling remained unstabilised, the Governor, Montagu Norman, also taking the purist line that available resources should be devoted to restructuring and re-equipping the British steel industry rather than offering it a crutch through 'non-competitive' orders.[34] Given the Governor's views on foreign lending, although they may well have been coloured by a fear of opening the floodgates to overseas issues, it is significant that the Bank itself had made available to Denmark a million pound credit in June.[35] This was to help maintain the stability of the krone, threatened, among other things, by an attempt of the agricultural exporters to force it down by withholding foreign exchange from the National Bank. The Treasury professed surprise that the Bank of England was attempting to assist the maintenance of exchange controls in Denmark while refusing loans which would be used for boosting British exports. The authorities changed their minds in February 1933. The documents do not make explicit what caused the reversal of opinion, but the shift in the Treasury's attitude was decisive. In 1932 the Treasury had opposed the loan, but by February Chamberlain's opposition had weakened: although the foreign balance did not leave enough for foreign investment, it was possible, for special purposes, to use funds borrowed short-term from abroad, and evidently the Storstrom Bridge project qualified as 'special purpose'.[36] Probably it was an offer from Germany to finance the bridge on very favourable credit terms that helped precipitate a decision in Whitehall.[37]

[32] T 160/655/F12917, Neville Chamberlain to Runciman, 23 Mar. 1932.
[33] *Ibid.*, Kavanagh (British Steelworks Association) to Sir Frederick Leith-Ross, 11 May 1932.   [34] *Ibid.*, Sir Ernest Harvey (Bank of England) to Leith-Ross, 18 May 1932.
[35] T 160/920/12659/08/2, minute by S. D. Waley, 2 June 1932.
[36] Runciman Papers, WR 265, Chamberlain to Runciman 14 Feb. 1933.
[37] T 160/655/F12917, minute by Leith-Ross on meeting with Bernstein, 8 Feb. 1933.

Even then it needed the combined persuasion of Chamberlain and Runciman to overcome Norman's reluctance to make an exception of the Danish bridge scheme.[38] Moreover, the funds were to be spent in Britain. So as to discourage a rush of other applications, Norman wanted the announcement buried away discreetly in the trade agreement; Runciman, on the other hand, wanted to use the decision in the negotiations with Denmark. In the event it was used as a sweetener in the negotiations, but was accompanied by warnings about the dangers to commercial relations of any further depreciation of the krone.[39]

By mid-March 1933 several important issues in British policy were either resolved or well on the way to being so. The Danish loan had been agreed, although it is doubtful whether this played a decisive role in the negotiations. Protests from the Sheffield steel industry were to be overridden in the interests of the Swedish negotiations. The formulation of UK fish policy, although not complete, was nonetheless fairly clear by this stage, while the Minister of Agriculture had agreed not to insist on Britain reserving the right to tax Danish bacon as well as control it by quotas. However, Elliot does appear to have secured his other objective, that is, to reserve the power to protect milk products and eggs by quotas as well as by duties. The reservation of this power was to make the Danish negotiations the most difficult in the final stages. This still, of course, left many issues unresolved. Quite apart from the degree to which the Scandinavians were prepared to meet British requests, there were important points of detail to be settled on bacon quotas, the formulae for dealing with butter and eggs, and acceptability of the UK fish proposals and a variety of tariff requests including timber and paper duties.[40]

The negotiations

British practice, as at Ottawa, was for ministers and officials to represent the UK in the negotiations. As a rule it was civil servants from the Commercial Relations and Treaties Department of the Board of Trade who ran the discussions with the occasional participation of Lt.-Colonel John Colville, Secretary of the Department of Overseas Trade, and with

---

[38] *Ibid.*, minute by J. R. C. Helmore of meeting between Chamberlain, Runciman and Norman held on 15 Feb. 1933.

[39] BT 11/177. Reception of Danish Trade Delegation by Colville, 24 Feb. 1933. Danish sources suggest Britain was so concerned about the devaluation of the krone that the Danes were threatened that unless assurances were given that there would be no further devaluation the negotiations would be terminated. Susan Seymour, 'Anglo-Danish relations and Germany: 1933–45' (Ph.D. University of London, 1979), 28.

[40] BT 11/177, Anglo-Danish Tariff Negotiations, meeting 2 Mar. 1933, and Note for Information of Col. Colville, 7 Mar. 1933.

Walter Runciman taking virtually no part in the formal negotiations. Businessmen played a direct role in the Scandinavian delegations. Bjorn Prytz, head of SKF and, after Kreuger's suicide, of the Swedish Match cartel, led the Swedish negotiating team, and did so very effectively. The Norwegian delegation was headed by Ivor Lykke, ex-premier, who took a prominent part in the discussions, but businessmen also participated directly. The Danes too were represented by politicians and officials, with Dr Peter Munch, Minister for Foreign Affairs, leading the delegation, but with a good sprinkling of business and agricultural advisers included.

Denmark

The main agricultural discussions were held with the Danish delegation. Bacon took up less time than might have been expected. The Danes, who saw advantages in supplies being controlled by quota, were mainly concerned with ensuring that their bacon exports were not also taxed. Once this was agreed, the agricultural talks concentrated on devising schemes of byzantine complexity aimed at limiting the extent to which Danish imports would be reduced if quotas were established for butter and eggs. Having been refused any modification of the duties which discriminated against the medium-size eggs in which they specialised, the Danes reluctantly agreed to a formula which would cut back their butter exports by double the amount the dominions might agree to restrict supplies. But what the Danish side wanted was some form of guarantee as to the actual minimum amounts below which their butter exports could not be restricted. Eventually this was agreed at 2·3 million cwts with a proviso that if UK butter imports exceeded 8·1 million cwts the Danish share would rise proportionately.[41] Eggs proved more difficult because British production interests were greater than for butter; here too the Danish team wanted a specified minimum figure for their exports, but eventually had to settle for less than watertight guarantees.

In return Britain obtained tariff concessions, and, much more important, a series of 'purchasing' agreements. The Danes offered only very modest reductions of duty on printed cottons, but more generous reductions on plain, unpatterned piece goods of cotton and artificial silk mixtures. There were particular difficulties here because they were nervous about freezing duties on cotton cloth for as long as three years, fearing the effects of competition from Central Europe or Japan on their own industry. Adjustments in the tariff structure on cars to favour smaller vehicles were secured, together with conventionalisation of the duty on motor cycles, this being pushed for at the expense of demands for footwear. The Danes

[41] *Ibid.*, meeting 12 Apr. 1933.

agreed to bind the duty on cotton yarns, and also on bananas and polishes, the only concession specifically to the benefit of the colonies.[42]

Some of the minor purchasing schemes had been more or less agreed before Christmas. Greater progress had been made with Denmark in some of the other special purchasing arrangements. A delegate's promise to use the 'considerable' influence of the Danish Committee to increase the use of British salt had been enough to satisfy the Department of Overseas Trade officials who later translated this into an increase in the 1931 share of the market of 23 per cent to one of 75 per cent.[43] For jute, it was pointed out to the Danes that while British prices might be 25 per cent or so higher than those of their competitors, by the time four sides of bacon were wrapped in it, the price discrepancy made little difference to the total cost.[44] Here, too, it was hoped that Britain might raise its share of the market to 75 per cent, a big advance on the 20 per cent share of 1931.[45] Something of the flavour of Anglo-Danish bargaining can be indicated from the negotiations about steel. British prices were in many cases higher than those of other suppliers to Denmark, which the Danes not unnaturally pointed out was an obstacle to greater purchases. Arthur Mullins, of the Department of Overseas Trade, 'expected, after the discussions which had taken place in Copenhagen, that the Danish side would have found a way to surmount this difficulty'.[46] That was before Christmas, but the issue remained as a major stumbling block to a treaty. The Danish administration took the view that while the state would give guarantees, and would use its influence with the municipalities, there was absolutely nothing they could do over private purchases of iron and steel. They were emphatic on this, arguing that it was out of the question to expect their nationals, often competing on world markets, to give a price preference to British steelmakers. The atmosphere of the negotiations is again apparent from the ready Danish acquiescence to a British suggestion that the Danish State Railways, having placed an order for 10,000 tons of rails in France, should compensate Britain with an order for 2,500 tons in anticipation of future requirements![47] Yet even the state purchases proved difficult to arrange. Eventually the Danes agreed to buy at least 80,000 tons a year of British steel of specified types,[48] about double the amount that would have been bought in 1932 if purchases had not been inflated by special measures to divert trade to Britain. The British

---

[42] *Ibid.*
[43] BT 11/174, Commercial Negotiations with Foreign Countries. The discussion took place on 15 Dec. 1932.   [44] FO 371/16297, Anglo-Danish discussions, 13 Dec. 1932.
[45] BT 11/174, Negotiations summary, 31 Jan. 1933.
[46] FO 371/16298, Anglo-Danish discussions, 16 Dec. 1932.
[47] BT 11/177, Trade Negotiations with Denmark, meeting 10 Mar. 1933.
[48] T 160/827/13090/04/4, Anglo-Danish Trade Negotiations, memorandum submitted by Danish delegation on iron and steel, 7 Apr. 1933.

side wanted to buttress this by incorporating a price preference in the agreement. The Danes agreed to a preference of up to 10 per cent for selected iron and steel products when government purchases were being made.[49] They would also give the UK the first offer on orders for state and municipal purchase, and the government would use its utmost influence with private purchasers to allow some margin of preference for British supplies. These proposals were to form part of a 'gentlemen's agreement', and although because of Denmark's mfn obligations it could not formally be incorporated in a treaty, the agreement eventually formed the subject of a letter from the Danish Minister in London to the Foreign Office. This was concealed in the treaty by a protocol referring to discussions which had taken place in London about increasing British sales of iron and steel in Denmark in view of the disparity in the balance of trade between the countries.[50] Coal too was a vital part of the treaty. Having had their suggestion of a 90 per cent share of the Danish coal market rejected, the British team had finally to accept 80 per cent together with a 70 per cent share of coke imports.

Norway and Sweden

The tenor of the negotiations with Norway and Sweden differed significantly both from each other and from those with Denmark. This had been apparent before Christmas when the Swedes gave every impression that they would be prepared to offer generous tariff concessions if in return their demands for steel and paper were met; in contrast, the Norwegians, in the view of Laurence Collier of the Foreign Office, and later ambassador to Norway, were 'living up to their reputation of being the least accommodating of the Scandinavian peoples'.[51] This created a 'technical' negotiating difficulty later in the proceedings. Where countries had interests in the same products, unless negotiations were carried out simultaneously, there were bound to be concessions made primarily to one country but from which the other also benefited. For example, if Norway was offered lower duties on planed timber, a reduction which Sweden also desired, should Sweden be told that this reduction would only apply if Britain and Norway reached an agreement? If so, offers to Sweden decreased in value as the list of reservations grew. Against that, if too many offers were made unconditionally to Sweden, the Norwegians, with their negotiations lagging behind, could sit back, offer little themselves and rely on their mfn rights, to obtain much of what they wanted through an

---

[49] Iron and steel in bars, sections, rods etc. and black plates for shipbuilding; a small preference on state purchases of rails would also be given.
[50] BT 11/177, Anglo-Danish Tariff Negotiations, meeting 11 Apr. 1933.
[51] FO 371/16298, minute, 5 Jan. 1933.

Anglo-Swedish accord. British officials attempted to work through the difficulty by drawing up lists of reserved products, but kept these as short as possible so as not to antagonise the Swedes unduly. They resolved to keep matters vague, make the reservations as generalised as possible and hope the Norwegian negotiations would catch up rapidly.[52]

Most of the running on agriculture had been made by Denmark, but Norway was interested in fisheries and also had some special requirements for farm products. The Norwegians generally welcomed the fish proposals as an attempt to make the fisheries more profitable, but thought the quotas they had been offered were based on unfavourable years to Norway and were too small. They accepted consolidation of the 10 per cent duty, but were refused their request for free entry during specified times of the year. Norway also wanted guarantees of unrestricted access for bacon, butter, cheese, eggs and poultry, all products which the Norwegians supplied in 'insignificant' quantities to the British market. In a response that was to have a bearing on later negotiations, a clause was agreed whereby these products would not be regulated unless they increased so much in quantity that it became necessary to control them.[53] The Swedes had to be content with mfn treatment for their butter and bacon.

Wood products and paper were of great importance to both Sweden and Norway. The British offered to maintain free entry for newsprint, a not unimportant concession in view of the UK newsprint industry's application for duties, as well as for wood pulp and various types of pit-props and mining timber.[54] They also agreed to reduce duties from 15 to 10 per cent on various semi-manufactured wood products and guaranteed not to raise the existing 10 per cent duties on sawn and planed softwoods. An offer was made to reduce the duty from 25 to 20 per cent on kraft, machine-glazed and greaseproof paper and on non-newsprint printing paper. Although the British offers on timber were not particularly contentious, those on paper were. Both Norway and Sweden considered them inadequate. However, on 30 March, following an application to IDAC for higher duties on the heavier grades of paper and board, an application of which the Board of Trade apparently knew nothing, further concessions were offered to Norway and Sweden. Duties on kraft and greaseproof papers would be reduced to $16\frac{2}{3}$ per cent, the old Safeguarding of Industry duty, and conventionalisation of duties on millboard and wallboard was proposed. In the final round of bargaining, Britain lowered duties on writing and

[52] BT 11/132, minute by Kilroy, 14 Mar. 1933, and minutes by Griffith, Kilroy and Hill, 18 Mar. 1933.

[53] BT 11/129, Anglo-Norwegian Tariff Negotiations, meeting 11 Apr. 1933.

[54] *Ibid.*, Colville to I. Lykke, 12 Apr. 1933. This became the 'insignificant supplier' clause, and was to cause problems in bacon regulation later when a number of countries took advantage of it to send up to 400 cwt of bacon a week to the UK.

tissue paper, and consolidated the tariff on boards at 20 per cent. The British team also moved some way further to accommodate Swedish steel demands.[55]

The Swedes were much more generous in their treatment of British tariff requests than the Norwegians. By late March Sweden could be described as having met about 90 per cent of these.[56] On textiles, the Swedish delegation had offered reductions on 1931 trade worth £720,000 and had refused only £40,000 of reductions, all of which were products supplied mainly by Germany and included rayons which the Board of Trade had been wary of asking for anyway. Consolidation on textiles was agreed on British 1931 trade to Sweden of over £1 million, and the refusals were thought to be more a gesture of independence than a signal of impending duty increases. On wool textiles, the British negotiators could write that they had got 'most of what we asked for and considerably more than we hoped for'.[57] Tariff manipulation had been exercised in the case of small cars, where the duty had been reduced from 20 to 15 per cent, and for footwear by a reduction of the tariff on men's shoes by a quarter. Other items of substantial importance on which Britain obtained full demands included gramophones and records (duty halved), oil cloth (duty reduced by one-sixth), cycle tyres (duty reduced by 25 per cent), and confectionery (duty reduced by 37 per cent). The delighted officials felt themselves in 'sight of an admirable bargain'.[58]

This all provided a stark contrast with the Norwegian tariff negotiations. Many UK requests for duty reduction or stabilisation were refused. For example, lower duties were rejected on film, gramophones, rubber footwear, liquid glue and door fittings.[59] Conventionalisations were either refused or the UK was asked not to press for them on a number of categories of cotton textiles. Where lower duties were offered, they were often nominal. After at first refusing duty reductions on varnishes, the Norwegians later agreed to reduce the duty from 15 ore to 14 ore per kilo. Their offer on textiles was little more than a gloss on conventionalisation. For example, Britain had asked for a lowering of the duty on cotton prints from 1·80 krone per kilo to 1 krone: the Norwegians offered 1·53 krone. The Norwegian delegation offered to reduce the duty on wool hosiery from 3·24 to 3·15 krone per kilo in response to a British request for a duty of 2·50 krone. When concessions were made at all, these examples were fairly typical of their extent.

[55] *Ibid.*, 30 Mar. 1933 and BT 11/88, minute by Kilroy, 25 Mar. 1933.
[56] BT 11/88, minute by Hill, 25 Mar. 1933.
[57] *Ibid.*, minute by Kilroy, 25 Mar. 1933.
[58] *Ibid.*, minute by Fountain, 26 Mar. 1933.
[59] BT 11/129, Anglo-Norwegian Tariff Negotiations, Statement communicated to United Kingdom Representatives at Meeting on 16 Mar. 1933.

Important though tariffs were in the British desiderata, it was progress on coal that was the major criterion when assessing progress in the negotiations. Here the offers on hand by early April varied widely. The Norwegians had been unwilling to name the percentage of their coal imports they would buy from Britain. This, they stated, was dependent on other matters, but Lykke 'expressed very definitely the opinion that British exports of coal could best be increased by relying on the good faith and good intentions of Norway than by an agreement which specified percentages of British coal to be used'.[60] If pressed, he said, then 50 per cent was suggested. Neither proposition appealed to the British negotiating team. At a private meeting to assess the state of the negotiations and to decide on the final stages, it was agreed that it was quite possible to extract 70 per cent from the Norwegians;[61] Whitehall considered that its treatment of the Norwegian requests had been quite generous (duties had been reduced or conventionalised on £5·5 million out of £6·7 million of 1931 imports from Norway). The Swedes had proposed to buy 44 per cent of their coal from the UK, as much as could be offered without bringing importers into the proposals. While the Mines Department wanted more, Colville argued that the Swedes had been more generous than the other two countries on tariffs, that coal was obtaining considerable help under the Scandinavian agreements as a whole and he would not like to see a treaty with Sweden jeopardised because of coal alone.[62] Earlier, Fountain had minuted similarly: 'I am strongly of the opinion that it would be foolish to throw away a good chance of a bargain because the Coal Mines Dept. (who have rather too single an eye) think we ought to get a bigger concession than the substantial one offered on coal.'[63] The negotiations with Sweden, which, apart from the steel problem, had progressed so smoothly through most of their course, had reached crisis point and a temporary breakdown during the final stages. The Swedes were not satisfied by the British response to their demands for bacon, butter or boards, and, in some late bargaining the UK had to accept a 47 per cent share of the Swedish coal import market.

Scandinavia: conclusions

The agreement with Denmark was estimated to increase coal exports and employment by the greatest margin of the three treaties. This was more a reflection of the size of the Danish coal market than anything else, because the proportional increase, based on 1931, was from 63·9 per cent to 80 per

---

[60] *Ibid.*, Anglo-Norwegian Tariff Negotiations, meeting 21 Mar. 1933.
[61] BT 11/174, meeting 5 Apr. 1933.   [62] *Ibid.*
[63] BT 11/88, minute by Fountain, 26 Mar. 1933.

cent of Denmark's imports, leading to an extra 1·3 million tonnes of coal a year and 5,300 more jobs.[64] The relative increase from the other two countries was in fact greater. In the Norwegian case the figures were 39·1 to 70 per cent, the additional tonnage 538,000 and employment 2,120.[65] The Swedish ratio of 1931 coal imports from the UK had only been 23·6 per cent, so there was plenty of scope for improvement. The figure in the agreement, with the grumbling acquiescence of the Mines Department, therefore represented a doubling of the percentage take, yielding another million tonnes and 4,180 jobs in coalmining.[66]

In other respects the Danish agreement did not appear conspicuously more productive than the other two pacts. Its distinctive elements, of course, were the purchase agreements: by far the most important of these was steel, calculated to generate at least another 30,000 tons of exports over and above the 1931 figure, and, on officials' more optimistic assessments, an extra 1,500 jobs.[67] Tariff reductions covered a very small part of UK trade, little over £400,000 of Danish imports from the UK in 1931.[68] Attention had been focused on cotton textiles, but the results were far from impressive. Lower duties had been won for printed and certain unbleached cotton piece goods, but according to the industries this represented only about one-quarter of Lancashire's exports to Denmark, and even then only brought duties back into line with the level of 1931.[69] The rest of the list bypassed the core of British industry: felt hats, carpeting, photographic plates, marmalade and apricot jam, pickles, biscuits and cakes. The binding of existing duties or of free entry was achieved for over £5 million of UK exports, little short of half the 1931 trade. Because Denmark was a low tariff country these were thought to be substantial and worthwhile guarantees, but it should be of little surprise that the treaty was generally accepted with relief in Denmark.[70]

Duty reductions covered a much larger proportion of British imports into Norway. On the basis of 1930 figures, lower duties were conceded on trade worth over £1 million, and consolidation of duties or free entry on nearly £3·5 million. There were few outright refusals, although one of these was on cars. Probably the most valuable concession was the introduction of a 30 per cent 'stop' on woollens. However, as emphasised above, the duty reductions were generally of the most nominal character.

The Swedish tariff concessions were far more generous. Most UK requests were met in full, although not those for concessions for cars and

[64] CAB 24/240 CP 107 (33), memorandum by Runciman, 11 Apr. 1933.
[65] POWE 16/214, note May 1933.   [66] *Ibid.*   [67] BT 11/167, note, Apr. 1933.
[68] CAB 24/240 CP 107 (33), memorandum by Runciman, 11 Apr. 1933.
[69] Sir J. Nall in *Hansard* (Commons), vol. 277, no. 83, 10 May 1933, col. 1641.
[70] Seymour, 'Anglo-Danish relations and Germany', 29.

textiles, the items at the forefront of their tariff objectives. Nonetheless, the readiness of the Swedes to accede to London's demands contributed to the cordial atmosphere in which the negotiations were conducted, and goes some way to explain why Sweden escaped with a coal obligation as low as 47 per cent. Negotiating skills and personalities may have had a bearing on the results. The charm of Bjorn Prytz perhaps made its contribution. Raymond Streat had expressed his surprise when he found, 'for the first time, a woman official with executive responsibility – a mere girl, Miss Kilroy, who had been given charge of "Sweden"'.[71] There was evident mutual attraction between Prytz and Alix Kilroy and they became life-long friends.[72] Frank Ashton Gwatkin was impressed with Prytz's skill as a negotiator.[73] But essentially the contrasting outcomes of the three sets of negotiations reflect the varying degrees of vulnerability to British pressure of each Scandinavian state. The Danes were peculiarly unfortunate, not only because they relied so heavily on the UK market in general, but because they depended on just those products where the competing demands of UK agriculture and imperial supplies were squeezing non-Commonwealth imports. The northern Scandinavians, with lower overall reliance on the British market, and with forest products predominating, were able to obtain better guarantees for their exports. They also had to concede less than Denmark. Although the Danes offered little in the way of tariff reductions, they had to grant the highest coal purchase guarantee, and, alone of the three countries, agree to various purchasing arrangements, most importantly for steel. The Norwegians and Swedes were in a position to drive tougher bargains, although it has to be kept in mind that they were opening their markets to the UK while at the same time stemming a retreat in the British market.

From the viewpoint of the UK the Danish agreement was to prove the most productive. The treaty itself was only partly responsible for this; it was through the agency of the import licensing system that a major trade diversion was to be engineered in favour of Britain – ironically, the agreement was concluded without a single specific guarantee as to how the import regulations would operate.

Reciprocal concessions had, of course, been made by the UK. Tariff reductions had been few, the most important being on wrapping paper and steel, but overall they were estimated to involve the loss of more than 2,000 jobs, and also about £200,000 in lost Customs' revenue.[74] The major

---

[71] M. Dupree (ed.), *Lancashire and Whitehall. The diary of Sir E. Raymond Streat*, I, *1931–39* (Manchester, 1987), 198, 5 Dec. 1932.
[72] Alix Meynell (Dame), *Public Servant, Private Woman: an autobiography* (1988), 136–40.
[73] FO 371/16297, minute, 20 Dec. 1932.
[74] CAB 24/240 CP 104 (33), memorandum by Runciman, 11 Apr. 1933.

Scandinavian objectives had centred on guarantees of security for their agricultural produce. While British concessions fell far short of satisfying their trading partners, they nonetheless contributed to the immense difficulties in formulating a coherent agricultural policy in the 1930s.

Germany

At Ottawa, and in the London talks with the Scandinavians, Britain had been dealing with countries that were predominantly exporters of primary products. This pattern was broken when the Anglo-German treaty was signed in 1933, the only occasion until 1938 that Britain made an agreement with a major industrial country.[75] The agreement was a limited one however, although insofar as Britain sought guarantees for its coal trade there were, of course, similarities with Northern Europe. But while in Scandinavia and the Baltic states the power of the UK's market was used to push aside competitors in the coal trade, in Germany Britain was attempting to salvage severe losses.

Germany had drastically curtailed coal quotas from Britain in the winter of 1931–2. While the quota for UK coal had been 420,000 tonnes per month, this had been reduced in a series of steps until it was only 100,000 tonnes by April 1932. Moreover, coal imports from other countries were not reduced. The official reasons for this were that Germany was bound by an agreement with Holland, that imports from France and Belgium were comparatively small, and in any case, Germany was also an exporter of coal to these countries.[76] But there were major problems in the German coal industry, consumption and production having fallen steeply since 1929, so the restrictions were an obvious response to these problems. Moreover, as emerged later, the Germans do seem to have been worried about the competitive strength of British coal after the depreciation of sterling. An increase in imports in late 1931, a seasonal rise according to British officials, was seen by German coal experts as heralding a major new penetration of the market, British coal appearing in areas where allegedly it had never been seen before.[77] The cutback was severe, however, and whatever the reasons, it was also discriminatory. It seems probable, although there is no decisive evidence from the British archives, that the

---

[75] An agreement was signed with France on 27 June 1934, but this was almost wholly a restoration of trade rights after a period of trade warfare. FO 371/18470, memorandum on Trade Agreements 1934, 3 Dec. 1934.

[76] FO 371/17319, memorandum Respecting Trade Agreements, 11 July 1933.

[77] BT 11/189, Anglo-German Commercial Negotiations 1932/3, 1st meeting on coal, London, 12 Jan. 1933.

motivation was in part retaliatory, a response to the way German exports to Britain had been hit by the new tariff legislation.

There was the possibility of legal redress for the UK because of apparent breaches of the 1924 Anglo-German Commercial Treaty. Although coal had been specifically exempted from the stipulation of the treaty, which provided for the abolition of import and export prohibitions and restrictions, there had been a secret undertaking that Germany would not act to the detriment of British coal exports.[78] Perhaps more to the point, the treaty had unconditional mfn clauses applying to duties and to other types of restriction. After unsuccessful protests had been made to Germany, arbitration in the international courts was considered. Germany was willing to accept arbitration, but in that event would insist on taking Britain to court on the grounds that the recent duties had been especially injurious to German trade and that Britain, contrary to the treaty's protocol, had been unwilling to discuss German complaints.[79]

Between 1929 and 1931 German exports to Britain had proved extremely resilient, but in the next year, as the Import Duties Act began to bite, retained imports from Germany fell 53 per cent from £62 to £29 million. Comparing the first ten months of 1932 with those in 1930, the value of imports of wool tissue fell by 96 per cent.[80] There were many instances where the decline was to a level of only one-third or less of the 1930 values, including important groups such as silk or rayon fabrics (74 per cent), electrical products (69 per cent), artificial silk hosiery (80 per cent), semi-manufactured iron (91 per cent) and toys (70 per cent). Although both the depression and the depreciation of sterling contributed to this, German products do seem to have been subject to particularly high duty loads. The incidence of duties, when they combined *ad valorem* with specific, was often very high. Safety-razor blades were taxed at 20 per cent from May 1932 until July 1932. When the IDAC recommendation that a specific duty of 2s per gross was accepted, the overall rate of duty rose to the equivalent of about 70 per cent and imports slumped.[81] The Germans particularly objected to the high incidence of the specific duties on their cheap goods such as artificial silk stockings.[82]

The German threat to take Britain to court on grounds of discrimination was interpreted in the Board of Trade as a device to secure negotiations. Officials were certainly not keen on the idea of arbitration. As Quintin Hill minuted, not only might it be politically awkward for the government to

[78] BT 11/138, memorandum by Hill, 21 Apr. 1932.   [79] *The Times*, 8 July 1932.

[80] BT 11/189. Some of these examples cover the first nine months of 1930 and 1932.

[81] CAB 24/240 CP 103 (33), Anglo-German Agreement, memorandum by Runciman, 11 Apr. 1933.

[82] BT 11/189, Anglo-German Commercial Negotiations, 1932/3, meeting 10 Dec. 1932.

announce it had been compelled to seek arbitration because of the Import Duties Act, but he was 'not at all sure that a Court composed of a majority of foreigners would not give a judgement against us'![83] Perhaps the best idea was to start negotiating but see that not too much progress was made. It also became clear that Britain's substantial point was about discrimination, and that it would be all too simple for the Germans to meet that by cutting back on other suppliers with little or no benefit to the British coal trade.[84] Since the Germans were willing to negotiate both on coal and tariffs, or to go to arbitration on them both, it was decided to negotiate.

The negotiations were very restricted in scope, a further agreement being left for some time in the future. The British objective was for a quota of 300,000 tonnes per month with little conceded in return. German requests were restricted to a number of fairly minor products. The industrial giants of heavy engineering, machine tools or electrical products were left on one side for musical instruments, toys, scissors, razor blades, stockings and a number of other relatively minor items. The first stage of the negotiations took place in Berlin in December 1932, but quickly foundered once the Germans put a figure to their coal offer; 125,000 tonnes, or a little more if Britain was prepared to concede to Germany on stockings, was considered by UK officials to be an unacceptable basis for negotiations, and the delegation was told to return to London.[85] It was agreed to present this as an adjournment rather than a breakdown of talks, but Runciman told the German ambassador that he (Runciman) wished to be taken seriously and that 'I would not waste my time over figures which were ridiculous.'[86]

Improved German offers were quickly forthcoming, and the eventual formula, after further talks in London, was for a minimum coal quota of 180,000 tonnes per month plus scaled additions to the quota if German coal consumption rose by 1 per cent or more above $7\frac{1}{2}$ million tonnes per month. Imports into German free ports and for bunkering were to remain unrestricted. There is no doubt that Whitehall thought that the partial restitution of the coal trade was being bought by employment sacrifices elsewhere at home. For the products on which concessions were being made, estimated losses of employment and Customs' revenue were calculated. Many of the products were in the luxury category and bore higher duties than average, around 30 or $33\frac{1}{3}$ per cent, and reductions were generally to the 20 or 25 per cent level. The Germans had put particular emphasis on lower tariffs on toys and stockings; nothing was conceded on

[83] BT 11/138, minute by Hill, 25 June 1932.
[84] *Ibid.*, minute by G. Jenkin, 31 Aug. 1932.
[85] BT 11/189, Board of Trade telegram to J. J. Wills, 19 Dec. 1932.
[86] *Ibid.*, note by Runciman on informal talk with German ambassador, 19 Dec. 1932.

stockings, but a cut in duty from 25 to 15 per cent on toys was calculated to increase imports by £300,000 per annum at a cost of 1,250 jobs, very nearly half the total price of the concessions as a whole.[87] In only a few isolated instances such as the production of mouth organs and the cheaper types of concertinas was there thought to be no domestic production. The additional 80,000 tonnes of coal – additional to the quota operating from April 1932, that is – were estimated to employ a further 3,800 miners, together with some auxiliary employment.

Argentina

Outside Europe the major foreign agreement of the early 1930s was that with the Argentine. The Republic was central to Britain's economic relationships in Latin America, accounting for more than half of import-export trade in the 1930s, and with over one-third of Britain's Latin American investments. Yet the Anglo-Argentine connection was in some senses a weakening relationship, and the agreements of 1933 followed years of attempts by the UK to stem German and American competition in the Republic. While the First World War had proved a major setback to Germany in the Argentine, the United States, mounting a determined onslaught on South American markets, had proved the major beneficiary, easily overhauling Britain as the principal seller.[88] Trade missions headed by Sir Maurice de Bunsen (in 1918) and Lord D'Abernon (1929) yielded little.[89] But, as Runciman later explained: 'I believe one reason why nothing came of (the D'Abernon Mission) was that we had no means of exercising any pressure. We are now in a position to do that.'[90]

Argentina, like the Scandinavian countries, was heavily dependent on the British market for export sales, and the return to protection, together with the tightening of links with the Empire, acted as a serious threat to its position. Approximately 40 per cent of Argentine exports went to Britain, but of even greater importance than this was the total reliance of the chilled beef trade on sales to Britain – and there was a close connection between ranching and political power in Argentina.[91] Hence Argentine anxiety in 1932 to negotiate some form of guarantee for the preservation of its export trade. While nothing substantial could be negotiated before the Imperial

---

[87] CAB 24/240 CP 103 (33), memorandum by Runciman, 11 Apr. 1933.
[88] R. Gravil and T. Rooth, 'A time of acute dependence: Argentina in the 1930s', *Journal of European Economic History*, 7 (1978), 373. In 1911–15 the UK had supplied 31·1 per cent of Argentine imports, the USA 16·1 per cent; by 1926–30 the figures were UK 19·1 per cent, USA 24·4 per cent.
[89] R. Gravil, *The Anglo-Argentine Connection, 1900–1939* (Boulder, Colorado, 1985), ch. 6.
[90] W. Runciman in *Hansard* (Commons), vol. 227, no. 83, 10 May 1933, col. 1544.
[91] P. H. Smith, *Politics and Beef in Argentina: patterns of conflict and change* (1969).

Economic Conference, Britain was careful at Ottawa not to concede too much on meat to the dominions.[92] Clearly, apart from Argentina's initiative in seeking trade negotiations, the fact that it was not interested in selling manufactured goods to Britain encouraged Whitehall to negotiate early. However, while the low tariffs of the Scandinavian countries made quick results from the negotiations all the more likely, there was some doubt as to whether Argentina really qualified as a low tariff country.

The height and purpose of the Argentine tariff has been a rich source of controversy for writers on its economy. For some commentators, Argentina, up until the Second World War, was a low tariff country. The tariff reflected the needs and interests of powerful anti-industrial forces, was primarily a revenue tariff and, because of its incidence, managed even to be negatively protective.[93] Many other commentators, one as early as 1908, described the tariff as protectionist, and the League of Nations placed Argentina as one of the more highly protected countries in 1925, behind the USA but ahead of Canada, France, Germany and Italy. Certainly the incidence of the tariff had changed markedly during the 1920s. The basic tariff had its origin in a law of 1905 which came into effect in January 1906. This measure placed an estimated unit value (*aforo*) on each imported item that could be changed by law. Most foodstuffs and beverages were subject to percentage duties, although, because of the *aforos* system, they too were in effect specific.[94] New valuations were made in 1920 and 1923, although in both cases this was little more than a catching-up operation, reflecting the decline in protection that had resulted because of the world-wide inflation of 1914–20. The combination of the new *aforos* together with falling world price levels meant a gradual rise in protection through the 1920s. Diaz Alejandro calculates that the ratio of all import duties collected to the value of all merchandise imports was by the late 1920s roughly the same as before the war and substantially higher than earlier in the decade.[95] It was measures taken in 1931, however, that really upset exporters. New valuations were charged for hundreds of items in 1931 and hundreds of new valuations made for items not previously specified.[96] In addition, in October 1931 a new surcharge of 10 per cent was introduced. When added to basic rates of duty and various surcharges it meant, for example, that goods subject to a basic rate of 25 per cent would pay a 42 per cent duty. The free list was considerably curtailed in 1931, although

---

[92] See ch. 3.
[93] The literature is reviewed and the matter fully discussed in C. F. Diaz Alejandro, *Essays on the Economic History of the Argentine Republic* (1970), 227–308.
[94] BT 11/143, Argentina: Note on the Nature, History etc. of the Customs Tariff System, June 1932.   [95] Diaz Alejandro, *Economic History of the Argentine*, 282.
[96] BT 11/143.

coal remained on it and, also of great importance to British trade, items imported by railway companies, most of them British owned and buying supplies from the United Kingdom, continued to be exempt from duties.

It was to this great increase in tariffs that many British firms referred when consulted about the Argentine negotiations. A number of London based companies wanted cancellation of the 10 per cent surcharge and a return to the customs valuation of 1923 or 1930.[97] Yet in the case of no other country was there such a consensus that the retention of the mfn principle would make a trade agreement practically worthless. The British Chamber of Commerce in Argentina asserted that the existing trade imbalance would not be eliminated without a 50 per cent tariff preference,[98] and many firms in Britain thought that a rebate of one-third to one-half was needed.[99] The Federation of British Industries held similar views, many of the firms stating that any benefits would otherwise 'be of equal or preponderating advantage to our competitors'.[100] Whitehall's view, as discussed above, was that they were not going to abandon mfn unless forced to do so, and although there had been suggestions before Ottawa that Argentina might be prepared to give Britain preferences, it was thought that when it came to the point Buenos Aires would be unwilling to face the wrath of the USA and other powerful countries.[101] Certainly, when negotiations started, the Argentine team refused to countenance any thought of tariff preferences.[102]

This obviously limited the scope of the tariff negotiations, the more so as investigation and consultation revealed little scope for tariff reclassification and sub-division, the classic subterfuge for circumvention of mfn articles. There were exceptions, such as electric cables and the important case of cars, where yet again Britain hoped to gain through tariff reductions being concentrated on smaller vehicles.[103] But consultations with industry did reveal difficulties about exchange control. Some British industries, such as the aircraft companies, had no trouble in winning orders but did find difficulty in getting their money out of Argentina. The FBI's special Argentine Committee recommended that as well as tariffs the negotiations should cover the provision of exchange for current payments, remittance of dividends etc. as well as trying to secure guarantees on the treatment of British capital invested in Argentine public utilities.[104] The allocation of

[97] *Ibid.*, various letters.
[98] *Ibid.*, Sir James Macleay (British Ambassador in Buenos Aires) to Simon, 24 May 1932.
[99] *Ibid.*, London Chamber of Commerce to Dunwoody, Secretary, Association of British Chambers of Commerce, 28 Oct. 1932.
[100] *Ibid.*, C. F. I. Ramsden (Divisional Manager for Foreign Trade, FBI) to A. E. Overton, 15 Feb. 1933.   [101] *Ibid.*, minute by Hill, 8 July 1932.
[102] BT 11/194, meeting by 17 Feb. 1933.   [103] *Ibid.*, and BT 11/143.
[104] BT 11/143, G. H. Locock (Director of FBI) to Runciman, 11 Oct. 1932.

exchange rapidly came to the forefront of British desiderata, and there is no doubt that the agreement on exchange came to act as the most effective form of preference for British trade in Argentina during the 1930s. Exchange control had been introduced in October 1931. The major problems for British interests were twofold: (1) to obtain payment for exports and remittance of profits from Argentina, and (2) the accumulation of frozen balances to such an extent that by February 1933 at least 373 British companies had balances frozen in Argentina to a total of about £10 million.[105] British firms needed to remit money from Argentina for four main purposes: to pay for imported goods; to pay British income tax; to meet the claims of debenture holders; to pay dividends on shares. The problem was especially acute because banks in the Republic, even when accepting deposits, were paying only 1·25 per cent interest.[106]

The early stages of the negotiations, largely concerned with Argentina trying to shield its beef industry from Ottawa, had been carried out by Argentina's ambassador in London, Dr Manuel Malbran. But the leader of the Independent Socialist Party, Dr Antonio de Tomaso, argued that if the negotiations were to be entrusted to an individual it should be to him in his role as Minister of Agriculture.[107] This was not a prospect welcomed by the Argentine government, and to head it off, a mission led by Dr Julio Roca, Vice-President, and including Malbran but not de Tomaso, came to London masquerading as a visit to repay that of the Prince of Wales, although with a brief to discuss trade relations as well.[108]

Argentina's requirements were relatively simple. The most important of these was for beef exports. On the face of it, it might appear odd that so much emphasis should be placed on beef, for, in 1929, beef accounted for a mere 10 per cent of Argentine exports, less than a third the value of wheat and flour exports, substantially below maize exports and less than even linseed. Apart from the political importance of the cattlemen, there was some justification for concentrating demands on a product which had only one outlet, the British market, and merely seeking mfn treatment for other, more market-diversified, products. So, as Roca said at the first official meeting of the negotiations: 'the fundamental matter for Argentina was to maintain her exports of chilled beef to the UK at the level laid down for the basic year 1931–2, free of customs duties, and to secure for her remaining exports to the United Kingdom a treatment at least equal to that afforded by the Ottawa agreements'.[109]

The Argentine government also wanted some degree of control over the allocation of meat quotas to the British market, at least enough to give

---

[105] Gravil and Rooth, 'Argentina in the 1930s', Table 6, p. 356 lists the most important of these.   [106] *Ibid.*   [107] FO 371/15800, Macleay to FO, 2 Nov. 1932.
[108] *Ibid.*, 29 Oct. 1932.   [109] BT 11/194, meeting 15 Feb. 1933.

scope for some national *frigorificos* to participate in the trade alongside the American and British companies that dominated the meat-packing industry.

Even before the Argentine delegation set sail, British officials were becoming alarmed that the negotiations might fail because Britain had nothing to offer them.[110] In the autumn of 1932, when the Ministry of Agriculture were becoming worried at the prospect of a meat crisis, the Argentines had been prevailed upon to cut chilled beef shipments temporarily to 10 per cent below their 'Ottawa Year' level. This temporary restriction continued in the New Year. Fountain minuted to Runciman that while it had been possible to argue that the Ottawa agreements had not prejudiced the possibility of making a favourable treaty with Argentina, he now felt that with the combination of the 'Ottawa Agreements and general meat situation it is becoming increasingly difficult to see on what basis Treaty arrangements with the Argentine can be concluded'.[111] When it became clear that the Minister of Agriculture's view was that the UK should reserve the right to impose duties on meat and bacon as well as the existing quantitative restrictions, Fountain's pessimism deepened. If the Ministry's views were to prevail, 'we do not stand any chance of making any agreement with the Argentine at all'.[112] After strenuous appeal from the Board of Trade Elliot relented, and one major obstacle to successful negotiations with Argentina was removed.[113]

Several meetings were held between Argentine and British representatives on UK tariff requests. But it became evident that the Argentine team did not have the authority of the Ministry of Finance to make any proposals.[114] Thereafter there was no discussion of detailed tariff requests in the first stage of the negotiations. Instead the talks concentrated on beef and exchange. The reluctance of Britain to concede any control to the Argentine of the allocation of beef exports stood in the way of a good exchange agreement. Britain wanted 40 per cent of available exchange after certain deductions for the servicing of government debts were made. Instead they were offered 20 per cent, and not only had to share it with the dominions, but were told it was conditional on British imports from Argentina being maintained at the 1932 level, and, moreover, that it did not include re-exports.[115] How was such a wide gap reconciled? Of key importance was an improvement in the British offer on meat. Roca was

---

[110] FO 371/15800, minute by R. L. Craigie, 3 Nov. 1932.
[111] BT 11/143, 12 Jan. 1933.   [112] *Ibid.*, minute 31 Jan. 1933.
[113] CAB 27/489 CFC (32) 11, memorandum by Runciman 6 Feb. 1933, and *ibid.*, CFC (32), 2nd meeting, 8 Feb. 1933. Elliot had agreed not to press for duties on meat at an earlier meeting: BT 11/143, note of a meeting held on 6 Feb. 1933.
[114] BT 11/194, Anglo-Argentine Trade Negotiations, meeting 21 Feb. 1933.
[115] *Ibid.*, meeting 9 Mar. 1933.

reported as saying that if the British government would give Argentina a fair deal on meat, they could have as much exchange as they wanted.[116] The final guarantee on meat was not given without further battle between Runciman and Elliot, but eventually Argentina was conceded duty free entry for chilled and frozen meats during the currency of the agreement. They also wanted assurances that there would be no further reductions in the volume of British imports beyond those fixed at Ottawa. The Ministry of Agriculture, without effective control over dominion imports, felt that any pledge to maintain foreign import levels would destroy its ability to protect meat prices. British livestock producers would be left at the mercy of world supply conditions at a time of unprecedented instability, and if Runciman's suggested 10 per cent cut was adopted, it would leave only a tiny margin to deal with the possible expansion of home and dominion supplies.[117] The Minister was very unwilling to name a specific figure, but if compelled to do so would reluctantly suggest a 15 per cent cut as the amount. In Cabinet he said the government would be accused of sacrificing agriculture to the interests of the rentier.[118] Runciman, asserting that the negotiations would fail if Britain could not give a better guarantee to Argentina, stated that if the negotiations were now to be abandoned, he would have to resign. Chamberlain 'could not put too strongly his sense of disaster that would result from a breakdown in Argentine negotiations ... the reaction of a failure on the negotiations with other countries would put in question the whole of our foreign trade policy'.[119] The eventual solution was to guarantee 90 per cent of the Ottawa Year levels (i.e. the amount being imported at the time); any reductions beyond this would not be made without consultation, and, more importantly, would need equivalent reductions by the dominions. The dominions, in defending themselves, would be defending Argentina. Moreover, the 10 per cent cut could only be maintained as long as the excluded beef was not replaced by other meats 'with the effect of neutralising the desired effect on prices'. This was partly vitiated by a clause which excluded 'experimental shipments' of chilled beef from the categories of other meats. Because there was a long history of false alarms in the chilled beef trade from the Antipodes, the Argentines accepted this clause. In fact both Thomas, Secretary of State for the Dominions, and Runciman knew that the technical problems had been largely overcome,[120] and that dominion supplies were likely to replace those of the Argentine to the limit of

[116] FO 371/16532, minute by Craigie of conversation with Dr E. L. I. Burgin, 29 Mar. 1933.
[117] CAB 24/239 CP 66 (33), memorandum by Minister of Agriculture, 14 Mar. 1933.
[118] CAB 23/75 CAB 18/33, 15 Mar. 1933.   [119] Ibid.
[120] I. M. Drummond, *Imperial Economic Policy 1917–1939* (1974), 312. The clause was inserted on the suggestion of Bruce, the Australian High Commissioner.

Thomas's phraseology. Britain also met the Argentine government's wishes to control some of the shipments of meat to Britain, a concession that Whitehall seemed reluctant to have made.

The improvement of British offers on meat was the key to a better deal on exchange. But there were other considerations. First, Argentina operated a sinking fund for the relief of the national debt which in times of stress could be suspended.[121] Secondly, a solution to the problem of the frozen balances was found. The British government agreed that after 11 or 12 million pesos were released in cash payments, the other balances could be met through an issue of 4 per cent bonds by the Argentine government. Thirdly, the Argentines seem to have believed that a generous offer on exchange would satisfy Britain, and British demands for tariff reductions would virtually cease. In this they were seriously mistaken. Apparently Dr Carcano, perhaps through disproportionate contact with Treasury officials, became convinced that Britain's priority was with the exchange control system, and persuaded President Justo that if exchange control could be adapted to give preference to Britain, then pressure for major tariff cuts would be relaxed.[122] Certainly the Treasury do seem to have regarded the exchange part of the deal as of 'far greater importance to British trade in present circumstances than reductions in tariffs'.[123] The Argentine delegation were told that a satisfactory solution of the exchange problem was an 'indispensable condition of progress in the negotiations as a whole'.[124] The original British intentions were to secure tariff reductions, and only as preparations advanced did the exchange question come to the forefront. There may have been some difference of emphasis in objectives between departments, but tariff reductions remained very much to the fore in the minds of Trade and Foreign Office officials. Tariff reductions are more politically saleable than the obscurer matters of exchange control, and export interests wanted a return to the easier tariffs of 1930 or before. Besides this, Runciman was still committed to his view of British protectionism as a trade liberalising device and anxious to show results. It is also possible that once exchange control was used in Britain's favour, the danger of most of the benefits of tariff reductions going to competitors was largely averted, although there is no reference to this point in the documents. But British officials were worried that if exchange conditions improved and controls were abolished, unless there were tariff concessions Britain would have nothing to show from the agreement: in these

---

[121] BT 11/166. Anglo-Argentine Tariff Negotiations, inter-departmental meeting 22 Dec. 1932. Leith-Ross suggested this, together with the idea that private remittances might be reduced.   [122] Gravil and Rooth, 'Argentina in the 1930s', 355.

[123] FO 371/16533, minute by Craigie of telephone conversation with Waley (Treasury), 3 Aug. 1933.

[124] BT 11/194, Anglo-Argentine Tariff Negotiations, meeting 16 Feb. 1933.

circumstances 'the Argentines would be left in the position of having immeasurably the best bargain'.[125] The first part of the agreement therefore included an article providing for the conclusion of a supplementary agreement dealing with tariffs, and a protocol to the convention contained a pledge 'to revert to the rates of duty...in force in 1930 so far as fiscal considerations and the interests of national industries permit'.

This therefore formed the basic objective of the British negotiating team although some tariff manipulation and in some cases a reduction of duties below the 1930 level were also wanted. Why the Argentines wanted the second part of the negotiations to be held in Buenos Aires is somewhat obscure. Officially the reason was that the Argentine mission to London did not include tariff experts.[126] If so, then it reflected the Argentine misconception that exchange preferences would be enough. But it is possible that a tariff battle was anticipated, and that the political constraints of public opposition to tariff concessions could be demonstrated clearly to the British team. Factory employees were even released from work on full pay to attend protest meetings.[127]

The early stages of the negotiations, which started on 16 June, made very little progress. By late July the position was so unsatisfactory, particularly for textiles, that Runciman prepared to break off the negotiations.[128] It had been expected that the supplementary agreement would be ready by the beginning of August, and although by then expecting delay, Runciman obtained Cabinet authority to denounce the existing Convention if the negotiations did not achieve more.[129] Yet this again exposed the division within government over the value of the existing agreement and the potential benefit of further tariff concessions. The Treasury felt it would be a great mistake to denounce the Convention of 1 May,[130] a view which found some echo in the Foreign Office. As an influential official, David Kelly, wrote:

It is therefore arguable that from the practical point of view the exchange agreement was by itself worth the price of the agreement – seeing that the matter is only for 3 years... The B(oard of) T(rade) on the other hand feel presumably that we are being tricked, and that only the exchange agreement combined with solid tariff concessions justify the pressure which was put on the Ministry of Agriculture to tie their hands as has been the effect of the agreement.[131]

[125] FO 371/16532, minute by P. Mason on meeting between Burgin and other British delegates, 27 Mar. 1933.

[126] FO 371/16533, conversation between Craigie and Malbran, 2 July 1933.

[127] *Economist*, 15 July 1933, 130–1.

[128] FO 371/16533, minute by Mason on conversation with Board of Trade officials, 27 July 1933.   [129] CAB 23/76 CAB 49 (33), 28 July 1933.

[130] FO 371/16533, minute by Craigie of telephone conversation with Waley, 3 Aug. 1933.

[131] *Ibid.*, minute by Kelly, 8. Aug. 1933.

In fact, progress started to accelerate. It is not clear whether this was because the Argentines learned unofficially of Runciman's authority from the Cabinet, or, as is more likely, because of changes within the Argentine government made a few days earlier. The Minister of Finance, who had been opposed to the Convention, resigned, leaving the conduct of the negotiations in the hands of the Minister of Foreign Affairs.[132] He arranged for the withdrawal of customs experts from the Argentine delegation, leaving matters in the control of Carcano. The British ambassador concluded that the Argentines had decided to meet requests for tariff reductions but to do so slowly in order to forestall criticism by appearing to put up a fight in the cause of local industries.[133] By mid-August the Argentine government was keen to conclude the negotiations as rapidly as possible. They were refusing to meet British requests for a tariff reclassification on a weight/capacity basis, largely, it seems, because of the opposition of interests in the US car trade.[134] On textiles mixed progress was made: reversion was offered on most cottons,[135] and also on woollens, but whereas the 1930 duties on cotton had been quite modest, the higher duties on woollens led the British delegation to press for further reductions below the 1930 level.[136] What aggravated the position was that the Argentines were now determined to keep the 10 per cent surcharge, and to make no useful pledges on its abolition, so this remained an obstacle to the agreement. By late August the negotiations had reached a critical stage. Judged in terms of the overall objective of a return to the 1930 rates of duty, the Argentine offer appears quite generous. The value of UK trade in goods subject to duty increases since 1930 was about 25 million gold pesos; for these the Argentine had offered a return to 1930 rates (or occasionally lower) for goods of a value 16·3 million pesos and rates intermediate between the 1930 and 1933 levels for goods worth 8·1 million gold pesos – requests refused accounted for little more than $\frac{1}{2}$ million gold pesos.[137] Moreover, reductions were also made on 6·6 million gold pesos worth of goods which had not been subject to tariff increases since 1930, and although rejections amounted to over 5 million pesos, much of this was accounted for by tinplate with a 5 per cent duty. Britain asked for

---

[132] The Finance Minister, E. Huego, was strongly opposed to major tariff concessions to the UK because the loss of customs revenue seriously threatened his attempts to balance the budget. By mid-July he was faced by almost united Cabinet opposition to his stand on tariffs. E. F. Early, 'The Roca-Runciman Treaty and its significance for Argentina, 1933–41' (Ph.D. thesis, University of London, 1981), pp. 179–80.

[133] CAB 24/242, Macleay to Foreign Office, 25 July 1933, attached to CP 199 (33), memorandum by Runciman, 27 July 1933.

[134] FO 371/16533, note by Mason on telephone conversation with Fraser, 4 Aug. 1933.

[135] BT 11/216, E. Millington Drake (Chargé d'Affaires) to Foreign Office 11 Aug. 1933.

[136] Ibid., note by R. M. Nowell on Present Situation of Tariff Negotiations with Argentina, 15 Aug. 1933.   [137] Ibid., undated memorandum, probably 27 or 28 Aug. 1933.

conventionalisation of existing duties on 1931 trade of 44·5 million gold pesos; all of this was granted apart from the relatively unimportant item of tyres.

Three courses of action were considered: (1) to denounce the Convention of 1 May; (2) to press for more substantial concessions, threatening serious damage to River Plate exports; and (3) to accept the present offers subject to some minor adjustments. The factors governing the decision are revealing. The first course was ruled out partly because the exchange agreement was providing major benefits to both financial interests and exporters. But there were other considerations: because denunciation, if it was to hurt Argentina, would involve punitive action against chilled beef exports, it was likely to penalise the substantial British interests in the meat packing trade as well as raising prices to British consumers. The second alternative was also ruled out. Congress was soon to rise, so delay was likely to mean that the duty reductions would be postponed until the summer of 1934. Moreover, undue pressure jeopardised the chances of the agreement being passed by Congress, and the good will of the government might also be forfeited. Therefore the decision to accept the Argentine offer, subject to a few adjustments, was made.

The exchange agreement, concluded in May, was of considerable benefit to the UK. All the exchange earned in Britain was to be allocated to it minus a sum fixed at £3 million maximum which was set aside for public debt payments to third countries.[138] Arrangements were also made for the gradual unfreezing of the blocked peso balances: some balances were to be paid in 1933, the rest through the issue of sterling bonds paying interest at 4 per cent, repayable within twenty years.[139] Coal was to be admitted duty free, and the Argentine government undertook to maintain the existing position of UK coal and coke in the Republic.[140] In addition there was a 'benevolent treatment' clause whereby the government pledged to protect the interests of British companies operating in Argentina. A tangible example of this were the euphemistically named 'traffic co-ordination' laws in Buenos Aires which assisted the Anglo-Argentine tramways in competition with the Argentine-owned motor buses.[141] The tariff agreement does appear to have got near to the pledge to return to 1930 basic

---

[138] BT 11/194, Declaration by the Plenipotentiaries of the Argentine Government on Exchange Allocation. (This was a confidential statement.)

[139] BT 11/596, United Kingdom–Argentine Commercial Negotiations, 3 Mar. 1936, lists the order of priority in the allocation of exchange: (a) Service of Argentine public debts held in the UK. (b) Payment of goods imported into the Argentine from the UK. (c) Payment of freights, insurance commissions etc. (d) Debenture interest and rents. (e) Private remittance by British subjects. (f) Dividends on preferred and ordinary stocks.

[140] Ibid., In a separate and confidential document the existing position was defined as 89·2 per cent of total imports of coal and 68·6 per cent of coke.

[141] Gravil and Rooth, 'Argentina in the 1930s', 365.

rates of duty. The problems lay in the determination of the Argentines to hold on to the 10 per cent surcharge. British export interests had emphasised the importance of securing the removal of this tax. While officials at the Foreign Office were pleased with the results of the tariff negotiations,[142] feeling among the British negotiating team and in the Buenos Aires Embassy was much less sanguine, and in this reflected the disappointment of local British opinion.[143] In textiles, failing the removal of the 10 per cent surcharge, the 'immediate practical value of textile concessions appears to have been little more than nominal'.[144] Representatives of the British Chamber of Commerce in Buenos Aires were 'unanimously agreed that without removal of ten per cent surcharge reductions proposed will be of no particular benefit to United Kingdom trade'.[145] Only when the surcharge was removed did local British opinion feel that UK industry would obtain a distinct competitive advantage. British officials hazarded a calculation that trade might benefit by £1 million to £3 million. Perhaps the best part of the tariff concessions was 'the undoubted value in guarantee they provide against further development of national industries'.[146]

The trade agreements before parliament

The trade agreements were not embodied into legislation without difficulty. Free trade sentiment in an overwhelmingly protectionist House of Commons made little impact, although given able expression by Sir Archibald Sinclair. Dismissing the pacts as 'insignificant and trivial agreements', he went on to expose the contradictory motivation behind the Import Duties Act: he argued that the objectives of protection, imperial integration, revenue raising and tariff bargaining were essentially incompatible.[147]

Opposition to the trade agreements did reflect some of the multiplicity of purpose that inspired the protectionist movement. More embarrassing to the government than the hostility of free traders was the criticism that not enough had been achieved. Not all Lancashire opinion agreed with *The Manchester Guardian Commercial* that in the trade pact with Denmark 'the British negotiators have used their bargaining weapons with devastating

[142] FO 371/16534, various minutes.
[143] See P. B. Goodwin Jr., 'Anglo-Argentine commercial relations: a private sector view, 1922–43,' *Hispanic American Historical Review*, 61 (1981), 29–51.
[144] BT 11/216, Millington-Drake to Foreign Office, 26 Aug. 1933. The major disappointment for the British side, apart from the weak Argentine commitment on the surcharge, was the failure to secure better terms on wool textiles and cars. Early, 'Roca-Runciman treaty', 200.   [145] BT 11/216, Millington-Drake to Foreign Office, 26 Aug. 1933.
[146] *Ibid.*   [147] *Hansard* (Commons), vol. 277, no. 83, 10 May 1933, cols. 1563–4.

effect in the first agreement concluded since the Imperial Conference'.[148] The Cotton Spinners' and Manufacturers' Association attacked the treaty because not only had the government allegedly failed to consult the industry, but, unlike the coal and iron and steel industries, no purchasing arrangements had been made for textiles.[149] Local MPs were mobilised in support of the industry, but Whitehall defused criticism by producing evidence of the full consultations they had conducted with the Manchester Chamber of Commerce, and by pointing to the very different circumstances in which the textile import trade operated in Denmark.[150] The criticism nonetheless appears to have stung Whitehall, and may explain the great emphasis in subsequent negotiations, both with Argentina in the summer of 1933 and with Northern Europe later, in securing concessions for textile exports.

The Argentine agreement was particularly open to attack. It was easy to portray it as a rentier's charter, and it was presented as such not just by the Labour opposition but by the *Daily Express*. The Beaverbrook paper stated that men were being put out of work on the farms of Britain in order to benefit City financiers. Investment holders should be prepared to risk their money; nor, if they lost it, would this be altogether undesirable, for it might force their sons and daughters out of their Mayfair idleness and there 'is much to be said for putting the West-End to work'.[151] Labour Party opposition derided the absurdity of deliberately forcing up import prices by import controls; C. R. Attlee argued that this was an attempt to cut real wages, chosen as an alternative to the more difficult method of actually reducing money wages.[152]

The greatest threat to the government came from those who opposed the trade agreements because they eroded protection and undermined imperial integration. The Germany treaty stimulated protests from the National Union of Manufacturers and from individual industries such as the Birmingham Jewellers' and Silversmiths' Association.[153] When the agreement first came before the House of Commons on 1 May there was strong

---

[148] *Manchester Guardian Commercial Industrial and Financial Review*, 29 Apr. 1933.
[149] *Manchester Guardian*, 3 May 1933.
[150] *Ibid.*, and *Hansard* (Commons), vol. 277, no. 83, 10 May 1933, cols. 1579–80, 1640–2, speeches by J. P. Morris and Sir J. Nall. Both MPs stated they were satisfied that the textile industry had had plenty of opportunities to express its viewpoint to the Board of Trade. The reasons advanced by Whitehall for not attempting purchasing agreements were that unlike coal the cotton industry had done quite well in the Danish market and, moreover, that buying arrangements for textiles in Denmark, because of the absence of major purchasing by government cooperative organisations, were not conducive to agreements of the type made for other industries.
[151] *Daily Express*, 8 May 1933.
[152] *Hansard* (Commons), vol. 277, no. 83, 10 May 1933, col. 1657.
[153] *Manchester Guardian*, 1, 5 May 1933.

opposition. According to Leo Amery, 'Runciman introduced his proposals in a short and very hoity-toity speech', and at the end of the debate 'made no real attempt to justify his figures but confined himself to saying he was a good negotiator and that if we thought otherwise he would resign'.[154] The *Manchester Guardian* reported that although the government won the vote, 'it has been the most uncomfortable day they have spent since they came into office (and) from the moment when the attack on the agreement opened with the speech of Sir Austen Chamberlain right to the end, the House was stirred and Ministers flustered'.[155] Eventually fifty-five Conservatives voted against the government on the resolution to approve the Anglo-German trade agreement.

The *Daily Express* castigated the treaties with Germany, Denmark and Argentina as the 'Three Black Pacts', but reserved its venom for the latter two agreements. It contrived to state that the benefits conferred on Britain by these pacts were 'utterly inadequate or completely illusory', while those conferred on Denmark and Argentina were 'colossal and explicit'.[156] The burden of complaint was fastened on the loss of protection: not only had a growing sector of British industry been sacrificed, but Runciman had 'handed over British agriculture in bondage to the foreigner for three years'. Amery, too, was worried about the lack of protection. Industry needed certainly, and agriculture had not been sufficiently considered. But his greatest concern was the derogation from the Ottawa spirit. While the letter of the imperial agreements remained undisturbed, 'the whole spirit of Ottawa Agreements is...contradicted by the conclusion, and even by the language of these agreements'.[157]

Opposition to the trade agreements was too fragmented to be effective. It was polarised between free traders, a relatively ineffectual force, and the 'die-hard' protectionists, occasionally supplemented by a few representatives of adversely affected interests. Sir Austen Chamberlain led the opposition to the German treaty, and seven out of twelve Birmingham MPs voted against it. But Chamberlain did not vote against the Argentine and Danish treaties. The government won the vote with ease.

[154] J. Barnes and D. Nicholson (eds.) *The Empire at Bay: The Leo Amery Diaries 1929–1945*, 1 May 1933.   [155] *Manchester Guardian*, 2 May 1933.
[156] *Daily Express*, 11 May 1933.
[157] *Hansard* (Commons), vol. 277, no. 83, 10 May 1933, col. 1586.

6   The World Economic Conference, Finland and Japanese competition

By the summer of 1933 the main lines of British commercial policy had been established. The bedrock was the Import Duties Act of March 1932. Within two months of its passage the standard tariff on imports of manufactures had been raised to 20 per cent, and the Import Duties Advisory Committee subsequently recommended additional duties. An inevitable concomitant of protection had been imperial preference, granted to the self-governing dominions on a temporary basis in March 1932 but confirmed and enlarged at Ottawa later that summer. The imperial agreements had still reserved plenty of bargaining power for negotiating other agreements, and by April 1933 the most important of these had either been signed or were well on the way to being completed.

The basic framework of protection and overseas commercial policy was therefore in place by 1933. This still left other issues to be decided, notably agricultural policy, and it still left other treaties to be negotiated, but the point is that they had to be accommodated within the framework already constructed. While the World Economic and Monetary Conference held in London during the summer of 1933 might have provided an opportunity for reviewing policy, perhaps leading to greater emphasis on multi-lateralism, there is no evidence that it induced any change in the main thrust of British policy. Although Ministers in London appeared convinced that world recovery demanded a rise in price levels, and some time was spent in discussing schemes of monetary reform that might have en-couraged mild inflation, there must be a suspicion that Whitehall's interest in this was stimulated by the need to divert attention from international pressure on London to stabilise sterling. From March 1933 attention switched to the dollar: there was genuine anxiety that the depreciation of the dollar might spark a European financial crisis, but in Whitehall it was tinged also by concern about the competitive edge the United States was gaining by devaluation. Although commercial policy featured at the conference, it was subsidiary to and indeed contingent upon currency stabilisation, the issue that dominated proceedings. Britain joined in a weak tariff truce, but otherwise treated the conference as a forum for self-justificatory pronouncements on the virtues of the British route to trade liberalisation.

The breakdown of the conference and of the tariff truce left Britain confirmed in the path of bilateral negotiations. Even during the conference Britain and Finland had been involved in trade discussions, and there had been debate in Whitehall about the next phase of negotiations. The continuing agricultural crisis led the Ministry of Agriculture to press for the formulation of a comprehensive policy of support for farmers. The further tightening of protection manifested itself in abortive discussions with Japan about limiting competition: after these talks failed, Britain unilaterally imposed quotas on Japanese supplies to colonial markets.

World Economic Conference

Officials involved in preparing the World Economic Conference were free of any false optimism about its chances of success. In December 1932 Sir Warren Fisher, Permanent Secretary to the Treasury, commenting on a colleague's pessimistic assessment of the prospects for the conference, referred to it as that 'precursor of Utopia'.[1] A few days later Leith-Ross drew parallels with the failure of an earlier conference at Genoa, disputing the view that this was a result of inadequate preparation, and emphasising instead that failure stemmed from 'the radical differences in policy of the principal countries concerned'.[2]

Doubts were not confined to British officials. The previous month the Preparatory Committee for the conference had postponed its work in Geneva, partly because of the American presidential election but also because their meetings had revealed profound differences of opinion.[3] Months later, in very different circumstances, the American State Department official Herbert Feis, an enthusiastic internationalist, drew a deep breath before unsuccessfully proposing to President Roosevelt and Prime Minister MacDonald that the conference be postponed.[4]

The objectives and analysis of the British and American governments were fundamentally similar – both regarded an increase in world prices as essential for economic recovery. The gold bloc countries, several with the great inflations of the early 1920s fresh in their collective memories, were sceptical; while they paid lip service to the idea, their methods of achieving it, through the restoration of business confidence in the wake of

[1] T 172/1814, Sir Warren Fisher, 12 Dec 1932.
[2] *Ibid.*, Sir Frederick Leith-Ross, 20 Dec 1932.
[3] CAB 58/183, Committee on International Economic Policy, Report on the Work of the Preparatory Committee for the World Economic Conference, Leith-Ross and Sir Frederick Phillips, 10 Nov 1932.
[4] Herbert Feis, *1933: Characters in Crisis* Boston, (1966), 143.

a return to the international gold standard, were extremely nebulous, and the main thrust of their policies was directed towards the stabilisation of currencies.

While the gold bloc countries were at least consistent in their position, the UK and the USA were never able to act in concert. Similarities of interpretation were obscured by tension over war debts, and, even more importantly, by a sharp switch in their respective stances towards currency stabilisation. In the early stages of preparation for the conference the American government tended to argue for stabilisation of currencies as a prerequisite to international accord, placing itself in alliance with the gold bloc and leaving the UK isolated in its refusal to countenance fixing a value for sterling. By the time the conference was held in the summer of 1933 the positions had been reversed and it was the Americans who were isolated: Britain had now joined forces with the gold bloc in pressuring the Americans to fix a value for the dollar. Roosevelt's refusal to do so scuppered whatever slender chances the conference had of achieving useful results.

The underlying purpose of the WEC has been traced back by Ian Drummond to a desire on the part of the Americans and the British governments to raise world commodity prices through joint action on monetary expansion.[5] The most proximate origins can be found in a League of Nations Conference held in Lausanne in July 1932. Because it was a League Conference, and because war debts and reparations featured prominently on the agenda, the United States had not been present. Aware of impending Anglo-American discussions on world commodity prices, and of the restricted nature of their agenda, the Lausanne delegates agreed that the League should convene a World Economic and Financial Conference and that the United States should be asked to attend.

Why were prices so important, and what was thought to have caused their spectacular decline? In the domestic economy, it was argued, the tendency for prices to fall faster than money wages had increased the level of real wages, encouraged firms to shed labour, and, by reducing profits, to cut investment. At an international level the collapse of primary product prices was one of the most striking characteristics of the depression. The deflationary process crippled purchasing power, dangerously impaired the ability of borrowers to maintain debt servicing and, because of balance of payments problems, encouraged the paraphernalia of exchange controls and quotas that were paralysing international trade. Uncertainty and lack

---

[5] I. M. Drummond, *The Floating Pound and the Sterling Area, 1931–1939* (Cambridge, 1981), 120–7. See also Kenneth Mouré, *Managing the Franc Poincaré: economic understanding and political constraint in French monetary policy, 1928–1936* (Cambridge, 1991), ch. 3.

of confidence had led to a virtual cessation of capital exports. Drummond has termed such an analysis 'Strakochism' after Sir Henry Strackosch, financier, Chairman of *The Economist* and indefatigable conference delegate. Certainly he was an able and energetic advocate of the absolute necessity for a rise in world price levels. He had been an influential member of the League of Nations Gold Delegation, and a key figure in the production of a minority report. Such a viewpoint gained greater authority through its support from the Swedish economist Gustav Cassel, one of the most influential economists of his generation. A member of the Gold Delegation, he paid tribute to the work of Strackosch and was unable to sign the minority report only because he was away lecturing in Oxford at the time of its preparation. His lectures, 'The Crisis in the World's Monetary System', analysed the causes of the problem.[6]

Cassel argued that the collapse of commodity prices was not a result of general over-supply, but was monetary in origin. The basic problem was the breakdown in the gold standard, the blame for which could be placed squarely on French and American policies. War debts and reparation payments had enabled France and the USA to run balance of payments surpluses, a process exacerbated by the protectionist policies pursued by both countries. While US lending up to 1928 had disguised potential liquidity problems, the subsequent cessation of this overseas investment accelerated the accumulation of gold by America between 1929 and 1931. If the gold standard mechanism had been allowed to operate normally, adjustment would have been secured by an expansion of the money supply in surplus countries, and the consequent rise in their prices. Instead, Cassel argued, the monetary authorities in both France and the USA had sterilised the new gold supplies, burying much of the gold in Central Bank vaults: 'The payment of war debts in conjunction with the unwillingness to receive payment in the normal form of goods led to unreasonable demands on the world's monetary stocks; and the claimants failed to use in a proper way the gold they had accumulated.'[7] Gold-losing countries were forced into deflationary policies, and the result of this was severe pressure on commodity prices, 'increased competition in world markets, and in consequence a world-wide price fall of unparalleled dimensions'.

This accorded with views in Whitehall, although not all accepted such an extreme emphasis on monetary factors alone. The centrality given to war debts made it less welcome to American ears, and it conflicted with the accepted wisdom of the gold bloc countries. In the view of the latter countries the worst obstacles to trade dated from Britain's departure from the gold standard in September 1931. Excessive tariff barriers, quota

---

[6] G. Cassel, *The Crisis in the World's Monetary System* (2nd edn Oxford, 1932).
[7] *Ibid.*, 64.

systems, exchange controls and clearing arrangements came in the wake of British devaluation, and were in large measure the direct consequences of a fluctuating sterling exchange.[8] Sporadic support from the Japanese representative apart, the British delegates were on their own. Yes, they agreed, some international standard was probably desirable and the gold system was probably the only one that held any chance of universal acceptance. But it was out of the question for Britain to return to it without fundamental changes in world monetary arrangements. In December Leith-Ross spelled out what these were: (a) the settlement of war debts; (b) agreement that the monetary policy of the Central Banks of the USA and France could and would be used to secure an increase in the price level; (c) lower tariffs, especially in France and the USA, and the abandonment of most quotas; (d) 'an agreement for the effective redistribution of gold and/or credits so as to enable the various "Still-stands" and exchange controls to be abandoned'.[9]

This last point referred to some schemes being considered by the UK government. If recovery from the depression was seen as being hampered by the world distribution of gold and by credit stringency among primary producers, their imaginative proposals, anticipating Clearing Union plans a decade later and some of the features of the Special Drawing Rights of the 1960s, might have gone a long way to secure it. Henderson and Keynes produced plans, and the British Treasury came up with the 'Kisch plan' (named after Sir Cecil Kisch, financial expert and a senior official at the India Office), which proposed that funds from surplus countries would be channelled through an International Credit Corporation to deficit countries at very low rates of interest. Borrowers would be expected to stabilise their exchanges, remove exchange controls and liberalise their trade.[10]

The Kisch plan held several attractions for the British government. By December London was still adamant in its refusal even to contemplate fixing a rate for the pound. The gold bloc view was that stabilisation would be followed by a rise in prices, although it was by no means clear how this would happen. In the opinion of the Treasury, however, reform of world monetary arrangements had to precede stabilising the pound, let alone returning to a gold standard. The Treasury was very sceptical of the willingness of France to pursue expansionary credit policies. Sir Frederick Phillips quoted the Bank of France Report for 1931 which in order to accomplish 'the austere and necessary task' of adapting the rhythm of production to diminished purchasing power, urged the necessity of further

---

[8] CAB 58/183.
[9] T 172/1814, Leith-Ross, Prospects of the Economic Conference, 20 Dec. 1932.
[10] See S. Howson and D. Winch, *The Economic Advisory Council 1930–1939* (Cambridge, 1977), 114–21.

monetary contraction. The Bank of France, Phillips argued, would 'go on obstructing to the end of the chapter'.[11]

To avoid a stalemate on the issue of stabilisation, it was necessary to encourage delegates to work on another range of ideas. The Kisch plan 'would get people's minds off the controversy of gold versus non-gold and direct them to the real point that debtor countries must be helped or they cannot continue to trade and that the help must come out of the clot of gold in Paris and New York'.[12]

The scheme was also a useful counter to the American view that what the debtors needed was an international scheme for scaling down debts. While London was all for scaling down war debts, it was unhappy at governments taking a hand in the reduction of excessive commercial debts, a job it thought best kept to the creditors and debtors concerned. War debts remained as a major source of friction between Paris and London on the one hand and Washington on the other. A pronounced sense of grievance, even of injustice, permeated British and French attitudes to the debts, but hostility to them was further stoked by the pressure they placed on the budget and the balance of payments (they absorbed 12 per cent of Britain's 1932 export earnings), and an awareness of their contribution to the breakdown of the world monetary system. Moreover, the cessation of German reparation payments presaged by the Lausanne Conference in 1932 gave an even greater incentive to eliminate the war debts.[13] But there was a danger that Washington might offer a deal on war debts if London would agree to stabilise the pound. Indeed, American officials, underestimating the strength of Britain's opposition to fixed exchange rates, do seem to have seen this as part of a package. Keenly aware of the tactical risks, the Treasury wanted to settle the war debts question ahead of the conference.[14]

While war debts were a running sore in Anglo-American relations, they were not to blame for the inability of London and Washington to act together in securing a rise in world prices. Failure was a consequence of the primacy given to currency stabilisation, a view shared by the gold standard countries of Europe, and to the belief that this was a prerequisite to a broader understanding.

US devaluation

The total configuration of the conference and of national alignments was transformed by the American decision to leave the gold standard and let

---

[11] T 172/1814, Phillips, 10 Dec. 1932.   [12] CAB 58/183, Leith-Ross and Phillips.
[13] Stephen V. O. Clarke, *The Reconstruction of the International Monetary System: the attempts of 1922 and 1933*. Princeton Studies in International Finance, no. 33 (Princeton 1973), 23.   [14] T 172/1814, Leith-Ross, 20 Dec. 1932.

the dollar depreciate. This was announced in April 1933 while the British delegation, headed by Ramsay MacDonald, was travelling on the *SS Berengaria* to New York. Although the Prime Minister rejected the advice of Leith-Ross to return home on the next available ship, there is no mistaking the anger felt by the British government. An appreciation of the new situation by Hopkins and Phillips was wired to the Prime Minister. They stressed the almost gratuitous nature of America's departure from the gold standard, 'when invulnerable to outside action and when still possessing favourable trade balance'. It was totally unlike Britain's enforced departure from gold in 1931, and it was the first time in history, they asserted, when a currency had been allowed to go under in circumstances when it could easily have been held; 'on top of its high tariffs, sudden withdrawal of creditors from Europe and demands for war debts, America now throws a new source of confusion into the world'.[15]

There was a line of consistency in Roosevelt's decision to leave the gold standard and allow the dollar to depreciate. The administration was under strong pressure to raise prices. Farmers, the silver lobby, forcefully led by Key Pittman, Senator from Nevada and Chairman of the Senate Foreign Relations Committee, academic economists as reputable as Irving Fisher, and influential sections of the business community, including bankers, who had formed the Committee for the Nation to Rebuild Prices and Purchasing Power, all campaigned for higher prices. But as Freidel emphasises in his careful analysis, none of the pressure for inflationary policies conflicted with the predilections of Roosevelt himself.[16] True, he might quibble about the means, showing little enthusiasm for the restorative properties of silver revaluation, but he was convinced of the need for price rises. The objective of mild inflation also influenced the welter of otherwise often contradictory policies that comprised the New Deal, lending it at least one element of consistency. This was reflected in a joint statement made by MacDonald and Roosevelt at the end of their talks in April: 'the necessity for an increase in the general level of commodity prices was recognised as primary and fundamental'.[17] This was one factor in Roosevelt's decision. It was given urgency because the administration became anxious that gold losses in March and April 1933 would lead to a tightening of domestic credit conditions, reinforcing what

[15] FO 371/16604, Sir Richard Hopkins and Phillips to Prime Minister, 19 Apr. 1933.
[16] F. Freidel, *Franklin D Roosevelt: launching the New Deal*, (Boston, 1973), esp. ch. 19. The following three paragraphs draw heavily on this source together with C. P. Kindleberger, *The World in Depression, 1929–1939* (1973), Feis, *1933*; A. M. Schlesinger Jnr, *The Age of Roosevelt* (Boston, 1959), and L. C. Gardner, *Economic Aspects of New Deal Diplomacy* (Madison, 1964).
[17] CAB 29/142, Joint statement by the Prime Minister and President Roosevelt, 26 April 1933.

they feared might be the deflationary consequences of federal government measures aimed at cutting the budget deficit. Paradoxically, leaving gold also allowed Roosevelt to head off pressure from Congress for more extreme inflationary measures. There was an international strand too. James Warburg, the 'shimmering bright' young banker who advised Roosevelt,[18] thought the dollar was too high, and that because of the strength of the balance of payments administrative action was needed to draw it down and thereby to restore American competitiveness. On 15 March Warburg had advocated the establishment of a stabilisation fund, modelled on the British Exchange Equalisation Account, which by buying and selling dollars could be used to force the dollar down. It would, moreover, give the Americans greater bargaining leverage on negotiations with Britain. The banker used the imagery of the west:

Irrespective of whether we ever use the fund, it is a very much healthier way for us to sit down at the table with the British if we have a gun on our hip so long as we know that they are coming with a gun on their hip. It is very much easier to suggest that we both unbuckle our belts and lay the guns on the table than for us to make the suggestion to the British if they know and we know that we have no gun.[19]

Letting the dollar depreciate therefore held out the hope of removing the threat of deflation posed by gold outflows, freeing the administration from international constraints on the New Deal programme, restoring America's diminished competitiveness on world markets and, while helping to reverse price movements, appeasing Congress and meeting Roosevelt's own objectives of moderate inflation.

Conference preparations

As the conference, scheduled to open in London on 12 June, drew nearer, its shape became clearer.

Ambitious British schemes for reshaping the international economy on the lines of the Henderson–Keynes or the Kisch plans had been removed from the agenda. Variation on the schemes in the shape of a Treasury memorandum had been discussed in Washington in mid-April, but when Feis raised doubts, Bewley, the British financial attaché, had not even left a copy of the memorandum he had brought with him.[20] On 18 May it was decided in London not to put forward the Henderson–Keynes plan, although the Kisch proposals might be raised by the delegation. Since the schemes depended on tapping the gold stocks of the French and Americans, it had no chance of acceptance without their approval. But it is worth

---

[18] Feis, *1933*, 152.   [19] Freidel, *Roosevelt*, 327.
[20] Kindleberger, *World in Depression*, 208–9.

recalling that UK enthusiasm for the proposals had been fanned by the need to divert attention from sterling, and by the pressure Britain had been under from the Americans and the gold bloc countries to stabilise the pound. With the devalued dollar now threatening to underbid sterling, London rediscovered an interest in discussing stabilisation – the stabilisation of the dollar.

This became the central issue of the conference. As Feis has suggested about the early emphasis on fixing a value for the pound, '[t]his was the start of a slide into a strategy for the conference which caused all the other measures which had figured in the original correspondence to pivot around a stabilisation accord. It was not foreseen that the demand for stabilisation would concentrate upon the dollar.'[21] When MacDonald met Roosevelt in April he was convinced of the American desire to fix a rate for the dollar. Warburg suggested a stabilisation fund to which Britain and France would contribute. The French, however, regarded stabilisation as essentially a matter for Britain and the United States, while Britain worried about the extent of the devaluation the Americans were aiming to achieve. As American ideas on this evolved, and as the dollar continued its slide, British and French anxieties grew. It was agreed that talks about currencies would be held in London, although they would be fenced off from the official conference, and would take place between American, British and French government officials and central bankers. The key role of these to the conference lies partly in the weight given to currency stabilisation during the preparatory talks, but also because other moves depended on resolution of the issue. Until this was settled it was virtually impossible to get any agreement on tariffs.

Tariffs interested the State Department, and particularly Secretary of State Cordell Hull who had an almost obsessive concern with trade liberalisation, which he saw as an integral part of harmonious relations between nations. Charles Kindleberger states that Hull had only one formula: 'stop raising tariffs and start lowering them. It was hard to see the mechanism by which this could lead to recovery.'[22] For the most part because everyone became weary of Hull's lengthy, rambling sermons, Feis handled the negotiations for the Americans as often as possible.[23]

By March 1933 British commercial policy was well defined, although it had changed little since the early preparations for the conference in October.[24] The crucial question centred on whether to retain the most

[21] Feis, *1933*, 115.   [22] Kindleberger, *World in Depression*, 201.
[23] Freidel, *Roosevelt*, 384.
[24] CAB 29/142, Board of Trade memorandum, 19 October 1932 and *ibid*. M.E. (B)5, Policy of United Kingdom on Main Questions Raised on Agenda: Trade Restrictions and Tariff Policy, 18 May 1933.

favoured nation (mfn) clause and whether to use clearing arrangements as a normal instrument of policy. As discussed in a previous chapter (ch. 4), there was strong domestic pressure to abandon multilateralism so as to secure maximum bargaining leverage; clearing agreements were another manifestation of the same objectives. The rejection of these arguments appears to have had no relation to the World Economic Conference or any external pressure. Preparatory British documents for the conference show little fresh thought in Whitehall, merely a justification for continuing with existing policies. London was strongly in favour of tariff liberalisation provided it was done by other countries. As a late starter in the tariff game, British protection was comparatively mild. Hull's proposals for multi-lateralism were looked upon sceptically in Whitehall. It was argued these would tend to involve moderate tariff countries in making disproportionate concessions, would on past experience be difficult to achieve and were shot through with technical difficulties over *ad valorem* equivalents for specific duties and the definition of 'revenue' tariffs. The most promising route to liberalisation lay through bilateral agreements precisely of the type Britain was making with the Scandinavians and Germany. These were defined as meeting Britain's requirements of securing the widest and most un-conditional interpretation of the mfn clause. In consequence, London looked upon regional or group agreements for exclusive tariffs with a jaundiced eye, permissible only in 'quite exceptional circumstances'. Although Washington expressed its anger at the Ottawa agreements on several occasions, protests were dismissed with the argument that the treaties were 'a domestic affair between the British nations'.[25] As Leith-Ross predicted, however, this question was to be raised again when bilateral negotiations were opened with the United States later in the decade. Quotas and similar restrictions were jointly condemned by the UK and the USA, although they feared that France, with quotas on more than a thousand articles, would be opposed to their abolition, especially without exchange rate stabilisation. But London's opposition was qualified: for was not Britain in the process of erecting virtually identical barriers to agricultural imports such as bacon and meat? A distinction had therefore to be made between quotas on agricultural products and those on raw materials and industrial goods, justified by the argument that the structure of farming, with numerous producers, meant that price falls often stimulated output rather than discouraged it.

Hull's suggestion of a tariff truce was pursued, however, although in Whitehall this was done with a martyred air. The French were doubtful,

---

[25] CAB 29/142, Leith-Ross, Discussions at Washington on the Programme of the World Conference, 12 May 1933.

arguing with some substance that pledges given on fixing existing tariff levels could be entirely nullified by currency movements. Stabilisation of the dollar was therefore a prerequisite to any agreement on relaxing tariffs and quotas. Nonetheless tariff truces were placed on the agenda, although in the event the schemes became so hedged about with reservations and qualifications as to be virtually worthless. A resolution was adopted by the Organising Committee of the Conference on 12 May by which governments pledged themselves not to introduce 'any new initiatives which might increase the many varieties of difficulties now arresting international commerce'.[26] It also envisaged a tariff truce to be arranged for the duration of the conference. Whitehall insisted that bacon quota schemes, already in the process of being implemented, should be exempted, as should applications for duty increases made to the IDAC by 12 May. On the same day the United States Agricultural Adjustment Act became law, legislation that allowed the administration to impose compensatory taxes on imports of commodities subject to processing taxes.[27] The French and Germans also made reservations which severely limited the value of the tariff truce.

The conference

The conference duly opened on 12 June. It soon settled into a process of waiting for the Americans to agree on stabilising the dollar. The official committees of the conference became dependent on the outcome of the tripartite negotiations on exchange rate stabilisation, talks lying outside the official framework of the conference and themselves ultimately reliant, as it transpired, on decisions made in Washington, or, more accurately, wherever President Roosevelt's sailing holiday took him.

The American delegation was a divided delegation without full authority and having to negotiate against a background of unsettled United States policy. Liaison between the official delegates and the finance group, the latter reporting direct to Washington and not to the Secretary of State, was poor. Hull, interested in tariff reductions and little else, was not close to Roosevelt, and alleged to MacDonald that there was no one in the delegation he could trust.[28] It included Senator Pittman, whose escapades were to provide good material for the gossip columns, Cox, an ex-presidential candidate and very able, and others there largely because of political favours or their position: 'a motley group' concluded Feis, one of the advisers, as he read the roster.[29]

[26] CAB 29/142, M.E. (B)5.
[27] R. M. Kottman, *Reciprocity and the North Atlantic Triangle, 1932–1938* (Ithaca, 1968), 54–6.   [28] CAB 29/142 Pt. 2, Meeting between PM and Hull, 19 June 1933.
[29] Feis, *1933*, 174.

Divisions in the delegation soon became public. With Hull's assent, Feis submitted to the conference secretariat a number of proposals for discussion in the field of international trade, including a suggestion of a 10 per cent cut in tariff rates. When published in the press on 17 June, Pittman issued a statement denying that the American delegation was sponsoring any such action. Hull, in turn, had to produce an explanation emphasising that it was a topic for discussion, not a statement of United States policy. Pittman appears to have taken the proposal unusually hard, and Feis records an episode when shortly after these events the senator drunkenly pursued him along the corridors of Claridges wielding a hunting knife.[30]

Tariff matters, as emphasised above, were of secondary importance: once the Americans had dropped off the gold standard the stabilisation of the dollar dominated proceedings. It assumed even greater importance because of the rapid fall of the dollar, which in itself worried the British, but also threatened a financial crisis in Europe as gold flowed out of the smaller European gold bloc countries.[31] American stabilisation was seen as essential if currency chaos in Europe was to be averted. In fact the Treasury and banking representatives had devised a scheme, based around a middle rate of $4 to the pound and to be backed by gold of up to 3 million ounces from each of the three central banks.[32] Agreed on 15 June, rumours of the scheme leaked, causing the dollar to rise and stocks and commodity prices to fall sharply. It appeared therefore to threaten the very objectives that Roosevelt was seeking, and it stirred up the inflationists again. As General Hugh Johnson, head of the newly formed National Recovery Administration, told Raymond Moley, 'an agreement to stabilise now on the lines your boy friends in London are suggesting would bust to hell and gone the prices we're sweating to raise'.[33]

Roosevelt refused to agree the proposals, instead sending Moley, who had the reputation of an economic nationalist, to London to see if he could work out a deal more to the liking of the President. While Moley took ship across the Atlantic the conference stalled. He arrived on 27 June as anxiety about the sustainability of the gold standard was reaching a new pitch. To calm speculation, an innocuous statement was drafted and despatched to Roosevelt for approval. Although it committed the signatories to virtually nothing, not even a temporary stabilisation, and it spoke of co-operation to calm speculation, it appears to have been misunderstood by the President as limiting his freedom of action. He elaborated his reasons in the infamous 'bombshell' message of 3 July which emphatically rejected any

[30] *Ibid.*, 188–9.
[31] CAB 29/142 Pt. 2, Meeting between UK and US delegations, 27 June 1933.
[32] Drummond, *Floating Pound*, 164.
[33] Quoted in Schlesinger, *The Age of Roosevelt*, 207.

thought of stabilisation, and in the process referred to the 'old fetishes of so-called international bankers'. It was, said Chamberlain, 'couched in language which could not fail to give deep offence to almost every other Delegation at the Conference. Its tone was arrogant and it lectured the Conference in a manner and circumstances which were hardly believable'.[34] It effectively killed the conference, although as *The Economist* remarked, it took 'an unconsciable time to die.'[35] It was kept going, more for psychological than for practical reasons, until it adjourned on 27 July. It did not reconvene.

Conclusion

The proximate causes of failure lay in the United States and in Roosevelt's refusal to contemplate anything that smacked of stabilisation. The price jitters of mid-June when rumours of a London agreement on exchange rates hit New York had probably helped confirm Roosevelt in his determination to avoid obligations to fix the dollar. The domestic programme had to be given priority. In March and April internationalism had been nearer the foreground, but in the next two months there was a swing towards isolationism, a trend that was widely recognised. It was referred to several times in the London press. Hull emphasised to MacDonald the isolationist shift in the United States, and a State Department friend warned Feis 'You fellows must not expect to find America the same as it was when you left.'[36] These factors were paramount. They were almost certainly encouraged by a sense of European duplicity and a fear of European entanglements. Britain had ruled the Ottawa agreements as out of contention, but had confirmed the main thrust of policy, as Norman Davis reported from London, by signing trade agreements with quotas and preferential clauses, one of the most objectionable of which was being negotiated with Argentina.[37] Behaviour over war debts fuelled American resentments. The French government refused to make its payment on 15 June, and although Britain paid $10 million, this was the equivalent of only 13 per cent of the amount due, and was paid in silver obtained cheaply from India. Feis records:

it is probable that the default washed away the remnants of Roosevelt's tolerance for the French effort to cause us to return to the international gold standard at a fixed rate to the franc, and made him more determined not to let the British

[34] CAB 29/142 pt. 1, Minutes of 19th meeting, 3 July 1933.
[35] *Economist*, 8 July 1933, cited by Feis, 1933, 252.
[36] For example, *The Times*, 13, 15, 29, 30 May 1933, and meeting between PM and Hull, 19 June 1933, CAB 29/142 pt. 2.   [37] Gardner, *Economic Aspects*, 28.

authorities ease him into an agreement about the relative pound–dollar value which might be to Britain's advantage.[38]

There was also a sense that the United States got the worst of deals when negotiating with Europe.[39] Roosevelt felt that although his message may have been rather brusque, it might nonetheless have given a psychological lift at home and have helped dispel the view that at every conference the Americans came out the losers.

The emphasis placed on exchange rate stability was understandable in the light of fears of a European financial crisis in the wake of the devaluation of the dollar and because tariff concessions, even a truce, could quickly be undermined by depreciation of currencies. Yet even if some currency accord had been achieved, it was little guarantee that much else could be accomplished as a result: as the Swedish delegate reminded the conference, trade restrictions were a consequence as much as a cause of the depression, and although exchange rates had been stable prior to September 1931, this had not prevented the erection and extension of trade barriers.[40]

The best hopes of contributing to international recovery had lain in the schemes that had been advanced earlier. The International Labour Organisation had advocated extensive public works schemes, but although the Americans expressed some interest, few other delegates did, and the British Treasury was well rehearsed in arguments against such projects (although it had no objection to schemes elsewhere, especially in France and the gold bloc countries).[41] The British proposals for international credits might have eased foreign exchange shortages and encouraged lending, but stood slender chance of acceptance by the gold standard countries: the inability of the United States and Britain to reach any accord over them guaranteed failure. So the conference was left with a feeble tariff truce to show for its endeavours. Because the conference was technically in recess the life of the truce was extended. It was observed in the breach. Many countries had reserved their positions, allowing additional restrictions, including France and Denmark. Britain raised schedules on fifty items on the grounds that applications had been made before 12 May. By late September the truce was in effect dead, with countries beginning formally to withdraw from it including the Netherlands and Sweden.[42] Whitehall had resisted pressure from the National Union of Manufacturers and other groups to withdraw earlier, but by

---

[38] Feis, *1933*, 182 and Gardner, *Economic Aspects*, 30.
[39] Kindleberger, *World in Depression*, 231.
[40] CAB 29/142 Pt. 1, Meeting of Bureau, 6 July 1933.
[41] For example, memorandum by Phillips on General Smuts's memorandum, 17 July 1933 and 25th meeting, 13 July 1933, CAB 29/142.
[42] Note prepared in the Board of Trade on the Tariff Truce.

November it was accepted that the pact was useless. Runciman's announcement in the House of Commons on 7 November that notice had been given to withdraw in one month was greeted by Tory cheers.[43]

Finland

If confirmation was needed of the total lack of influence that the World Economic Conference exerted on British commercial policy, the negotiations with Finland provided it. Starting on 23 May, the Anglo-Finnish talks continued during the course of the conference and concluded shortly after its adjournment.

From a British viewpoint, Finland was an ideal choice for trade bargaining. Exports were narrowly concentrated on forestry products which accounted for around 85 per cent of Finnish foreign sales. The British market was an important outlet for all the major timber products and also absorbed a high proportion of dairy exports.[44] In 1929, 38 per cent of Finland's exports had been sold in Britain and by 1932 the figure had risen to 47 per cent.[45] As with Denmark and Sweden, the chief supplier of Finnish imports was Germany, and the trade balance was highly unfavourable to Britain. In the late 1920s Britain was importing around £13–14 million from Finland, and selling only £3½–4 million worth of exports. Finland had therefore the classic hallmarks of high trade dependence on Britain and a heavy bilateral surplus. Nor, apart from timber and paper products, was Finland particularly interested in selling manufactured goods, so there was little risk of stirring the opposition of British industry to the agreement.

One potential obstacle to a good treaty was that as much as 85 per cent of Finland's trade with the UK was already covered by the agreements with Norway and Sweden.[46] This was a problem that was to recur in later negotiations. The negotiating tactic was simple, however: Finland must pay for the most-favoured-nation (mfn) privileges it enjoyed by making concessions to Britain – if it was not prepared to make sufficiently attractive offers, the existing treaty would be denounced and Finland would lose its mfn rights in the UK. This was to prove a perfectly effective negotiating stance, both with Finland and with the other countries which stood to lose heavily by exclusion from the British market. A more fundamental problem was the size of the Finnish market. The Scandinavian countries as a whole were small and sparsely populated, but they made up for this with high income levels and remarkably high import propensities.

---

[43] Kottman, *Reciprocity*, 76.
[44] Department of Overseas Trade, *Economic Conditions in Finland in 1935* (1936), 13.
[45] BT 11/200, notes on negotiations with Finland, 24 Jan. 1933. The 1932 figure is for the first 11 months.   [46] *Ibid.*

Table 6.1 *Exports of selected UK produce to Finland, 1929–1932* (£000s)

	1929	1930	1931	1932
Herrings	61	52	8	—
Sugar	79	45	49	265
Meal and flour	481	390	239	258
Coal	332	259	156	265
Cotton-yarns	72	53	53	63
piece goods	214	140	101	89
Machinery	336	189	101	106
Iron and steel	245	188	121	133
Wool tops	89	100	84	171
Wool and worsted yarns	48	31	31	53
tissues	151	123	60	34
Total	3,363	2,414	1,604	2,263

Source: UK *Annual Statement of Trade, 1932.*

Finland, mid-way between a Scandinavian and Baltic state, reflected its geographical position in lower living standards. Only $7\frac{1}{2}$ per cent of the land was cultivated, growing seasons were short, and, apart from the southern and south-western coastal plains, soil fertility was low.[47] Although hydro-electric power and mechanical cutting were in the process of transforming living standards through exploitation of the forests, incomes in the 1930s remained substantially below those of Finland's Scandinavian neighbours.[48] The Finnish population, at 3·6 million, was greater than that of Norway by nearly a million, but total imports were considerably less than half those of Norway.[49]

Table 6.1 above shows the main British exports to Finland. The depression had taken hold as early as 1928 in Finland, but tariff increases had contributed to the decline in imports, and the Finnish tariffs had of course an important bearing on the scope of the negotiations and the shaping of Britain's desiderata.

Even in 1929 Finnish mills had been producing three-quarters or more

[47] Royal Institute of International Affairs, *The Scandinavian States and Finland* (1951), 73 and 116.
[48] In 1929, Finland's gnp per capita (expressed in 1960 $US), has been calculated at $530. The equivalent incomes in Denmark were $945, in Norway $1,033 and in Sweden $897. P. Bairoch, 'Europe's gross national product: 1800–1975', *Journal of European Economic History*, 5 (1976), 297.
[49] Between 1930 and 1932, Finland's imports averaged the equivalent of $38·9 million while Norwegian imports averaged $206·1 million. League of Nations, *Review of World Trade, 1934* (Geneva, 1935), 89.

of the market's cotton requirements,[50] and in 1931 Finland raised almost every duty on textile goods, taking them to levels 85 to 105 per cent above those of 1913.[51] Exports of wool piece goods to Finland had been dropping steadily since 1923, but had been hit also by tariff increases between 1930 and 1932.[52] Tariffs had been raised on a variety of other manufactured goods.[53] In other areas the duties remained modest enough for Britain to request conventionalisation of those on machinery and textile yarns and to feel there was no real point in asking for a reduction in the 14 per cent duty on motor cycles.[54] There was the familiar danger for a country supplying only a small part of the market that tariff reductions would benefit competitors more than itself. Germany's dominance of the import market meant there were few types of manufactured goods where these considerations did not apply. Machinery duties were already low, so the question barely arose there, but even textile requests had to be finely tuned to the particular strengths of the British industry. Any concessions won on footwear duties were likely to work mainly to the advantage of Sweden or Germany which supplied lasts, shapes and fittings better suited to local requirements.[55]

The British desiderata for manufactured goods echoed those for Scandinavia. There was considerable emphasis on tariff manipulation. It was hoped to steal some advantage from the USA by restructuring the duties on cars to suit British vehicles. Tariff reductions on textiles might be concentrated on a new category of wider cloths.[56] There were other instances where customs practices led to disproportionately high duty levels. The Board of Trade wanted cloths to be allowed an admixture of up to 5 per cent silk or artificial silk without duties being increased. Another important request was for an *ad valorem* 'stop' of 20 per cent on woollen cloths – on some of the cheaper cloths the specific duties amounted to as much as 100 per cent.[57]

Although all of this was fairly familiar territory after the negotiations with Scandinavia, there were some distinctive features in the trade discussions with Finland concerning herrings and wheat flour. British flour exports had been badly hit by tariffs,[58] and protection had virtually

---

[50] BT 11/199, memorandum from Manchester Chamber of Commerce for the information of Sir Alan Anderson, Chairman of Mission to Finland, Feb. 1933.
[51] H. Liepmann, *Tariff Levels and the Economic Unity of Europe* (1938), 152.
[52] BT 11/200, notes 24 Jan. 1933.
[53] BT 11/199, Anglo-Finnish Trade Negotiations, meeting, 25 May 1933, and Department of Overseas Trade, *Economic Conditions in Finland in 1931* (1931), 22.
[54] BT 11/200, notes, 24 Jan. 1933.
[55] BT 11/199, notes by the Commercial Secretary at Helsingfors on possible UK requests, nd.
[56] BT 11/200, note by J. J. Wills on explanation of UK textile proposals, 29 Apr. 1933.
[57] *Ibid.*   [58] BT 11/200, note, 24 Jan. 1933.

eliminated the trade in herrings. The Finns were determined to protect the livelihood of fishermen who had been hit by the fall in demand for stromling (a small Baltic herring) and by the ending of prohibition in 1932 which had killed a useful income from smuggling.[59] Britain wanted a specific quota at low duty rates.

It was clear, however, that even if these demands had been met in full, they would contribute little to rectifying the trade gap. At its peak, the herring trade had only been worth around £60,000 a year, and these concessions, together with tariff adjustments and manipulations were unlikely to expand UK trade much, certainly not enough to make major inroads into a £10 million balance of trade deficit. All this was recognised at the Board of Trade early in the preparations for the negotiations: the chief value of the tariff requests, it was argued, would be in checking the growth of protection in Finland.[60] If the trade negotiations were to yield anything of much value, the Finns would have to be persuaded to make purchasing agreements. Coal, yet again, was at the forefront of British requests. As in the rest of northern Europe, British dominance of the coal import trade had been ceded to Poland. In 1924 the UK had supplied 96 per cent of coal imports; by 1931 that share had fallen to $29\frac{1}{2}$ per cent.[61] The Mines Department thought the chances of a favourable agreement were good, partly because the balance of trade argument was so formidable and partly because the main coal consumers, outside the state institutions, were the major export industries of Finland. In 1930 the timber, pulp and paper industries took well over half of the total industrial requirements,[62] and it was these industries which were so dependent on exports to Britain. The problem, however, was the size of the Finnish market. Heavy reliance on wood and water as alternative sources of power and warmth meant that total annual coal imports had never reached as much as a million tons. With prospects for the coal industry muted, other purchasing agreements were sought. Apart from coal, these had not featured in the negotiations with Norway and Sweden, and were playing little part in the Argentine discussions. Only in the case of Denmark had they formed an important aspect of the trade pact. In the next phase of negotiations, purchasing agreements were to take a far more prominent role in the circumvention of the mfn clause and in the expansion of Britain's exports. A list of products thought suitable for purchasing agreements was forwarded to the Finnish government. For the most part it consisted of products such as jute bags,

[59] BT 11/199, Anglo-Finnish Trade Negotiations, meeting, 29 May 1933.
[60] BT 11/200, notes, 24 Jan. 1933.
[61] CAB 24/242 CP 188 (33). Anglo-Finnish Negotiations, memorandum prepared in the Board of Trade, 21 July 1933.
[62] BT 11/200, Tariff Negotiations with Finland. Coal and coke, note by Mines Department, 18 Jan. 1933.

Table 6.2. *Selected imports into UK from Finland, 1928–1932* (£000s)

Commodity	1928	1929	1930	1931	1932
Butter	1,737	1,952	1,597	1,487	1,080
Eggs in shell	2	2	8	28	126
Bacon	—	—	22	100	95
Paper-making materials	1,683	2,150	2,175	2,740	3,431
Wood and timber					
hewn – soft	135	78	72	46	73
sawn – hard	78	100	109	75	49
sawn – soft	142	5,942	4,276	3,235	3,060
planed or dressed	298	318	373	422	266
pitprops or pitwood	1,053	995	822	508	767
staves	156	226	117	34	17
Paper, cardboard etc.	1,612	1,572	1,625	1,650	1,556
Mfrs. of wood & timber	1,135	1,337	1,232	1,072	997
Total	13,240	14,948	12,634	11,630	11,733

Source: UK *Annual Statement of Trade 1932.*

salt, creosote or china clay, all of which formed a direct input to Finnish exports to the British market, but iron, steel and commercial vehicles also featured strongly.[63] Because open agreements between governments would have been too blatant a breach of the mfn principle, the general technique was either for a 'gentlemen's agreement' to be made, or for representatives of the industries concerned to make their own agreements while keeping in close touch with their governments.[64]

When it came to the Finns' requests there was little they could ask for that had not already been granted in the Scandinavian negotiations. The main British imports from Finland are shown in Table 6.2. Finland was one of the countries least affected by British protection and imperial preference.

The agreements with Norway and Sweden had incorporated concessions on important Finnish exports such as sawn and planed softwood (10 per cent duty consolidated) and wood pulp, newsprint and pit-props, all of which had free entry guaranteed and, together with timber, had in 1931 accounted for nearly £7½ million of imports from Finland. Some Finnish

---

[63] *Ibid.*, note for information of the Finnish delegation sent to the Finnish Minister on 29 Apr. 1933. The full list was iron and steel, commercial vehicles and tractors and cars used for commercial purposes, wheat flour, cattle, foodstuffs, salt, jute bags and wrappers, china clay, sulphate of alumina, creosote, glue and gelatine and coal and coke. Machinery felts were later added to the list.

[64] BT 11/199, Anglo-Finnish Trade Negotiations, meeting, 24 May 1933.

requests betrayed a complete lack of realism. The Finns thought they might persuade the dominions to forego the butter duty.[65] They also hoped to qualify for 'insignificant supplier' status for their bacon exports, but were told they furnished far too much to qualify and would have to be satisfied with mfn treatment. There were however a number of Finnish specialities not covered by the earlier treaties. Included among these were sawn and planed birch, threadreels and imitation kraft and greaseproof paper. The extreme frustration of the Finnish negotiating team is easy to understand. It was exceedingly difficult for them to extract anything from the negotiations over and above a continuation of mfn treatment. By no means all of the 15 per cent of their exports not already covered by the other agreements were likely to win concessions. Finnish requests were typically rejected because either the maximum limit had already been reached in the Scandinavian agreements or because Finland was too small a supplier of the product to warrant a concession.[66]

Given that the British side were able to concede so little to Finland, the somewhat hectoring manner in which Whitehall conducted the negotiations is surprising. Perhaps the initial obduracy of the Finns contributed to this. At the very outset of the negotiations they were unyielding on British textile requests, making, as Fountain pointed out, 'a very inauspicious opening'.[67] The discussion on British demands was being carried out in three sub-committees, dealing with coal and coke, tariff requests and purchase agreements. At the end of the first week of talks the overall position was assessed at a full meeting of the delegates. The Finnish side had been unable by then to make any offer on the percentage of coal imports they would take, nor, a vital point for Britain, had they been able to give a guarantee that duty free entry for coal and coke would be maintained. The purchasing agreements made had been confined to the minor commodities, and the tariff position was described as 'unsatisfactory'. The Finns were told by Colville that unless they could improve their offers Britain would 'have no option but to denounce (the) treaty'.[68]

The threat seemed to work. During the next two weeks the Finnish negotiators offered 70 per cent of the coal and coke market, guaranteed free entry,[69] made purchasing arrangements for jute[70] and salt,[71] improved their tariff offers,[72] and moved towards a general undertaking from the

[65] *Ibid.*, meeting, 26 May 1933.   [66] *Ibid.*, 7th minutes, meeting, 24 May 1933.
[67] *Ibid.*, 5th minutes, meeting, 24 May 1933.
[68] *Ibid.*, 14th minutes, meeting, 30 May 1933.
[69] *Ibid.*, 18th minutes, meeting, 12 June 1933 and 21st minutes, 13 June 1933.
[70] *Ibid.*, 17th minutes, meeting, 7 June 1933.
[71] *Ibid.*, 20th minutes. Both agreements were to purchase as much jute and salt as was used in the manufacture or wrapping of the bacon, hams and salt destined for the UK market.
[72] *Ibid.*, 22nd minutes, meeting 14 June 1933.

export industries that for products not covered by the purchasing agreements the industries would nonetheless, whenever possible, make their purchases in Britain.[73] By the time the next overall assessment of the negotiations was made on 19 June, the Finnish delegates had also agreed to buy 30,000 tons of wheat flour a year, roughly the amount that had been imported from Britain in earlier years, although not to reduce the tariff: Whitehall thought this a good offer, not least because the brunt of import reductions had fallen on American supplies, and they feared that with the devaluation of the dollar the United States might regain its market share.[74]

Nonetheless the British response was again to apply pressure by threatening to terminate the negotiations. Although London seems by then to have considered the overall position of the negotiations as quite satisfactory, Finnish textile duties remained a major stumbling block.[75] The British delegates decided to take a tough line, and the next day Colville again told the Finns that unless their offers were improved, the treaty was threatened.[76] Dr Henry Ramsay, leading the Finnish delegation, had to return home for further consultations while the Finnish Minister in London anxiously sought assurances that no drastic action would meanwhile be taken.[77]

Ramsay came back to London in mid-July with offers sufficiently improved to warrant a stay of execution.[78] He seems to have concentrated his efforts in Finland on persuading the textile interests to accept bigger tariff reductions and adjustments.[79] The negotiations dragged on with some discussion on Finlands's agricultural requests, and limited progress on Britain's textile demands. London's behaviour may have been rather heavy-handed, but there were limits to the pressures that could be applied. Too overbearing an attitude might create such an unfavourable reaction that either Finland would refuse to sign an agreement or ill-will would neutralise many of the apparent concessions. Gentlemen's agreements and other rather nebulous undertakings played a sufficiently important part in the Finnish agreement to make the retention of goodwill in Finland a tangible influence on British export prospects. This placed a measure of constraint on British behaviour; it also made it necessary to grant at least some minimal concessions specifically to Finnish requirements over and above the maintenance of mfn treatment. Late in the negotiations, and

[73] *Ibid.*, 24th minutes, meeting, 15 June 1933.
[74] *Ibid.*, BT 11/200, Anglo-Finnish Tariff Negotiations. Summary of Finnish offers up to 19 June 1933.   [75] BT 11/199, 27th minutes, meeting, 19 June 1933.
[76] BT 11/199, 28th minutes, meeting, 20 June 1933.
[77] FO 371–17213, Sir John Simon to R. A. C. Sperling (Helsingfors) 23 June 1933.
[78] BT 11/199, 31st minutes, meeting, 13 July 1933.
[79] FO 371/17209, note by R. Keith Jopson (Commercial Secretary in Finland), 30 June 1933 and Keith Jopson to C. F. Monier-Williams, 4 July 1933.

subject to the Finns improving their offers to the UK, they were conceded the freezing of the 10 per cent duties on birchwood as well as on plywood, and a reduction of duty from 20 to 15 per cent on wooden thread reels.[80] The UK refused even to discuss agricultural products until the Finns were more forthcoming on British requests, but even when they were discussed there was little scope for movement without upsetting the whole structure of import control, actual or potential. Finland was given assurances of minimum quantities and consultations if quantitative restrictions were going to be used to control butter and egg imports,[81] and mfn treatment for their bacon exports.

What did Britain obtain from the agreement? The most important tariff requests were for textiles. In the Danish treaty the absence of purchasing agreements for textiles had caused strong criticism. In the Finnish case, Lancashire did not think one was feasible.[82] Tariff requests therefore became all the more important. Finland did concede a differentiation of cotton piece goods with bigger reductions on wide cloths, a concession the industry thought would be of value in meeting European competition. Finland also agreed a 30 per cent 'stop' on wool piece goods, met certain requirements about silk admixtures and consolidated the low duties on woollen yarns, and, with some reservations, on cotton thread and yarns.[83] The tariff reductions made were quite substantial on some of the more important cotton textiles, but less for woollens.[84] A reduced duty for specified quantities of herrings gave the fishing industry prospects of recovering some of the lost trade, and a wide range of other, less important, duty reductions were made. But the chief tariff objectives of the British government had been to guard against further Finnish protection. More immediate advances were to be gained through the purchasing arrangements. Finnish undertakings on coal (where at 75 per cent they had offered more than the 70 per cent acceptable to the British delegation) were worth an extra 400,000 tons on 1931 figures, but not so much extra on the greater

[80] BT 11/199, 38th minutes, meeting, 20 July 1933. Both thread-reels and plywood were made to a limited extent in the UK but it was thought users' interests were more important than the producers'.

[81] The butter quota guarantee was for 195,000 cwts: the Minister of Agriculture would have greatly preferred a percentage guarantee rather than, for him, the more inhibiting quantity guarantee. CAB 23/76 CAB 48 (33) 10, 26 July 1933.

[82] BT 11/206, A. R. Knowles (Assistant Secretary of Manchester Chamber of Commerce) to A. Mullilns, 29 May 1933.

[83] CAB 24/242 CP 188 (33), Anglo-Finnish Negotiations. Note prepared in the Board of Trade, 21 July 1933.

[84] Britain's most valuable trade to Finland was in medium-weight cottons, bleached, dyed or printed. The duty of 18 F.mks per kilo was reduced to 10.80 F.mks. for wide prints, 15 F.mks. for narrow prints and 13 F.mks. for bleached and dyed. The duty on medium-weight wool piece goods was reduced from 45 to 27 F.mks. per kilo – but the *ad valorem* 30 per cent 'stop' was to be of real use for lower priced textiles.

market share of 1932. The Finns gave secret guarantees on coke which would substantially reverse the decline of an important trade. Other purchasing agreements, some more specific than others, covered a wide range of mostly unimportant exports such as salt, jute wrappers and cloth, sulphate of alumina and creosote.[85] They also included wheat flour, iron and steel where the UK hoped to increase its market share from around 10 per cent,[86] and commercial vehicles, the market for which was dominated by the USA.

No estimates were made of the likely value of the treaty for British exports. Although minimum calculations of herring, wheat and coal sales could be made with reasonable certainty, the undertakings for other products were too vague.[87] Goodwill was to be important, as were the efforts of British exporters. A British Week was arranged for September to publicise UK products. Widespread publicity in the Finnish press reflected the goodwill that existed, but it was ominous that British industry gave only lukewarm support: the Commercial Secretary wrote of the 'incredible difficulties of persuading United Kingdom firms to participate in this joint drive for British trade, let alone subscribe to its funds'.[88]

Anglo-Japanese competition and trade diplomacy, 1932–1934

Intensified competition between Lancashire and Osaka threaded through Ottawa, the World Economic Conference in London and the deteriorating diplomatic relations between Britain and Japan. Following the end of the short-lived postwar boom, Lancashire had struggled for the greater part of the decade; but the export decline from 1929 was precipitate, the volume of exports dropping by more than half within two years.

The collapse of purchasing power, especially among impoverished rural populations, and the accelerated rise of local mill production, often behind exchange controls and higher tariffs, squeezed world trade in cottons. Yet in the midst of contracting international markets, the volume of Japanese cotton textile exports continued to expand. In 1929 Britain had sold overseas nearly 3·7 billion square yards of cotton piece goods, twice the volume of Japanese exports. By 1933 Japan had overhauled Britain as the

[85] CAB 24/242 CP 188 (33), 21 July 1933.
[86] BT 11/199, 40th minutes, meeting, 24 July 1933. The understanding was that the UK would supply about 30,000 tons of an assumed import of around 100,000 tons.
[87] The undertakings for steel and for commercial vehicles contained clauses such as 'The Finnish Government will instruct the State Purchasing Department, when buying from abroad motor vehicles of all kinds, to bear in mind the proportion of Finland's total exports taken by the United Kingdom.' In the instance of steel, as the previous footnote suggests, there was a firm commitment however.
[88] FO 371/17209, Sperling to DOT, official report by Keith Jopson, 28 Oct. 1933.

world's major supplier, and in 1934 sold nearly 2·6 billion square yards as against Lancashire's 2 billion.

Japan's export success was sparked by a savage depreciation of the yen in December 1931 to a level far below sterling.[89] The collapse of silk exports to the USA gave added impetus to a search for markets, while the cotton industry itself suffered losses in China, especially following a widespread boycott of Japanese products after the Japanese take-over of Manchuria in September 1931. The complacency with which much of Lancashire viewed Japanese competition in the late 1920s was now shattered.[90] It was suspected foul play lay behind the surge in Japan's exports, and there were rumours of dumping, subsidies, exploitation of labour and of other malpractices. In fact little evidence could be found to support accusations of subsidies or of dumping, and they were refuted by the distinguished historian of Japan, G. B. Sansom, who was Commercial Counsellor in Tokyo.[91] Perhaps with greater justification, low wages, 'the rice bowl standard of living', could be brought into account. Wages of women workers, who contributed the bulk of the workforce, were already low in 1930, but starvation in the countryside forced an influx of peasant daughters to the mills, facilitating a 22 per cent cut in wages by 1932.[92]

Yet the much of the groundwork for this trade drive had been laid in the 1920s. Rationalisation of the industry had led to huge advances in productivity.[93] Furthermore, as Hiroshi Shimizu has demonstrated, Japanese companies often encouraged by the government, had been laying the basis for subsequent market growth well before the depression.[94] The rapid expansion of textile sales to the Middle East would have been far more difficult without the establishment of consular posts, direct shipping services, banking facilities and trading organisations in the 1920s. By the 1930s the major firms were setting up their own sales offices in the chief distribution centres such as Teheran, Baghdad, Casablanca, Alexandria

---

[89] From $48·8 to $25·2 per 100 yen in 1933. Japan's total exports grew in volume by 29 per cent between 1929–33 while world trade contracted by a quarter. T. Nakamura, 'The Japanese economy in the interwar period: a brief summary', in R. Dore and R. Sinha (eds.) *Japan and the World Depression: then and now* (New York, 1987).

[90] Alex J. Robertson, 'Lancashire and the rise of Japan, 1910–1937', Mary B. Rose (ed.), *International Competition and Strategic Response in the Textile Industries Since 1870* (1991).

[91] Hiroshi Shimizu, *Anglo-Japanese Trade Rivalry in the Middle East in the Inter-War Period* (1986).

[92] Ouchi Tsutomi, 'Agricultural depression and Japanese villages', *The Developing Economies*, V (1967) and A. Waswo, 'Origins of tenant unrest', in B. S. Silberman and H. D. Harootunian (eds.), *Japan in Crisis: essays on Taisho democracy* (Princeton, 1974).

[93] G. C. Allen, *A Short Economic History of Japan*, (3rd edn 1972), 120, and G. R. Saxonhouse, 'Productivity change and labour absorption in Japanese cotton spinning, 1891–1935', *Quarterly Journal of Economics*, 91 (1977).

[94] Shimizu, *Anglo-Japanese Trade Rivalry*, esp. 70–94.

and Beirut. Driven out of Chinese markets, desperate for foreign exchange, armed with a heavily depreciated currency, the Japanese were well placed to launch an export drive.

Lancashire had been anxious about the rising tide of Indian protectionism long before it started to worry about Japan. The cottonocracy's power was being eroded, in part because the industry was diminishing in size, but perhaps more tellingly because of a change in the nature of British politics as the provinces lost force in an increasingly centralised and class-based party system.[95] Yet it could still carry considerable clout. In 1930–1 this was far from evident. A Labour government, much as it detested tariffs, was unwilling even to contemplate overruling Delhi's freedom of action. When the National government assumed control later in 1931 it was much less reluctant to make representations to the government of India about tariffs. But the interests of Lancashire had to be subordinated to the overriding needs of financial stability in India and in the financial crisis of 1930–2 to ensuring that the British taxpayer did not have to meet the costs of Indian defaults. Despite vigorous opposition from the government of India, the threatened resignation of the Viceroy and all of his executive council, London forced a tough budget and tight monetary policy on India. Under these circumstances Whitehall could hardly object to revenue raising tariff increases.[96]

By 1932, with the currency crisis receding, one impediment to the implementation of effective pressure by cotton interests was reduced. But it was the political controversy in Britain over constitutional reform in India, and Churchill's powerful campaign against it, that momentarily enhanced Lancashire's leverage. The campaign was assured of strong support in the Home Counties' Conservative and Unionist Associations, and sought to draw on the grievances of the cotton constituencies to bolster support in the north-west. There was frequent tension in Lancashire between those who campaigned for more vigorous government action and the moderates of the leadership, particularly of the Manchester Chamber of Commerce, who, in close touch with Whitehall, were more aware of the constraints on policy.[97] In December 1932 the Cotton Trade League had been formed to press for a stronger policy. The Indian section, which had suffered the most catastrophic losses, and which was involved with a country where the British government might be expected to control events,

[95] C. Dewey, 'The end of the imperialism of free trade: the eclipse of the Lancashire lobby and the concession of fiscal autonomy to India', in C. Dewey and A. G. Hopkins (eds.), *The Imperial Impact: studies in the economic history of Africa and India* (1978), esp. 56–60.

[96] B. R. Tomlinson, 'Britain and the Indian currency crisis 1930–32', *Economic History Review*, 2nd ser., 32 (1979).

[97] See, for example, Marguerite Dupree, *Lancashire and Whitehall. The Diary of Sir Raymond Streat*, I, *1931–39*, (Manchester, 1987).

was the most restless and critical. The industry's frustrations manifested themselves in some potentially controversial evidence to the Joint Select Committee on Indian Constitutional Reform. This in its original form had apparently contained some forceful arguments that Indian constitutional reform would be harmful to Lancashire, and had sought some safeguards. In the event two senior members of the committee, Lord Derby, an immensely powerful force in Lancashire, and Sir Samuel Hoare, Secretary of State for India, exerted strong pressure on the Manchester Chamber of Commerce to scrap its original evidence and substitute something altogether blander and less explosive. In the ensuing controversy, Churchill in 1934 obtained a hearing of the Parliamentary Committee of Privileges, which, probably wrongly, concluded no breach had been committed.[98] Senior members of the Manchester Chamber were able to persuade the Indian section to alter the evidence they had sent in June.[99]

The cooperation of Manchester was reflected in a determination in Whitehall that it should be rewarded, and help extended to it in other ways. Hoare argued that Lancashire had been more reasonable recently, dropping its opposition to Indian fiscal autonomy, and that its evidence to the Joint Select Committee had produced an 'excellent effect'.[100] So appeasing Lancashire might keep the more restless spirits quiet. In a perverse way the privileges issue had shown how opinion there carried weight. Meanwhile, Raymond Streat continued to foster Whitehall contacts while Lancashire MPs were able to raise a stream of parliamentary questions. What was being done, they demanded to know, to check Japanese competition in overseas markets, and, most particularly, within the British Empire?

Action against Japan was also being demanded by the India Office. Even in the 1920s Japanese competition had been causing problems for Indian producers, particularly in Bombay. Bombay was a relatively high cost producer, especially after the wartime and immediate postwar boom had swollen capital values in much the same way as in the British industry. The resulting higher overheads, together with output geared to the coarser varieties of cloth made the industry particularly vulnerable to competition both from up-country mills and from Japan.[101] The intensification of Japanese competition in the early 1930s created additional problems for the Indian industry, and growing political ferment encouraged the Indian government to press for further action against Japanese imports. Although

---

[98] M. Gilbert, *Winston S. Churchill*, V, *1922–39* (1976), 511–48.

[99] Dupree, *Diary of Sir Raymond Street*, 201–2.

[100] Memorandum by Hoare, CAB 27/556 Committee on Indian Cotton, CP 282 (33), 27 Nov. 1933.

[101] B. Chatterji, 'Business and Politics in the 1930s: Lancashire and the Making of the Indo-British Trade Agreement, 1939', *Modern Asian Studies*, 15 (1981), 527–73.

duties on non-British cottons had been raised in August 1932 from $31\frac{1}{4}$ per cent to 50 per cent, this was regarded as insufficient protection against the Japanese onslaught. What the Indian government wanted was the power to discriminate specifically against Japanese imports, action that was barred by the 1904 Indo-Japanese convention which stipulated mfn rights. In March 1933 the India Office asked the Cabinet to sanction India's denunciation of the convention.

The India Office was joined by the Board of Trade, energetically supported by Cunliffe-Lister at the Colonial Office, in pressing for action against Japanese competition in other markets. Lancashire had been rocked by Japanese competition in many parts of the world, especially in areas where there was little or no domestic production and where therefore Japanese competition posed the main threat. Ceylon provided a stark example, but Japanese suppliers had made rapid incursions into East Africa and Middle Eastern markets too. Little could be done in the Middle East, but action could be taken in some, although not all, colonial territories. In early March Runciman pointed out that Britain could unilaterally withdraw its West African colonies from the Anglo-Japanese commercial treaty, and thus be free to use quotas. Later in the month he reported that the situation had deteriorated still further, and advocated that West Africa and the West Indies should be withdrawn from the Anglo-Japanese treaty.[102]

This does not mean that Whitehall opinion was unanimous. The Foreign Office in particular was worried by the drift of events. Sir Francis Lindley, UK ambassador to Japan, warned that the timing was bad. Britain had instituted an arms embargo against Japan and China in February, and he hoped 'nothing would be done until the atmosphere here has cleared... [d]enunciation at this moment would be interpreted as due to desire mark disapprobation of Japanese policy in China and is most undesirable'.[103] Having failed to achieve League of Nations recognition of 'Manchukuo', Japan had announced in March that it would leave the League. In the wake of Ottawa, Britain's involvement in two virtually simultaneous acts of discrimination against Japan smacked of sanctions.

The issue highlighted the dilemmas of British policy towards Japan.[104] The Manchurian crisis having revealed the impotence of the west to counter Japanese aggression, what should UK policy now be? Should Tokyo be appeased? How could relations be improved? One line of action would be to seek an accommodation with Japan. Important constituents of

---

[102] Notes by President of the Board of Trade, CAB 24/239, CP 54 (33) and 55 (33) and FO 371/17153, 3, 6, 31 Mar. 1933.
[103] FO 371/17153, telegram, Lindley to Foreign Office. 2 Mar. 1933.
[104] Ann Trotter, *Britain and East Asia 1933–1937* (Cambridge, 1975).

such an arrangement might include recognition of Manchukuo and collaboration with Japan in China. However, the 'fabulous wealth of the orient' syndrome was still alive: the nationalist movement of Chiang Kai-shek held the promise of carrying through the sort of reforms that would unlock the economic potential of China, but British cooperation with Chiang, already strong, would be fatally compromised by overt collaboration with Japan. The increasingly active China lobby, although it did not speak with one voice, would not have countenanced such a threat to its interests. Moreover, collaboration with Japan would have been opposed by public opinion both in Britain and overseas.[105]

With full scale cooperation with Japan ruled out, the alternative of market sharing arrangements was sought. Withdrawal of west Africa from the 1911 treaty was seen as helpful in several ways. It might mollify Lancashire and forestall more extreme demands for complete abrogation of the treaty. At the same time, while the actual impact on Japanese trade would be minimal because the west African markets were still unimportant to its exporters, Japan might be induced to enter talks on market sharing.[106] And, if such talks were to be held, they had better be held while Britain was still a major exporter of textiles and had some bargaining power. It would take a year before denunciation of the treaty took effect, and both Runciman and Simon, when explaining action to Matsudaira, the Japanese ambassador, said that they hoped negotiations would take place in the interval.[107]

Talks between Britain and Japan were preceded by Indo-Japanese discussions.[108] The Japanese were galvanised by denunciation of the convention on 10 April, and, because it could not take effect for six months, by an increase from 50 to 75 per cent of the tariff on foreign imports. Osaka had trouble understanding the Indian grievance. Although India bought nearly one-third of Japanese cotton exports in 1932, in contrast to Britain Japan was also a major customer for Indian raw cotton, absorbing over half of Indian exports in 1932–3. Moreover, although 1932 was an exception, in most years Japan ran a balance of payments deficit with India. The Japanese industry responded by boycotting Indian supplies.

Lancashire, hoping to benefit from tough measures against Japan in the sub-continent, pressed the British government to strengthen the hand of the Indian negotiators by guaranteeing the government there against loss

---

[105] *Ibid.*, 45–6.
[106] FO 371–17153, Overton (Board of Trade) to VAL Mallet (Foreign Office), 23 Feb 1933, minute by Orde, 8 Mar. 1933 and telegram, Lindley to Foreign Office, 13 Mar. 1933.
[107] *Ibid.*, Runciman, 25 Apr. 1933 and Simon, 16 May 1933.
[108] Ian M. Drummond, *British Economic Policy and the Empire 1919–1939* (1972).

on the purchase of $1\frac{1}{2}$ million bales of cotton that might be lost to the Japanese boycott.[109] Stiffened by this assurance, the Indians were able to force the Japanese negotiators to accept a quota deal linking Japanese sales to purchases of Indian raw cotton, but in any case entailing a sharp cutback in the amount of imports from Japan.

The treaty was initialled in January 1934. Discussions between representatives of the British and Japanese textile industries, which had been holding fire during the autumn, began in February, got nowhere and broke down in March.[110] No basis for agreement could be found. The Japanese wished to limit the agreement to competition in the British colonies, while the UK side wanted a world-wide agreement. With no common ground, and fearing loss of face from a failure of inter-governmental talks, London embarked on a programme of unilaterally restricting Japanese trade.

In fact Britain's formal sway was very limited, and action was precluded in large parts of even the dependent empire, the terms of mandates or treaties making it impossible to practise discrimination in East Africa, for example, and with many of the entrepôt ports, including Aden, Gibraltar and Hong Kong, also outside the system. Britain could take action in markets which had absorbed only about 14 per cent of cotton textile exports in 1932.[111] Nevertheless there was some room for action. Tariff preferences, it was agreed by the Board of Trade, the Colonial Office and the Manchester Chamber of Commerce, were ineffectual against Japanese competition, so quotas would be used.[112] Japanese imports were to be restricted to the average levels of 1927–31, when competition had still been muted. Because of the great surge of imports from Japan after 1931, this often entailed spectacular cutbacks. In Ceylon, for example, Japan had accounted for 14 per cent of textile imports in 1929, but 68 per cent four years later.

Colonial governors were often far from happy at the results. Low price Japanese imports often tapped new markets, finding customers who could not afford Lancashire's products, and because local opposition would have ruled out the Ceylonese State Council enacting the legislation it had to be carried out in London by Order in Council. It was the interests of local populations that limited the concessions made by the Dutch East Indies: quotas were agreed, but at the higher levels of 1929–33.

Certainly Lancashire benefited in the markets directly affected. Between 1934 and 1935, while imports of Japanese cotton goods fell from 165

[109] CAB 27/556, Committee on Indian Cotton.
[110] Dupree, *Diary of Sir Raymond Streat*, esp. pp. 298–304.
[111] FO 371/17153, memorandum by Runciman, 31 Mar. 1933.
[112] CAB 27/568, Committee on Japanese Trade Competition, meetings, 27 Mar., 11 Apr., 6 June 1934.

million yards, imports from Britain more than doubled from 136 to 278 million yards.

Conclusion

Although world economic recovery began in 1933, it was hesitant and for most countries domestically based. The nearest approach to coordinated international economic action, the World Economic and Monetary Conference, was a spectacular failure. British commercial policy was barely touched by the conference; instead, Whitehall represented bilateral trade treaties as the only practicable route to liberalisation. While the power of these treaties to lower the protectionist barriers of other countries was demonstrably weak, they proved more effective in achieving a measure of trade diversion to Britain. This was secured despite the retention of the mfn clause as the basis of non-imperial trade and the rejection of clearing agreements as a mechanism for bilateral trade balancing. British trade gained in the short run through judicious manipulation of tariff structures, consistent with mfn practice, and through purchase agreements that were a blatant abuse of the clause. The retreat from economic internationalism went further in Britain's dealings with Japan: Manchester and Osaka having failed to reach a market-sharing agreement, London unilaterally applied discriminatory quotas against Japanese cotton exports to colonial territories.

The Baltic states and Poland

Negotiating stragegy: the next phase

While the World Economic Conference had been in progress discussions with Finland had continued and a harassed Board of Trade had conducted preliminary talks with the Baltic states of Estonia, Latvia and Lithuania. In considerable part the Baltic state negotiations represented a victory for the views of Laurence Collier, head of the Northern Department of the Foreign Office, who had first had to overcome the indifference of the Board of Trade.

Early doubts in the Board of Trade had centred on the supposed inability of British negotiators to wrest much from the Baltic states in the wake of the new restrictive bacon policy, a pessimism shared in the Economic section of the Foreign Office. Frank Ashton Gwatkin wrote of the Baltic states, 'negotiations will start, if they ever do start, on a basis so unfavourable to them that they can hardly be expected to offer much advantage to us'.[1] The Northern Department had different priorities. Anxious in case the historical and geographical pull of Moscow and Berlin might otherwise be reasserted over the Baltic states, particularly now that regional agreements were becoming so important, Collier wanted Britain to move quickly to tighten economic ties. The Board of Trade began to think that negotiations might be fairly easy with these countries once the main lines of policy towards Scandinavia had been settled, and was induced to give some commitment to negotiate once the other agreements were concluded.[2] In the event, substantial negotiations with the Baltics were delayed because the Commercial Relations and Treaties Department of the Board of Trade was too small and too busy. Further negotiations would have to wait until those with Finland were finished and the World Economic Conference was over.[3] The Foreign Office, or at least Collier,

[1] FO 371/16296, T. St Q. Hill to L. Collier, 2 Dec. 1932 and FO 371/16294, minute by Ashton Gwatkin 27 Oct. 1932.
[2] FO 371/16296, minute by Collier on inter-departmental meeting.
[3] FO 371/17213, Board of Trade to Foreign Office, 12 May 1933.

were not to be deterred. Arguing that British motives for delay would be misunderstood, and that Lithuania would be drawn into the arms of Germany, he prevailed upon the Board of Trade to undertake at least token negotiations with the small Baltic states while their Ministers were in London for the conference.[4]

By the summer of 1933 future strategy was being mapped out further, and the results of the deliberations were circulated to the Cabinet for confirmation.[5] Two dominant considerations helped narrow the choice of candidate countries: whether their balance of trade with the UK was favourable and whether their trading structure was complementary. As a rough guide, countries which had less than half their imports into the UK classified as manufactures qualified as suitable candidates under the second criterion. On the basis of 1931 figures, and leaving aside the Scandinavians, Finland and Argentina, the following countries met the two conditions: Russia, the three Baltic states, Poland, Holland, Portugal, Spain, Romania, Egypt, Persia, the USA, Cuba, Mexico, Costa Rica, Peru, Chile, Brazil, Uruguay and Bolivia. Of these, Brazil and Portugal had since started to run trade deficits with the UK. With the exceptions of Brazil and Uruguay, all the Latin American countries were ruled out on grounds of their unimportance or instability. Brazil, however, was excluded because of the change in the balance of trade, and because the UK was a poor market for Brazilian coffee and oranges, the latter having been displaced after Ottawa by South African supplies. The USA was dismissed because it offered 'special difficulties'.[6] Portugal was thought likely to demand concessions on port which Britain would be unable to meet, and Persia and Romania offered no special attractions. Negotiations were already being held with Russia, and Whitehall felt committed to the Baltic states,[7] including Poland, for all of which the necessary preparations in the Board of Trade had been made. That left Holland, Spain and Egypt. The Dutch tariff was too liberal to offer much scope for increasing British trade. On the other hand, although Egyptian textile duties did worry the Board of Trade, it was felt that Britain lacked leverage since no obstacles were likely to be put in the way of Egyptian raw cotton. Spain was considered an altogether more promising candidate: the market for UK goods was already quite large, the tariff level on manufactures was high, and the surplus together with its

---

[4] Ibid., minute by Collier, 13 May 1933.
[5] CAB 24/242 CP 187(33), Commercial Negotiations with Foreign Countries. Note by Runciman, 21 July 1933.   [6] Ibid.
[7] Not with any enthusiasm however: in a note to Runciman on future trade negotiations, Fountain wrote: 'these tiresome little countries will involve the expenditure on the part of the United Kingdom Ministers and officials of an amount of energy altogether disproportionate to the value of the trade actual or prospective which might conceivably benefit as a result'. 1 June 1933. WR 257.

heavy dependence on the British market seemed to augur well for successful negotiations. After Northern Europe, Runciman therefore asked for authority to prepare negotiations with Spain and Uruguay, and for Egypt and Holland to be considered later. The programme was approved in Cabinet, although the Secretaries of State for India and for the Colonies wanted greater priority for Holland because of various treaty ramifications affecting their departmental interests.[8] Significantly, France and Germany were to be excluded because any concessions made on industrial products would arouse the maximum of opposition in Britain. Commenting on the rather indefinite postponement of negotiations with the major industrial powers, Ashton Gwatkin observed, the 'power of our tariff policy to reduce foreign tariffs is clearly very limited'.[9]

There was some criticism within the Foreign Office of the Board of Trade's inability to conduct a sufficient number of negotiations simultaneously. Britain was failing to capitalise on trading opportunities: R. L. Craigie wrote that the Board's methods were 'incredibly dilatory' and that the staff should be increased.[10] With this was merged a suspicion that the Board of Trade's strategy was wrong and that the choice of countries should be reassessed. David Kelly minuted that constant pressure had to be exerted on the Board on the question of policy, although 'on the technical side once negotiations get started that department is excellent'.[11] The criticism stemmed in part from the growing anxieties the American section of the Foreign Office had about a commercial offensive by the United States in Latin America. The Board of Trade discounted the American initiative in Latin Amercia as being a reaction to the failure of the World Economic Conference and also thought that any concessions would be hard to get through Congress (this was before the passage of the Reciprocal Trade Agreements Act which from 1934 gave the administration power to reduce tariffs in trade negotiations). Nonetheless the Board was pessimistic about Britain achieving much in the rest of Latin America. Selling most of their coffee and fruit in the American market, Brazil and Colombia were to be abandoned to the USA. Chile was dismissed as a hopeless proposition because of its export structure and its insolvency.[12] Peru was hardly considered a better prospect because Britain's chief imports, raw cotton and wool, were unlikely to be taxed, and sugar was discriminated against through imperial preference. Despite this, although further obstacles were posed by high Peruvian tariffs and the development of local industries, the Board agreed to examine prospects.

The Board of Trade was therefore confirmed in its position. Collier, in

---

[8] CAB 23/76, CAB 48(33) 9, 26 July 1933.   [9] FO 371/17319, minute, 26 July 1933.
[10] *Ibid.*, 27 July 1933.   [11] FO 371/16534, minute, 1 Sept. 1933.
[12] FO 371/16530, Hamilton to Vansittart, 10 Oct. 1933.

arguing that the next batch of negotiations should be held with the Baltic states had been able to present the negotiations as the 'resumption' of the discussions held earlier in the summer.

The Baltic states

In accordance with the overall policy agreed in July 1933, the next phase of negotiations involved Britain with three of the smallest and most impoverished states in Europe. While in area slightly larger than England and Wales, the total population of Estonia, Latvia and Lithuania was just over $5\frac{1}{2}$ millions.[13] They were primarily agricultural communities, the proportion of the working population ranging from about 60 per cent in Estonia to 77 per cent in Lithuania.[14] Purchasing power was low – in Latvia in 1928–9 approximately 95 per cent of the population had a declared income the equivalent of less than £1 per week[15] – and total imports of the three countries in 1932 had amounted to only £12·2 million, of which a mere £1$\frac{1}{2}$ million came from the United Kingdom.[16]

By the end of the 1920s the successor states were firmly within Germany's commercial orbit, Britain having lost opportunities to establish a stronger presence at the beginning of the decade.[17] In 1919 and 1920 there had been intense British interest in the Baltic states, although not so much for themselves as because they were seen as a commercial highway to the potentially vast Russian market. But changing British attitudes to the Soviet Union, together with a realisation of limited resources, led Britain to withdraw military guarantees that had been given earlier. An opportunity was lost to capitalise on the undoubted goodwill that existed because of the British role in the achievement of independence, and Germany, more consistent in its eastern policies, and better commercially organised, was able to increase its economic penetration of the area. It was

---

[13] Royal Institute of International Affairs, *The Baltic States. A Summary of the Political and Economic Structure and the Foreign Relations of Estonia, Latvia and Lithuania* (1938), 103. The population figures come from censuses in the mid-1930s.   [14] *Ibid.*

[15] BT 11/218, memorandum, Anglo-Latvian Commercial Negotiations, 1 Jan. 1934.

[16] T 160/664/F13090/08/1, memorandum for Overseas Trade Development Council, 8 Sept. 1933.

[17] This is fully discussed by Merja-Liisa Hinkkanen-Lievonen, *British Trade and Enterprise in the Baltic States, 1919–1925* (Helsinki, 1984), 'Britain as Germany's Commercial Rival in the Baltic States 1919–1939' in Marie-Luise Recker, ed. *From Competition to Rivalry: the Anglo-German Relationship with countries at the European Periphery, 1919–1939* (Stuttgart, 1986), and 'Exploited by Britain? The Problems of British Financial Presence in the Baltic States After the First World War', *Journal of Baltic Studies*, 14 (1983), 328–39. See also John Hiden, *The Baltic States and the Weimar Ostpolitik* (Cambridge, 1987).

this that Collier was seeking to reverse. The Baltic states also met the criteria used for determining negotiating partners. All three were anxious for trade discussions and had made the first approaches to the British government.[18] All three, following the transformation of their agricultural sectors in the early stages of independence and the loss of markets in Russia, had come to rely on a Scandinavian export pattern with bacon, butter and timber prominent. All three ran substantial trade surpluses with the United Kingdom. In addition to this, specific sectors of British trade had suffered tangible losses in these markets which it was felt could be remedied. In the late 1920s herrings had been Britain's single biggest export item to Estonia and Latvia. Import duties and surcharges, together with a switch in demand to cheaper local supplies, had cut British herring exports to Latvia from £540,000 in 1928 to £74,000 in 1932, and the Estonian herring market had also been lost.[19] Temporary agreements had been made with the three Baltic states during July 1933 to give some safeguards for British herring sales. Coal sales had also been hit, generally by Polish competition. In 1924 Britain had supplied 93 per cent of the Latvian market; by 1931 Poland supplied 96 per cent and Britain 1 per cent.[20]

Using the leverage that stemmed from unequal dependence and from a balance of trade deficit, Britain could hope to achieve some amelioration of these setbacks. But Whitehall had its reservations about the sum total of benefits likely to accrue from the negotiations. Debt defaults were common, agents often incompetent or dishonest, and 'commercial morality' low.[21] Evidently little had changed since the early twenties when the Baltic states abounded with some of the shadier members of the international business community, described by the Foreign Office as 'sinister figures', at least one of whom would be 'quite likely to go off with the spoons if you were to leave him alone in your house'.[22] Legal redress was difficult. All this weakened the chance of achieving major increases in trade, but the fundamental obstacle was the poverty of the markets. It was, noted a Board of Trade official, 'hardly a matter for pride or congratulations that Lithuania (and Estonia) should be so high up in the list of countries negotiating with this country under the new tariff system'.[23] There was a determination not to waste much time on the trade talks, Arthur Mullins recording: 'Those on the spot are very definitely of the opinion – and that opinion I share – that very early in the negotiations

---

[18] CAB 24/242 CP 187(33), 21 July 1933.

[19] BT 11/207, Anglo-Estonian Commercial Relations, note on the herring position, 7 June 1933.   [20] BT 11/218, memorandum, 1 Jan. 1934.

[21] T 160/664/F13090/08/1, memorandum by E. F. Crowe, 8 Sept. 1933.

[22] Quoted by Hinkkanen-Lievonen, 'Exploited by Britain', 333.

[23] BT 11/121, note by Turner, 18 Jan. 1933.

Table 7.1. *Distribution of exports from the Baltic states to Germany and the UK, percentage of total value, 1927, 1930 and 1932*

	Estonia			Latvia			Lithuania		
	1927	1930	1932	1927	1930	1932	1927	1930	1932
United Kingdom	31·4	32·3	36·7	34·1	28·4	30·8	24·8	19·5	41·4
Germany	29·8	30·1	26·2	26·4	26·6	26·2	51·6	59·9	39·1

Source: RIIA *The Baltic States, A Summary of the Political and Economic Structure and the Foreign Relations of Estonia, Latvia and Lithuania* (1938), 126–65.

they should be told what is expected of them, and told in such a manner as to leave nothing to the imagination.'[24] These attitudes implied considerable bargaining leverage on Britain's part. By 1932 the UK had become the most important market for all three Baltic states (see Table 7.1).

While the proportional dependence of Estonia and Latvia had not changed very drastically, the value of imports into Britain from both countries had fallen heavily by 1932, in part because both had stayed on the gold standard and were suffering heavy competition in timber and dairy exports from countries with depreciated currencies. Estonia's exports to Britain were roughly balanced between wood and agricultural produce; Latvia, heavily dependent on timber and wood products, was less threatened by British imperial and domestic policies. Lithuania's position *vis-à-vis* Britain had been transformed during the depression. Exports had boomed, but because of its heavier reliance on the UK, and particularly for sales of agricultural produce, Lithuania was the most vulnerable of the Baltic states. The rise of the bacon trade had been very rapid: British imports of Lithuanian bacon had risen from £7,000 in 1928 to £1·2 million in 1933. Butter imports had also increased substantially. Lithuania was the Denmark of the Baltics, and on that analogy likely to have the maximum pressure applied in the negotiations.

How could the British use the trade talks to provide a better basis for future exports? Tariff stabilisation and reductions were one obvious objective. But as with the Nordic countries, resort to tariff reductions alone was likely to achieve little. In the case of the Scandinavians one reason for this was because tariffs were mostly low, but with the Baltics it was because exchange and licensing restrictions had become key determinants of trade.

[24] T 160/664/F13090/08/1, minute by Mullins. 20 Sept. 1933.

Additionally, as in the rest of northern Europe, Germany was a powerful competitor and would have been likely to reap the main benefit from lower tariffs. Therefore guarantees on licence and exchange allocations, specifying quantities and values of individual products, were to become a central feature of the agreements. Coal again featured prominently in British requests, and purchasing agreements on the Finnish model were also an important part of the overall package.

Estonia and Latvia

The imports of both countries had contracted sharply during the depression. Lower export volumes and prices had reduced purchasing power early in the depression, while later, with the German financial crisis of July 1931, capital withdrawals and flight had aggravated the balance of payments position. Since both Estonia and Latvia held much of their reserves in sterling, the devaluation of the pound in September caused losses in reserves, precipitating the introduction of exchange controls.[25] Under the twin pressures of deflation and direct controls, total imports by 1932 had fallen to a third or less of their 1928–30 levels. However, the introduction of controls meant that an instrument had been created which, whatever its serious immediate impact on British exports, had the potential to divert trade from Germany to Britain. Between 1928 and 1930, 40 per cent of Latvia's imports had come from Germany, only 8·8 per cent from Britain, and from a British perspective the position was only slightly better in Estonia.

The main objective of London in the negotiations became the restoration of trade in those products which had suffered severely in the slump. Estonia's total imports of coal and textiles were low. Local shale-oil deposits and plentiful timber provided alternative sources of power and heat, and even in 1928–30 coal and coke imports had formed only 1·4 per cent of Estonia's imports.[26] Estonia had long had a cotton and woollen textile industry, before the war possessing at Krainsholm one of the largest cotton mills in the world, processing imported raw cotton for the Russian market. After independence a smaller cotton industry managed to find some outlets in the Baltic and Balkan states during the 1920s, and supplied much of the domestic market. All this was reflected in low textile imports even before 1929, but once the depression started, textile imports were further cut so as to save foreign exchange and compensate for the loss of export markets. Although Latvia had a more varied and larger industrial

---

[25] RIIA, *The Baltic States*, 172–3, and League of Nations, *International Currency Experience: Lessons of the inter-war period* (Geneva, 1944), 162.

[26] RIIA, *The Baltic States*, 162–3.

sector than Estonia, the structure was less of an obstacle to British exports. Coal sales were low not because Latvia imported little coal but because Poland had most of the market. Despite the presence of cotton and woollen mills in Latvia, imports had been nearly three times the Estonian level before the depression.

Tariff requests for textiles featured prominently in the British demands. It was considered necessary to reduce duties both because these had been raised sharply after 1929, and because if licensing systems were later to be abandoned, Britain would be left with nothing to show for the trade agreements. Estonia was requested to guarantee licence allocations for up to 60 tonnes of cottons and 25 tonnes of woollen cloth, and Latvia 357 tonnes of cotton and 40 tonnes of woollens.[27] The Estonians were asked for tariff reductions for coal, flour and galvanised sheets together with a specified proportion of coal imports and a stated minimum tonnage. Purchase agreements, on the Finnish pattern, would be made for a range of other products. Broadly similar requests were made of the Latvians. Both treaties were to include balance of trade clauses for future use as a lever to increase British exports. The basic objectives were to secure an expansion of exports from a narrow range of specified products – textiles, coal, herrings and the purchase agreement goods – while other imports from Britain were to be stabilised at the 1932–3 levels unless and until conditions improved.

The principal concerns of both Estonia and Latvia were for their agricultural exports. Although forestry products earned more export revenue for Latvia than food, and were by no means negligible for Estonia, these had already been covered by the Scandinavian agreements, so continuation of mfn treatment was largely all that was required (Estonia also wanted the duty fixed at 20 per cent for two of their specialities, plywood chairbacks and seats). The negotiations thus centred around what would happen to their exports if Britain introduced quotas for potatoes, dairy and poultry products, and how much they might be entitled to under the bacon quota scheme. The Letts, for example, wanted assurances that they could supply about 200,000 cwts of butter, three times the amount they would have qualified for under the criteria used in the Scandinavian agreements. The delegation argued that they would otherwise return from London entitled to export two-thirds less than they were already doing.[28] Eventually they were offered 113,000 cwts.[29] The Estonians argued that

---

[27] The documents do not always make clear whether imperial or metric tons were specified, but since import figures were to be used it is reasonable to assume that it was tonnes.

[28] T 160/664/F13090/08/4, Anglo-Latvian Commercial Negotiations, meeting, 29 Jan. 1934.

[29] T 160/664/F13090/08/5, *ibid.*, meeting of UK delegation, 29 Mar. 1934.

they needed a substantial butter quota because, unable to subsidise butter exports, their shipments had fallen sharply. In the event a contingency quota was guaranteed well below the level of Estonian demands and they were refused a minimum quota for bacon. Latvia, on the same basis as Norway, would be able to claim 'insignificant' status for their exports of cheese, eggs and poultry, and for non-agricultural products received assurances of free entry for flax and duties of 20 per cent for match splints and 10 per cent on raw gypsum.

The crux of the negotiations, however, was the price the Estonians and Letts were prepared to pay to retain mfn status in the British market. The main stumbling blocks were the various textile desiderata. The Estonians argued that if they were to grant even a 40 tonne cotton quota, their mfn obligations to other countries would force them to increase total cotton imports by 150 to 200 tonnes.[30] Similar problems were involved with woollens. Eventually they offered to purchase perhaps 60 per cent of import requirements from the UK, and to give quotas for 50 tonnes of cottons and 20 tonnes of woollens – provided the guarantee was confidential.[31] Britain had maintained its share of Estonian coal imports better than in other north European markets, accounting for more than 60 per cent of sales in 1932. But although the agreement conceded 85 per cent of coal imports and the duty was lowered to a quarter of its existing level, this was thought to generate only a little over £6,000 extra trade above the 1932 level. The textile quotas and purchase agreements were valued at £127,000, the major slice being wool yarns, the herring guarantees were calculated to be worth £69,000, and the other purchase agreements £38,000 over the value of 1932 trade. The total was estimated at £240,000 over 1931 (but only half that over 1932 trade), although no figure was included for the fairly extensive list of tariff concessions.

The Latvian market was more important for Britain, but officials were not particularly optimistic – indeed with protectionist pressures from local industries and the general decline in Latvian trade it was feared that Britain might end up with less trade after the agreement than before.[32] In fact British exports to Latvia had risen from £591,000 in 1932 to £1 million in 1933, largely through trade diversion, and once London's requests were more fully formulated, they did look ambitious. By September 1933 the Board of Trade's Alix Kilroy was noting that 'our requests are rather excessive and will no doubt have to be substantially modified in the negotiations'.[33]

[30] BT 11/207, note by Hill, 7 Mar. 1934.
[31] T 160/735/F13090/09/5, Estonian note handed to British officials, 6 Apr. 1934, and meeting, 10 Apr. 1934.   [32] BT 11/218, notes by Kilroy, 22 Aug. 1933.
[33] Ibid., minute by Kilroy, 20 Sept. 1933.

Certainly the Latvian delegation's instructions nowhere approached the British demands, and in early February negotiations were suspended while the delegation head returned to Latvia to seek a fresh mandate. The anxiety of the Latvian government to conclude an agreement was evident in a marked improvement in their offers. The delegation proposed 300 tonnes for cottons with the understanding that a generous allocation of 140 tonnes for printed cottons would forestall the establishment of a textile printing works in Latvia, something the British government had been anxious to stop. Licences were allocated for 30 tonnes of woollens. Compromises were made about herrings, an offer made to buy a minimum of 9,000 tonnes per annum of steel,[34] and Latvia guaranteed a minimum of 70 per cent of its coal market to the UK, with a private undertaking to issue licences, if requested, up to 85 per cent, and to import an agreed minimum of 235,000 tonnes.[35] There was one additional matter, the Riga loan, issued before the war but on which no interest or sinking fund payments had been paid since 1917. Although not forming part of the agreement, it was understood that ratification would not take place until a satisfactory settlement had been made.[36] Runciman suggested that the main effect of the treaty would be to consolidate the £500,000 increase in British exports between 1932 and 1933, but that an extra £200,000 of trade might be generated over and above the 1933 figure.[37]

Lithuania

The negotiations with Lithuania, which were held after the agreements with Estonia and Latvia had been concluded, differed both in form and result. Lithuania was the poorest and least industrialised of the three states and, at the end of the 1920s, although the most populous, imported less than either of them. Yet, while badly affected by the depression, Lithuania does not appear to have been quite as severely hit as Estonia or Latvia. The decline in foreign trade was more protracted but less severe, and certainly the financial crisis of 1931 had a less traumatic effect than on its neighbours. There was less foreign capital in the banking system, and nor was Lithuania, with foreign exchange reserves held mostly in dollars rather than sterling, so vulnerable to Britain's departure from the gold standard.[38] Official exchange control was not introduced until 1935. Lithuanian exports were also better maintained than those of its neighbours, but there was a marked shift in the composition and direction of trade. In 1928–30

---

[34] T 160/665/F13090/08/5, meeting of UK delegation, 29 Mar. 1934.
[35] *Ibid.*, draft of a letter to form unpublished part of agreement, n.d.
[36] T 160/664/F13090/08/4, copy of CP 88(34), memorandum by Runciman, 23 Mar. 1934.
[37] *Ibid.*   [38] RIIA, *The Baltic States*, 175.

Table 7.2. *UK retained imports of selected products from Lithuania 1929–1932* (£000s)

	1929	1930	1931	1932
Butter	102	100	139	324
Eggs	15	18	30	6
Bacon	23	250	869	1,189
Pulpwood	247	230	139	111
Wood – sawn, soft	5	16	89	205
manufactures	51	36	52	56
Total	582	753	1,410	1,943

Source: UK *Annual Statement of Trade 1932.*

the main exports had been timber and livestock with flax and butter an equal third. By 1932 timber, livestock and flax had all lost heavily, and bacon and butter had become the most important export earners. This was associated with much heavier dependence on the UK market, with the result that exporters were exposed to the British bacon restriction scheme: by 1933, as Tom Preston, the British Chargé d'Affaires, observed, 'the whole of Lithuania was crawling with disappointed pigs'.[39]

These increases were achieved despite the non-depreciation of the lit. It has been suggested that the very poor standard of living in Lithuania enabled farmers to accept lower prices than their competitors in neighbouring countries,[40] but low fodder prices also helped and bacon exports were aided by government payment of export premiums.[41] So while its Baltic neighbours were losing ground in the British market, Lithuania was becoming far more dependent. Initially, no efforts seem to have been made to increase imports from the UK, with British exports declining between 1929 and 1931 before staging a modest recovery in 1932. Import licensing had been introduced in December 1932, and tariff increases also threatened British sales, notably of coal and textiles. This became the ostensible reason for postponing negotiations with Lithuania until after those with Estonia and Latvia had begun,[42] – this pressure, together with a threat to terminate existing commercial relations, was to encourage Lithuania to switch trade to the UK.[43] The import licensing system, although applying

[39] T. H. Preston to H. M. Knatchbull-Hugessen, cited in Hughe Knatchbull-Hugessen, *Diplomat in Peace and War* (1949), 64.   [40] RIIA, *The Baltic States*, 149.

[41] Department of Overseas Trade, *Economic Conditions in Lithuania During 1931* (1933), 15.

[42] CAB 24/242, CP 187(33), 21 July 1933.

[43] BT 11/233, Anglo-Lithuania Commercial Relations, note of meeting with Lithuanian delegation, 30 June 1933.

to only about one-third of Lithuanian imports, covered sufficiently important products to provide a means of trade diversion.

While Latvian and especially Estonian industry had posed an obstacle to British exports, the undeveloped state of Lithuania's industrial sector offered no such problems.[44] Moreover, because Britain was so poorly represented in Lithuanian imports, accounting for only 11 per cent in 1932, there were plenty of opportunities for increasing trade at the expense of its competitors if mfn clauses could be circumvented. The main requests included a number of purchase agreements, initially the most important of which were for coal and steel. Since the UK was the major supplier of very few commodities, and the trade gap was relatively great, tariff reductions alone were going to achieve little. Whitehall made the usual request for coal – a return to the 1924 share of the market which had been 93 per cent, an ambitious demand, since by 1931 Poland supplied 66 per cent and Germany 32 per cent of coal imports. But the growing dispute with Poland over Vilna led to a 100 per cent duty on Polish coal imports, and British suppliers were also helped by rail rate reductions between the port of Memel and the capital Kovno.[45] The British representative in Kovno thought the best prospects lay in asking for purchase agreements or quotas.[46] The Lithuanians themselves suggested a similar course of action, arguing that duties were important fiscally, and that reductions would bring less benefit to Britain than to its competitors.[47] Accordingly Whitehall relaxed the tariff requests for textiles and substituted a number of purchase demands for specified minimum market shares and tonnages.[48] Of the other purchase arrangements wanted, the most important was for iron and steel. Reduced duties, of course, also featured in the desiderata, and were requested for coal and coke, herrings, textiles and a variety of other products, including a differential duty favouring small cars.

The early Lithuanian requests were ambitious. High and expanding quotas were wanted for butter and bacon, and were described by a Board of Trade official as 'manifestly absurd'.[49] The Lithuanians wanted a bacon quota of 800,000 cwts by 1935, but were granted one of 350,000, 'which is more than they deserve'.[50] The Lithuanians, having at first delayed making

---

[44] There were, for example, apparently only 600 employed in Lithuania's cotton industry while Estonia employed over 3,000 and Latvia 5,000. T 160/735/F13090/09/4, Knatchbull-Hugessen to FO, 8 Jan. 1934.

[45] Department of Overseas Trade, *Economic Conditions*, 20.

[46] BT 11/255, Preston to C. S. Toseland, 8 Mar. 1934.

[47] CAB 24/249, CP167 (34), 29 June 1934.

[48] T 160/828/F13090/010, Anglo-Lithuanian Commercial Negotiations. Memorandum by UK Delegation handed to Lithuania on 10 May 1934.

[49] BT 11/121, note by Kilroy, 18 Jan. 1933.

[50] *Ibid.*, quotas were based on supplies during two years ending October 1932.

offers until they knew the size of their bacon allocations, seem, once they did know them, to have been genuinely shocked and, having commenced negotiations, broke them off while further instructions were obtained.[51] The negotiations, which had started in February 1934, were suspended in late March and did not restart until May.

Impatience in Whitehall at what was regarded as Lithuanian prevarication manifested itself in a document that was virtually an ultimatum. The visiting delegation was presented with a provisional draft of an agreement together with a memorandum.[52] Subject to minor modification, the memorandum constituted Britain's minimum requests, and should the Lithuanians not agree to these terms and initial at least the heads of an agreement within a reasonable time, the Anglo-Lithuanian Exchange of Notes of 1923 would be denounced.[53] Negotiations were not in fact completed until after the expiry of the suggested deadline, but Britain got most of what had been demanded.[54] Tariff requests had been moderated, but it was the purchase agreements which had been more central. The Lithuanians agreed to take 80 per cent of coal imports from the UK with a minimum figure of 178,000 tonnes and a reduction of the tariff; some late haggling produced a 60 per cent guarantee for cement purchases and 25 per cent of steel imports with a minimum figure of 8,000 tonnes. The final guarantees for textile imports were remarkably near the British requests, producing a grand total of 1,350 tonnes with specified minimum quantities and percentages for each major grouping – these were for actual purchases whereas the agreements with Estonia and Latvia dealt only with exchange and licence allocations. The textile quotas were calculated to be worth an additional £200,000 over 1932 export values.[55] The coal clauses were worth about £70,000. There were other purchase schemes, including guarantees for licence allocations for superphosphates, the total value of which, excluding coal, textiles and superphosphates, was estimated at £120,000. Tariff reductions included one for the herring trade, and there were other clauses covering the issue of licences and exchange, the encouragement of British shipping and the taxing of commercial travellers. The total value of the concessions was thought to be worth about £400,000 in extra trade over the 1932 level, plus an uncalculated amount for tariff concessions. If these hopes were realised they promised more valuable additions to British exports than the Estonian treaty, but were worth a little less in absolute gains than the Latvian agreement (although this had included estimates for tariff concessions). In practice, but mainly because of the Lithuanian

---

[51] BT 11/255, memorandum by Nowell on meeting with B. K. Balutis, Head of the Lithuanian Delegation, 26 Mar. 1934.   [52] BT 11/233, meeting 10 May 1934.
[53] *Ibid.*   [54] *Ibid.*, meeting, 29 June 1934.
[55] CAB 24/249 CP 167(34), 29 June 1934.

disputes with Germany and Poland, this was to be the most fruitful of the Baltic treaties for Britain.

Poland

The negotiations with Poland were long delayed and, once started, protracted. The Polish Embassy had made enquiries as early as October 1932 about trade talks, and expressed dissatisfaction that the Scandinavians should take precedence.[56] The delay was partly because of the difficulties of negotiating with a high tariff country,[57] but also because Whitehall did not want the Poles in London at the same time as it was pushing British coal to the Scandinavians at Poland's expense. While there was some fear that there might be common action between the Poles and the Scandinavians,[58] another view looked to secure concessions from Poland in return for leaving it with at least some of the Nordic market. The Polish ambassador had told the British government that if Polish trade could be guaranteed at least a foothold in its present markets, especially for coal, 'they would find the Polish Government most businesslike and accommodating in the forthcoming negotiations'.[59] Pursuing this theme, Fountain reported that before they started any conversations with the Poles the Board of Trade wanted to determine how much of the Scandinavian market could be secured for British coal. Britain would not be able to monopolise the market, 'in which case we would be prepared to see what we could get out of the Poles in return for an agreement to leave them that part of it which we should be obliged to leave in any case...'[60] Later a third market coal agreement was to form an integral part of the trade negotiations, but any concessions the Poles made were within the coal agreement itself rather than taking the form of greater openings for British exports to Poland.

Eventually other factors delayed the start of the talks. In October 1932 Poland had announced much higher tariffs that were to come into force a year later.[61] Britain was the main supplier of only very few commodities, and it was considered far better that countries such as France, Czechoslovakia, Belgium or Austria should obtain concessions which would automatically be extended to British goods.[62] Ultimately administrative

---

[56] FO 371/16294, memorandum by Ashton Gwatkin, 27 Oct. 1932.
[57] The Nordic countries were chosen partly because their low tariffs were likely to facilitate agreement. CAB 27/489 CFC (32) 3, memorandum by Runciman, 22 Oct. 1932.
[58] BT 11/120, minute by Hill of discussion with Collier, 14 Dec. 1932.
[59] FO 371/16294, memorandum by Collier on talks with Polish Ambassador, 30 Nov. 1932.
[60] Ibid., minute by Collier reporting conversation with Fountain, 7 Dec. 1932.
[61] BT 11/120, W. Erskine (British Ambassador to Poland) to Simon, 17 Oct. 1932.
[62] BT 11/266, unsigned memorandum, n.d. but probably Oct. 1933.

considerations played their part; negotiations with Finland dragged on, preparatory work for the Baltic states prevented any being done for Poland and meanwhile the Poles themselves became involved in a series of trade discussions.[63]

When finally the negotiations did start, the prospects were poor. The population of Poland, at 32·3 million in 1931, far exceeded the combined populations of the Scandinavian and Baltic states. But this was a long way from indicating the size of the market. Despite a population more than a dozen times that of Norway, Polish imports in the early 1930s were below the Norwegian level.[64] Poverty was deep and widespread. In 1929 Polish incomes had been below even the spartan standards of the neighbouring Baltic states.[65] Of the countries of Northern Europe, only Lithuania had a relatively much larger rural population than Poland's 60 per cent.[66] Even before the depression Poland's farming community had been scarred by deep poverty. Gross income per hectare was estimated at less than one-third of the West European level,[67] and rural population density was far higher. These averages obscure vast regional differences. Farm productivity was high in western Poland and declined towards the south and east where the underlying problem was not so much one of bad farming technique as of over-population and extreme land fragmentation.[68] Six and a half million of the population of central, southern and eastern Poland were incapable of satisfying their basic needs for food.[69] Farm labourers by 1930–1 were earning only 54 per cent of their low wages of two years earlier, and, one recorded: 'we eat potatoes, of course, without any seasoning. We are crawling with lice because we cannot afford soap...A slice of bread is only for a big occasion.'[70] Southern Poland, wrote Doreen Warriner, was 'a nightmare of degradation and poverty'.[71] By the second half of 1934 the purchasing capacity of the rural population was calculated at only 43 per cent of the 1928 level.[72]

While falling agricultural prices may have aided the urban worker as a

---

[63] *Ibid.*, and T 160/830/FI3090/011/3, notes on Anglo-Polish trade, 25 June 1934. By 1933 there had been some anxiety to negotiate early with Poland so as to capitalise on its trade dispute with Germany. Note by Fountain for Runciman, 1 June 1933. W.R. 257.

[64] League of Nations, *Review of World Trade 1934* (Geneva, 1935), p. 89.

[65] P. Bairoch, 'Europe's Gross National Product: 1800–1975', *Journal of European Economic History*, 5 (1976), 297 gives GNP per capita at $350 US dollars, one of the lowest levels in Europe and comparing with $468 for the Baltic states. Both figures, Bairoch warns, are subject to a high margin of error.

[66] J. Taylor, *The Economic Development of Poland, 1919–1950* (Ithaca, 1950 and Connecticut, 1970), 63.

[67] D. Warriner, *Economics of Peasant Farming* (Oxford, 1939 and London, 1964), 80. The figures are from a Rome Institute of Agriculture study of 1934–5.   [68] *Ibid.*, 132.

[69] *Ibid.*, 88.   [70] Taylor, *Economic Development of Poland*, 71.

[71] Warriner, *Economics of Peasant Farming*, 26.

[72] Department of Overseas Trade, *Economic Conditions in Poland in 1935*, 23.

consumer, the collapse of rural purchasing power affected jobs. Industrial production in 1932 fell to only 58 per cent of its pre-depression level, worse than the world average, while unemployment exceeded 40 per cent in each of the years 1932 to 1934.[73] Orthodox economic policy aggravated the crisis: Poland stayed on gold and maintained the value of the zloty, interest rates remained high, and the commercial banks contracted credit severely.[74] Total imports fell from 3,111 million zloty in 1929 to 827 million zloty by 1933.[75] Impoverishment was a major factor, but import restrictions were a contributory cause of the decline. Poland was heavily indebted abroad both in terms of state borrowing and of direct investment; remitting profits and servicing debt placed a heavy burden on the balance of payments,[76] and although exchange controls were not introduced until 1936, import restrictions were considerably extended in January 1932 and again in March and June of 1933. Even in 1927 Polish industrial duties were among the highest in Europe,[77] but had been raised subsequently; under the impact of the depression, surtaxes on customs duties were imposed and in October 1933 a new and considerably higher tariff came into force.[78]

Britain's share of Polish trade was small. In 1929 only 8·5 per cent of Polish imports came from the UK and by 1933, 10 per cent of a seriously curtailed trade. On the eve of the depression Britain had only been Poland's fourth largest customer, but had moved up to first place by 1931, taking 17 per cent of Polish exports.[79] Poland's trade dependence on the British market was therefore smaller than that of the other countries of northern Europe, but as the depression deepened it was sufficient to give some leverage to London. Officials considered Britain was tactically strong for two other reasons.[80] The balance of trade, with imports in 1933 of £6·6 million and exports of £2.7 million, was strongly in Poland's favour, and German–Polish relations were bad. A trade war had been conducted since June 1925,[81] intensifying between April 1932 and March 1934.[82] A protocol in March relaxed some of these restrictions, and a clearing agreement was made in October 1934 which involved Germany being accorded mfn rights,

---

[73] Z. Landau and J. Tomaszewski, *The Polish Economy in the Twentieth Century* (Beckenham, 1985), 87 and 106.
[74] League of Nations, *International Currency Experience*, 82.
[75] T 160/830/F13090/011/3. Statement on Polish Trade.
[76] A. Teichova, *An Economic Background to Munich: International Business and Czechoslovakia 1918–1938* (Cambridge, 1974), 16–20.
[77] H. Liepmann, *Tariff Levels and the Economic Unity of Europe* (1938), 153.
[78] T 160/830/F13090/001/3. Statement on Polish Trade.
[79] League of Nations, *International Trade Statistics* (Geneva, 1932).
[80] T 160/829/F13090/0111/2. Note by Mullins on Trade Mission to Poland, 13 Feb. 1934.
[81] Taylor, *Economic Development of Poland*, 117–19.
[82] T 160/830/F13090/011/3. Note on Anglo-Polish Trade, 25 June 1934.

but only for about 100 commodities, and even then limited to a quota for each product.[83] In effect Britain had a preference for many goods and this was taken into account in formulating requests for tariff reductions on products supplied largely by Germany.[84] Another aspect of the situation in Germany likely to operate to Britain's advantage was the oppression of the Jews. Nearly half the commercial enterprises of Poland were controlled by Jews, and some industries, notably textiles and the leather and fur industries were completely dominated by Jewish enterprises.[85] The boycott against Germany was encouraging a switch of purchases to Britain, opening up opportunities for example, for the products of Sheffield and for the chemical industry.[86]

Yet British opportunities were likely to be restricted not merely by Polish poverty but by the determination of the government to protect and develop the industrial sector. Clearly one case was coal. This had dominated British requests in all negotiations except those with Estonia, but in dealing with a competitor the discussions inevitably took a different shape. Polish industry generally was far more widely based than that of the Nordic countries. The steel industry met practically the entire domestic needs, and exported about 30 per cent of output at very low prices. Steel industry members of a British trade mission to Poland concentrated on securing some understanding about sales policy in third markets.[87] The electrical and textile industries were well established, and engineering output was diverse.[88] Army influence, which was powerful, was exerted in the expansion of the Polish motor industry for strategic purposes.[89] The Poles aimed at encouraging local assembly and manufacture of standardised products, and already had contracts with Fiat, but the British industry was adamantly opposed to any such scheme. UK officials had been made conscious of the Polish government's determination to adhere at all costs to the development of industries essential to the military potential of the country.[90] Trade opportunities had to be sought therefore in highly specific sectors or in trade diversion principally at Germany's expense. The most important of British exports are indicated in Table 7.3

[83] Department of Overseas Trade, *Economic Conditions in Poland*, 8.
[84] T 160/830/F13090/011/3, note, 25 June 1934.
[85] Taylor, *Economic Development of Poland*, 103.
[86] BT 11/321. Reports of UK Trade Mission to Poland, Mar. 1934.
[87] *Ibid.* Report of Trade Mission, memorandum on Polish Heavy Steel Industry by J. L. Piggott.
[88] *Ibid.* memorandum on Electrical Industry by W. G. Bass, and Taylor, *Economic Development of Poland*, 83–4.
[89] BT 11/321. Report of Trade Mission, Report of Motor Delegation by L. Walton and W. E. Rootes.
[90] T 160/829/F13090/011/2, memorandum by Mullins on the UK Trade Mission to Poland, 20 Mar. 1934.

below. The main trade requests centred on herrings, textiles and vehicles, although Polish discrimination against Germany gave opportunities for other products too. The trade mission had discovered openings in other previously unimportant trades, such as chemicals and various types of machinery. Britain wanted tariff reductions, quota allowances and purchase agreements. As in other Baltic markets, there had been a major decline in the landing of herrings. In part this was because herrings, which had constituted the staple diet in certain religious fasts, were being replaced by cheaper fish or other food. Yet suppliers from Britain had fallen further than total fish imports, and although British shippers contributed to their own plight by concentrating on Danzig and ignoring the fast growing port of Gdynia, their problems were aggravated by the lower duties imposed on the bigger herrings from Iceland and Norway.[91]

London wanted the duty on small herrings reduced to a quarter its existing level.[92] Britain had only a tiny export of cars, lorries and parts but wanted extensive tariff reductions – these requests were to play a major part in the negotiations. The duty on motor cycles had been raised from 132 to 700 zloty per 100 kilograms in October 1933 and had virtually killed British sales.[93] Altogether, reductions were asked for on some 120 items together with 7 items of interest to the colonies; with a small number of duty consolidations added, the total number of items involved was about 150 out of the 1,275 items in the Polish tariff. Nevertheless it was felt that the British tariff claims covered about three-quarters of recent trade. There were a number of developments arising out of the trade mission's activities in Poland. Mostly these concerned potential purchase agreements, which included a number of by now familiar requests. Purchase arrangements were likely to draw out some of the peculiarities of the Polish import control system. It was quite common to waive or substantially cut duties on products needed by Polish industry, so guarantees had to be secured that purchase agreement goods would be treated this way. The other hurdle was the import licensing system, and here the British negotiators wanted the Poles to suggest the quotas they would allow.

There were two other major items in the British negotiating objectives. Shipping was to play a prominent part in the commercial discussions and to prove an important obstacle to agreement. Essentially, it was felt that in the carrying trade the Poles discriminated in favour of their own shipping and the UK wanted a more equitable share of the tramp and liner business. In addition, Whitehall wanted the abrogation of the Emigration Decree of 1930 which required that emigrants to North America should go directly

---

[91] Department of Overseas Trade, *Report on Economic Conditions in Poland 1934*, 24.

[92] T 160/830/F13090/011/3, note on Anglo-Polish Trade, 25 June 1934.

[93] *Ibid.* The rest of the paragraph is based on this document.

Table 7.3. *Principal UK exports of domestic produce to Poland,
1929–1933* (£000s)

	1929	1930	1931	1932	1933
Herring	1,300.6	1,011.3	581·9	398·8	363·9
Iron and steel scrap	355·9	135·2	126·4	21·2	137·1
Raw wool	71·3	21·2	33·4	56·1	106·2
Cotton – yarns	419·6	247·3	133·2	141·4	247·9
piece goods	204·0	109·6	74·9	89·8	163·2
Electric goods	63·3	54·4	79·3	66·4	146·7
Machinery and parts	529·5	193·3	123·9	137·7	154·0
Road vehicles, etc.	208·0	206·4	129·0	113·0	175·6
Cycles and parts	54·8	56·9	28·4	4·0	31·0
Woollens & worsted					
yarns	128·7	66·6	50·0	44·2	60·2
tissues	87·8	68·8	41·7	23·2	26·3
Total	4,504·8	3,564·2	2,003·8	2,001·4	2,738·1

Source: UK *Annual Statement of Trade 1933.*

from Gdynia; it was uneconomic for British lines to operate such a direct
service.

Secondly, as mentioned above, an integral part of the negotiations was
an agreement between British and Polish coalowners to limit competition
in third markets. The Mines Department had suggested to the Board of
Trade that while negotiations on other matters would go ahead con-
currently with the coal talks, they would not be brought to an end until the
coal negotiations were satisfactorily concluded.[94] Such an idea was put to
the Poles, and Runciman in his welcome to the Polish delegation in June
said he hoped the coal discussions would be completed before the end of
the negotiations for a trade agreement.[95] Discussions between representatives of the two industries had been held in 1929. Initially the British side
had deprecated any idea of an understanding, asserting that the competitive power of the UK industry would soon drive Polish coal out of
Scandinavia.[96] A truer appreciation of the organisational and technical
strength of the Polish mining industry later led to talks about the
possibilities of restrictions, but, largely because of the lack of central
organisation of the British industry, came to nothing. The Coal Mines Act
of 1930 had brought greater centralisation to British mining, and,

[94] FO 371/17775, note by Mines Department Minister to Runciman, 9 Feb. 1934, enclosed
in Cole to Ashton Gwatkin, 15 Feb. 1934.   [95] BT 11/321, 3rd meeting, 27 June 1934.
[96] POWE 16/181, R. E. Kimens (Commercial Secretary in Warsaw) to Sir Austen Chamberlain, 10 Feb. 1928.

Table 7.4. *Selected imports into UK from Poland, 1929–1933* (£000s)

	1929	1930	1931	1932	1933
Butter	538·2	398·5	158·0	11·4	0·7
Eggs	1,240·4	1,580·3	1,015·0	624·8	508·5
Sugar	616·1	319·2	889·1	482·3	176·7
Bacon	1,482·0	1,883·8	2,704·8	2,658·6	2,289·0
Other meat	173·7	184·6	334·5	354·8	287·5
Poultry & game	0·1	1·0	27·5	57·6	72·0
Timber – hewn, hard	195·5	170·2	69·5	37·9	15·8
sawn, hard	248·9	280·8	303·3	307·0	422·0
sawn, soft	533·0	6,932·8	792·8	548·1	1,385·1
Sleepers	423·5	959·3	418·7	144·5	146·4
Timber m/fctrs.	400·1	232·9	210·0	134·9	116·2
Total	6,908·4	7,948·6	8,612·2	6,184·4	6,551·1

Source: UK *Annual Statement of Trade 1933.*

naturally, the use of the trade agreements to recapture the Scandinavian markets for UK coal also sharpened Polish interest in an export agreement. This was achieved through a series of meetings in Warsaw and London between industry representatives. Certain price arrangements were made (the Poles had been quoting very low prices in Scandinavia, feeding dissatisfaction with the agreements there), and quarterly quotas were established for Polish coal at 21 per cent of British coal exports.[97] In effect Polish coal exports were to be dependent on the ability of the British industry to sell abroad.

British demands, apart from the coal stipulations, therefore centred on a larger share of shipping and a number of trade requests, the most important of which were for herrings, vehicles and textiles. What did the Poles hope to achieve, beyond the continuation of mfn treatment? British imports from Poland, as Table 7.4 shows, followed a typical Scandinavian/ Baltic pattern. Dairy products, important on the eve of the depression, had declined rapidly, in part because of the overvalued zloty. There had been some compensation in more valuable timber exports, but the major advances had been in the emergence of the bacon trade, relatively unimportant in the late 1920s but by far Poland's most important export

[97] FO 371/17781, Mines Department to Foreign Office, 19 Dec. 1934. These figures excluded certain markets, but otherwise Polish exports would be 21 per cent of British exports up to 8·75 million tons per quarter and 10 per cent of any figure beyond that. For a full and useful discussion of the whole issue, see P. Salmon. 'Polish–British Competition in the Coal Markets of Northern Europe, 1927–1934', *Studia Historiae Oeconomicae*, 16 (1983), 217–243.

to Britain by the early 1930s. Poland wanted a range of tariff reductions and consolidation on agricultural, timber and manufactured goods, and, particularly for farm products, guarantees about minimum quantities. Ideally, the delegation wanted not just a minimum percentage of British bacon imports but a stipulated minimum absolute amount of 1 million pigs. This was the most important item in their overall claims and they declared it would be difficult to agree to a treaty without satisfactory assurances for their bacon.[98] The problem with butter was the sudden drop in exports in 1931 and 1932, but the Poles hoped to achieve 'insignificant' status which would enable them, if import controls were introduced, to expand exports freely as long as the market was not endangered. Egg duties were to be consolidated, but again the Polish delegation wanted a definite percentage of the market, and suggested $14\frac{1}{2}$ per cent.[99] Among requests on other products were a range of duty consolidations on timber and wood products – some were already guaranteed through the earlier trade agreements and the UK side wanted further detail so as to give concessions only on closely defined products.[100] Tariff concessions were also wanted, *inter alia* for ready-made clothing, kilims and bentwood furniture.

The negotiations, which began in June 1934, were long and difficult. Problems stemmed from the fact that the Poles regarded the British agreement as a key one, setting a precedent for later commercial pacts with other countries. But the extensiveness of the Polish import restrictions also complicated discussions: prohibitions covered about 75 per cent of imports from the UK, and it was necessary to discuss quotas for nearly 200 classes of product. The Poles also proved very determined negotiators, and were not only extremely reluctant to make concessions on shipping and vehicles, for example, but were also insistent on securing precise guarantees for their agricultural exports.

Discussions about motor vehicles were especially difficult, not helped by the determination of the Polish government to develop its own industry, and by the reluctance of the British motor industry to specify the range of cars it was most interested in selling. Another major item in the trade requests, herrings, was more easily agreed, with Britain accepting a halving of the duty on small herrings.[101] Neither did cotton textiles present much of a problem in the negotiations: the duty on cotton yarns was brought down to practically the level Manchester wanted, and duties on the relevant cotton piece goods were reduced to pre-depression levels.[102]

[98] T 160/831/F13090011/8, 78th meeting, 28 Nov. 1934.

[99] *Ibid.*, 82nd meeting, 5 Dec. 1934.

[100] FO 371/17779, UK–Poland Commercial Negotiations, notes for Col. Colville for Reception of Polish Delegation on 10 Oct. 1934.

[101] T 160/830/F13090/011/6, 55th, 59th and 69th meetings, 30 Oct., 3 and 20 Nov. 1934.

[102] *Ibid.*

Woollens created greater difficulties, only a small reduction on woollen yarns being achieved, and little progress was made on other products.

The other matter of major importance in the British desiderata was shipping and discussions on this proved to be the most protracted of all. Agreement on tramp shipping, by which British owners would be informed of opportunities of Anglo-Polish trade, and of the results of tenders, was reached comparatively easily. Proposals on emigrant shipping, allowing British lines to participate in the American routes by transhipment, and which involved the abrogation of the Polish Emigration Decree of 1930, stipulating direct sailing from Gdynia, were settled in principle.[103] The most difficult of the shipping issues was the short-route sea liner trade. Eventually British companies were assured a higher share of the trade, and, if additional shipping was needed, British lines were to have first option of providing the necessary tonnage until the carrying trade was approximately equal.[104]

Purchasing agreements, an important part of the British desiderata, proved less of an obstacle in the negotiations than vehicles or shipping. Progress on state purchases was hampered by Polish reluctance to give written guarantees which might cause embarrassment if leaked to other countries, and also by the Poles' insistence that British prices should be competitive. As Arthur Mullins expressed it, 'if "competitive" meant that the United Kingdom side, in order to obtain the benefits of Purchase Arrangements, were required to quote at the lowest price, the Arrangements would be valueless'.[105] The eventual agreements covered a large number of products, but for state purchases Britain had to be satisfied with an oral undertaking only.[106]

Most concessions on British products were useless unless the Polish government was prepared to issue licences. Quotas were fixed for nearly 200 classes of goods, the general basis being that the 1933 volume of trade would be increased by 20 per cent plus larger quotas for products where trade opportunities looked especially good. It was here that the paucity of British guarantees for Polish agricultural exports restricted the value of the return concessions. The Poles were primarily interested in getting a steady market for their bacon, and this was crucial to the negotiations as a whole. In the end they were guaranteed that their percentage of foreign bacon imports would not be reduced, and were given a quota for 1935. Because of Polish pressure, a decision was made that total imports of bacon from foreign countries would not be reduced in 1935 by more than $12\frac{1}{2}$ per cent,

[103] FO 371/18885, United Kingdom–Polish Commercial Negotiations, note by Runciman, 24 Jan. 1935, Annex.   [104] *Ibid.*, 95th meeting, 19 Dec. 1934.
[105] FO 371/18885, UK–Polish Commercial Negotiation, note by Runciman, 24 Jan. 1935, Annex.   [106] T 160/830/F13090/011/5, 44th meeting, 16 Oct. 1934.

thus enabling a firm minimum figure for 1935 to be given.[107] But it was not possible to provide definite figures for 1936 or beyond, and this inability led to the inclusion of a clause which entitled 'either party at the end of one year to raise the question of the revision of the quotas it had been granted, and, if agreement is not reached, either party may denounce the whole agreement'.[108]

Their failure to obtain long-term security for bacon exports was a source of major dissatisfaction for the Poles, and they also failed to achieve much for their other products. They were granted a minimum of $13\frac{1}{2}$ per cent of foreign imports for their eggs,[109] and, a matter complicated because of unusually low shipments in 1932 and 1933, a guarantee that their butter exports would not be regulated until they reached the 1929 level (a high one). All relevant duties on agricultural produce were consolidated, largely items already covered by earlier trade treaties, but with some additions for Poland.[110]

The final assessment of the trade value of the agreement for Britain was hedged with qualifications and was modest enough. Much depended on UK competitive ability, and on Polish economic recovery – but it also hinged on Polish goodwill. The purchase agreements were calculated to produce at least an extra £200,000, and much more if state purchases were substantially increased. Estimates for other products were extremely tentative but thought to be worth a minimum of £300,000. Probably £500,000 was an understatement of the trade value of the agreement for Britain, but even so it reflects the difficulties of securing much from medium sized powers with industrial pretensions. The Poles were determined to develop their industry, both for military reasons and as part of their economic strategy for coping with the gross agricultural poverty that resulted from land shortage. This partly accounts for their obduracy. But they also felt, rightly enough, that they were getting precious little in the agreement. The negotiations were long and tortuous, and had none of the bullying tones that had characterised Britain's trade discussions with the smaller Baltic states. But they were unproductive if the Board of Trade's estimates were anything to go by: after well over a hundred meetings a trade agreement emerged that was to last less than two years and produce less extra trade than with Latvia.

---

[107] FO 371/18885, note by Runciman, 24 Jan. 1935, Annex. Amongst others, there were agreements for purchasing textile machinery and parts, leather, chemicals and agricultural and dairy machinery. The Poles also agreed to buy at least 50 per cent of the jute wrappers required for bacon exports to Britain, despite a strong jute industry of their own.

[108] CAB 27/560 PMS (33), 11th meeting, 17 Oct. 1934.

[109] FO 371/18885, note by Runciman, 24 Jan. 1935, Annex.

[110] T 160/831/F13090/011/9, 92nd meeting, 18 Dec. 1934.

This chapter examines the influence of British policy on imports from the
trade agreement countries. By the 1920s, as discussed in chapter 3, the
dominions had a larger share of the British market than before the war. But
in the last four years before the depression the dominions began to lose
ground to their Scandinavian, Baltic and Argentine competitors. The
struggle for the British market was most intense in temperate foodstuffs,
world imports of which were dominated by the UK, a domination which
became even more marked as the depression worsened. Britain's return to
protection signalled that a third major group of competitors, domestic
farmers, were likely to have first call on their own home market. But
although the Import Duties Act and the subsequent treaties had established
a formal hierarchy between domestic, imperial and foreign suppliers, these
were not absolute priorities but were highly qualified and contingent, and
reflected the value placed by British policy makers on the maintenance of
overseas markets, both dominion and foreign. One of the principal benefits
of the treaties to Britain's suppliers was the way in which they constrained
and shaped British agricultural policy in the 1930s.[1]

Agricultural policy

By the summer of 1933 the major legislation and agreements had been
completed. The Import Duties Act, the Ottawa conference legislation and
the completion of the agreements with Denmark and Argentina had set the
framework for British protection. This status quo, however, was soon
under attack. The attack came from two sources and highlighted the

[1] I. M. Drummond, *Imperial Economic Policy 1917–1939: Studies in expansion and
protection* (1974), ch. 7, and J. S. Eyers, 'Government direction of Britain's overseas trade
policy, 1932–37' (D.Phil. thesis, University of Oxford, 1977). See also T. J. T. Rooth,
'Trade agreements and the evolution of British agricultural policy in the 1930s',
Agricultural History Review, 33 (1985), 173–90, for a fuller account, and A. F. Cooper,
British Agricultural Policy, 1912–36. A Study in Conservative politics (Manchester, 1989).

conflict between the three main groups of contestants for the British market. It was the Ministry of Agriculture, seeking to protect domestic agriculture, that presented the first challenge, and because this involved possible modification to the existing treaties it opened up the possibility of further pressure from imperial suppliers to oust their foreign competitors.

British farmers

Sir John Gilmour had been largely unsuccessful at Ottawa in protecting British agriculture against the dominions. His successor, Walter Elliot (as was seen in chapters 4 and 5), had a measure of success in restraining the largesse of the Board of Trade in the subsequent treaty making. Nonetheless, by the time the first major series of trade treaties had been completed, Britain had a range of obligations that strictly curtailed the government's freedom of action in assisting home farmers. For meat, foreign supplies of frozen mutton, lamb and beef were being progressively reduced so that by mid-1934 they would be at 65 per cent of their Ottawa Year (the year ending 30 June 1932) level. From July 1934 Whitehall would, in theory at least, be able to control empire supplies by import quotas; Argentina had rights to 90 per cent, or in some circumstances 100 per cent of its Ottawa Year *chilled* beef supplies, although these might be restricted below 90 per cent if dominion meat imports were cut by similar proportions. But Britain had also bound itself not to tax meat imports during the currency of the Argentine and Ottawa agreements, i.e. until November 1936 or August 1937 respectively. The bacon situation was a little more straightforward: Canada was guaranteed a market for $2\frac{1}{2}$ million cwts, but foreign supplies could be cut to whatever level was thought wise or desirable. Here too, though, free entry had been conceded, so if duties were to be introduced this would involve acquiescence of the trade partner. A mixed bag of obligations on dairy products and eggs also hampered freedom of action. Foreign supplies could be quantitatively controlled if domestic sales were also regulated by a marketing scheme. Dominion produce was to be free of duties or quotas until mid-1935, but minimum preference margins were fixed until 1937. Because existing duties were stabilised until 1936 in the various foreign agreements, it was therefore impossible to tax dominion supplies without infringing the preferential tariff margins.

The scope of action available to the Ministry of Agriculture was thus severely curtailed, although more so for import levies than in the field of quotas. This accorded with Neville Chamberlain's ideas that producer control offered the best prospects for raising prices. As early as November 1932 the Pacific dominions and countries of South America had been induced to cut back their meat shipments, and these arrangements had been carried through into 1933.[2] Mutton and lamb prices were fairly well maintained, partly because of restricted supplies, partly because demand trends were relatively favourable. Beef prices continued to fall during 1933, however, and pressures built up from domestic producers and landowners for further help.[3] The structure of the industry was such that the fatteners, principally located in the East Midlands (summer grazing) and East Anglia (winter feeding), were able to wield more political influence than the breeders, who were geographically more remote and operating on a smaller scale. The fatteners were also more vulnerable to price falls. The cattle they bought cost them 75 to 80 per cent of the price they hoped to realise for the finished beef, so when prices fell at the rate they did in 1932 and 1933, this margin could be eliminated during the six months they normally kept the animals.[4] Elliot's solution to these problems, first mooted when the ink on the agreements with Argentina was barely dry, proposed the introduction of a levy-subsidy, and, as an inducement to Argentina's acquiescence, suggested the waiving of British rights to reduce chilled beef imports below 90 per cent of the Ottawa Year level.[5] At this stage Ministers were lukewarm about or opposed to the idea of a subsidy, Chamberlain, for example, asserting that if beef producers had a subsidy, every other industry would demand one.[6] Ideas reverted to supply restriction. The Canadians were to be persuaded to stabilise their cattle exports, and a 50 per cent cut was made in imports of Irish cattle. Although this arose out of the dispute with the Irish Free State, it involved a reduction of over 5 per cent in total supplies of fresh beef, the type most directly competitive with home produced beef, and was aimed at helping British producers.

The emphasis on restriction of supplies as the main method of holding or raising prices was to last until the middle of 1934. It has been severely criticised by Ian Drummond who argues that it failed to generate budgetary revenue, and 'raised everyone's price'.[7] Because price elasticities were high, cutbacks in supply were likely to lead to less than proportionate increases in price: the total sales revenue of overseas suppliers would be reduced and

[2] CAB 27/495, Cabinet Committee on Meat Policy. This committee met only once and produced no report. The one meeting, at which Elliot pressed for the Board of Trade to be given powers to regulate meat supplies from abroad produced the usual opposition from the Board of Trade, Dominions Office and Treasury as well as from the Prime Minister. The voluntary restrictions, also involving bacon, did serve to firm prices temporarily.

[3] CAB 27/560 PMS (33), 1st meeting, 1 Dec. 1933 (the landowners included the bursars of Oxford Colleges).

[4] Viscount Astor and B. S. Rowntree, *British Agriculture. The principles of future policy* (1938), 194.   [5] CAB 27/560 PMS (33) 2, memorandum, 5 Dec. 1933.

[6] *Ibid.*, 3rd meeting, 14 Dec. 1933.   [7] Drummond, *Imperial Economic Policy*, 302.

their purchasing power, together with their ability to service debt, impaired. Instead, a fall in prices might have done the trick. Drummond suggests that policy makers, although aware that lower prices would stimulate consumption, failed to appreciate their power in reducing production.[8] Perhaps this is to romanticise the efficacy of the price mechanism, for in the conditions of the 1930s, supply elasticities for agricultural output as a whole were low. Certainly prices fell dramatically, and output did not contract. Capital was tied up in farms, and opportunities for alternative employment in industry were virtually non-existent.[9] Governments committed to maintaining agriculture and rural population frequently had resort to subsidies, particularly for export crops. Exchange depreciations could nullify tariff imposts. In the circumstances, therefore, lower prices would either fail to reduce output, or, at best, do so only very slowly.

If the price mechanism was a weak instrument of adjustment, import controls alone were unlikely to render much assistance to British farmers. The high price elasticities that characterised several imported meats,[10] and probably dairy products as well, meant that only very severe cuts in production would be successful in raising prices significantly, and not least because consumers would switch from one type of meat to another if relative prices changed. For example, they were more likely to regard good quality lamb as an alternative to fresh Scotch beef than chilled Argentine beef. For these reasons, import restrictions were unlikely to be very effective in raising the price of home produced meats. It was also understood at the time that when dealing with products of which Britain was the major buyer, the incidence of tariffs was likely to be borne by producers rather than reflected in higher prices. Nor, as was suggested above, was there reason to think that this would have any immediate impact on production. Thus the objective conditions of supply and demand, together with the maze of treaty obligations, severely restricted the British government's scope in protecting its farmers from the crisis.

Quite apart from their relative ineffectiveness there were other problems in regulating imports by quota. The government found the actual implementation of voluntary supply regulations fraught with difficulties. After Elliot's proposals on levy-subsidies for meat producers had been

---

[8] *Ibid.*, 329.

[9] For a review of various explanations of supply inelasticity of agricultural output during depression, see D. G. Johnson, 'The nature of the supply function for agricultural products', *American Economic Review*, 40 (1950), 539–64. Johnson argues that during a depression it is the absence of alternative uses for factor inputs that accounts for inelastic supply functions.

[10] F. H. Capie, 'The British market for livestock products, 1920–1939' (Ph.D. thesis, University of London, 1973), 64–5, 76–82.

rejected in 1933, London remained committed to restricting the quantity of imports by direct methods. Foreign meat supplies were being compulsorily reduced. But the dominions were guaranteed unrestricted entry until July 1934; until then their cooperation in regulating their shipments was necessary. Through 1933 and 1934 attempts were made to control meat imports, by negotiation, on a quarterly basis. This involved almost continuous wrangling with the dominions, and both the administrative burden and the costs to imperial goodwill were high.[11]

The lost battle for expansion

These manoeuvres arose out of the crisis afflicting British farmers. Emergency assistance to the UK farmer was one thing, but how far should British agriculture be allowed to expand? In what directions should it expand? With a slow-growing population and with food consumption virtually static, the answers to these questions were clearly vital for overseas suppliers. Two key reports were produced in the autumn of 1934, one by the Committee on Economic Information (the Stamp report), and the other by a powerful inter-departmental committee chaired by the government's chief economic adviser, Sir Frederick Leith-Ross.[12] The gist of the reports, stated more clearly in the Stamp report than in the Leith-Ross document, was that there was little scope for a substantial increase in British consumption of agricultural produce, that an increase in domestic production would entail a corresponding reduction in imports and that this in turn would lead to reduced exports. Other, broader, approaches to stimulating economic activity, advocated by Keynes, were abjured by the rest of the Stamp Committee.[13]

J. S. Eyers argues that Elliot was unable to challenge successfully the assumption that agricultural expansion at home must entail lower imports. Although the reports were discussed in Cabinet and at a series of meetings of the Produce Markets Supply Committee, no explicit decision was taken on the larger issues of policy. Elliot's memoranda on the possibilities and implications of agricultural expansion were challenged by those from Runciman. In what may have been a crucial encounter, Elliot lost the battle for any notable agricultural growth. While Elliot, as Eyers suggests, may have contributed to this failure by poor tactical leadership and mobilisation of argument, the real problem for the Ministry of Agriculture was the formidable array of assumptions and departmental interests ranged against it. Britain's long reliance on a free trade policy, a tendency

---

[11] The process is traced in Drummond, *Imperial Economic Policy*, 307–17.
[12] CAB 27/560 PMS (33) 26 and 27, 1 Nov. 1934 and 8 Jan. 1935.
[13] Eyers, 'Government direction of British overseas trade policy', 99–147.

to regard agriculture as an industry much like any other industry, and a tradition of cheap food for the urban population, coupled with the long period of British expansiveness overseas during which export levels had been built up and investments made – all this militated against a sudden development of agriculture at the expense either of overseas producers or of domestic consumers. High unemployment made the government all the more wary of losing markets for industrial exports. The Board of Trade was the main guardian of the export interest, but received frequent assistance from the Foreign Office and Dominions Office. The Treasury was keen to safeguard overseas investments and also, when subsidies were introduced, not to make them so generous as to stimulate a large increase in subsidised output. From early 1935, therefore, although discussion did not end, a major expansion in British output at the expense of overseas suppliers or of the cost of living was ruled out, and the main thrust of policy was directed merely to propping up British agriculture.

Levy-subsidies

This left vital issues unresolved. The actual method of agricultural support was obviously of crucial concern to farmers, and was also likely to affect British consumers and taxpayers. Furthermore, in the conditions of the 1930s even a policy directed largely towards stabilising home agricultural output might incur considerable costs for overseas suppliers – much would depend on the choice of method. One of the outcomes of the policy reviews of the autumn and winter of 1934–5 was to confirm the government in its switch to levy-subsidies as the main technique of agricultural support. Disillusion with quantitative controls stemmed from the fact that they either failed to work or, if they did work, did so at heavy cost. The bacon restriction scheme had been a disaster. Here was one case where British agriculture was being expanded, and directly at the expense of foreign imports. By 1934 these had fallen from their 1932 peak of 11 million cwts to only 6·3 million cwts. In contrast to other meats, Danish bacon had a distinct brand image and low price elasticity, and the result was sharply rising import prices.[14] The Leith-Ross Committee was strongly against quotas, and had been influenced by the operation of the bacon quota restrictions which had been 'admittedly a failure'.[15] Runciman and J. H. Thomas both expressed the resentment felt by consumers at the increasing price of bacon, reporting that the Danes and the Dutch were selling

[14] W. Beckerman, 'Some aspects of monopoly and monopsony in international trade as illustrated by Anglo-Danish trade, 1921–38' (Ph.D. thesis, University of Cambridge, 1952).
[15] T 188/101, Leith-Ross papers, memorandum by Leith-Ross to Runciman, 6 Dec. 1934.

surpluses abroad at 30s per cwt below the London price.[16] Another major source of disillusion had been the trouble and ill-feeling generated in the regulation of meat imports from the dominions. It was widely felt within government that the cost was too heavy and that alternatives, more acceptable to overseas suppliers, should be sought. In June 1934 Elliot had brought forward the idea of deficiency payments only because the 'political difficulties with the Dominions in regard to restriction of imports were of so grave a nature'.[17] It was a view shared by Chamberlain, anxious about antagonising the dominions with meat restrictions, and by the Foreign Office, which stressed the damage caused to relations with Northern Europe and South America.[18]

Although deficiency payments for the Milk Marketing Board had been announced in parliament in 1934, import quotas had then been the favoured instrument of Ministers. By the summer though, for the reasons suggested, opinion was swinging toward the levy-subsidies, and on 13 June the Produce Markets Supply Committee decided in principle to introduce them for beef producers.

If British Ministers had hoped such proposals would be more acceptable to the dominions, they were soon to be disillusioned. The proposals were formally published in a White Paper in July.[19] They were presented in the form of alternatives and show how far Britain had travelled since Ottawa: (a) drastic restriction of imports by quantitative regulations; (b) a levy on imports of meat (apart from bacon and ham) without import regulations; (c) a levy on imports 'coupled with some degree of direct supply regulation in the interest of all suppliers'. The threat of tougher quantitative restrictions was essentially a device to induce the dominions and Argentina to waive their treaty rights and agree to the levy-subsidy. It failed.

The Australian reaction was particularly vehement.[20] Already agriculture was severely depressed. Long-term prospects were clouded by fears of stagnant or declining population in the UK. Now Britain proposed to shore up its livestock industry in ways which were directly at the expense of Australian output. These trends and actions cut right across prevailing Australasian assumptions. Australians especially had long assumed that if they could produce foodstuffs and raw materials then a grateful world would buy them. An Inter-State Commission, discussing in 1916 the tariff and employment prospects had stated:

---

[16] CAB 27/560 PMS (33), 12th meeting, 7 Dec. 1934.
[17] *Ibid.*, 7th meeting, 12 June 1934.
[18] See *ibid.*, PMS (33) 30, Simon to Baldwin 9 Jan. 1935, for an emphatic account of the difficulties caused in relations with those countries, and for a demand that quotas be abandoned immediately.   [19] Cmd. 4651, *The Livestock Situation*, July 1934.
[20] DO 35/255/9105/198. Response summarised.

We need have no anxiety in regard to our export trade in those natural products for which there is an increasing world wide demand ... Fortunately, Australia offers the possibility of unlimited expansion in agricultural, mining and pastoral industries, for the products of which the world's demand is practically unlimited.[21]

To many Australians the whole basis of national development still appeared to depend on the expansion of such production and exports; the growth of population, central to Australian national aspirations, was seen as stemming from the associated settlement. Broadly similar views were held in New Zealand. In replying to the British threat of 1934, the New Zealand Governor-General telegraphed:

A proposal of the character that has been mentioned goes to the heart of the economic life in this country and must cut disastrously across our national development...The essential fact is that, since New Zealand became British Territory and particularly since British capital has been invested on a large scale in this country...it has been implicit in the development of New Zealand that production should be increased and that in payment of principal, an increasing volume of primary products should flow to the United Kingdom. Payment in goods is imperative. The investments proceeded, and the debts were incurred, on the implicit understanding, by virtue of the development thereby financed, higher standard of living would result to the investing and consuming countries and also to producers here – producers who it is needless to emphasise are either immigrants from the United Kingdom or their immediate descendants...the suggested policy would tend permanently to restrict immigration.[22]

The Pacific dominions therefore felt intensely such a blow to their underlying assumptions about national development. But if heavy shadows were cast over their long-term future, more immediate and urgent preoccupations sharpened their reaction. Acute balance of payments difficulties could be relieved by export expansion. Exports appeared to offer the only route out of the depression. J. A. Lyons, the Australian Premier, claimed that 'only by full restoration of our exporting industries can internal purchasing power be re-established, leading to the employment of the workless and to renewed progress'.[23] This explains the force of the Pacific dominions' reaction, and their negotiating tactics. In a framework of virtually stagnant demand the main prospect for recovery and for the continuation of traditional patterns of national development appeared to be through the progressive displacement of the foreigner in the British market. Wherever it was technically possible or economically

[21] Quoted by A. J. Reitsma, *Trade Protection in Australia* (Leiden, 1960), 20.
[22] DO 35/317/9513/98, Telegram from Governor-General of New Zealand to Thomas, 9 July 1934.
[23] CPP, 1932–4, vol. IV, p. 510. Quoted by C. B. Schedvin, *Australia and the Great Depression* (Sydney, 1970), 317.

feasible, Britain, they thought, should help them achieve this by use of commercial policy.

Australia, Argentina and the emergence of deficiency payments

It was in this context that the second challenge came to the post trade agreements status quo. After considerable experiment, it at last became technically possible to ship chilled meat from the Pacific dominions and to land it in the UK in a marketable state.[24] This potentially transformed the prospects for Australian and New Zealand beef. Previously they had been confined to exporting frozen beef, the demand for which was rapidly declining. By 1930 Australian frozen beef had been virtually eliminated from the UK retail trade and depended on institutional demand; even then, irregular shipments made it difficult to secure large contracts.[25] It is true that there remained a formidable range of problems for Australian beef producers – poor quality stock, bad grazing conditions, including sporadic droughts, and the fact that breeding and fattening was carried out on the same ranches and at considerable distance from the meat works.[26] But with the first wholly successful shipment of chilled beef from Australia in 1934, the prospect, at least to Australian eyes, became brighter. Instead of an unyielding market for frozen beef, offering little or no chance of expansion, there was now the opportunity to supplant Argentina as supplier of the huge British market for chilled beef. Australian energies were now turned to the twin tasks of holding off British attempts to restrict beef imports generally, and of seeking the gradual displacement of Argentine chilled beef supplies. Given the state of Australian beef, and to a less extent that of New Zealand, they were only going to be able to supplant Argentina if the British could be persuaded to use their commercial armoury to improve the Australasian position.

London's response to these pressures is significant: while wanting a solution to the low prices crippling British livestock producers, it did not want a solution that penalised foreign suppliers markedly more than imperial suppliers. The concessions to the Empire had been made in 1932 – after Ottawa there was extreme reluctance in London to further jeopardise foreign markets for the benefit of the dominions. Consequently, the Australians considered Whitehall unduly sympathetic to Argentina. Explanations of Britain's alleged pro-Argentine inclination centred on the scale and pattern of British investments in Argentina. John Curtin, Leader

[24] See e.g. K. Burley, *British Shipping and Australia 1920–39* (1968), 85–87.
[25] R. Duncan 'The Australian beef export trade and the origins of the Australian Meat Board', *The Australian Journal of Politics and History*, 5 (1959), 192.
[26] R. Duncan, 'The Australian export trade with the United Kingdom in refrigerated beef, 1880–1940', *Business Archives and History*, 2 (1962), especially 108–11.

of the Opposition, claimed in a debate in November 1935 that UK policy towards Argentina was governed by the fact that British investments there were largely in trading companies with variable returns whereas British investments in Australia, although larger than in Argentina, were in government fixed interest securities. Therefore 'Britain has an interest in making investments in Argentina profitable, while it is completely indifferent to the fate of companies operating in Australia because the bulk of British capital is invested, not in private ventures, but in Government securities'.[27]

Lyons expressed similar views to the UK government.[28] Australian ill-feeling even led to the suggestion that foreign supplies were being given precedence over the dominions: 'Argentina's favoured situation in her Agreement with the United Kingdom is an incomparably superior one to that which was granted to Australia at Ottawa, despite the very high and special price which we paid for the meat concession.'[29]

This piece of nonsense was described by Whitehall officials as an 'abuse of language'. The Australians used a combination of threats and cajolery to secure concessions. The main threat was to play on British fears of the Australian Labour Party, which was strongly protectionist and highly critical of the Ottawa agreements, getting back into power.[30] But the Australians could also offer improved conditions for UK exports. There seems little doubt that the Australian trade diversion policy, introduced in 1936 and helpful to British exports, was used in the meat negotiations to secure better terms for Australia.[31] While restrictions on motor chassis imports were mainly designed to help develop the Australian motor industry (although the UK did get some temporary benefits), a major objective of the steep tariff increases on foreign textiles was to divert trade from Japan to the UK. As in other parts of the world the Japanese textile exporters had been making enormous inroads into the Australian market since 1932 and making a mockery of the intentions of the Ottawa agreement. In return for rectifying this position the Australians hoped that

[27] DO 35/259/9105/3/157, J. Curtin speaking on Meat Export Control Bill in Australian House of Commons, quoted by UK representative, 19 Nov. 1935.
[28] DO 35/256/9105/446, Telegram from Lyons to Baldwin, 17 June 1936.
[29] CAB 32/124 E.D.A. (a) 35. Statement by J. A. Lyons to Ministers of HM Government in the United Kingdom, Apr. 1935.
[30] DO 35/256/9105/236 and DO 35/256/3/15.
[31] For further details and discussion of the motivation behind these measures see D. P. Copland and C. V. James (eds.), *Australian Trade Policy – A Book of Documents 1932–1937* (Sydney, 1937); N. F. Hall, 'Trade diversion – an Australian interlude', *Economica*, ns, 5 (1938), 1–11; H. Burton, 'The trade diversion episode of the 'thirties', *Australian Outlook*, 22 (1968); K. Tsokhas, *Markets, Money and Empire: the political economy of the Australian wool industry* (Melbourne, 1990), ch. 7. As mentioned in the text above, the motivation behind the sets of measures was probably distinct and it seems possible that they were combined together so as to divide and confuse internal opposition.

Britain would adopt a more helpful attitude to Australian imports. Indeed as political opposition to the measure rose in Australia, it became imperative to obtain something of value from Britain.

Possibly this move tipped the balance in favour of the Australians. Malcolm MacDonald, successor to Thomas as Dominions Secretary, argued that:

One of the essential factors of the position in Australia was the step they had taken, simply in order to help the United Kingdom textile manufactures, of imposing high tariffs against Japanese textiles. Japan had threatened serious retaliation, and it was not certain that Australia would stand up to her. If the terms of the present United Kingdom offer remained unmodified, the new tariffs would stand every chance of defeat in the Commonwealth Parliament... Mr. Menzies had told him at their last interview that even a very small modification of our terms would help Australian Ministers greatly... for the sake of our textile trade, we ought to make such a modification.[32]

It is worth pursuing this saga further because it demonstrates the relatively small gain Australia eventually made over Argentina, and also because it led to a key decision which established the fundamentals of British agricultural policy between 1936 and the 1970s. In part the Australian response was so hostile because they had regarded meat as their major gain from the Ottawa conference.[33] The British proposals were therefore particularly unwelcome, despite offering the prospect of Australian advances at Argentina's expense. But how far did the eventual solution differ from the earlier proposals?

At one time, in 1935, when the levy-subsidy principle was in the ascendant, Britain wanted levies of $1\frac{1}{4}$d per pound on foreign chilled beef and $\frac{1}{4}$d on imperial supplies, and, envisaging future reductions in the levy, was prepared to guarantee the dominions a minimum preference of a half-penny. Various proposals were outlined for additional levies if supplies increased and prices fell further, and there were to be smaller levies on frozen beef. In addition there was to be a conference to deal with meat imports as a whole, fixing total quantities and allocating these among suppliers.[34]

The final arrangements allowed Empire beef free entry and charged a $\frac{3}{4}$d per pound levy on foreign chilled beef and $\frac{2}{3}$d on foreign frozen supplies. Two conferences, one imperial, the other international, were to be set up, but to deal in the early stages only with beef. The international conference was to operate for three years under 'instructions'. Negotiations in 1936

---

[32] CAB 27/619 TAC (36), 6th meeting, 24 June 1936.

[33] DO 35/258/9105/3/125, Sir H. S. Gullett (Australian Minister for Trade and Customs) to Elliot, 15 July 1935. This is one of several references to the Australian view.

[34] E.g. CAB 32/126, 3rd draft of meat proposals, 6 June 1935.

had concentrated on the length of time during which the conference was to be given instructions and the precise nature of those instructions. Eventually it was decided that total beef imports were not to exceed 'recent' levels, but within this total there was to be a 5 per cent cut in supplies of foreign chilled beef, not replaceable by frozen beef. These cuts were to be staged over three years, not exceeding 2 per cent in any one year. Cuts in foreign supplies could be replaced by Empire supplies, which would allow these a 14 per cent expansion.

This represented a substantial modification in the stance the UK had taken in 1934. The crucial decision, allowing a way out of the impasse, was Chamberlain's announcement in May 1936 that the Treasury was prepared to subsidise cattle producers on a long-term basis.[35] This was a major step in British agricultural policy. Its immediate result was to remove pressure on the UK negotiators to raise all the money from the levies: indeed the decision had been made as a result of dominion and Argentine recalcitrance. Now Britain could acquiesce to dominion demands for continued free entry and at the same time impose a less onerous levy on the Argentine beef industry.

The Australasian achievement was not insubstantial: free entry was maintained, the UK agreed to all the post-Ottawa expansion of beef exports as well as conceding room for further growth, and also gave dominions the freedom to switch from frozen to chilled beef within the overall quotas. The 1934 White Paper threat had been largely contained.

But if the Australian achievement in warding off UK restrictions was a considerable one, the extra gains over Argentina were trivial when compared to the amount of diplomatic energy spent.[36] The principal gain was the preference, but the main impetus for this came from the British government's attempts to protect its own agriculture, and the preference had anyway been offered to the dominions at the outset in 1934. The extra concession achieved was the 5 per cent reduction in foreign supplies from the level of 1935. This was little more than an irritation to Argentina, and certainly did not represent any more than the most nominal of concessions towards the Australian viewpoint that their supplies should gradually

[35] CAB 27/619 TAC (36), 3rd meeting, 4 May 1936.
[36] Delegations of Australian Ministers were in the UK in 1935, 1936, 1937 and 1938 although also of course for ceremonial events such as the Silver Jubilee and Coronation. Meat dominated the discussion in 1935 and 1936. In 1935, when the delegation included J. A. Lyons (Prime Minister), Sir H. S. Gullett (Minister for Trade Treaties) and R. G. Menzies (Attorney General), they left Australia in February and the discussions did not end until July. The 1935 discussions were attended for New Zealand by G. W. Forbes (Prime Minister) and J. G. Coates (Minister of Finance, Customs and Transport). Walter Nash, New Zealand's Labour Minister of Finance, arrived in the UK late in 1936, stayed for much of 1937 and was back again in 1939. The tone of some of these discussions can be gauged from the quotations in the text above.

replace those of foreigners in the British market whenever possible. While it is true that the Empire had not the physical capacity wholly to replace foreign chilled beef supplies (indeed Australian producers could not even reach their chilled 'quotas' in the UK market), there is no evidence that this really influenced British negotiators or made them less tender towards Australian ambitions than they otherwise would have been. Essentially, to have responded to Australian pressure would have been to have jeopardised Anglo-Argentine relations and the valuable Roca–Runciman treaty. Argentina had simply too much to offer Britain.

Both Australia and Argentina, however, had used their treaty rights to block British attempts to tax their meat. Only on the expiry of the Roca–Runciman agreement had a duty been put on Argentine supplies, and that at a lower rate than first proposed: London had by then abandoned the original plan to cover all of the beef subsidy from the levy.

The end of levy-subsidies

It was the attempts to grapple with the problems of Britain's beef producers which had led towards greater acceptance of the levy-subsidy idea in mid-1934. Subsequently various other commodities were considered, including bacon.[37] The import restriction scheme had failed. Leith-Ross summarised the conclusions of a ministerial sub-committee. While foreign bacon imports had halved, prices had increased sharply: 'The restriction of supplies of foreign bacon is unpopular with the foreign countries but the increase of price of foreign bacon has compensated them, in monetary value: so we get the odium of restriction, without any financial benefit.'[38] Higher prices were not only unpopular at home and difficult to defend, but British bacon producers had not experienced anything like the same price increase as the foreign supplier. What was now proposed was a virtual stop to the expansion of the home industry. This was to be achieved by introducing a subsidy to home producers, and by distributing the subsidy only for an agreed limit of up to 3·5 million cwt it was hoped to discourage further production.[39] The subsidy was to be paid for by a levy on foreign imports. The snag with this was that until the expiry of their treaties in 1936, foreign suppliers had rights to free entry. The offer of larger quotas as an inducement to the renunciation of their rights proved unpersuasive, not least because some suppliers now admitted that they liked the advantages of the higher prices that had resulted from the squeeze

---

[37] CAB 27/560 PMS (33) 29, memorandum, 11 Jan. 1935. PMS (33) 35, memorandum, 1 Feb. 1935. and PMS (33), 16th meeting, 4 Feb. 1935.

[38] T 188/112, Leith-Ross papers, note by Leith-Ross to Runciman, 5 June 1935.

[39] CAB 27/561 PMS (33) 39, Report of Sub-Committee on Pigs and Bacon, 15 May 1935.

on imports, and perhaps also because they doubted the ability of the British bacon industry to expand in the face of rising fodder prices.[40]

Treaty rights also frustrated the introduction of levy-subsidies for butter and milk. Although the dominions had assured free entry only until 1935, they had been guaranteed preferential margins until at least 1937: since the UK had fixed dairy duties in the 1933 agreements, the dominions could on this occasion hide behind the foreign treaties.[41]

The trade agreements, both imperial and foreign, were therefore a major obstacle to the formulation of a plan for protecting British agriculture, and particularly to the introduction of levy-subsidy schemes. But the idea of levy-subsidies lingered on. Promises had been made to the farming community that they would be introduced as soon as was feasible, so that although by 1936 the worst of the agricultural crisis was over, it was inevitable that as the treaties approached their expiry dates, the battle within Whitehall would be renewed. It had been decided in principle to protect the bacon industry by levy-subsidies. Applications had been made to the Import Duties Advisory Committee for new or higher duties on butter and cheese and for eggs, and, in addition, a Reorganisation Commission had recommended higher egg duties. If these duties were to be implemented, the treaties would have to be revised.

During 1936 and 1937 first Elliot and then his successor as Minister of Agriculture, W. S. Morrison, suffered a number of setbacks, ending with the abandonment of the levy-subsidy idea. Elliot was unable to persuade his colleagues to denounce the trade agreements at the earliest possible moment, and Morrison failed to obtain the insertion of a clause in a new Anglo-Canadian treaty specifically reserving British power to impose duties.[42] Eventually, faced by the danger of serious political action developing in the rural constituencies, with the establishment by farmers of a political fund to fight for effective tariff protection, and with the prospect of angry deputations, Baldwin and Morrison set up an interdepartmental committee under the chairmanship of Sir Horace Wilson to consider the whole issue of levy-subsidies.[43] The committee advanced several reasons for scrapping them. First, the cost of living was rising, so any measure

---

[40] FO 371/20326, Ramsay to Eden, Annual Report on Denmark and Iceland for 1935, 25 Mar. 1936. CAB 27/620 TAC (36) 28, memorandum, 21 July 1936. FO 371/30323, A. W. E. Randall (Chargé d'Affaires) to Eden, 27 Aug. 1936, Survey by the Commercial Secretary of the Economic and Financial Situation in Denmark, Jan. to July 1935.

[41] Rooth, 'Trade agreements and the evolution of British agricultural policy' for fuller discussion.

[42] CAB 27/620 TAC (36) 23, memorandum, 22 June 1936 and ibid., 6th meeting 24 June 1936 and TAC (36) 32, memorandum, 1 Dec. 1936.

[43] The Times, 31 July 1937. For instance, the policy was denounced as 'a betrayal of promises' by the Dorset Farmers Union which planned to send an emphatic protest to the government. The Times 13 Aug. 1937 and 17 Sept. 1937. Minutes of the committee

likely to exacerbate this should be avoided. Secondly, the Treasury objected in principle to assigning revenues from particular sources to specific objects. It was, however, a third set of considerations that was decisive in the rejection of levy-subsidies, the impact on overseas suppliers.

Duties on milk products would hit New Zealand, nearly 40 per cent of whose exports would be affected, particularly hard. Since, after some protracted negotiations, Britain was in the process of rejecting New Zealand proposals for a bilateral clearing scheme, the timing could hardly have been worse, and would have jeopardised British exports to New Zealand.[44] Exports to Australia and Canada would also have been put at risk. In each case commercial issues were involved. But there was another vital aspect of imperial relations involved, the planned Anglo-American trade negotiations. If these were to have any hope of success, meeting American demands would mean the dominions surrendering preferences in the British market without receiving any tangible reciprocal benefit. Australian–American relations were already strained, feelings in Australia running sufficiently high for Britain to have to postpone an announcement of the formal start of talks with the USA until after the Australian elections of November 1937.[45] Hardly less important were the likely political and trade ramifications on north European countries. The Wilson committee had emphasised how valuable the trade agreements had been in boosting UK exports, arguing that it hardly seemed worthwhile putting at risk an export trade of over £80 million for the sake of raising £1 million on imports of dairy produce. Oliver Stanley, Runciman's successor at the Board of Trade, stressed that in the context of trade relations levy-subsidies were the most onerous form of agricultural protection. Overseas suppliers, both foreign and commonwealth, objected with particular vehemence to a system that forced them to subsidise directly their British competitor. He asserted that a heavy price would have to be paid in the trade agreements, something that was all the more likely, the Wilson report suggested, because Britain's bargaining position was no longer as strong as it had been in 1933.[46] In November 1937 the Cabinet agreed to the recommendations of its Agricultural Policy Committee to abandon the levy-subsidy principle for meat and livestock, bacon, milk and dairy products.[47]

meetings are in CAB 27/632 AP (37) and its report to the Cabinet is in CAB 24/272 CP 268 (37) 5 Nov. 1937.   [44] Drummond, *Imperial Economic Policy*, 358–61.

[45] M. R. Megaw, 'Australia and the Anglo-American trade agreement of 1938', *Journal of Imperial and Commonwealth History*, 3 (1975), 191–211.

[46] CAB 27/620 TAC (36) 29, 20 July 1936, TAC (36) 23 memorandum by Runciman, 25 June 1936 and BT 11/735, draft memorandum, Ashton Gwatkin to Brown, 4 Jan 1937.

[47] CAB 24/272/275 (37), 12 Nov. 1937; CAB 23/90 42 (37), 17 Nov. 1937. The Cabinet later included eggs and poultry in this category.

Conclusions

By the end of 1937, therefore, the UK government had accepted the principle of Exchequer-subsidised agriculture. It appears as an inevitable consequence of the obligations that London had entered into in the trade agreements of 1932 and 1933. If major sectors of British agriculture were to be preserved, and an increasingly effective agricultural lobby was to be appeased, protection was necessary. Quotas had been disastrous, either because they unduly raised prices to consumers, or because they involved constant wrangling with suppliers, above all suppliers in the dominions. Moderate duties on foreign products were possible, but particularly if combined with commonwealth free entry, generally did not provide adequate protection. Duties on imperial produce, if the preferential margins were to be maintained, meant very high tariffs on foreign imports – this might have raised consumer prices to unacceptable levels and been very harmful to overseas relations. Levy-subsidies looked as though they might provide a way out, but the reaction of overseas suppliers, both dominion and non-imperial, was hostile. The political and economic cost was simply too great. The maintenance of the trade agreements in the late 1930s was regarded in Whitehall as essential: the abandonment of the levy-subsidy plans was the price.

To summarise, from 1933 there were important changes in British policy towards domestic agriculture. But these were principally in the methods used to ensure its survival rather than in any dramatic increase in protection or the introduction of new schemes aiming at a major expansion of output. After the middle of 1933, attempts to maintain the solvency of British farmers had to be carried out within the complex constraints laid down by the various imperial and foreign trade agreements. From late in 1934 it was at least tacitly accepted within government that there was to be no great expansion of agricultural production, least of all where it was likely to reduce imports. The Ottawa agreements had also established the limits of imperial preference – subsequently the only significant extension had been the small tax on foreign beef. Whitehall therefore showed itself extremely reluctant after 1933 to take measures that were likely to penalise foreign suppliers further.

Imports from the agreement countries

Sufficient discriminatory restrictions and taxes had been introduced in 1932–3 to alter substantially the structure and source of imports. This is not particularly apparent in the broad import categories, although the

Table 8.1. *Imports into UK of major groups of commodities by total values and percentages, 1928–1939 (£m)*

Years	Food, drink & tobacco	%	Basic materials	%	Fuels	%	Manufactures	%
1928–31	1,946	45·0	1,089	25·2	164	3·7	1,104	25·6
1932–5	1,407	49·1	752	26·3	132	4·6	555	19·4
1936–9	1,633	44·4	1,025	27·8	185	5·0	812	22·0

Source: London and Cambridge Economic Services, *The British Economy Key Statistics 1900–1970* (1972)

figures do show a relative decline in the import of the more highly taxed manufactured goods (see Table 8.1).

Protection worked to the extent that in 1932 there was a distinct break in the link between the volume of manufactured imports and of British industrial production, the result also of devaluation.[48] Measured by volume, food imports in the late 1930s were above the 1929 level, and imports of manufactures about a quarter below. The differential in prices disguises much of this volume change however, with the results shown in Table 8.1. In broad terms, then, primary producers might have expected to make some very small relative gains because of the changing structure of imports, although most of these would have accrued to oil suppliers.

Imports from the Empire

In fact, the Empire made major advances in the British market during the 1930s, and appears to have done so exclusively through increasing its share in the imports of individual commodities rather than through any shifts in the commodity composition of trade. Table 8.2 shows the substantial gains that the Empire as a whole made, and, in particular, those made by the self-governing dominions which had played such a prominent role at Ottawa and were most intensively involved in the competition for the temperate foodstuffs market. A similar analysis to that carried out in chapter 3 reveals that, if anything, the movements in the structure of imports worked slightly against the commonwealth. The full details are given in Appendix E, while the results are summarised in Table 8.3.

There were very few groups in which a larger proportion of supplies did not come from imperial sources at the end of the decade than in 1931. The switch to cane sugar imports at the expense of the beet sugar suppliers, a

[48] M. Fg. Scott, *A Study of United Kingdom Imports* (Cambridge, 1963), 152–4, and 244–5.

Table 8.2. *Total retained imports into the UK and share of Empire and selected dominions, 1929–1938* (£000s *and percentages*)

	1929	%	1930	%	1931	%
Empire	298,922	26·9	258,824	27·0	216,104	27·1
South Africa	14,440	1·3	11,853	1·2	8,600	1·1
Australia	45,253	4·1	38,983	4·1	40,920	5·1
New Zealand	40,673	3·7	40,287	4·2	33,656	4·3
Canada	43,684	3·9	35,761	3·7	30,876	3·9
Total	1,111,193		957,140		797,385	
	1932	%	1933	%		
Empire	220,958	34·0	221,904	35·5		
South Africa	10,124	1·6	9,462	1·5		
Australia	40,920	6·3	43,888	7·0		
New Zealand	33,221	5·1	31,907	9·1		
Canada	40,431	6·2	43,720	7·0		
Total	650,648		625,935			
	1934	%	1935	%	1936	%
Empire	242,758	35·7	254,274	36·3	297,864	37·8
South Africa	8,045	1·2	10,307	1·5	9,721	1·2
Australia	45,334	6·7	48,593	6·9	56,123	7·1
New Zealand	35,085	5·2	34,237	4·9	38,389	4·9
Canada	48,176	7·1	52,593	7·5	71,191	9·0
Total	680,170		700,738		952,691	
	1937	%	1938	%		
Empire	364,648	38·3	337,838	39·4		
South Africa	13,829	1·5	11,341	1·3		
Australia	65,044	6·8	66,645	7·8		
New Zealand	43,541	4·6	41,767	4·9		
Canada	83,568	8·8	73,159	8·5		
Total	952,691		857,984			

Source: UK *Annual Statement of Trade* (various years).

continuation of the trends of the 1920s, benefited imperial sources although it did not spare them the misery of devastatingly low prices.[49] Some of the biggest gains were in grain and meat products, and relatively great advances were made in imports of timber supplies, although from a low

[49] Bill Albert and Adrian Graves (eds.), *The World Sugar Economy in War and Depression, 1914–40* (1988), 8–9.

Table 8.3. *Selected UK imports from the Empire: percentage changes 1931–1937*

1931	Actual share	33·1
1937	Actual share	42·4
1937	Hypothetical share	31·7
1931–7	Change due to structural movements	−1·4
1931–7	Change due to competitive factors	10·7
1931–7	Net change	9·3

Source: Parliamentary Papers, *Statistical Abstract for the British Empire 1929–1938* (Cmd 6140).

base. By 1937 the Empire was supplying about half of British butter, cheese and egg imports, which, given the margin of preference involved, was only a modest advance over the 45·5 per cent share of 1931.

Wheat

Not all of these gains necessarily represented a net advantage for the dominions. The general assumption has been that where the Empire produced a net surplus, imperial preference would lead merely to a redirection of supplies rather than to any greater share in world markets or higher prices for producers. Imperial supplies might oust foreign supplies from the British market, but would not necessarily receive higher prices there and would have to face competition in other markets from the displaced foreign supplies. Accordingly there had been no demands for wool preferences at Ottawa, although there had been demands for a preferential duty of wheat; this was conceded, although nobody apparently expected anything other than some political kudos for the Canadian government in the prairie provinces[50] – certainly the Australians had shown little interest. This view has been challenged, but in the event it was a combination of weather conditions and grain policies in the supplying

[50] CAB 32/102, 46th and 47th meetings of the UK delegation at Ottawa, 11 and 12 Aug. 1932. See also A. F. Cooper, 'The transformation of agricultural policy, 1912–1936: a study in conservative politics' (D.Phil. thesis, University of Oxford, 1979), 190, who reports that briefs had been submitted to the Canadian government by the Winnipeg Grain Exchange, the Wheat Pool and the United Grain Growers Ltd., the constant theme of which had been that having looked at the possibilities of the quota plan and the preferential system, neither scheme was thought helpful and that the best prospects lay in the maintenance of as many free ports in Europe as possible. These views are also recorded in the National Archives of Canada, RG 25, vol. 1591, F159, but they were not shared by many of the grain farmers (NAC, Bennett papers, M1178, Press comments on the Conference).

countries that proved to be the decisive influences on the international cereals trade of the mid-1930s.[51]

Undoubtedly one group of beneficiaries from British policies were wheat growers in the United Kingdom. The subsidy, guaranteeing a minimum price of 10s per cwt up to a stated maximum domestic sale, encouraged an increase in wheat acreage and enabled British farmers to increase their share of the market.[52] The proportion of imports coming from imperial sources also rose: from 39·8 per cent of imports by value in 1929–31, they increased to 64·6 per cent by 1934–6. But it would be wrong to attribute much of this to imperial preference. With Russian supplies well below the peak levels of 1930 and 1931, and with US output devastated by weather conditions (in some years of the thirties, America imported wheat), the Empire share of UK cereal imports would have increased without a preference. The major gainer in the British market was Australia, yet the Australians failed to make any significant inroads into the world market as a whole. The Canadian gain, in volume terms, was limited initially by the government's stabilisation scheme which raised sale prices above the world level, and then, after the abandonment of the operation in 1935, by poor harvests. Argentina was not as badly penalised as it might have been. Argentine wheat sales to the UK slumped, their share of imports falling from 27 per cent to 15 per cent in 1934–6. Yet assisted by the decline in Soviet sales, by the catastrophic US harvests and by Canadian policies and harvests, which were both poor, Argentina was able to hold on to its share of world markets despite unfavourable weather conditions in 1935–6.[53]

---

[51] The argument that they would bring no benefit to imperial suppliers tends to assume that wheat is homogeneous and that one country's supply is interchangeable with another's. For a view that Canada did stand to benefit both from European tariffs and British preferences, see D. A. MacGibbon, *The Canadian Grain Trade 1931–51* (Toronto, 1952), 21–3.

[52] G. Egerer, 'Protection and imperial preference in Britain: the case of wheat, 1925–1960', *Canadian Journal of Economic and Political Science*, 31 (1965), 384. Sales of domestic grain as a percentage of total grain and flour sales rose from 12·9 per cent in 1925–33 to 21·3 per cent in 1933–9. The area of wheat grown in England and Wales increased in the mid-1930s, but farmers grew less barley: 'The Wheat Act thus checked, but did not reverse, the fall in the area of arable land in England and Wales', *The Agrarian History of England and Wales*, VIII by E. H. Whetham (Cambridge, 1978), 244. For a fuller discussion and a quite favourable assessment, see Alan Webber, 'Cereals production and policy, 1932–39: the background to the international trade agreements of the 1930s', Centre for Banking and International Finance, Discussion Paper Series, no. 59.

[53] International Institute of Agriculture, *World Trade in Agricultural Products: its growth, its crisis and the new trade policies* (Rome, 1940), 1048, 1023, 1068–9. For an authoratative discussion, see C. F. Wilson, *A Century of Canadian Grain: government policy to 1951* (Saskatoon, 1978).

Beef and lamb

However, there were few alternative outlets to the meat market, so Argentina was far more exposed to trade restrictive and diversionary devices for meat than for wheat. Table 8.4 shows the extent of the Republic's losses and the gains made by Australia and New Zealand in UK imports of mutton and lamb. The Australians had practically doubled shipments between 1930 and 1931 after very low wool prices led to heavy slaughterings, although a similar development in Argentina had also enabled it to achieve high shipments during the 'Ottawa Year'.[54] Then came the 35 per cent cutbacks, although Argentina mitigated the impact of this by substituting the higher priced lamb for mutton within the total quota.[55] Of much greater importance to Argentina was beef. Here the results of Ottawa had not been particularly harmful, and, after all, greater security for its beef had been the major Argentine objective in the Roca–Runciman negotiations. Frozen beef shipments were cut by 35 per cent, but chilled beef, the more valuable export, was merely stabilised, although later reduced by 10 per cent. However, the dominion share of the market for chilled beef, initially gained in the guise of 'experimental' shipments, rose from 0·1 per cent in 1932 to 12·4 per cent in 1939.[56] The other major group of competitors, the British farmers, do not appear to have posed a major challenge. There was an increase in the supply of home-killed beef up until 1936, but probably most of this came from low quality cow-meat; the number of animals kept for the production of beef seems not to have risen.[57]

Bacon

The other major treaty country to have suffered as a result of Britain's protection and imperial preference was Denmark. Denmark dominated the bacon market and was therefore an inevitable loser from British attempts to stimulate local bacon production. Total bacon imports had reached huge proportions by 1931–2, increasing from 8·3 million cwt in 1929 to 11·4 million in 1932, two-thirds coming from Denmark. Prices fell dramatically. The reduction of imports, a central feature of the Lane–Fox plan, was carried out exclusively at the expense of foreign supplies. These fell from their 1931 level of 11 million cwt to settle around 5 million cwt between 1936–8. Dominion shipments meanwhile expanded, rising from a

---

[54] Imperial Economic Committee, *Mutton and Lamb Survey, 1935*, 31.

[55] In 1930 lamb accounted for 55 per cent of mutton and lamb shipments; in 1936 its proportion was 86 per cent.

[56] MAF 40/101, International Beef Conference (Statistical Bulletin) 1/40.

[57] Whetham, *Agrarian History*, 289.

Table 8.4. *Percentage shares of UK imports of mutton and lamb by volume, 1929–1937*

	1929	1930	1931	1932	1933	1934	1935	1936	1937
New Zealand	48·5	51·4	48·7	56·4	55·8	54·8	53·8	55·9	52·8
Australia	10·5	12·7	21·4	16·6	19·5	25·1	26·4	23·7	27·6
Argentina	27·3	22·7	21·8	19·8	17·1	14·2	13·4	14·2	13·1

Source: Imperial Economic Committee, *Meat: A Summary of Figures of Production and Trade 1936* 43, 44, and *1938*, 48, 49.

low of 348,000 cwt in 1931 to a peak of 1·90 million in 1937, by which time they accounted for more than a quarter of total imports. Canada was the main beneficiary, although imports from Eire also increased after 1933. The restrictions at least had their effect on prices, the decline in the value of imports being less pronounced. Home production, 1·7 million cwt in 1934, was 2·8 million in 1936, but fell to slightly below that level in 1937 and 1938.[58] Leaving aside the British consumer, the principal losers from restricted imports and from imperial diversion were foreign exporters. With quotas allocated on the basis of supplies at the beginning of the decade, there were few changes in the relative position of foreign exporters. Those which had emerged suddenly as suppliers in the late 1920s or early 1930s, notably Poland and Lithuania, obtained larger market shares and shipped more in the later 1930s than they had a decade earlier. Those whose supplies had fallen in the early stages of the depression, such as Russia and Latvia, tended to obtain very small allocations. Most foreign suppliers of bacon, though, suffered huge cuts in shipments, partly offset by the greater resilience of prices after 1933.

Butter

Denmark was also a major potential loser from changes in the butter market. In this case there was no real attempt to encourage UK production, which rose only from 950,000 cwt in 1930–1 to slightly over 1 million in 1935–6 before higher fodder prices caused a decline of output in 1937.[59] But the dominions, with free entry, had a great advantage over their foreign competitors, burdened with duties of 15s per cwt. In contrast to bacon, however, there was a substantial absolute increase in the total volume of butter imports (from a 1929 total of 6·4 million cwt to 9·7 million

[58] Imperial Economic Committee, *Dairy Produce Supplies, 1938*, 123. These figures refer to Great Britain and exclude Northern Ireland output.   [59] *Ibid.*, 1937, 7.

in the peak year of 1936). Under the impact of this major expansion in supplies, prices fell sharply, with the result that during the 1930s the total value of imports never quite regained the pre-depression levels. Nevertheless, while bacon accounted for a smaller proportion of imports by value in the later 1930s than on the eve of the depression, butter increased its share of imports. The problem then, for foreign countries, was what advantage could the dominions take of their preferential position? This turned out to be quite considerable, although mainly limited to Australia and New Zealand, and, in Australia's case, inhibited by drought. Overall, the Empire share of butter imports, by weight, rose from 42 per cent in 1929 to a 1936 peak of 57 per cent. New Zealand overhauled Denmark as the leading supplier in 1934. Imports from Australia rose from 768,000 cwt in 1929 to over 2 million in 1934 and 1935 before bad weather adversely affected production and exports during the 1935–6 and 1936–7 seasons.[60] Foreign shipments, by share, weight and value, regained some ground between 1936 and 1938, although never recovering to pre-depression levels. In a more competitive market, the fortunes of foreign suppliers tended to vary far more than in the case of the carefully regulated bacon market. Argentina, the second greatest foreign source at the end of the 1920s, proved unable to compete, so steadily lost ground. Finland too, shipped decreasing quantities down to 1935. Poland virtually disappeared as a supplier in the early 1930s before staging some recovery. Subsidies were clearly one factor enabling countries to compete, and appear to have helped Latvian shipments after the government there had raised them in August 1932.[61] Other major gainers were Lithuania, which rapidly increased shipments after 1932, and the Netherlands which was furnishing about 7½ per cent of imports by 1936–8, although it is difficult to determine the role of price support schemes in these advances. Currency depreciation was another influence on market shares. Both New Zealand and Denmark engaged in competitive currency depreciation between 1930 and 1932 before Denmark was warned that further devaluation of the krone would jeopardise an agreement with Britain.[62] Although the volume of Danish shipments was quite well maintained, their share of imports slipped from over one-third in the late twenties to less than one quarter by 1936–8.

[60] Imperial Economic Committee, *Dairy Produce Supplies*, *1935*, 65 and *1936*, 65.

[61] Latvian butter subsidies were calculated at 200 per cent of the export price. Department of Overseas Trade, *Economic Conditions in Latvia, 1934*.

[62] C. P. Kindleberger, 'Competitive currency depreciation between Denmark and New Zealand'. *Harvard Business Review*, 12 (1934), 416–26. New Zealand, the instigator, was depreciating the currency against sterling starting from 1930; Denmark did not respond until late 1932. Because depreciation was immediately reflected in lower prices, Kindleberger argues that the only beneficiary was the British consumer. New Zealand, with preferences as well, nonetheless steadily advanced its market share and maintained total receipts until 1933.

Table 8.5. *Imports of wood and timber into the UK, 1929–1938, percentage share of selected countries (value)*

Country	1929	1930	1931	1932	1933	1934	1935	1936	1937	1938
Finland	16·7	13·5	14·9	16·5	20·5	19·7	21·8	19·5	17·9	19·2
Estonia	1·5	1·2	0·9	0·4	1·3	2·0	1·3	1·1	1·0	0·6
Latvia	4·6	4·9	4·3	4·6	4·8	3·8	5·9	2·2	4·6	3·4
Lithuania	—	—	0·4	0·6	0·7	0·5	0·7	0·7	0·9	0·7
Sweden	15·0	13·3	12·5	14·3	17·0	14·5	11·8	12·4	12·9	13·7
Norway	3·9	3·5	2·8	2·3	1·6	1·6	1·4	1·3	1·2	1·4
Poland	3·4	5·5	6·2	4·6	7·5	7·8	6·6	8·0	8·3	8·5
Total foreign	90·5	91·1	91·5	89·9	87·2	83·0	82·2	80·5	80·6	77·7
Total Empire	9·5	8·9	8·5	10·1	12·8	17·0	17·8	19·5	19·4	22·3

Source: UK *Annual Statement of Trade* (various years).

Other products

There remained a number of products where geographical proximity to the British Isles enabled North-west European countries to effectively counter competition from the dominions, even when the latter were armed with preferences. Eggs are one example. The Danes were able to escape from the worst effects of Australian competition by switching from preserved to fresh eggs, and, despite tariffs, were able to increase shipments and maintain their share of imports.[63] Nor did the dominions possess decisive advantages in the timber trade. A preferential margin, generally of 10 or 15 per cent, was only a limited offset to high transport costs, although applied on a price that included freight and insurance charges it gave British Columbia a clear advantage over American west coast competition from Oregon and Washington, encouraging a more than threefold expansion in the value of imports from Canada. Nordic countries, nearer and with devalued currencies, were better able to withstand this competition, and, of course, were fortunate in other ways: the housebuilding boom contributed to a rapid recovery in demand, and there was little in the way of domestic competition to intrude. By 1936–8, the value of timber imports was 13 per cent above the level of 1928–30, and they contributed a higher proportion of total imports than before the depression. Imperial supplies did increase, more than doubling their share of the market to 20 per cent by 1936–8 (see Table 8.5). As with butter supplies, the fortunes of individual exporters varied. The most notable trends were the absolute losses experienced by Norway and the substantial absolute and relative gains made by Polish and

[63] Imperial Economic Committee, *Dairy Produce Supplies, 1938*, 37–43.

Finnish timber interests. Imports from Finland rose from an average of £6·8 million in 1928–30 to £9·3 million by 1936–8.

Similar trends occurred in paper and cardboard imports. Although total values did not regain pre-depression levels, the proportion coming from the Empire rose only modestly from around 10 per cent to a little under 15 per cent by 1936–8. Sweden enhanced its position as principal supplier, Norway lost some share in the market and by the end of the decade Finland had increased exports markedly, easily overtaking Norway to become the second supplier. The Finnish industry achieved major cost reductions during the depression.[64]

Winners and losers

Competitive ability was clearly one factor determining the success of countries in the British market in the 1930s. The dominions gained because of the preferences they had secured in 1932 or because foreign supplies of meat were cut back by administrative action. But even here individual experience varied considerably. India and South Africa got few preferences of real value to them, while Canada (wheat, timber and bacon), Australia (wheat, meat and butter) and New Zealand (meat and butter) stood to gain much more from Ottawa. The net benefit of the wheat preferences was doubtful, but Canadians lost because in the mid thirties output was devastated by drought and disease. That in the face of this Canadians more than doubled their overall market share owed something to imperial preferences but not everything: ironically the most massive gains were in non-ferrous metals, virtually unaffected by the trade pact.[65] It is therefore also obvious that countries' prospects were influenced in large degree by the composition of their exports. North Europeans, much more interested in timber and ores than bacon, and therefore relatively immune from protection or preference, had at least a potential chance of benefiting from the buoyancy of the British market in the 1930s. Major suppliers of bacon and butter – and Denmark was the prime instance, of course – were

---

[64] J. Ahvenainen, 'The competitive position of the Finnish paper industry in the inter-war years', *Scandinavian Economic History Review*, 22 (1974), 1–21. Jussi Raumolin, 'Natural resources exploitation and problems of staple-based industrialisation in Finland and Canada', *Fenna*, 163: 2 (1985), 395–417. The two biggest economies were in, first, the cost of procuring the raw material, secured by lower stumpage prices paid to forest owners and by severe wage cuts for lumberjacks, and, secondly, in reducing the consumption of wood per ton of pulp produced. Stumpage prices and logging costs fell from 59 Fmks per cubic metre in 1928 to 34 Fmks in 1932, economies which would also have been available to sawmills.

[65] T. Rooth, 'Imperial preference and Anglo-Canadian trade relations in the 1930s – the end of an illusion?', *British Journal of Canadian Studies*, 1 (1986), 205–29.

Table 8.6. *Imports into UK from the foreign trade agreement
countries 1929, 1932 and 1937* (£000s *and percentage of total UK
imports*)

	1929	%	1932	%	1937	%
Finland	14,945	1·2	11,733	1·7	22,437	2·2
Estonia	2,497	0·2	1,260	0·2	2,254	0·2
Latvia	5,467	0·4	2,683	0·4	5,339	0·5
Lithuania	587	—	1,882	0·3	3,275	0·3
Sweden	25,709	2·1	13,424	1·9	26,191	2·6
Norway	14,149	1·2	8,283	1·2	11,574	1·1
Denmark	56,178	4·6	40,570	5·8	36,570	3·6
Poland	6,908	0·6	6,184	0·9	10,834	1·1
Total Above	126,440	10·3	86,021	12·2	118,474	11·5
Argentina	82,447	6·8	50,885	7·3	59,836	5·8
Total Above	208,887	17·1	136,906	19·5	178,310	17·3

Source: UK *Annual Statement of Trade* (various years).

extremely vulnerable to British protection and imperial preferences. Beyond Europe, Argentina, heavily dependent on meat and wheat, and with some interest in butter as well, was another country whose export structure exposed it to the full force of British protection. For wheat growers there was the prospect of compensation in supplying other markets – but for meat, including bacon, and to some extent butter also, the British market was completely dominant and prospects elsewhere slim. These factors are reflected in individual countries' performances in the British market in the 1930s.

The market share of the main foreign countries with which agreements were made is summarised in Table 8.6. One of the outstanding, if not unexpected factors, was the behaviour of imports from the two major agreement countries, Argentina and Denmark. Both countries were sending substantially less to Britain at the end of the 1930s than in 1929, and both, having registered a peak share of the market in 1932, then suffered major losses in their share of sales. Imports from Denmark continued to decline until as late as 1935. Two of the smaller Baltic states, Estonia and Latvia, managed to hold their market shares, although never quite regaining the values of their 1929 trade. The same is more or less true of Norway – there was a rapid decline in its share of British imports – but in view of Norway's favourable export structure, the failure to achieve more in the 1930s must be accounted for by competitive weaknesses. Sweden, another country favoured by the composition of its exports,

achieved more: exports to Britain began to recover as early as 1933 –
arguably exports may have initiated the Swedish recovery of the 1930s –
and by 1937 were above the levels of 1929. The greatest advances were
made by Lithuania, Finland and Poland. The Lithuanian case defies the
generalisation made above, because by the early thirties Lithuania had
become heavily dependent on bacon and butter. But by making rapid
advances in bacon shipments to secure a reasonable quota, and by
subsidising butter exports and diversifying other exports, the Lithuanians
achieved a fivefold expansion of trade between 1929 and the later 1930s.[66]
Poland also made gains, not so spectacular relatively, but in absolute
values worth more, and by 1936–8 had a considerably larger share of UK
imports than in 1929. Finland too made substantial progress: its export
structure was favourable, but as seen above the Finns were also able to
increase their share of individual commodity groups, so that imports,
having bottomed in 1931, then recovered so rapidly that between 1929 and
1937 they increased by 50 per cent and the Finnish share of the British
import market nearly doubled.

Conclusion

To sum up, imperial preferences, confirmed and extended at Ottawa, were
effective in increasing the Empire's share of the British market. The trends
of the late 1920s and early 1930s were thus reversed. Where foreign
countries lost in the British market the prime cause was imperial
competition, not the expansion of protected British output. The foreign
agreements provided a buffer against the attempts of the Ministry of
Agriculture either to increase domestic farming output or to support it by
methods foreign countries thought inimical to their interests. But, in
general, foreign trading partners with a heavy dependence on agricultural
exports tended to suffer lower export values and shares whereas those
specialising in forest products were faced by more buoyant demand
conditions and by less intense imperial competition.

[66] Bacon exports were subsidised until higher prices made them unnecessary, and butter and
egg exports were also subsidised. Department of Overseas Trade, *Report on Economic
Conditions in Lithuania, November 1935*, 3, 10.

9 British exports to the trade agreement countries

British export performance has to be seen in the context of the dismal record of world trade as a whole during the 1930s. Even in the peak year, 1937, world trade, whether measured by volume or value, was still below the level of 1929, although world production both of primary commodities and of manufactures was higher than it had been before the depression.[1] International trade in primary products was better maintained than that in manufactured goods, although there was no dramatic shift in the proportion between the two categories. In 1927 manufactured goods comprised 38·4 per cent of world trade, and in 1937 they accounted for 36·5 per cent.[2] Alfred Maizels estimates that world exports of manufactures in constant (1955) prices were £19,895 million in 1937, still 16·6 per cent below the 1929 level of £23,841 million.[3]

The greatest absolute and relative contraction in imports of manufactured goods was into the markets of the industrial countries. By 1937 the volume of world manufactured exports to this group was 29 per cent below the amount in 1929.[4] The other principal groups of countries, the semi-industrial and the 'rest of the world', had proved to be more resilient markets. In 1937 world exports of manufactures to the semi-industrial countries were 14 per cent below the 1929 volume, while those to the 'rest of the world' had increased marginally.[5] Britain, with its unusually heavy dependence on the markets of the semi-industrial countries, was therefore less vulnerable to the decline in total world trade than major competitors which depended relatively more for their sales on the drastically curtailed outlets of the industrial countries.[6] Moreover, the UK's bargaining power

---

[1] By 1937, world production of foodstuffs was 8 per cent above the level of 1929, that of raw materials 16 per cent and that of manufactures 20 per cent higher. W. A. Lewis, *Economic Survey 1919–1939* (1949), 58.

[2] P. Larmartine Yates, *Forty Years of Foreign Trade* (1955), Table 16.

[3] A. Maizels, *Growth and Trade* (Cambridge 1970), Table A4. In current prices the fall was from $12,201 million in 1929 to $9,266 million in 1937, a reduction of 24·1 per cent. Table A3, 274–5.   [4] *Ibid.*, Table A4.   [5] *Ibid.*

[6] Maizels's classification, based on criteria applying in 1955, does not conform neatly with the agreement countries. Nonetheless, the Scandinavian group proved to be buoyant markets in the 1930s, in contrast to other 'industrial' countries.

enhanced the prospect of gaining an increased share of these semi-industrial countries' imports through the mechanism of the trade agreements. The influences on UK trade performance in these markets, and the ability of British exporters to capitalise on their opportunities, are analysed in each of the main groups of agreement countries.

The Nordic countries

One of the most conspicuous features of British export performance in Scandinavia during the 1930s is that sales to the more dependent economies, Denmark and Finland, increased substantially more than to Norway and Sweden. The overall expansion of 20·7 per cent is all the more remarkable when seen in the context of a decline in Britain's total domestic exports of 29·2 per cent between 1928–30 and 1936–8.

The trade agreements, of course, were only one of several influences on Britain's exports to its trade partners. Generally, income levels and foreign exchange earnings determined the import capacity of countries. In turn, Britain's share of these imports was affected by changes in the commodity composition of purchases, by the sterling exchange rate and general levels of competitiveness, as well as by the specific benefits accruing from the trade agreements.

Assessed from an international perspective, the four Scandinavian states recovered well from the depression and all experienced a growth in income during the 1930s. Estimates of gnp suggest that Denmark's 18 per cent expansion between 1929 and 1938 was the most sluggish, while Sweden's gnp rose 26 per cent, Norway's 31 per cent and that of Finland by 65 per cent.[7] In a decade notable for accelerated import substitution, it is surprising how much of this additional income was spent on imports. Although League of Nations' figures, expressed in pre-1933 gold dollars, show a marked decrease in imports for each country, when presented in their own (depreciated) currencies, a different picture emerges, as shown in Table 9.2.

Except for Denmark, all countries experienced some growth of imports, even when measured in current values. This makes for a fair comparison with British exports to these markets, also quoted in current values. UK domestic exports increased slightly faster than Swedish imports (15·8 per cent against 13·3 per cent) and considerably faster than Finnish imports (66·7 per cent against 20 per cent). The UK appears to have failed dismally in Norwegian trade, but the picture is distorted by the exceptionally large

[7] P. Bairoch, 'Europe's gross national product: 1800–1975', *Journal of European Economic History*, 5 (1976), 295.

Table 9.1. *UK exports of domestic produce to Scandinavia, 1928–1930, 1931, and 1936–1938 (averages) £000s (current values)*

	1928–30	1931	1936–8
Denmark	10,226	9,213	15,875
Finland	3,126	1,773	5,213
Norway	10,239	7,860	7,883
Sweden	10,109	9,213	11,709
Total	33,700	28,059	40,680

Source: UK *Annual Statement of Trade* (various years).

Table 9.2. *Total imports into Scandinavian countries, 1928–1930 and 1936–1938 (averages) millions (current values)*

	1928–30	1936–8
Denmark (Kroner)	1,753	1,604
Finland (Markkoissa)	6,754	8,094
Norway (Kroner)	1,054	1,137
Sweden (Kronor)	1,718	1,946

Sources: Denmark: Statistiske Department, *Danmark's Handel* (Copenhagen, various years). Finland: Suomen Tilastollinen Paatoimisto, *Suomen Tilastollinen Vuosikirja* (Helsinki, various years). Norway: Statistisk Centralbyrå, *Norges Handel* (Oslo, various years). Sweden: Statistiska Centralbyrán, *Statistisk Årsbok* (Stockholm, various years).

export of ships early in the decade, especially in 1930, when British trade statistics record sales of £6·3 million.[8] If new ships are excluded from the figures, British exports were actually higher in 1936–8 than they had been in 1928–30, albeit by a modest 8 per cent. Sales of UK produce to Denmark rose by 55 per cent, an astonishing performance in view of the overall decline of Denmark's imports.

There is a measure of confirmation for this in the British share of imports into the different countries. In all four Britain appears to have improved its relative position, most notably in Denmark and Finland. These figures need to be interpreted cautiously. All are based on country of payment as opposed to origin, and greatly exaggerate the volume of British business. When, from 1935 in Finland and Norway, and 1937 in Sweden, alternative data using country of origin became available, Britain is revealed as a

[8] This was 31 per cent of total British ship exports in 1930.

Table 9.3. *UK share of imports into Scandinavian countries, 1929–1938 (by country of payment)*[a]

	1929	1930	1931	1932	1933	1934	1935	1936	1937	1938
Denmark	14·7	14·5	14·9	22·3	28·1	30·1	36·0	36·6	38·1	34·6
Finland	13·0	13·6	12·6	18·3	20·6	22·8	24·2	23·6	22·2	21·7
Norway	21·2	25·8	20·4	21·6	22·9	23·0	23·4	23·9	24·6	23·1
Sweden	17·3	15·8	14·1	16·8	17·9	19·5	19·3	19·0	19·9	18·2

Source: League of Nations, *International Trade Statistics* (Geneva, various years).
[a] Except for Sweden, the figures include imports from the Irish Free State.

much less important supplier.[9] Danish statistics were notoriously misleading. Nonetheless it seems probable that the figures provide a tolerably
accurate guide to the main trends even if they are unreliable as an indicator
of the real level of trade share. The UK position began to improve after
1931. Clearly therefore the trade agreements were not alone responsible for
Britain's export performance. The depreciation of sterling from September
1931 gave the UK a competitive advantage against the USA and the gold
bloc countries. But the Scandinavians, aware of their precarious position,
had also taken measures to switch trade to Britain even before the
negotiations began in late 1932. The UK's share of imports continued to
increase until 1934 in Sweden and 1935 in Finland. In Norway and
Denmark the expansion appears to have been sustained until as late as
1937. In 1938, as is discussed below, Britain's position deteriorated in all
four countries.

One of the objectives of the British negotiators had been to limit further
protectionism and to discourage the expansion of local output where it was
likely to harm British exports. Hence the wide-ranging stabilisation of
duties. This certainly did not prevent all the Nordic countries experiencing
substantial industrial growth during the 1930s. Swedish industrial production rose by 46 per cent between 1929 and 1938 (well ahead of gnp),
that of Norway by 27 per cent, Finland by 56 per cent and Denmark 36 per
cent. Some import replacement occurred. Alfred Maizels calculated that
the import content of supplies of manufactured goods into Sweden fell
from 18 per cent in 1929 to 14 per cent by 1938.[10] The British Commercial
Secretary in Stockholm reported in 1935 that the Swedish government was
raising duties on a list of more than twenty-five articles of interest to British

[9] In 1938, for example, the UK accounted for 18·2 per cent of Sweden's imports based on
country of payment, but only 12·2 per cent by country of origin.
[10] Maizels, *Growth and Trade*, 136.

exporters.[11] Even when duties had been lowered or frozen, as for many textiles, the industry had been rationalised to meet foreign competition, and in the mid-1930s at least, was experiencing high levels of production and employment.[12] Much the same was happening in Finland where production of consumer goods increased 78 per cent between 1929 and 1938.[13] Since investment goods production rose by only 22 per cent, there was some compensation for suppliers, imports of machinery more than doubling in value between 1930 and the late 1930s.[14]

There is also evidence that the trade agreements did limit protection. Since most duties in Scandinavia were levied on a specific basis, the real level of protection declined as prices began to recover after 1933. By binding existing rates, as well as reducing tariffs, the treaties served British industry well. The Finns had only agreed to lower textile duties under considerable duress. In subsequent treaties some of the advantages conceded to Britain, notably the textile duties, were specifically withheld from Germany, Poland and Czechoslovakia.[15] When from 1934 the incidence of Finnish tariffs began to fall industrialists started to complain of inadequate protection against foreign competitors:[16] there is some suggestion that local production was being restrained since between 1935–7 raw cotton imports increased by only 26 per cent while imported cotton tissues more than doubled in value.[17]

By the later 1930s Swedish industry too was experiencing the growing severity of foreign competition. German export prices were so low that even Swedish machinery manufacturers were seriously threatened, woollen manufacturers feared Italian and German dumping, and worsted spinners were suffering because of European competition.[18] Norway made relatively little headway in import replacement, and it is significant that industrial production probably lagged behind gnp during the decade.[19] In Denmark the tariff guarantees were potentially valueless because of the import licensing system employed by the authorities. But although a wide range of new industries emerged, the Danes were careful to minimise the damage to British trade.[20]

Curbing protection where it affected British exports had been one

---

[11] Department of Overseas Trade, *Economic Conditions in Sweden, 1935*, 84.
[12] *Ibid.*, 25.
[13] League of Nations, *Statistical Year Book, 1938/9* (Geneva, 1939), 182.
[14] Tilastollisen Paatoimiston, *Suomen Tilastollisen Vuosikirja*, Helsinki, various years.
[15] Department of Overseas Trade, *Economic Condition in Finland, 1935*, 33.
[16] *Ibid.*, 34 and *1938*, 43–4.   [17] *Ibid., 1938*, 52.
[18] Department of Overseas Trade, *Economic Conditions in Sweden, 1939*, 44, 48.
[19] Maizels, *Growth and Trade*, 136, calculated that the import content of manufactured supplies fell only from 38 to 36 per cent between 1929–37.
[20] T. J. T. Rooth, 'Limits of leverage: the Anglo-Danish trade agreement of 1933', *Economic History Review*, 2nd ser., 37 (1984), 221–2.

objective of the negotiations. The other principal aim had been to secure trade diversion in Britain's favour; the main methods had been tariff manipulation and the purchase agreements. The coal schemes were successful in raising exports to all four countries, particularly if compared with 1931. Despite the continued development of hydroelectric power in Scandinavia, the consumption of coal remained high, resulting in a growth of shipments far exceeding the estimates originally made in Whitehall; 1931 exports had been 3·7 million tons; by 1936–8 they averaged 8·8 million tons.[21]

Purchase agreements for steel had been made only with Denmark and Finland. However, world trade in steel was dominated by international cartel agreements during the 1930s, 85 per cent of British exports being affected in 1938, and for some steel products Scandinavia was allocated to Germany as a 'domestic' market.[22] This probably explains why much less British steel was shipped to Norway and Sweden in 1936–8 than in 1928–30. But despite the steel agreement with Finland not being observed, the UK share of the market remained comfortably beyond pre-depression levels so that exports were worth 42 per cent more in 1936–8 than in 1928–30. Curiously, sales to Denmark rose by precisely the same proportion, but these increases only just offset the losses elsewhere in Scandinavia.

Where tariffs were concerned, Whitehall had concentrated on improving conditions for the textile industries. Total exports certainly increased, even measured by value, and the volume record was better still. The quantity of cotton yarn exports more than doubled between 1928–30 and 1936–8, and piece goods exports rose by more than half. Yarn exports did well in all markets, especially Sweden, although by the late thirties British suppliers were tending to lose ground to Finnish and Swedish exporters and to Czechoslovakian producers.[23] Piece good exporters had a more varied experience. In Sweden, British supplies tended to lag behind total imports, and in Norway too Britain continued to lose its share of imports, especially to Japan. In Finland, duty reductions in medium weight cottons were a major factor in the growth of British sales, although here again Japanese competition was intense and the UK share of imports fell after 1935. Denmark provided the best market, with volume doubling and earnings rising substantially. Wool and worsted yarn exporters achieved little. Belgian, French and Czechoslovakian competition was severe in the later

---

[21] Average exports between 1928–30 had totalled 5·5 million tons.
[22] Board of Trade, *Survey of International Cartels, 1944*, I, and E. Hexner, *The International Steel Cartel* (Chapel Hill) 1943.
[23] Department of Overseas Trade, *Economic Conditions in Norway, 1936*, 37 and *Economic Conditions in Finland, 1938*, 26.

1930s in most of Northern Europe. The clearest beneficiaries from tariff manipulation were the manufacturers of woollen and worsted fabrics. Since Britain had an established reputation as a supplier of quality woollens, there had been scepticism about its ability to capitalise on the *ad valorem* 'stops' when they had been negotiated in 1933, yet subsequently the duty reductions and the 'stops' were singled out as major factors in the growth of exports to Norway and Finland.[24] The total export rose from 4·5 million square yards to 10·5 million square yards per year (1928–30 to 1936–8), with sales to both Finland and Denmark more than tripling. But even woollens were not immune to the tougher conditions prevailing in the latter part of the decade: subsidised German and Italian competition was rife, and Belgian and Czechoslovakian woollens and worsteds were also making inroads into north European markets. Serious losses were experienced throughout Scandinavia between 1936 and 1938.

Tariff manipulation for road vehicles, another prominent element in the negotiations, achieved much less. The Norwegians had refused to concede it at all, and UK vehicle exports remained unimportant, averaging only £126,000 at their peak in 1936–8. British vehicles also remained a rare sight on Finnish roads, and although sales to Sweden increased in the later thirties, the United States reasserted its predominance as a supplier, with UK sales slipping. Only in Denmark was substantial progress made, and that was probably more a result of the allocation of import licences than of tariff adjustments.

By contrast, machinery exports to Northern Europe increased sharply. It is unlikely that the gains in Norway or Sweden had much to do with the trade agreements. Both markets were thriving in the later 1930s, but in Norway Germany remained the chief supplier with Sweden also well ahead of Britain.[25] The main reason for the virtual doubling of sales to Sweden was the expansion of the market, although there was a modest increase in share. Only in the Finnish trade pact had there been much for Britain's engineering industry; the purchasing arrangements offered potential advantages for the suppliers of woodworking and paper-making machinery. A major increase in trade share accounted for a surge in exports to 1935. Early in the decade Britain supplied a tiny proportion of Finland's imports of machinery[26], but by 1935 it had passed Sweden to become second only to Germany. Textile and paper machinery imports were both at high levels. From 1935 relative losses were experienced, this partly reflecting a diversion of orders to Germany for paper and textile-making machinery, but also the growing demand for electrical and metalworking

[24] DOT, *Norway, 1936*, and FO 381/19437, Economic Report on Finland, 1935.
[25] DOT, *Norway, 1938*, 51. Only in the supply of belts and packings did Britain take first place.   [26] In 1931, for example, only 6 per cent.

equipment, little of which came from the UK.[27] The dynamism of the market provided compensation, however, so that total British machinery exports continued to increase. Sales to Denmark, the licence system notwithstanding, made only a small advance. Overall, however, sales of UK machinery to Scandinavia increased from £1·4 million per year at the end of the 1920s to £2·4 million by the late 1930s.

From a British perspective the trade agreements with Norway and Sweden were far less productive than those with Denmark and Finland. Nonetheless, coal exports to Norway and Sweden were given a substantial lift, and the concessions on textiles, especially the tariff 'stop' on woollen textiles, were useful. Other factors supplemented the trade agreements in increasing Britain's share of imports, notably the devaluation of sterling in late 1931, and possibly the linking of the Scandinavian currencies to the pound as the sterling area developed. A high volume of Swedish purchases of machinery helped the overall level of UK exports towards the end of the decade.

With the other two Scandinavian states, Denmark and Finland, Britain's bargaining leverage was substantially greater and the trade agreements were correspondingly advantageous for the UK. British exports were aided by the extraordinarily strong recovery of the Finnish economy from the depression. But assisted by tariff reductions and by the purchase agreements, Britain also benefited from trade diversion. Up until 1936 the UK increased its import share of nearly every major commodity group. The agreement with Denmark was also valuable. The major instrument in securing a diversion of purchases to British exporters was the import licensing system introduced by the Danes in 1932. Ironically, the trade pact contained not a single guarantee about the allocation of licences, and yet they were to be a key factor in trade relations. The results achieved by British exporters in Denmark are all the more extraordinary in view of the serious losses experienced by the Danes in Britain. Ultimately, however, lower British purchases restricted Danish foreign exchange earnings and were a crucial constraint on the overall allocation of licences. Increased sales to Denmark were entirely the result of trade diversion and had to be sustained in the face of the decline in total Danish imports.

The Baltic states

The small Baltic states experienced a deeper depression and slower recovery than their northern neighbours in the Baltic and North Seas. Estimates of gnp indicate that for the three states together it was 9 per cent higher in

---

[27] DOT, *Finland, 1938*, 29–30; by 1937, lengthening dates were added to the price difficulties of British machinery salesmen. BT 11/911, memorandum on exports to Finland, nd.

Table 9.4. *UK exports of domestic produce to Estonia, Latvia and Lithuania, 1928–1930 to 1936–1938 (average) (£000s) (current)*

	1928–30	1936–8
Estonia	484	988
Latvia	1,314	1,539
Lithuania	367	1,879
Total	2,165	4,406

Source: UK *Annual Statement of Trade* (various years).

1938 than in 1929.[28] Figures for industrial production, where they exist, suggest marked expansion however. Latvia officially recorded output levels 75 per cent higher by 1938 than on the eve of the depression.[29] Estonia, its industries more dependent on export markets, nonetheless experienced an increase of 46 per cent between 1929 and 1938. A combination of export difficulties, very modest economic recovery and continued industrialisation served to restrict imports. Despite this, British exports, worth £2·2 million in 1928–30, had doubled by 1936–8, a relatively much better performance than to the more buoyant markets of northern Scandinavia. Although this was the result of Britain's strong leverage, it was only possible because all three states possessed instruments of import licensing and exchange controls which made possible such a large degree of trade diversion.

Exports to Estonia more than doubled, and manufactured goods alone nearly tripled. Advances were made principally in the exports of refined sugar and woollen textiles, together with machinery, vehicles, and, in 1937–8, iron and steel. By 1937–8 nearly half Estonia's total import of 1,100 tonnes of manufactured textiles came from the UK, a considerable advance on the 17 per cent share in 1929, and made largely at Germany's expense.[30] Overall, however, the Germans retained their share of the Estonian market. After slipping in the mid-1930s, Germany had by 1938 surpassed its 1929 market share, remaining Estonia's largest supplier. The UK, with only 10 per cent of Estonia's imports in 1929, reached a peak in 1935 and nearly held that position with 18 per cent in 1938. Poland was a major loser, but mainly in the Estonian case because of a decline in food exports.

[28] Bairoch, 'Europe's gross national product', 295. Bairoch cautions that these figures are subject to a wider margin of error than for most countries.
[29] League of Nations, *Statistical Year Book 1938/9* (Geneva, 1939).
[30] Riigi Statistika Kesburoo, *Valiskaubandus 1938* (Tallinn, 1939).

Latvia, the most important market for Britain of the three Baltic states in the late 1920s, proved the most disappointing. This was not so much because of any failure to gain a larger share of the market (this rose from 8·4 per cent in 1929 to a peak of 22·6 per cent in 1934 before receding to 19·3 per cent in 1938) but because of the severity of the depression; Latvia paid the penalty for refusing to devalue until 1936. It was the very slow recovery of imports prior to 1936 that principally concerned British officials, together with difficulties UK firms had in securing payment, and Latvia was considered the most unsatisfactory of the Baltic markets.[31] The sharp recovery of Latvian imports from 1936 provided some amelioration, so on average British exports were 17 per cent higher in 1936–8 than they had been in 1928–30. Sales of woollen tops and yarns and, above all, coal, increased. Latvia had guaranteed to take 70 per cent of coal from the UK with a minimum tonnage of 235,000 tons; in the event, coal exports averaged over 400,000 tons by 1936–8.[32] Poland, consequently, was the principal loser in the Latvian market. Although Latvia agreed to take at least 9,000 tons of iron and steel from Britain, this promise failed to be honoured, and only in one year, 1937, did steel exports even approach this figure.

By far the most spectacular gains for British trade occurred in Lithuania. Although Lithuanian imports did not recover their 1929 levels, UK domestic exports increased more than fivefold from 1928–30 to 1936–8, reaching £1·9 million. This was a major exercise in trade diversion: Britain's share of Lithuanian imports, only 8·5 per cent in 1929 and 7·1 per cent in 1931, at one time rose to 37·2 per cent before declining to 30·9 per cent in 1938. No important sector of British trade failed to register a gain, with outstanding beneficiaries being the cotton industry and woollens (woollen exports secured a fourteenfold expansion between 1930 and 1938). Coal, iron and steel, together with electrical and other machinery, all increased sales markedly. Although the trade agreement was a factor in these remarkable developments and British imports from Lithuania grew very rapidly, the major cause was the dispute that Lithuania ran simultaneously with its Polish and German neighbours over the status of Vilna and Memel.[33] Trade featured prominently in these disputes, Poland all but disappeared as a supplier, and Germany, which had furnished nearly half of Lithuanian imports in 1929, provided less than a quarter by

[31] FO 371/19439, Report on Trade Relations and Economic Conditions in the Baltic Area, Summer 1935. Ashton Gwatkin, 20 Sept. 1935 and FO 371/19398, Board of Trade Memorandum on Recent Discussions respecting the working of the Anglo-Latvian Trade Agreement of October 1934, 15 Oct. 1935.
[32] The 1928–30 average export was 27,000 tons.
[33] Royal Institute of International Affairs, *The Baltic States, A Survey of the Political and Economic Structure and Foreign Relations of Latvia and Lithuania* (1938), 89–102.

1938. The poverty of the Lithuanian market meant that the huge proportional gains accruing to Britain were worth little in the context of total exports; nevertheless, Lithuania had become Britain's largest market among the three Baltic states before 1939.

Poland

The depression in Poland was extremely severe, and the recovery, when it came, very modest. The government's refusal to devalue the zloty not only placed an additional burden on exports but as a corollary involved restrictive fiscal and monetary policies, the commercial banks playing a leading part in the contraction of credit.[34] Industrial production had slumped by 1932 to 62·5 per cent of the 1929 level, an unenviable record, which only Canada and the USA surpassed by a significant margin.[35] Revival was slow, and despite the high priority given by the government to industrial development, it was not until 1937 that production regained its previous peak. With rapid population growth the expansion in gnp of 18·5 per cent between 1929 and 1938 is much less impressive when expressed in per capita terms.[36] Imports, worth 3·1 billion zlotys in 1929 had only recovered to 1·3 billion by 1937.

In this context it is surprising that UK exports increased at all, particularly when so much negotiating energy had been spent in dislodging Polish coal from the markets of Northern Europe. The expansion was moderate, an increase from £4·4 million in 1928–30 to £5·3 million in 1936–8, or 20 per cent. The reality, of course, was Britain's bargaining leverage; the UK market remained Poland's most important outlet between 1931 and 1937.

There was, however, a marked change in the composition of British exports, reflecting a radical shift in the structure of Poland's imports. Imports of non-essentials were rigidly controlled, while raw materials and capital goods were treated far more leniently. This resulted in a much sharper rise in British re-exports than of domestically produced goods. Notwithstanding this, Poland's direct imports from countries such as Australia, India and Argentina also increased sharply. Tariff concessions meant little unless the Polish authorities granted import quotas; although Britain had secured guarantees on these in the trade agreement, for the most part they were based on the low levels prevailing during the worst years of the depression. Increased quotas were often obtained by the Commercial Secretary, but, as he emphasised, they were far easier to secure

---

[34] League of Nations, *International Currency Experience* (Geneva, 1944), 82.
[35] League of Nations, *Statistical Year Book, 1938/9* (Geneva, 1939).
[36] Bairoch, 'Europe's gross national product', 295.

for machinery, tools and raw materials than for luxuries.[37] By the end of the 1930s items which had dominated British exports before the depression had failed to regain their previous value; this is true of herrings (worth over £1 million on average, 1928–30), cottons, and, unusually, woollen tissues. The greatest advances were made in raw materials – cotton waste, raw wool and wool rags. Armaments supplies exceeded £1 million in 1937, but the rise in machinery exports from an average of £489,000 in 1928–30 to £931,000 in 1936–8 was more consistent. The trade agreement undoubtedly contributed to this; purchase arrangements and special reductions to only 10–20 per cent of the level stipulated in the Polish tariff were important permissive elements, but the willingness of the government to issue the licences was essential. Buoyant demand from the cotton and woodworking industries was also vital.[38] German competition was intense, however, and was aided by an agreement in 1937 whereby German railway debts were liquidated in large measure by the supply of German machinery and capital goods in Poland.[39] The increase in British exports to Poland was secured entirely by trade diversion; competitive strength was of secondary importance compared with the use of the import licensing system by the Polish government. The UK's share of Poland's imports rose from 8·5 per cent in 1929 to a maximum of 14·1 per cent in 1936, but German competition, aided by Clearing agreements, was largely responsible for a decline in share to 11·4 per cent by 1938.

The self-governing dominions

British exports to the dominions mattered far more than those to Northern Europe. In 1929 Australia alone bought more British goods than all the trade agreement countries of Europe put together. If the four dominions most competitive with Europe and Argentina (Australia, Canada, New Zealand and South Africa) are taken as a whole, total exports in 1929 were £143 million, more than three times as much as to Northern Europe. Moreover, the Ottawa pacts should have been even more favourable to Britain than the foreign agreements. The dominions had been given privileged access to the British market in 1931 and 1932. They could and did give explicit preferences rather than the more devious variety characteristic of relations with Northern Europe. In the event, the Ottawa

[37] Department of Overseas Trade, *Economic Conditions in Poland 1937*, 9.
[38] *Ibid.*, *1939*, 20.
[39] *Ibid.*, *1937*, 11 and *1938*, 12, and BT 11/735. Observations by DOT on certain aspects of United Kingdom export trade to the Scandinavian and Baltic countries and Finland, Sept. 1937, which reported 'a considerable proportion of the payments in kind thus arranged have taken the form of government orders for machinery and equipment and in many cases this has meant a direct loss of trade to United Kingdom suppliers'.

Table 9.5. *UK exports of domestic produce to four dominions, 1928–1930 and 1936–1938*

	1928–30	1936–8
South Africa	30,167	39,479
Australia	47,189	35,980
New Zealand	19,516	18,913
Canada	32,871	24,441
Total	129,643	118,813

Source: UK *Annual Statement of Trade* (various years).

pacts proved extremely disappointing, and yielded far less than the European trade treaties. If 1928–30 and 1936–8 are compared, British exports rose to every trade agreement country of Northern Europe except Norway; to three of the four dominions, on the other hand, they fell. Overall, British exports to Northern Europe rose by 25 per cent (in current values). By contrast, as is summarised in Table 9.5, UK exports to the self-governing dominions declined by 9 per cent.

Why, then, were the dominions such poor markets for British exports during the 1930s? Among the most important influences were income levels, the degree of import replacement achieved, and Britain's competitive position compared with other suppliers. It is significant, and ironic, that only South Africa, which Britain conceded least to and received least from at Ottawa, should have experienced sufficient prosperity to have exceeded its pre-depression import levels. South Africa's gold resources were a major factor in the relative prosperity of the decade. For the other countries discussed here, the record was mixed. Australian real gdp rose 20 per cent between 1928–9 and 1937–8,[40] roughly in line with that of Denmark and Poland. In New Zealand the current value of commodity production between 1929–30 and 1937–8 increased 11 per cent (although by one measure gnp in 1937–8 was 27 per cent above the 1929 level).[41] The Canadian experience was truly disastrous, and despite a growing population, gnp by 1938 had still not recovered its 1929 level.[42]

[40] N. G. Butlin, *Australian Domestic Product, Investment and Foreign Borrowing 1861–1938/9* (Cambridge, 1962), 33. Gdp is expressed in 1911 prices.
[41] M. F. Lloyd Prichard, *An Economic History of New Zealand to 1939* (Auckland, 1970), 417. Values in current £NZ, which was at a discount against sterling from 1929–30. G. R. Hawke, 'Depression and recovery in New Zealand', in R. G. Gregory and N. G. Butlin (eds.), *Recovery from the Depression: Australia and the world economy in the 1930s* (Cambridge, 1988).
[42] A. E. Safarian, *The Canadian Economy in the Great Depression* (Toronto, 1970), 2 and 223.

Import policies were another key determinant of British export prospects. Any reduction of Commonwealth protection in the years following Ottawa must be seen, as discussed in chapter 3, against a backcloth of sharply rising tariffs and protection in the years preceding the conference.

As in many primary producing or semi-industrialised countries during the 1930s, the process of import substitution accelerated in the dominions. There was clear evidence of this in Canada, where the overwhelming impression gained from statistics and reports on industries is of the productive potential and broadening range of secondary industries. For example, there were notable advances in the woollen industry, production increasing two-and-a-half fold between 1930 and 1933, while worsted production doubled. Ninety-five per cent of the market for boots and shoes was met from national production. Canada was manufacturing a growing range of chemicals and national producers captured a larger slice of the market for primary iron and steel, cars and electrical equipment.[43] J. H. Dales claims that increased protection probably prevented manufacturing output from falling quite so far in Canada as it did in the United States.[44] Protection also played a major part in strengthening the competitive position of Australian manufacturing industry *vis-à-vis* imports. Devaluation, an 80 per cent jump in the tariff and the difficulty importers experienced in obtaining sterling exchange created this position, and, in C. B. Schedvin's view, the manufacturing expansion of the 1930s and the Australian recovery in general were founded on a boom in import replacement.[45] The major breakthrough by Australian industry came before the Ottawa conference. After Ottawa the share of the market held by Australian producers of textiles, chemicals, clothing and metals and machines tended to level off. Schedvin explains the slow-down in the growth of Australian textile production as being largely due to the lowering of British preferential tariff rates along with the easing of quantitative restrictions on sterling exchange and a rise in domestic wage

---

[43] Department of Overseas Trade, *Report on Economic Conditions in Canada, 1934/5* (London, 1935), 60 and *1935/6*, 85. H. E. English, *The Role of International Trade in Canadian Economic Development since the 1920s* (California, 1957, microfilm), 213, 257, 342, 373.

[44] J. H. Dales, *The Protective Tariff in Canada's Development* (Toronto, 1966), 114.

[45] C. B. Schedvin, *Australia and the Great Depression* (Sydney, 1970), 303. See also Helen Hughes, *The Australian Iron and Steel Industry 1848–1962* (Melbourne, 1964) for the expansion of the industry during the 1930s, 111–29. However, Schedvin's view has been challenged by Mark Thomas, who places great emphasis on the role of deflation in cutting the import share between 1929–31, and on improvements in the productivity and competitiveness of Australian manufacturing during the recovery phase. M. Thomas, 'Manufacturing and economic recovery in Australia, 1932–37', in Gregory and Butlin (eds.), *Recovery from the Depression*.

Table 9.6. *Import content of supplies of manufactured goods* (*percentages*)

	1913	1929	1937
Australia	39	37	25
Canada	23	24	16
New Zealand	46	46	40
South Africa	97	69	60
Norway	35	38	36
Sweden	14	18	14

Source: Maizels, *Growth and Trade* (Cambridge, 1963), 136.

Table 9.7. *Total imports into selected dominions, 1929–1930 and 1936–1938* (*averages*)

	1929–30	1936–8
South Africa (£SA)	74·8	96·9
Canada ($Can)	1,153·8	709·4
Australia (£A)	135·8	117·5
New Zealand (£NZ)	45·6	51·4

Source: League of Nations, *Statistical Year Book, 1938/9* (Geneva, 1939).

rates.[46] From the British perspective this therefore signalled some success and by 1933–4 the weighted British preferential tariff had fallen considerably from the pre-Ottawa level.[47] Import replacement also occurred in New Zealand and South Africa during the 1930s, although as the figures in Table 9.6 suggest, not as rapidly as in Australia and Canada. The experience of Norway and Sweden provides an interesting comparison. It suggests limited development in Norway but more rapid import replacement in Sweden than in either New Zealand or South Africa.

The twin pressures of the slump and of import replacement are reflected in the total imports of each country. Table 9.7 compares the position in 1929–30 with that in 1936–8. The strength of the South African recovery is apparent, the comparison with Australia and New Zealand being understated because of the depreciation of their currencies against sterling. While the agreement countries of Northern Europe increased their share of

[46] Schedvin, *Australia and the great depression*, 304.
[47] A. T. Carmody, 'The level of the Australian tariff: a study in method', *Yorkshire Bulletin of Economic and Social Research*, 4 (1952). The weighted British Preferential Tariff (1919/20 = 100) was 221 in 1931/2, 212 in 1932/3, and 155 by 1933/4. By the end of the 1930s it stood at 133.

Table 9.8. *Percentage of total imports coming from the United Kingdom, 1929–1938*

	1929	1930	1931	1932	1933	1934	1935	1936	1937	1938
South Africa	43·1	46·9	45·5	46·3	50·3	48·8	48·7	46·3	42·4	43·2
Canada	15·0	16·1	17·4	20·7	24·4	22·1	21·2	19·4	18·2	17·6
Australia	39·7	39·6	40·6	42·5	43·4	43·6	41·5	43·6	42·1	41·5
New Zealand	48·7	47·4	49·0	49·8	51·3	50·4	50·3	49·4	49·6	48·5

Source: League of Nations, *International Trade Statistics* (Geneva, various years).

world imports during the 1930s, the four dominions, in total, merely maintained their position.

However, if low incomes and accelerated import replacement frustrated the recovery of imports into these countries then at least Britain should have gained some offset by increasing its market share at the expense of other competitors. As Table 9.8 shows, the UK's progress in this direction was very modest. Superficially the pattern is remarkably clear. From the start of the depression until 1933 (1934 for Australia), Britain increased its share of imports. But as the depression started to lift, and following the depreciation of the dollar, the secular tendency for Britain's share of imports to fall was reasserted. By 1938 these were still above the 1929 level in Australia and Canada, but back where they had been in New Zealand and South Africa.

One obvious and significant point is that Britain was increasing its market share before the Ottawa conference. Two major influences helped to account for this. The first was the depreciation of sterling from September 1931, but this only assisted a process that was already in train. The other major part of the explanation is that the structure of import demand for British products aided them relatively as incomes fell and was unfavourable to them as incomes rose.[48]

[48] Part of the decline in Britain's share of world exports this century has been due to changes in the commodity composition of trade towards products in which it was badly placed and away from products in which its world market share was high. See Maizels, *Growth and Trade*; H. Tyszynski, 'World trade in manufactured commodities, 1899–1950', *Manchester School of Economic and Social Studies*, 19 (1951); R. E. Baldwin, 'The commodity composition of trade: selected industrial countries, 1900–1954', *Review of Economics and Statistics*, 40 (1958).

To the extent that the changing commodity structure of trade is partly a function of income it seems probable that a fall in income would slow or reverse trends that have been unfavourable to Britain. In Maizel's study, 1929–37 was the only period in which the area/commodity pattern of trade was favourable to Britain (200–1). A two country study laying considerable stress on structural factors in Britain's declining share of trade is G. L. Reuber, *Britain's Export Trade with Canada* (Toronto, 1960). He argues that 'in the

Table 9.9. *Comparison of UK percentage shares of selected imports, 1931 and 1937*

Country	Actual share 1931	Actual share 1937	Hypothetical share 1937	Changes due to competition	Changes due to structure	Total change
Australia	40·9	41·2	43·4	−2·2	+2·5	+0·3
Canada	18·8	19·8	15·3	+4·3	−3·3	+1·0
New Zealand	47·8	50·2	54·3	−4·1	+6·5	+2·4
South Africa	44·7	42·0	45·1	−3·1	+0·4	−2·7

Source: Calculated from Parliamentary Papers, *Statistical Abstract for the British Empire, 1929–1938*, Cmd 6140.

It is this kind of structural movement in trade which allows a fuller assessment of Britain's competitive position in these markets. On the face of it, the influence of the Ottawa agreements appears slight merely because most of the gains were made before the conference and most of the losses started to be made soon afterwards. A closer examination reinforces this impression. An attempt is made below to distinguish between structural and 'competitive' elements in the UK's changing share of dominion imports between 1931 and 1937.[49]

The results, summarised in Table 9.9, show that with the important exception of Canada, Britain made large 'competitive' losses in the other markets discussed here. In Australia and New Zealand the structural movements worked sufficiently strongly in its favour to outweigh these losses and Britain therefore made a net relative gain between 1931 and 1937. In South Africa the structural movement in Britain's favour was very slight and insufficient to offset substantial 'competitive' losses. In Canada the structural movement was severely unfavourable to the UK, but such was the extent of the 'competitive' gain that Britain, on balance, came out

short term the structure of Canadian demand has largely accounted for the tendency of Britain's share of Canadian sales to increase in periods of recession and to decrease in periods of expansion...', 125. This is not, however, entirely consistent with the findings of this study of the Canadian market in the 1930s.

[49] These years are chosen because 1931 is the nearest full year before the Ottawa Conference, and 1937 because (a) it marked the latest year in the 1930s relatively undistorted by war and preparation for war and (b) it was the year preceding the UK/US trade agreement which involved reductions in the Ottawa preferences. (D. MacDougall and R. Hutt, 'Imperial preference: a quantitative analysis', *Economic Journal*, 64 (1954), 233–57, also chose 1937 as the most suitable year of the decade for comparison). The method used is to calculate the UK's hypothetical share of each country's import trade in 1937 assuming that it had retained its 1931 share in 1937 and the actual share in 1931 reflects structural changes. The difference between the hypothetical share in 1937 and the actual share is then attributed to 'competitive' factors.

with an enlarged share of the market. But even here the gains were restricted to the years before 1934; as elsewhere, between 1934 and 1937 the UK lost ground in individual commodity groups. In Australia and New Zealand, Britain even made 'competitive' losses between 1931 and 1934 when devaluation and increased preferences should have operated strongly in its favour. This analysis casts considerable further doubt on whether the Ottawa agreements brought benefits to British trade with the dominions. Canada was a major exception; and these calculations suggest that the British achievement in increasing its share of Canadian imports was greater than is at first apparent because it was done in the face of unfavourable structural movements. The devaluation of sterling played a part, although the UK made small 'competitive' gains between 1929 and 1931 before devaluation could have had any discernible effect. From 1930 Britain should have benefited relatively from Canadian tariff changes and the various administrative devices which made it difficult for Canadians to purchase goods from the United States.[50] Clearly the bigger preferences from 1932 reinforced this favourable movement, and Ottawa may also have helped by bringing home to Canadians their dependence on the UK market and the advantages of reciprocity – at least so the UK Trade Commissioner suggested, pointing out that the Canadians were being encouraged to buy British.[51] The competitive gains were spread over nearly every commodity group analysed here. These included all the major classifications of textiles, chemicals, electrical machinery and iron and steel. In the case of iron and steel, for example, United States Steel sold their Canadian plant in 1937 because the preferences were so high that the company had had to switch its purchases of semi-finished steel away from the US parent company to British sources.[52] The relative advances made by the UK in Canada were associated with the largest extensions of preference made by any of these dominions. The proportion of imports from the UK enjoying preferences rose from 62–63 per cent in 1929 to 88 per cent by 1937, and preferential margins were also increased. Together these two factors helped to raise the average margins of preference on all UK imports from 7 per cent in 1929 to 20 per cent in 1937.[53]

The antipodean dominions already gave preferences on a wide range of imports, and therefore the major gains had to come through an enlargement of existing margins.[54] It is extraordinary just how high a

[50] J. B. Brebner, *North-Atlantic Triangle: the interplay of Canada, the United States and Great Britain* (New York, 1945), 290.

[51] Department of Overseas Trade, *Report on Canada 1933–34* (1934), 44–6.

[52] M. Wilkins, *The Maturing of Multinational Enterprise: American business abroad from 1914 to 1970* (1974) 185.   [53] MacDougall and Hutt, 'Imperial preference', 241.

[54] *Ibid.* Over 80 per cent of British trade to Australia and New Zealand received preferences in 1929.

proportion of particular products already came from the UK. In 1929 Britain accounted for 90 per cent of Australian and New Zealand iron and steel imports, 91 per cent and 87 per cent respectively of their cotton piece goods imports and four-fifths or more of the imports of woollen tissues. Obviously the potential for increasing sales lay more in market expansion than in trade diversion. What in fact happened was that with the exception of woollens to New Zealand, losses of market share were experienced in every instance. This was compounded by the failure of total imports of these commodities to regain their pre-depression levels. There were, of course, better prospects for some manufacturers. Cars were an outstanding example. Australia had imported more cars than any other country, and in 1929 had drawn 27 per cent of supplies from the UK while New Zealand took 22 per cent. Because the depression had such a devastating impact on the rural areas, where the USA had a virtual monopoly of the market, and a lesser impact on the urban areas, the relative position of the UK manufacturers was improved. As early as 1934 British road vehicle sales had passed their 1929 volume. No doubt the greater competitiveness of Morris and Austin contributed towards this, and the growing interest of consumers in the lower depreciation and running costs of British vehicles has been cited as a factor.[55] Preferences were extended, especially by Australia in 1936. By 1937 Britain's market share had risen to 44 per cent in Australia and 54 per cent in New Zealand, with sales of £7·3 million, twice the 1929 level; probably they would have been higher still if the industry had been prepared, like its competitors, to set up assembly works in the dominions to take advantage of lower taxation. There was nothing else to equal this degree of success. Sometimes market shares were increased – electrical machinery and apparatus for example – only for total imports to fall, outweighing the trade diversion. Preferential margins were raised: in Australia the average margin of preference on all imports from the UK was increased from 13–14 per cent in 1929 to 19–20 per cent in 1937, and the corresponding figures for New Zealand were 16 per cent and 23–25 per cent.[56] It seems generally that this extra margin of preference was not sufficient to offset the declining competitiveness of British exports, particularly after the 1933 American devaluation. For various reasons the Australians and New Zealanders were not prepared to go further. Surprisingly, in 1936, the Australians did take measures which gave Britain substantial further advantages in meeting American competition in vehicles and in stemming the Japanese textile onslaught. The motivation behind the Australian trade diversion episode is a matter of controversy,[57]

[55] Imperial Economic Committee, *A Survey of the Trade in Motor Vehicles* (1936), 38.
[56] MacDougall and Hutt, 'Imperial preference', 241.
[57] For some discussion see ch. 8.

but two of the consequences are significant: it caused a furore with Australia's trading partners, and Britain's gain was short-lived: its share of the Australian market increased in 1936 but the downward trend was soon in evidence again.

Where Britain already had a high proportion of a country's imports, such as in the southern dominions, and where the prospects of being offered dramatic extensions of preference were slim, the best chances for British exports lay in trade expansion rather than in trade diversion. Nowhere was this more clearly demonstrated than in the case of South Africa. The scope for increasing preference was enormous – the average margin of preference on imports from the UK in 1929 was only 1 per cent. The political difficulties of increasing preference were also enormous. As a result, by 1937 the margin of preference on all imports had risen to only 3 per cent. Yet of the four dominions discussed here South Africa was the only one to buy more British produce in 1937 than in 1929. There were products for which Britain captured a larger share of the market, notably cars and most types of textiles.[58] But often it was enough to maintain the market share and to rely on the buoyancy of the South African economy to expand British sales (e.g. electrical and non-electrical machinery).

In summary, the preferences extended by Australia and New Zealand were insufficient to prevent competitive losses; Britain only held its relative position in these markets because of favourable movements in the composition of imports. Lower total imports meant lower British sales at the end of the 1930s than on the eve of the depression. Technically the Canadian agreement was the most successful; with greater scope for trade diverting preferences, competitive gains were so substantial as to outweigh unfavourable structural movements of imports. All this, however, was more than nullified by the deep and prolonged depression. Only South Africa expanded imports on the scale of some of the Scandinavian countries, but here there was virtually no trade diversion to buttress this growth.

Argentina

Whitehall was remarkably sanguine about the results of the Roca–Runciman treaty. Judged by trade performance alone it is difficult to understand why the agreement should have been looked on so favourably, for it was one of the most unfruitful of those signed. By 1936–8 British exports to Argentina still averaged only around £18 million, a third less

---

[58] Although South Africa gave no preferences on motor vehicles, British sales increased continuously from 1931, the market share advanced modestly and by 1937 sales values of £2 million were nearly twice as much as 1929.

than in 1928–30. The pact with Argentina must be viewed, however, in a different light from the trade agreements with other countries. In 1933 there had been confusion both in London and Buenos Aires about whether Britain was primarily interested in trade or in unblocking frozen assets.[59] The existence of British capital in Argentina, estimated at £500–600 million, acted as a brake on the trade possibilities of the commercial agreement. Sterling exchange was only to be made available for British imports after Argentine public debt held in the UK had been serviced.[60] Too harsh an agreement would have run up against Argentine solvency and have jeopardised the goodwill necessary for the successful operation of the British-owned public utilities in the Republic. Before the depression the existence of British-owned companies in Argentina had served to stimulate trade because many of their requirements had been imported from the UK. By the 1930s, however, with many of these companies in difficulty, with profits low or non-existent, imports had been slashed anyway. British ownership of the bulk of the Republic's rail system had boosted exports of locomotives and rolling stock to a 1928–30 average of £2·3 million; by 1936–8, after some recovery, the export was worth only £562,000. The existence of these companies may have limited the pressure the British side could exert in the negotiations. But there is no indication that the priorities in the allocation of sterling actually hampered British trade: importers of UK goods were reported as obtaining all the exchange they required.[61]

What, then, held back British exports to a level where they apparently failed to press up against the limits of foreign exchange? The slow recovery of the economy was clearly one factor, and of course contributed to the troubles of British companies operating in the country. By 1938 Argentina's real gdp was about 12 per cent higher than in 1929.[62] Imports, however, fell. By 1936–8 they were 43 per cent less than their 1928–30 average in current prices, and 24 per cent less in constant prices.[63]

Carlos Diaz Alejandro lays great stress on the role of import substitution in the expansion of manufacturing output after 1925–9.[64] But this should not be taken as support for the dependency view that wars and depression weaken metropolitan pressure, thus encouraging a measure of independent development in the periphery. On the contrary, this has been specifically

[59] R. Gravil and T. Rooth, 'A time of acute dependence: Argentina in the 1930s', *Journal of European Economic History*, 7 (1978), 337–78, esp. 354–9.
[60] BT 11/596, Board of Trade memorandum, 31 Mar. 1936.   [61] *Ibid.*
[62] L. Randall, *An Economic History of Argentina in the Twentieth Century* (New York, 1978), 2–3. Gdp at factor cost (1935–9 prices).
[63] C. F. Diaz Alejandro, *Essays on the Economic History of the Argentine Republic* (New Haven 1970), 463–4.
[64] *Ibid.*, 219 and 232. Merchandise imports as a percentage of the value of gross domestic manufacturing production plus imports fell from 34 per cent in 1925–9 to 22 per cent in 1937–9.

rejected for Argentina in the 1930s.[65] The indications of excess capacity in
the 1930s, the decline in the industrial growth rate and the tendency for the
share of industry to grow more slowly than in the previous decade all
suggest that the conditions in the 1930s were less favourable than in the
1920s.[66] There is a widespread view that the industrial growth of the 1930s
was uneven and distorted, and Diaz Alejandro claims that the structure of
protection, because it created vested interests in the light industries hostile
to taxation of their imports, was unsuited to the smooth transition from
one stage of industrialisation to another.[67] The Roca–Runciman treaty
may well have contributed to this distortion by limiting Argentine access to
North American equipment.[68] Industrial growth undoubtedly continued
in the 1930s, and, when it incorporated a vast expansion in the output of
cotton textiles, served to restrict British exports. But Britain had received
major tariff concessions in 1933, especially for textiles, and it seems
probable that these operated both to lift exports from the basement levels
of the depression and to restrain the expansion of Argentine production.
Certainly the pace of the Republic's import substitution slowed. In 1929
national production had satisfied 48·9 per cent of final demand for
manufactured products; in 1930–4 the share rose to 62·7 per cent, but it
then levelled out at 63·3 per cent between 1935–9. It was not until 1940–4
when Britain was physically incapable of supplying the products that the
great leap forward to 80·5 per cent occurred.[69]

Even if total Argentine imports had failed to recover their pre-depression
levels, the trade agreement provided an opportunity for British exporters
to displace their competitors. From 1929 to 1935 this occurred, Britain's
stake in the Argentine market rising from 17·6 per cent to 24·7 per cent.
Tariff manipulation, the operation of exchange control, devaluation and
the income elasticity of Argentinian import demand all played their part.
That the last factor was important is suggested by the increase in market
share obtained by 1931. Britain also benefited from a 20 per cent exchange
surcharge operated from 1935 against, *inter alia*, Japan and the USA.
Nonetheless the UK failed to maintain this position, losing heavily from
1937 so that by 1938 its share of the Republic's imports had slipped again
to 18·3 per cent, barely above the level of 1929. Competition stemmed from
a variety of sources, although, curiously, Japan had little responsibility for
British losses after 1935. Germany made a modest recovery, the Netherlands and Belgium advanced their share of imports to 1937, and a number

[65] Gravil and Rooth, 'Argentina in the 1930s', 337–78.
[66] *Ibid.* 375–6, and Randall, *An Economic History of Argentina*, 125.
[67] Diaz Alejandro, *Economic History of the Argentine*, 259–60.
[68] Gravil and Rooth, 'Argentina in the 1930s', 374.
[69] For a discussion of these figures, see *ibid.*, 372–3.

of suppliers of primary products such as India, the Dutch East Indies and Peru all made considerable headway. The USA was also making a comeback after very severe losses before 1933, and although not quite regaining its position as first supplier, was by 1938 running the UK a close second. Britain thus achieved some trade diversion, but it proved too difficult to hold at the end of the decade.

From a British perspective, how is the Argentine agreement to be assessed? Whitehall's view by 1936 seems unduly favourable, even when it is remembered that the main losses in market share were still to be suffered. Such a rosy outlook can only be justified if the main criterion for success was the unblocking of frozen funds and the payment of remittances. There is no doubt that the payments parts of the agreement worked well: debts were serviced, interest and dividend payments were unhampered and sterling was made available for current imports from the United Kingdom.[70] In other respects the agreement was less successful: trade failed to recover its pre-depression levels; British railway and public utility companies in Argentina, suffering discrimination from the authorities, thought that the 'benevolent treatment' clause of the treaty had not been observed;[71] and British importers in the Republic were bitterly disappointed by the results of Roca–Runciman.[72] Depressed incomes, particularly the poor fortune of British owned companies, and the forces of import substitution were too powerful to be outweighed by the transitory gains of trade diversion. It is possible that a harder trade bargain might have been struck if there had not been British capital to act as hostage; as it was, a major part of Argentina's sterling receipts was allocated to payments on non-trade account. Nor could Argentine goodwill be forfeited if British companies were to operate unmolested. Perhaps, too, there had been a feeling in London that an agreement not too unfavourable to the *Concordancia* would bolster the stability of a regime sympathetic to British interests. These hopes proved unfounded. Instead the agreement became symbolic of a sell-out to foreign interests and a focus of nationalist resentment that contributed ultimately to the establishment of Peronism.[73]

---

[70] BT 11/596, Board of Trade memorandum, 31 Mar., 1936.   [71] *Ibid.*

[72] P. B. Goodwin, Jr, 'Anglo-Argentine commercial relations: a private sector view, 1922–43', *Hispanic American Historical Review*, 61 (1981), 29–51.

[73] Gravil and Rooth, 'Argentina in the 1930s'. For a contrary view, stressing the benefits of the agreement to Argentine economic recovery, see Peter Alhadeff 'Finance and the economic management of the Argentine government in the 1930s'. (D.Phil. University of Oxford, 1983.) Alhadeff places emphasis on the Roca loan, which he argues allowed a controlled depreciation of the peso and contributed to the refunding of government debt to lower interest rates. However, the fact that the peso depreciated by 24 per cent *after* the agreement, and that the government possessed some power over the external value of the currency because of exchange controls must place doubt on the connection between the loan and exchange rate stability.

The trade agreements and British exports: an overview

The discussion of Britain's export trade above is suggestive of some of the possibilities as well as the limitations of trade bargaining. What mattered most for British exporters was the growth of sales, and whether this stemmed from trade creation or diversion was immaterial. Thus it was the prosperity of South Africa rather than any trade diversion which led to the greatest absolute growth of exports to any country. Very often it was the British market itself that was a key to the prosperity of suppliers, and thus of UK exports. Of the dominions discussed here, this was probably true only of New Zealand, which in 1931 sold 89 per cent of exports to Britain. In Australia's case, although dependence was high (50 per cent of exports in 1931), the principal exports of wool and wheat depended on world market conditions, so the UK could provide only limited compensation as an outlet for newer products such as beef or the 'close settlement' commodities. Canada's prosperity hinged much more on conditions in the USA – the deep depression there and the related collapse of investment in the confederation dealt a double-blow to the economy. In Scandinavia and Finland prosperity was quite clearly tied to the British market, although Swedish domestic economic policy has long been upheld as a model for economic recovery.[74] The structure of UK protection and demand was not unfavourable to northern Scandinavia and Finland, although the Norwegians were unable fully to capitalise on it. Denmark, however, was peculiarly discriminated against, and its limited foreign exchange earnings were a serious restraint on British exports. Probably Argentina's prosperity was adversely affected by discrimination against its products and by the sluggishness of British demand for them, but there is no evidence that foreign exchange shortages limited imports from the UK, however much they blocked imports from elsewhere. The prosperity of Poland and the Baltic states had been compromised by the collapse of German imports; this served to throw them much more onto Britain, although recovery was not helped in the case of Poland and Latvia by long adherence to the gold standard at pre-depression parities.

While trade bargaining might have some influence on a country's income by affecting the openings for its trade in Britain, the same negotiations could create opportunities for British exports by restricting the expansion of the trade partner's domestic industry and by diverting

---

[74] See, for example, H. W. Arndt, *The Economic Lessons of the Nineteen-Thirties* (1944), ch. 8 and D. Winch, 'The Keynesian revolution in Sweden', *Journal of Political Economy*, 74 (1966), 168–76, and references cited there. For a later view emphasising the role of monetary policy rather than fiscal policy, see Lars Jonung, 'The depression in Sweden and the United States: a comparison of causes and policies', in K. Brunner (ed.), *The Great Depression Revisited* (Boston, 1981).

trade from other suppliers. With high unemployment, poor export prospects for primary products and balance of payments difficulties, countries were very reluctant to expose their protected secondary industries. There is some isolated evidence of concessions made to Britain inhibiting later expansion, particularly in the case of textiles in Australia, Canada, Sweden and Finland. The drive towards protection was also blocked by tariff rate fixing, although by the time most treaties were negotiated in 1932–3 the protectionist momentum was weakening anyway. When it came to trade diversion, prospects were good, but even here the scope was not unlimited. Explicit preferences, for example, offended against mfn clauses, and so should have been ruled out for the non-imperial agreements. Since within the Empire most dominions already granted preferences to Britain, these could be used as a trade diverting mechanism. But it is worth considering what proportion of a country's imports the UK could reasonably expect to supply. In 1929 Australia and South Africa already drew around 40 per cent of their imports from the UK and New Zealand little short of half. These were relatively sophisticated markets: per capita incomes, by international standards, were high, economic structures diversified and imports therefore wide-ranging. When the limited natural resources of Britain are taken into account, and after more than a century of increasing international specialisation, there was clearly a ceiling on the proportion of imports that could be drawn from the UK without jeopardising economic performance. Moreover, the dominions had to preserve relations with their overseas customers: specialisation had encouraged production in the Empire of wool, wheat and other commodities on a scale well beyond the absorptive capacity of even the United Kingdom. At a time when they were becoming more than ever aware of the finite nature of the British market for foodstuffs, and of the need to cultivate other outlets, the Commonwealth was unlikely to make huge sacrifices for the sake of Britain. From London's point of view large investments in Empire countries might be put at risk by driving a bargain that undermined their ability to service these debts: indeed, the enormous deterioration in Britain's trade balances with the dominions was a necessary part of the adjustments required if they were to continue making interest and dividend payments.[75] Nor, as was emphasised in chapter 3, could imperial goodwill be forfeited.

In the foreign negotiations not all these constraints applied. Perhaps goodwill, at least outside Argentina, had to be less jealously preserved. But the National government would have been more vulnerable to attack from free trade opponents if it had emerged empty-handed from the trade

---

[75] P. J. Cain, 'Free Trade, Protection and the Sterling Area in the 1930s', Discussion Paper, Institute of Commonwealth Studies, 2 Mar. 1989.

negotiations – so negotiations had to result in treaties, at least in the more important discussions. Again with the exception of Argentina, British investments in these countries could be virtually ignored. Turning to trade, Britain was a relatively modest supplier of its foreign trading partners' imports. In principle this therefore left plenty of scope for trade diversion, although economic viability generally demanded that these countries were left with a margin of free exchange for imports of raw materials. In the absence of explicit preferences, the problem was how to put this potential for trade diversion into practice. The way these difficulties shaped the trade negotiations has been discussed in chapters 4 to 7. One of the usual remedies was to use purchasing agreements, although these were in blatant contravention of mfn treaty rights. With the exception of coal, purchasing agreements did not feature in the treaties with Argentina, Norway and Sweden. Ostensibly this was because there was insufficient time to make the agreements,[76] although the fact that purchasing undertakings were an important part of the concurrent negotiations with Denmark suggests that there may have been other considerations: compared with Denmark the lesser dependence of Norway and Sweden on the UK reduced London's leverage and may account for the absence of such undertakings. Really successful agreements with foreign countries hinged on two factors. The first of these was their relative dependence on the British market. Where this was high, as for Denmark, Finland and the smaller Baltic states, the agreements paved the way for a major expansion of British exports, or at least for a substantial increase in market share. This occurred even when in return Britain offered only the prospect of discrimination against their exports. Secondly, import licensing or exchange control was a powerful instrument for diverting trade to the UK. It is notable that when such instruments did not exist, for example in Finland, the British share of the market slipped rapidly at the end of the decade. The Danish agreement proved that even in the absence of specific guarantees about the allocation of licences, the existence of import controls worked for the benefit of British trade. Argentina, relying heavily on Britain as an export outlet, and operating exchange control, proved an exception to this generalisation. However, in this case, as argued in the section above, the UK had objectives beyond export expansion, and was inhibited in other ways from pressing fully its trade advantage.

[76] BT 11/735, A. Mullins (DOT) to F. A. Griffiths, 8 July 1937.

Exports and the British economy in the 1930s

By 1936–8, British domestic exports to the trade agreement countries stood at £187 million, £10 million below the average for 1928–30.[77] Since export prices by 1936–8 were more than 12 per cent lower than in 1928–30, this does represent a gain in the volume of exports.[78] As Table 9.10 indicates, the export record to Northern Europe was considerably better than to the other agreement countries (South Africa excepted). But, in current prices, the trade gain to Northern Europe only just outweighed the losses in Argentina alone, and could not offset the decline in British exports to the dominions. The problem for Britain was that the countries where the largest increases in exports occurred (Denmark, Finland and the Baltic States) were simply too small to compensate for declining sales elsewhere.

When seen in the context of total British exports, the trade agreement countries came to occupy a more central role. While in 1928–30 these countries had bought 29·3 per cent of exports from the UK, by 1936–8 they took 39·2 per cent. Even the four dominions advanced from 19·2 to 24·9 per cent, while Northern Europe increased its percentage from 6 to 10·6. Only Argentina absorbed a smaller proportion of British exports by the end of the period.

One possible reason for Britain's greater reliance on these markets might have been because these countries increased their share of world imports. The years 1929–37 are the only period in Maizels's study of world trade in manufactures when the commodity/area pattern of trade was actually favourable to Britain.[79] The analysis of the structure of dominion imports made earlier in this chapter acts as some confirmation to Maizels' conclusion. Certainly the North European countries increased their share of world imports, but the dominions, on the other hand, took exactly the same proportion of world imports in 1937 as they had in 1929, and Argentina's share declined.[80] For the most part the UK's increased dependence was a consequence of additional market penetration.

Not all of this greater market share necessarily represented a net gain for British trade. It has been suggested that Britain's use of bargaining

---

[77] The trade agreement countries referred to are Denmark, Norway, Sweden, Finland, Estonia, Latvia, Lithuania, Poland, Argentina, Australia, Canada, New Zealand and South Africa.

[78] C. Feinstein, *National Income, Expenditure and Output of the United Kingdom, 1855–1965* (Cambridge, 1972), T. 139.

[79] Maizels, *Growth and Trade*, 200–1. His analysis covers the years 1929–37.

[80] In 1929 the North European trade agreement countries accounted for 5·3 per cent of world imports, and by 1937 and 1938 the share had risen to 6·4 to 7·0 per cent. The four dominions accounted for 7·5 per cent in 1929 and 1937, and for 7·8 per cent in 1938. Argentina's share declined from 2·3 to 1·7 per cent between 1929 and 1937. League of Nations, *Review of World Trade 1938* (Geneva, 1939), 91–2.

Table 9.10. *British domestic exports to selected trade agreement countries, average of 1928–1930 and 1936–1938 (£m and percentage)*

	1928–30	Per cent of total exports	1936–8	Per cent of total exports
Northern Europe	40·3	6·0	50·4	10·6
Argentina	27·4	4·1	18·2	3·8
4 Dominions	129·6	19·2	118·8	24·9
Total[a]	197·4	29·3	187·4	39·2

Note. [a] Does not necessarily tally with the above figures because of rounding up.
Source: UK *Annual Statements of Trade* (various years).

leverage to secure a privileged market, particularly in Northern Europe, merely diverted competition elsewhere.[81] Coal is often specified as an example.[82] Polish and German coal, driven out of Scandinavian markets, reappeared elsewhere to the detriment of British coal sales. Scotland and northeast England's gain was South Wales' loss. There can be no question that British coal export performance in Europe in the 1930s was dismal. The UK alone accounted for the whole of the decline in European coal exports between 1929–37,[83] and while total British coal exports fell by one-third in these years, those from Germany increased by nearly one-half. It is doubtful, however, whether the trade agreements had much to do with this. First, German coal was not displaced from Scandinavia. Secondly, while Polish coal exports to West European markets did increase, the absolute gains were far smaller than the losses in Northern Europe. Moreover, the British coal owners had their 1934 agreement with Poland which tied Polish exports to 21 per cent of the UK figure.[84] The main cause of declining British coal sales in Europe was the cut back in imports by the major producing and net exporting countries of Germany, the Netherlands and Belgium. Structural changes also hit Britain particularly hard because

---

[81] F. Benham, *Great Britain Under Protection* (New York, 1941), 146–7 and Political and Economic Planning, *Report on International Trade* (1937), 286. Unaccountably, and wrongly, of course, Benham asserts that Britain did not succeed in obtaining any reduction in duties, except for a tariff quota on herrings granted by Finland, from any country apart from Denmark, 130.

[82] Benham, *Great Britain*; J. H. Richardson, *British Economic Foreign Policy* (1936), 102; and W. R. Garside, 'The north-eastern coalfield and the export trade, 1919–1939', *Durham University Journal*, 83 (1969), 9. P. Salmon, 'Polish–British competition in the coal markets of Northern Europe 1927–1934', *Studia Historiae Oeconomicae*, 16 (1983).

[83] League of Nations, *Europe's Trade* (Geneva, 1941), 74.   [84] See above, ch. 6.

France and Belgium obtained most of their steam coal from the UK and their metallurgical coal from Germany. The competing power sources of hydro-electricity and oil weakened demand for steam coal, a tendency accentuated by the ability of France and Belgium to produce their own steam coal, while Germany, close to the consuming areas, could supply the more resilient market for metallurgical coal at lower cost.[85]

Extending the argument to trade diversion as a whole, Germany has been portrayed as the major victim and subsequently the major protagonist. There is no doubt that British protection directly harmed German trade, and Germany's foreign exchange shortage was aggravated by its reduced surplus with the United Kingdom. Probably the severe and discriminatory restrictions on British coal exports into Germany were in retaliation against the Import Duties Act.[86] But it does not follow that British action bore much responsibility for German losses in Northern Europe. Germany lost markets primarily because German agricultural protection led to a drastic curtailment in imports – it was action by the Reich that eased Britain's way into the markets of Northern Europe. Far from compensating for this by displacing British goods in the non-agreement countries, Germany lost trade there as well. The pattern is remarkably consistent in the major countries: Germany increased its share of imports between 1929 and 1931, but thereafter steadily lost ground.[87] After 1934 Germany achieved some compensation in a series of trade agreements, especially in South-eastern Europe, but these had been markets of little consequence for Britain anyway.[88]

How did the trade agreements affect Britain's international economic position? Certainly they were unable to haul back total British exports to the modest levels of 1929 or even to prevent a small decline in Britain's share of world trade in manufactured goods by 1937. The calculations of Maizels show that in 1929 the UK had still been the world's leading exporter of manufactures, accounting for 21·7 per cent of trade; by 1937 that share had slipped to 20·7 per cent.[89] The corresponding figures from Tyszynski, using a different classification, are 23·6 and 22·4 per cent. The competitive performance, judged by the world share held of trade in individual commodity groups listed in Table 9.11, was mixed, although

[85] M. Asteris, 'Britain and the European coal trade 1913–1939' (M.Soc.Sc. dissertation, University of Birmingham, 1971), 56.

[86] BT 11/138, Note on German restrictions on coal, Hill, 21 Apr. 1932.

[87] This applies to Austria, Belgium, France, the Netherlands, Switzerland, Czechoslovakia, Japan and the USA. Exceptions are Spain, Italy and Brazil.

[88] A good study of these is D. E. Kaiser, *Economic Diplomacy and the Origins of the Second World War. Germany, Britain, France and Eastern Europe, 1930–1939* (Princeton, 1980). Highly critical of British policy, Kaiser takes insufficient account of the utter unimportance of these markets for British exports.   [89] Maizels, *Growth and Trade*, Table A.4.

Table 9.11. *Shares in world trade held by the UK, 1929 and 1937* (*percentages*)

	1929	1937	Change
Iron and steel	25·1	19·9	−5·2
Non-ferrous metals	13·9	12·7	−1·2
Chemicals	18·8	17·4	−1·4
Non-metalliferous metals	16·4	18·4	+2·0
Miscellaneous materials	10·4	13·3	+2·9
Industrial equipment (non-electrical)	20·8	21·5	+0·7
Electrical goods	21·3	22·5	+1·2
Agricultural equipment	7·7	12·3	+4·6
Railways, ships etc.	45·9	28·6	−17·3
Motor-cars, aircraft etc.	11·7	17·5	+5·8
Spirits and tobacco	38·3	45·0	+6·7
Textiles	36·0	35·7	−0·3
Apparel	20·3	21·9	+1·6
Metal manufactures nes	16·9	15·4	−1·5
Books, films, cameras etc.	23·6	21·2	−2·4
Finished goods nes	23·8	23·8	0·0
Non-classified	33·8	26·6	−1·2
Total	23·6	22·4	−7·2

Source: Tyszynski, 'World trade in manufactured commodities, 1899–1950', 19.

worth contrasting with the almost universal retreat suffered between 1913 and 1929 (see chapter 1). In aggregate the commodity structure of world trade was mildly unfavourable, but, as mentioned above, Britain's relatively slight dependence on the industrialised countries again paid dividends, Maizels calculating that the area/commodity structure of trade was favourable to British exports for the only time this century (his study covers the years to 1959). The problem, then, appears to have been the enduring one of British uncompetitiveness, although it was far less marked than in earlier decades, and was mainly apparent again only towards the end of the decade. Looking at world trade as a whole, rather than just trade in manufactures, the evidence points to Britain having lost between 1929 and 1931, then staging a rapid recovery to 1935 before slipping again in the years before the war.[90]

This experience is borne out by other measures of exchange rate behaviour and of competitiveness. Redmond's estimates of multilateral exchange rates, a weighted average of a basket of currencies, show that

[90] A. Maddison, 'Growth and fluctuations in the world economy, 1870–1960', *Banca Nazionale del Lavoro Quarterly Review*, 15 (1962).

after the pound sterling depreciated from late 1931 to 1932, subsequent appreciation took it back to just below the level of 1929–30.[91] Using perhaps a more appropriate measure that focuses on the exchange rates of major competitors suggests that the UK retained an exchange rate advantage from late 1931 until the end of the decade, a result achieved in part by the government's policy of using the Exchange Equalisation Account to keep sterling low.[92] This, however, takes no account of prices. Maizels's figures for the benchmark years of 1929 and 1937 indicate not only that Britain's export prices remained higher than those of competitors, but that in the 1930s the gap widened further: while UK export prices, expressed in gold dollars, fell by 10 per cent, those of competitors declined by 18 per cent.[93] This is confirmed by the calculations of Michael Kitson and Solomos Solomou which reveal that the real exchange rate, having shown a substantial decline in the wake of devaluation, more than recovered its former rate by 1937.[94]

Competitive weakness was one cause of the persistent deficits in the current account of the balance of payments. For more than a century before the depression this had generated a surplus, but in 1931 had moved sharply into deficit where it stayed for the remainder of the decade, albeit on a more manageable scale than in 1931. Although devaluation and protection had quickly reduced the 1931 deficit, they did not eliminate it. Several factors contributed to its persistence. Imports, with a preponderance of foodstuffs and raw materials, were price inelastic and thus insensitive to exchange rate changes. The fact that more than two dozen countries, the majority of them primary producers, allowed their currencies to depreciate along with sterling tended to negate the effect of devaluation on the import of primary products.[95] Nor, as emphasised earlier, was British tariff policy directed principally at cutting the flow of foodstuffs and raw materials. Moreover, to the extent that devaluation and tariffs stimulated domestic recovery, they paradoxically weakened the trade balance. The merchandise trade gap widened substantially in volume terms, and measured in current prices increased as a proportion of total trade from under 20 per cent in the late 1920s to 26 per cent by 1936–8. This

[91] J. Redmond, 'An indicator of the effective exchange rate of the pound in the nineteen-thirties', *Economic History Review*, 2nd ser., 33 (1980), 83–91.

[92] N. H. Dimsdale, 'British monetary policy and the exchange rate 1920–1938', in W. A. Eltis and P. J. N. Sinclair, *The Money Supply and the Exchange Rate* (Oxford, 1981). For government policy, S. Howson, *Sterling's Managed Float: the operations of the exchange equalisation account, 1932–39*, Princeton Studies in International Finance, 46, 1980.

[93] Maizels, *Growth and Trade*, 205.

[94] Dimsdale, 'British monetary policy', and M. Kitson and S. Solomou, *Protectionism and Economic Revival: the British inter-war economy* (Cambridge, 1990).

[95] A. Cairncross and B. Eichengreen, *Sterling in Decline: the devaluations of 1931, 1949 and 1967* (Oxford, 1983), 90–7.

Table 9.12. *Bilateral trade balances, 1928, 1931 and 1937* (£m)

Area	Balance		
	1928	1931	1937
N. and NE Europe	−88·7	−84·9	−64·4
W. Europe	−54·8	−53·0	−18·9
Eire	−0·4	+2·5	+6·2
Central and SE Europe	+4·5	−46·4	−21·4
S. Europe and N. Africa	−2·2	−10·1	−8·8
Turkey and Middle East	−20·3	−7·5	−14·8
Rest of Africa	+9·7	+12·8	+13·6
Asia	+30·2	−12·4	−46·1
USA	−119·6	−77·8	−71·8
British North America	−20·9	−12·2	−62·0
West Indies	−14·3	−7·3	−25·0
Central and South America	−49·5	−52·4	−54·7
Australia and New Zealand	−23·6	−56·7	−62·8

Source: Mitchell and Deane, *Abstract of British Historical Statistics*, Overseas Trade 12.

may have been bad enough, but it was compounded by a decline in the surplus on invisibles which before 1931 had almost invariably covered the trade gap with something to spare. Lower earnings from shipping and financial services were part of the problem, but the major cause of the deterioration was the fall of investment income from abroad. This resulted from a combination of defaults, loan conversion operations to lower rates of interest, and reduced earnings from equity and direct investments which were hit particularly hard by the collapse of primary prices.[96] Only through adjustment on the capital account was a major crisis in Britain's international payments avoided. Capital embargoes were important, but it is likely that investors may have lost their taste for overseas lending after bitter experience with defaults; there were few favourable opportunities anyway, not least because many creditworthy governments were not only wary of burdening themselves with more debt, but were actually in the process of repaying it. Britain probably experienced a net inflow of long-term capital in the 1930s.[97]

The geographical structure of the balance of payments changed, as the trade balances summarised in Table 9.12 indicate. British trade deficits with the dominions deteriorated sharply. In part this may have reflected

[96] *Ibid.*   [97] Redmond, 'Pound in the 1930s', 89.

the need for debt to be serviced, British exporters paying the price for the benefit of the rentier, and arguably for some shadow of stability in the international financial system. Certainly very few Empire countries defaulted, and the rate of return on imperial loans stayed remarkably stable.[98] The settlement problem was compounded by the reversal of Britain's surplus with Asia, a key element in the pre-war and pre-depression multilateral settlements system. Although increased surpluses with Africa and Eire eased the position, the principal mechanism of adjustment lay with reducing deficits with the USA and with Northern and Western Europe. Since this was mainly the result of protection and the trade agreements, it gave rise to the well-known and well-publicised argument, discussed in the next chapter, that British commercial policy was hindering the access of Europe, and particularly of Germany, to raw materials.

Whatever the problem with the balance of payments, there is no evidence that it hampered economic growth. Indeed, the chain of causation runs in the other direction, with the early and sustained recovery of the British economy drawing in imports. This did not stop the government worrying about the external account, Leith-Ross producing a widely circulated document in December 1936, one result of which was the attempt to negotiate an export agreement with Germany.[99] But de-valuation, and perhaps the tariff too, were prerequisites of the cheap money policy implemented so speedily after February 1932. Although bank rate remained at 2 per cent from June 1932 until August 1939, sterling tended to appreciate, the best efforts of the monetary authorities notwithstanding. Nor was budgetary policy inhibited by external con-straints after 1931.

Studies of devaluation attribute to it an important role in the process of economic recovery, not so much for what it did for exports or imports or even the balance of payments but because it released policy-making from the straitjacket imposed by defending the external value of sterling. Caincross and Eichengreen, for example, conclude that '[t]here would be general agreement that going off the gold standard in 1931 helped lay the basis for economic recovery in Britain. Perhaps the most important contribution came not from any change in the external account but from the greater freedom that a floating rate lent the monetary authorities.'[100]

---

[98] Cairncross and Eichengreen, *Sterling in Decline*, 92–5, and Cain, 'Free trade, protection and the sterling area'.

[99] CAB 24/265 CP 339(36), 18 Dec. 1936. This is discussed in the next chapter.

[100] Cairncross and Eichengreen, *Sterling in Decline*, 230. See also Dimsdale, 'British monetary policy', 334 and 338–41 and S. Howson, *Domestic Monetary Management in Britain, 1919–1938* (Cambridge, 1975) for similar views.

The literature on protection has tended to be more dismissive. Two influential studies made by economic historians are those by H. W. Richardson and by Forrest Capie.[101] Richardson points out that since the fall in imports in the newly protected industries between 1930 and 1935 was less than the fall in imports of the older protected industries, other explanations are needed for the high growth rates of the new industries. Generally, he concludes, 'the evidence so far suggests that it is difficult to show that the tariff had much effect in stimulating recovery in those industries newly protected in 1931 and 1932', and 'its overall effects on employment and productivity were almost negligible'.[102]

Capie produces calculations of the effective incidence of the tariff, concentrating on the ratio of nominal tariff rates to the value added in production, but also allowing for the offsetting influence of tariffs on input costs. These calculations reveal that the steel industry received low effective protection and that the construction sector experienced negative effective protection (that is, there were no protective duties on the final product, but input costs for timber, window frames and so on were raised by tariffs). Since these industries, particularly construction, were central to economic recovery, there seems to be little connection between protection and the structure of recovery. These conclusions are criticised by J. Foreman-Peck who, arguing that the assumption that industries raised prices by the same amount as the tariff was false, then provides estimates of the effect of protection on sales growth.[103] Foreman-Peck also injects a new element into the debate by calculating the macroeconomic impact of the tariff, assessing the effect of the legislation on income and output. On this basis, the fall in imports of manufactures and semi-manufactures induced an increase of 4·1 per cent between 1930 and 1935.[104] Since gnp increased by 9·6 per cent, clearly this was a major contribution. T. J. Hatton confirms the view that the tariff was not unimportant, and although cautioning that the precise magnitude of the impact is debatable, produces an estimate that between 1931 and 1937, the tariff may have contributed a 7·2 per cent boost to aggregate demand, the greater part concentrated between 1931–3.[105]

---

[101] H. W. Richardson, *Economic Recovery in Britain, 1932–1939* (1967) and F. Capie, 'The British tariff and industrial protection in the 1930s', *Economic History Review*, 2nd ser., 31 (1978), 399–409.   [102] Richardson, *Economic Recovery*, 251 and 264.

[103] J. Foreman-Peck, 'The British tariff and industrial protection in the 1930s: an alternative model', *Economic History Review*, 2nd ser., 34 (1981), 132–9.

[104] Foreman-Peck in fact gives a figure of 2·3 per cent, but recalculations by T. J. Hatton, 'Perspectives on the economic recovery of the 1930s', *Royal Bank of Scotland Review*, 158 (1988), 18–32, and by Kitson and Solomou, *Protectionism*, both give a result of 4·1 per cent.

[105] Hatton, 'Perspectives on the economic recovery', and 'The recovery of the 1930s and economic policy in Britain', in Gregory and Butlin (eds.), *Recovery from the Depression*.

The findings of Kitson and Solomou provide further evidence of the importance of the tariff.[106] They identify four major routes through which a fall in import propensities might increase domestic demand. First, an increase in the relative competitiveness of domestic industry leads to import substitution. Secondly, the consequential increase in incomes spreads beyond the newly protected sector. Thirdly, the presence of increasing returns to scale may raise incomes and, finally, investment may be stimulated by increased confidence engendered by protection. They provide evidence of marked acceleration in the 1930s in the growth of those industries that experienced the sharpest reductions in import penetration following the introduction of the tariff.

Little attention has been paid to the contribution of the trade agreements to British economic growth. Nor is this surprising in the light of UK export performance in the 1930s, for not only had exports at their peak in 1937 failed to regain the level of 1929, but they represented a smaller share of national income, the trade gap was tending to widen, and the staple industries being still scarred by heavy unemployment. Ian Drummond suggests that the Ottawa agreements may have increased British exports by £13 million in 1933 and by £28 million in 1937 – even by deliberately erring on the generous side by allowing for a multiplier of two, he calculates that the imperial agreements raised British output by only 0·5 per cent in the first year and by 1·0 per cent in 1937.[107] Kitson and Solomou dismiss exports as a source of growth in the 1930s, concentrating instead on the benefits of import substitution.

Yet two points need to be made. The first concerns timing, particularly around the turning point of 1932–3. There were few sources of expanding demand between these years. The government's fiscal stance was sharply contractionary,[108] and although fixed investment rose by £10 million it was completely outweighed by inventory depletion, leaving the net contribution of investment as negative. Rising real wages may have fuelled consumers' expenditure which was estimated by Feinstein to have risen by £13 million, but in aggregate total domestic expenditure, measured in current prices, fell in 1933.[109] The fact that gross national product rose was only because of the contribution of the external account. Between 1932–3 exports to the agreement countries increased by £14 million, just enough to offset trade losses elsewhere and to raise overseas income by £8 million. In this context, Drummond's estimate that the imperial agreements swelled national

[106] Kitson and Solomou *Protectionism*.
[107] I. M. Drummond, *Imperial Economic Policy 1917–1939: studies in expansion and protection* (1974), 286.
[108] R. Middleton, 'The constant employment budget balance and British budgetary policy, 1929–39', *Economic History Review*, 2nd ser., 34 (1981), 266–86, and Hatton, 'Perspectives on the economic recovery'.   [109] Feinstein, *National Income*, T.9.

income by £26 million in 1933 assumes a new significance. Nonetheless, much more important was the decline in imports and payments abroad of £39 million. Between 1932 and 1934 exports to the agreement countries expanded by £38·5 million and income from abroad by £57 million. By 1934 other components of expenditure were also registering increases, consumption rising by £119 million, and investment, with housebuilding to the fore, also featuring strongly in the recovery.

The second point concerns the part played by the trade agreements in holding at bay the retaliation that might otherwise have been sparked by British protection. From a national viewpoint one of the major dangers of tariff raising is that suppliers and competitors will react by further closing their own markets. Yet there is little evidence that this happened in 1932, although reduced German coal purchases might have been a direct response to the Import Duties Act. There were several reasons for this: Britain was a follower rather than a leader in the protectionist game, and British tariffs were quite modest by the standards of 1932. But the size of the UK market gave leverage, and this was used to claim privileged access both within and outside the Empire. At the same time that British manufactured imports were falling sharply, exports were increasing; this was an earlier recovery than German or American exports experienced, and through to 1935 British exports continued to expand at a faster rate than world trade despite a rise in the effective exchange rate.

By late 1936 German competition was manifesting itself in several unwelcome ways. The British government's response was made within the context of anxieties about the effect of rearmament on the domestic economy, particularly its likely impact on inflation and the balance of payments, the conflicting pressures for trade liberalisation and more effective protection, and with a worsening political-strategic position that created its own impetus for economic appeasement. One result was the Anglo-American trade agreement of November 1938 which has been interpreted by some as marking the end of the Ottawa system.[1] If so, this view can only be accepted with considerable reservations: although there were arguments and even pressures for liberalisation, they were never decisive, for not only was the treaty the product of diplomatic imperatives but the actual form of the agreement between Britain and the USA was distinctly illiberal.

German competition

In hammering out future agricultural policy in 1936–7, levy-subsidy schemes had been opposed on the grounds that they were likely to accelerate inflation, thus endangering Britain's international competitiveness, and that they were likely to alienate trade partners.[2] With the trade agreements coming up for renewal, Whitehall was anxious to keep any modifications to them to a minimum, not least because the UK's bargaining leverage was no longer as strong as it had been in 1932–3. A major cause of Britain's weaker position was the expansion of Germany's

---

[1] R. F. Holland, *Britain and the Commonwealth Alliance, 1918–1939* (London, 1981), 150, and S. Howson and D. Winch, *The Economic Advisory Council, 1930–1939* (Cambridge, 1977), 144. See also W. K. Hancock, *Survey of British Commonwealth Affairs*, II; *Problems of Economic Policy, 1918–1939* (Oxford, 1942), 266–7; R. J. Skidelsky, 'Retreat from leadership: the evolution of British economic foreign policy, 1870–1939', in B. H. Rowland (ed.), *Balance of Power or Hegemony: the interwar monetary system* (New York, 1976), 186–8.   [2] See ch. 8.

buying power and the resurgence of German international economic competition. This manifested itself in several unwelcome ways, not the least of which was that it contributed to Britain's balance of payments problems. The merchandise trade deficit increased sharply from £275 million in 1935 to £346 million in 1936 and was to rise further in the next year. At Runciman's suggestion, Leith-Ross prepared a memorandum on the causes and possible remedies.[3] The major source of the increasing deficit, he concluded, was the growth of imports, particularly of raw materials and semi-manufactures, brought about by higher levels of economic activity in the UK and aggravated by a rundown of stocks in the previous year. Exports had failed to keep pace. Sterling had appreciated because of an influx of money from the gold bloc countries, but a more buoyant domestic economy had perhaps diverted potential exports, contributing to what was described as 'export weariness'. Greater competition was being met in third markets, especially from Germany and Japan; a major part of Leith-Ross's memorandum was devoted to this issue. Although it was thought that sterling was likely to depreciate once a revival of confidence in the gold bloc countries led to an outflow of the 'refugee' money, there were two recommendations made that are significant for this present analysis. One was that further import reductions should be avoided, the balance of payments weakness notwithstanding. The Committee of Economic Information, which as far back as 1934 had recommended that protection in the UK had gone far enough, had reiterated this in their Economic Survey in December 1936.[4] Leith-Ross, worried that rearmament would not only stoke inflation but by diverting resources into armaments production would impair the future exporting ability of the affected sectors, suggested that a balance of payments deficit of £10 million should be tolerated so as to ease these pressures. Moreover, only by an expansion of British purchases from Central and Eastern Europe could the prosperity of these countries, and therefore of the UK export trade, be revived. The second significant recommendation was that the problem of German and Japanese competition might best be dealt with by British industrialists entering market-sharing agreements with their rivals.

This was one of two fundamental ways that might have been used to stem German competition. The other way was to counter Germany by a more aggressive deployment of commercial weaponry. Subsidies might have been used, but there is little evidence that they were seriously considered in Whitehall as a general weapon, and they had been rejected in

[3] CAB 24/265 CP 339 (36), 18 Dec. 1936.
[4] Howson and Winch, *Economic Advisory Council*, 139–40.

1936.[5] The major instrument, in the view of sections of the Foreign Office, should be clearing powers, which could be used to force countries to buy more from Britain, either by threat or by implementation.[6] Moves to introduce such measures went back at least to 1933, but the critical decisions had been taken in 1934 when clearings legislation was introduced. In a draft Bill, the Treasury was to have been given powers to impose a clearing, 'if it appears to the Board of Trade that having regard to the balance of trade between any foreign country and the United Kingdom it is desirable so to do'.[7] The proposed inclusion of these clauses had been prompted by the troubles Britain was experiencing with Denmark, and by the fear that if Argentina abandoned exchange control, the UK would be left with little to show from the agreement. Besides, other countries had taken powers, and it was therefore 'no more difficult to justify the taking of similar powers by the United Kingdom than it [was] to justify the protection of British subjects by the use of gas masks or the use of anti-tank guns'.[8] It was also hoped to use clearing powers in forthcoming commercial negotiations. Apart from T. St Q. Hill, however, there was little enthusiasm for clearing orders amongst senior officials at the Board of Trade. Although the legislation was envisaged as being held in reserve, it was argued that protectionist opinion in parliament might strengthen the terms, and that once on the statute book, the Board would come under pressure from industrial interests to use the powers.[9] The clause was dropped from the Debts Clearing Offices and Import Restrictions Act, 1934, which became largely a debt collecting device. D. E. Kaiser points out that the Foreign Office did not participate in the discussions. Board of Trade officials later noted that while the bill was being considered, Denmark had become more forthcoming in meeting British demands for extra licences.[10] When the question of clearing powers was raised again in 1936 it was as a method of countering German competition. London was anxious about Germany's growing influence over Eastern Europe. Frank Ashton Gwatkin and his assistant Gladwyn Jebb of the Economic Section of the Foreign Office went so far as to suggest that Britain should renounce its mfn rights in South-eastern Europe in return for Germany agreeing to limit competition in Scandinavia and the Baltic area.[11] Primarily concerned that German

---

[5] BT 59/22/540 A, meeting of officials, 30 Oct. 1936, at which reference was made to this decision as having been made two days earlier.

[6] This is discussed in D. E. Kaiser, *Economic Diplomacy and the Origins of the Second World War, 1930–1939* (Princeton, 1980), 95–7, 175–7 and 184–6.

[7] BT 11/274, Draft of Foreign Trade and Finance (Powers) Bill, 14 May 1934.

[8] *Ibid.*, memorandum, 30 Apr. 1934.   [9] *Ibid.*, note of a meeting, 25 May 1934.

[10] BT 11/354, minute by R. Kelf-Cohen, 12 Mar. 1936. The observation was originally made by E. G. Cable, Commercial Secretary in Copenhagen.

[11] Kaiser, *Economic Diplomacy*, 172–3.

devaluation might damage British trade, they also suggested a possible restitution of German colonies and easier trade facilities for Germany in the British Empire. Even Sir Robert Vansittart was prepared to countenance the establishment of a German 'special area' in Central Europe. Britain had far more at stake in Northern Europe, and in Laurence Collier, head of the Northern Department at the Foreign Office, it had a man committed to countering German expansionism. As in 1934 it was problems with Denmark – a breakdown in negotiations for a revision of the trade agreement – which initiated a Foreign Office inquiry as to whether Britain had the power to set up a clearing under the 1934 Act, and whether such action would contravene Britain's seventeenth-century treaties with Denmark. Collier and E. G. Cable, the Commercial Secretary in Copenhagen, were keen to threaten the Danes with a clearing, but S. D. Waley of the Treasury explained that the Board of Trade took 'a less impetuous view', and that he felt sure the Chancellor would not agree to set up a clearing in this case.[12] During the summer Collier managed to enlist the support of Ashton Gwatkin, who reluctantly agreed that clearing powers might be necessary because of the nature of German competition. However, while the Foreign Office was in the midst of discussions with the Board, Runciman pre-empted the issue by renouncing in the House of Commons any increased use of clearing powers.[13] Again, commitment within government to a multilateral trading system had blocked measures which might have proved effective in protecting Britain's position in Northern Europe.

The pursuit of cartels as the alternative method of neutralising German competition emerged from the preparation of a Department of Overseas Trade memorandum in 1936.[14] In the memorandum the problem of German competition was examined, and an accompanying minute suggested that there were no grounds for feeling it was such as to 'give rise to serious apprehension'. In general, German competition was localised, being strongest in those countries from which it was obtaining supplies. Where UK sales had fallen in 1935, as in Italy, France and the Netherlands, this was the result of factors other than German competition. What really worried Department of Overseas Trade officials was the use of subsidies because 'it gives Germany an instrument which can be used with devastating effect in procuring any *particular* contract'. Such competition, because of its ruinous effect on prices, was bad for both countries. The

[12] T 160/921/12659/08/6, S. D. Waley to C. F. Cobbold (Bank of England), 13 Mar. 1936.

[13] The various minutes are in FO 371/20460, 6 June to 7 Sept. 1936, and FO 371/20323, the latter specifically concerned with Germany's use of its clearing agreement to expand sales to Denmark.

[14] BT 59/22/540, 'German competition in overseas markets', various drafts, May–Aug. 1936.

memorandum was given wide circulation in other departments, where the conclusion gained ground that the best course would be to reach some form of agreement with Germany. This was discussed at a meeting of officials in October 1936, and subsequently given Runciman's blessing.[15] There seems to have been remarkably little opposition to the idea. Apparently, none was expressed at the meeting. It was not until late in December that Collier heard what was happening, and, expressing amazement at Foreign Office concurrence, notified Vansittart.[16] Jebb's presence at the October meeting, with the Central Department's knowledge, together with Ashton Gwatkin's approval of Jebb's views, was enough to satisfy Vansittart that the proper procedures of consultation had been followed, and he reluctantly sanctioned the decision. The October discussion had centred not on whether to initiate cartel agreements with Germany but on how and at what level to do so. It was noted that German government officials had been present at other negotiations carried out by industrialists. However, too direct an official approach was ruled out on the grounds that, first, it would be taken by the Germans as a sign of weakness, encouraging greater demands, secondly, that it would have an adverse effect on customer countries, and especially in the dominions where it might further encourage them to develop secondary industries and, thirdly, that Germany might take the opportunity to extend the negotiations to questions about raw materials and other unwelcome subjects. It was therefore decided to encourage industrialists to get in contact with their German counterparts, moves which might be facilitated by the Commercial section of the Embassy in Berlin.[17] The Federation of British Industries was receptive to government suggestions which coincided with a paper by R. G. Glenday, Economic Director of the FBI, arguing the same course of action. The FBI obviously had hopes of reaching accord with the Reichsgruppe Industrie, but, on a visit to Berlin in March, reached the conclusion that talks would have to be carried out from 'below', that is, by agreements between individual industries.[18]

[15] BT 59/22/540 A, meeting of officials, 30 Oct. 1936, and Runciman to E. Wallace (Secretary, Department of Overseas Trade), 18 Nov. 1936.
[16] This is discussed in Kaiser, *Economic Diplomacy*, 187–8. The relevant minutes are in FO 371/20731. Collier wrote on 28 Dec. 1936 that 'this strengthens the view I have long held that we should at least take powers to threaten "clearings" in those foreign markets where German competition is so intense, if only to avoid being driven into undesirable expedients, such as Anglo-German cartels'.
[17] BT 59/22/540 A, minute by D. H. Lyall of meeting between Ramsden of FBI and A. Mullins, 1 Dec. 1936, and R. F. Holland, 'The Federation of British Industries and the international economy, 1929–39', *Economic History Review*, 2nd ser., 34 (1981), 287–300, which mentions Glenday's paper and the approval given to Anglo-German industrial talks by the Grand Council of the FBI in January 1937.
[18] This coincided with Whitehall's beliefs and intentions. The higher the level of contact, the more likely it was to be influenced by Nazi officials who were unenthusiastic about an

In the next eighteen months the Department of Overseas Trade and the FBI attempted to keep in touch with any cartel discussion between British and German businessmen. It was not until the renegotiation of the Anglo-German Clearing Agreement, concluded in July 1938, when the Germans agreed to further trade talks, that fresh momentum was imparted to the cartelisation movement. This resulted in a coal agreement, eventually reached in January 1939. The coal agreement was significant in at least two respects. In the first place, when the Rhenish-Westphalian Coal Syndicate demurred at the British coal exporters' terms, it was diplomatic action that led to the Reich government exerting pressure on the syndicate to reach an agreement.[19] The second significant fact was that when British officials hinted at the use of coal export subsidies, the Germans conceded. Threats also worked in the negotiations over the Payments Agreement: once Leith-Ross said he would suspend the agreement and introduce unilateral clearings, Berlin readily compromised.[20] It would be misleading to generalise from these incidents to suggest that strong measures would always have forced German concessions. They were not interested in selling abroad simply to raise coal output: miners were fully employed, and in the winter of 1938–9 there had been fuel shortages. What principally concerned the Reich government was the maintenance of foreign exchange earnings. Once they had been assured that a lower volume of coal exports would earn at least as much foreign exchange as before, and a break clause was inserted in the agreement to that effect, the German government was prepared to give its blessing. In the case of payments agreement, Britain had a strong bargaining position because of its still substantial trade deficit with Germany.

Contact between the FBI and the Reichsgruppe Industrie was also encouraged by the 1938 payments agreement discussions. The approval now given to the talks by the German government was clearly one factor; the intensification of international competition in 1938 was another. There were plans for Oliver Stanley and also the Secretary of the Department of Overseas Trade, Robert Hudson, to be in Germany to celebrate the conclusion of the Dusseldorf industrial conference. On the day the talks started German troops launched their Prague offensive. British govern-

---

Anglo-German accord. See report by Lyall, who had been sent to Berlin to keep an eye on the industrialists' informal talks, and FO minute in FO 371/20731, 7 Apr. 1937. A note by Ashton Gwatkin records that Ramsden was 'not very pleased with his visit to Berlin', reporting a 'Moscow' atmosphere and that officials and businessmen seemed afraid to talk. For Glenday's conclusion, see Holland, 'The Federation of British Industries', 298.

[19] T 188/158, various notes by the Secretary for Mines, and letters from W. A. Cole to Leith-Ross which outlines the course of the discussions.

[20] C. A. MacDonald, 'Economic appeasement and the German "Moderates" 1937–1939', *Past and Present*, 56 (1972), 105–35.

ment support for the talks was withdrawn and the official visits cancelled. The talks, however, continued. The eventual agreement has been subject to different interpretations. R. F. Holland stresses the wideranging nature of the agreement and the FBI's euphoria.[21] J. H. Magowan, the British commercial attaché in Berlin, dubious of the whole rationale of economic appeasement, sounded a more sceptical note, pointing out major omissions in the agreement and reporting that Goering had told the German delegation, 'it is a most difficult diplomatic task to put the onus of the breakdown on the other side'.[22]

The search for cartel agreements yielded little of benefit to British exporters. In the meantime it had become a substitute for more vigorous government action to protect UK trade.

Trade liberalisation

The attempt to achieve an industrial accord with Germany was one aspect of the British policy of economic appeasement. A perceived need to appease Germany was, in turn, one impulse behind the discussion of trade liberalisation in the UK between 1936 and 1939, and therefore potentially of the dismantling of the trade agreements system.

Economic appeasement certainly had more than one objective, one perceptive observer, Gustav Schmidt, listing nine of what he describes as only the most popular variants of the term.[23] At one level it was an attempt to cope with German competition and to ease British economic problems, particularly in export markets. There was some bad conscience in London that the foreign exchange repercussions of the Versailles settlement, revealed so starkly in the wake of the withdrawal of funds from Germany after 1928, together with British protectionism in 1931–2, had pushed Germany towards autarky and had intensified competition with Britain. In particular, it was thought that Britain's turn to an 'imperial economy' had encouraged Germany's drive towards domination of central Europe.[24] If Germany could be offered relief from its foreign exchange problems, perhaps by means of a British loan or by a wider margin of 'free' exchange in the Anglo-German Clearing Agreement, then it might be persuaded to

[21] Holland, 'The Federation of British Industries', 298.
[22] MacDonald, 'Economic appeasement', 126–7.
[23] Gustav Schmidt, *The Politics and Economics of Appeasement. British Foreign Policy in the 1930s* (Leamington Spa, 1987), 33–7. The following paragraph is based largely on this, MacDonald, 'Economic appeasement', and J. S. Eyers, 'Government direction of Britain's overseas trade policy, 1932–37' (D.Phil. thesis, University of Oxford 1977), chs. 5, 6.
[24] E.g. FO 371/21701, Leith-Ross, 25 Feb. 1938 and note by Ashton Gwatkin for Leith-Ross, 10 Mar. 1938.

abandon autarky and to stop subsidising exports. Greater availability of sterling would reduce the pressures of German competition, and, by expanding German purchases, especially in Central and Eastern Europe, would create more buoyant demand conditions in those markets for British and Empire products. Alternatively, as mentioned above, spheres of influence, or economic zones, might be demarcated, at least in part with the idea of restricting competition. But there were other objectives that stretched beyond the mere limitation of competition. It was hoped that measures such as these would break the fatal chain of progression from economic nationalism to militarily driven protectionism to a third stage where the German economy became dependent for its survival on the spoils of war. Easing access to foreign exchange might relieve these pressures, and as part of the same process, buttress the position of the German 'moderates', first identified as Hjalmar Schacht, and then, when by 1937 Schacht had lost influence, rather more improbably in the person of Hermann Goering. These ideas, which were pushed most persistently by Ashton Gwatkin and Gladwyn Jebb, were also discussed informally by a group initiated by Frank McDougall, economic adviser at Australia House, and including Professor Noel Hall, Barrington Ward of *The Times* and Lester Pearson from Canada House together with Rex Leeper and Jebb in attendance from the Foreign Office.[25] Essentially, the 'keep Germany fat' schemes involved relaxation of the Ottawa agreements and even perhaps a measure of colonial restitution. Intermittent support came from the influential Leith-Ross, who had close contacts with Schacht and was particularly keen on securing an orderly devaluation of the German mark. The essential conflict was between the 'lean' and the 'fat' Germany exponents. Even the regional bloc schemes could draw support for diametrically different reasons: while some saw them as a way of relieving German difficulties (and perhaps relaxing competitive pressures on British exporters), others envisaged that the problems Germany would encounter in absorbing and integrating these countries would dissipate its energies, thus impairing its capacity to launch an assault on the west. Basically, however, the economic departments were hostile, and the idea of economic appeasement made little headway within the Foreign Office itself where it was felt that a political settlement was a necessary precondition for economic concessions. German foreign exchange and raw material problems, it was argued, stemmed in large part from the process of rearmament. Far from increasing the chances of maintaining the peace, economic concessions and the provision of foreign exchange would merely speed the process of German militarisation.

[25] H. M. G. Jebb, *The Memoirs of Lord Gladwyn* (1972), 63–4.

Quite apart from its ultimate uselessness, economic appeasement never appears to have contributed towards liberalisation of external economic relations. Perhaps the nearest it came to doing so was in 1937 when an inter-departmental committee, chaired by Leith-Ross, produced a report recommending a reduction of colonial preferences by an extension of the Open Door principle, but this proposal was rejected by Ministers.[26] J. S. Eyers distinguishes the impetus behind trade liberalisation that aimed primarily at the direct economic appeasement of Germany from that which sought to reduce government restraints on trade for the sake of easing international tensions.[27] The issue of negotiating with or about Germany, he argues, was preponderant at the expense of the wider issue of trade liberalisation.

The Anglo-American Trade Agreement

The search for peace by the removal of international trade barriers was in accord with the ideas of the American Secretary of State, Cordell Hull.[28] Hull's persistence eventually bore fruit when, on 17 November 1938, a series of trade agreements between Britain, Canada and the USA were signed in the East Room of the White House. Around the Lincoln Table brought down for the occasion, were grouped President Roosevelt, the Canadian premier, Mackenzie King, Secretary of State Cordell Hull, the British Ambassador to Washington, Sir Ronald Lindsay, and Arnold Overton who had headed the British negotiating team. Discussions had been going on for four years, with growing intensity in 1938, and, as one participant observed, 'it was the big day in Mr Hull's career'.[29]

As mentioned, some historians interpret it as marking the end of the Ottawa experiment. Britain had grown to see the follies of bilateralism, and with Lindsay's signature of the Anglo-American Trade Agreement, turned its back on the imperial preference system. Holland expresses this viewpoint with great clarity: the agreements

signified the end of that economic nationalism which had governed world events since at least the late 1920's. They represented a recognition by the two greatest international traders (both of whom, Britain with her sterling alliances and the USA with her New Deal experiment, had tried to cut an independent route through the commercial jungle of the 1930's) that recovery could only be permanently stabilised on the basis of freer exchange.

S. Howson and D. Winch cite the agreement as 'one of the many ways in which the Ottawa policy was more or less abandoned by 1939'.[30]

---

[26] Eyers, 'Overseas trade policy', 214–15.   [27] *Ibid.*, 190–1.
[28] Cordell Hull, *The Memoirs of Cordell Hull* (1948), I, 81, 364–5.
[29] J. Pierrepont Moffatt, cited by R. N. Kottman, *Reciprocity and the North Atlantic Triangle, 1932–1938* (Ithaca, NY, 1968), 264.   [30] See note no. 1.

Although these authors acknowledge the political context of the negotiations, the extreme reluctance with which the British participated does not always emerge. Yet to read the UK account of the proceedings leaves a powerful impression of the huge doubts that were harboured about the whole enterprise, and the absence of a British Cabinet Minister from the ceremony was significant. During a discussion about whether to accede to American demands the Cabinet agreed 'to place on record the importance they attached, from a political and international point of view, to the conclusion of a trade agreement with the United States'.[31] A Foreign Office official summed up a widespread feeling in Whitehall when he commented that the agreement was 'highly unsatisfactory from the point of view of our foreign trade and our inter-imperial commercial relations'.[32] There can be little doubt that more was conceded and less gained than had ever been envisaged. From the outset London had been reluctant to negotiate, and persistent American pressure had been needed to draw the UK into talks.

Cordell Hull and American trade policy

In substantial part, American policy in these matters was that of the Secretary of State, Cordell Hull. He was a crusader, a tireless advocate of liberalising trade, the virtues of which he would extol frequently and at length. At one level, it was in Hull's view a policy for peace: 'To me, unhampered trade dovetailed with peace; high tariffs, trade barriers and unfair economic competition with war.'[33] The removal of trade barriers, the free flow of goods and exchange would foster economic interdependence and the peace of nations. Such an equation, which had a respectable antecedent in the ideas expressed so forcibly by Cobden and other English liberals in the mid-nineteenth century, found in the deteriorating international situation of the 1930s continued and widespread acceptance. While there seemed little doubt that Hull held these views with genuine, fierce conviction, he nonetheless had, as one commentator has observed, an 'awesome faculty for transmuting American interests into universal moral principles'.[34]

The passage and implementation of the trade agreements programme was, however, the product of various pressures. Along with events such as the establishment of an Export–Import Bank and diplomatic recognition of Soviet Russia, the trade agreements marked a commitment by the

---

[31] CAB 23/94 36 (38) 28 July 1938.
[32] Minute by Balfour, 12 Oct 1938, FO 371/21506, cited by C. A. MacDonald, *The United States, Britain and Appeasement 1936–1939* (1981).   [33] Hull, *Memoirs*, I, 81.
[34] B. M. Rowland, *Commercial Conflict and Foreign Policy* (New York, 1987), 178.

United States to a world economic role, a commitment that was to grow stronger over the next decade. In 1934 Leon Trotsky had written in the journal *Foreign Affairs* that the power of American capitalism was such that it 'must open up ways for itself throughout the length and breadth of our entire planet'.[35] F. V. Meyer has subsequently argued that trends within the US economy created pressure for international markets: as product life shortened, and research and development costs grew ever more massive, it became imperative for corporations to maximise sales world-wide.[36] The Reciprocal Trade Agreements Act of 1934 was the turning point in American policies, the watershed between the high protectionism of the 1930 Hawley-Smoot tariff and 1932 Revenue Act duties, and the forceful American pursuit of trade liberalisation in the 1940s.[37] Such trade expansionism accords with the view of how dominant economic powers behave: those with the technological and competitive edge have an interest in maximising sales through an open multilateral economy. There may be a delay between the establishment of economic leadership, a country's recognition that it has achieved it, and consequently the adoption of the appropriate policies. Inevitably some lagging sectors of the economy will cling to protectionism, but it is notable that export interests were behind Hull's programme. The American Automobile Manufacturers Association had backed Roosevelt in 1932 because they thought he would pursue a tariff policy designed to open up markets abroad, and he was still getting support from sections of the motor industry in 1936 on the grounds that however much they disagreed with his other policies they approved of what he had done for foreign trade.[38] Some conservatives supported an active foreign trade programme precisely because they saw it as an alternative to increasing government regulation.

By 1934 Hull had overcome powerful opposition from industries that felt threatened by foreign competition, from isolationists and, most strongly of all, from farmers. George Peek, director of the Agricultural Adjustment Administration, was an influential opponent of Hull within government, and there had been an epic contest between them in 1934. Once Peek had resigned in July 1935, Hull was the dominant voice on trade in the Roosevelt administration. Armed with the powers of the Reciprocal Trade Agreements Act, Hull could make an onslaught on the Ottawa system. The imperial trade agreements, embodying just about everything

---

[35] Quoted in Lloyd C. Gardner, *Economic Aspects of New Deal Diplomacy* (Madison, 1964), 26.   [36] F. V. Meyer, *International Trade Policy* (1978).

[37] David A. Lake, *Power, Protection and Free Trade. International Sources of U.S. Commercial Strategy, 1887–1939* (Ithaca and London, 1988), who emphasises that the United States was firmly committed to protectionism, and that the 1934 Act was intended as a complement to protection, enabling the US to reopen foreign markets for its exports. 7, 184 and 207.   [38] Gardner, *New Deal Diplomacy*, 39.

Hull detested in commercial policy in the 1930s, drew his special ire. Some years later he described the system as 'the greatest injury, in a commercial way, that has ever been inflicted on this country since I have been in public life'.[39] Not only had tariff barriers been raised, but American exports were being discriminated against both in their most valuable market, the UK, and in Empire countries. Furthermore, in Hull's view Britain's economic empire undermined a peaceful world order. With the object of attacking the imperial preference system, the State Department in the summer of 1934 set up the British Empire Committee. It involved a twofold strategy, first an attack via the periphery through agreements with the dominion countries, and secondly an assault on the system by direct bilateral negotiations with Britain.

The first part of this move met with early but limited success in the form of a trade agreement with Canada announced on 11 November 1935.[40] This was achieved easily because of the desperate concern of the Canadians to regain some of their lost markets in the United States. The initiative had come from R. B. Bennett, the Conservative Prime Minister, but Washington held back from concluding a treaty until after the 1935 Canadian elections. American officials had discussed matters with Liberal leader Mackenzie King, and judging a more favourable deal could be made with him, delayed concluding an agreement until after the Liberal victory. While as a result the USA almost certainly gained more from the agreement than would have been possible from Bennett, the pact nonetheless highlighted the limitation of the peripheral approach. It is true that the United States gained mfn treatment for its exports and freedom from arbitrary customs regulations, but the Canadians coralled off the British preferential rates from mfn coverage, so the Americans were failed to secure larger concessions on many items because the Ottawa agreements limited Canada's freedom of manoeuvre.

In pursuit of the second arm of Washington's assault on the Ottawa system, direct negotiations with London, various informal soundings were made of British officials and ministers in 1934 and 1935, but met with little positive response. The attack through the periphery had temporarily exhausted itself after the Canada–US pact of 1935, an agreement that had

---

[39] US Congress Hearings, 1940, cited Rowland, *Commercial Conflict*, 180.

[40] This is discussed by Marc Boucher, 'The politics of economic depression: Canadian–American relations in the mid-1930s', paper presented to the Association of Canadian Studies meeting, Montreal, 1985; Kottman, *Reciprocity*; Ian M. Drummond and Norman Hillmer, *Negotiating Freer Trade: The United Kingdom, the United States, Canada and the Trade Agreements of 1938* (Waterloo, Ontario, 1989), and for some of the background, Tim Rooth, 'Britain and Canada between two wars: the economic dimension', in Colin C. Eldridge (ed.), *From Rebellion to Patriation: Canada and Britain in the Nineteenth and Twentieth Centuries* (Lampeter, 1989).

in itself highlighted the trade restricting power of the Ottawa treaties. Washington had brushed off approaches from Canberra and by 1936 found itself embroiled in a trade war with the Australians.[41] Moreover, Hull's reciprocal Trade Agreements Act was in jeopardy because of opposition from farmers. By 1936 fourteen trade treaties had been signed, practically all with primary producing countries and therefore incorporating agricultural concessions by the United States in exchange for improved access for American industrial exports. If angry farmers were to be appeased, Hull badly needed an agreement with an industrial country.[42] The UK, by a wide margin the most valuable external outlet for United States farm produce, fitted the bill.

Hull therefore intensified his pressure on Britain in 1936. He twice interviewed Sir Robert Lindsay early in the year, drawing out the political implications of restrictive trade policies and causing the ambassador to comment that not only economic recovery but 'world peace itself' would emerge from the trade agreements programme. As the year wore on, the deteriorating international position made 'world peace itself' look increasingly fragile. Most ominously, German troops re-entered the Rhineland in March 1936, in July Austria declared itself a German state, and by September there were 40,000 Italian 'volunteers' in Spain. Direct approaches were made to Anthony Eden who was considered sympathetic to the United States; memoranda and speeches were composed and delivered.

British attitudes and responses

For the first eight months of 1936 London stalled, much as it had done in 1934 and 1935. There existed a distrust of America among the British political elite. Stanley Baldwin, during the 1931 Manchurian crisis, had remarked that 'you will get nothing out of the Americans but words. Big words, but only words', a comment on a subsequent occasion echoed by Neville Chamberlain.[43] Baldwin admitted that 'he had got to loathe the Americans so much' he hated meeting them. Chamberlain, whose distrust had been fed by what he saw as Roosevelt's torpedoing of the World Economic Conference in 1933 and by American bad faith at the Washington Naval Talks of 1934, feared being manoeuvred into an exposed position and then abandoned. Sir Robert Vansittart's attitude was

---

[41] M. R. Megaw, 'Australia and the Anglo-American Trade Agreement of 1938', *Journal of Imperial and Commonwealth History*, 3 (1975), 191–211.

[42] George Schatz, 'The Anglo-American Trade Agreement and Cordell Hull's search for peace, 1936–1938', *The Journal of American History*, 57 (1970), 90.

[43] MacDonald, *The United States*, 20.

similar. Head of the American Department of the Foreign Office in the late 1920s, and Permanent Secretary from 1930 until his removal in 1938, he was probably much more sympathetic, but even he wrote, in 1934, 'it is still necessary, and I still desire as much as ever that we should get on with this untrustworthy race... We shall never get very far; they will always let us down.'[44] He was certainly outdone in his anti-Americanism by Sir Warren Fisher, whose business as Permanent Secretary to the Treasury and as Head of the Civil Service none of this should have been, but who was closely involved nonetheless. Many felt, including Walter Runciman and his successor as President of the Board of Trade, Oliver Stanley, that any serious attack on the Ottawa system must be resisted. Distrust of America was often less a distrust of Washington's intentions than scepticism over its ability to deliver in the face of strong isolationism. After all, it was reasoned, if the dictatorships were to be deterred by gestures of solidarity among the democracies, why not modify or repeal the Neutrality Laws that inhibited America from giving assistance in time of war? Instead, the Americans insisted on trade liberalisation, and trade liberalisation that was targeted at the imperial preference system. Uncertain gains from an Anglo-American accord were to be pursued at the expense of the more dependable Empire. As J. M. Troutbeck of the Foreign Office expressed it:

> it was perfectly true that we want to keep on the best possible terms with the United States Government in the present critical situation in the world. But for precisely the same reason it is imperative to keep on good terms with the Dominions. And clearly if it comes to the point, the Dominions must come before the United States.[45]

If the political gains from an accord with the USA looked uncertain at best, the economic case was even weaker. America was an important market for British producers, accounting in 1936 for 6·3 per cent of domestic exports, but it was exceeded by each of South Africa, Australia and India. The prospect of a major gain in British exports was thin: even if maximum tariff reductions of the 50 per cent allowed by US legislation were obtained, many American tariffs would stay at a high level; 'moreover, a considerable part of our export trade is in luxuries, the market for which depends more upon internal prosperity within the U.S.A. than upon anything else'.[46] There was an uncomfortable recognition that any trade arrangement might widen the trade gap rather than narrow it. While London had been able to use balance of payments deficits to its advantage in negotiating with trading partners in Northern Europe, there was little chance of repeating this success with the USA. American

[44] Norman Rose, *Vansittart. Study of a Diplomat* (1978), 127.
[45] Troutbeck, FO 371/19834, 23 Nov. 1936, cited Rowland, *Commercial Conflict*, 213.
[46] BT 11/918, Draft instructions to UK delegates, nd but Jan. 1938.

dependence on the British market was too small for leverage to be exercised and the realities of political power also dictated otherwise.

What also became abundantly clear was that the Americans were not interested in a token agreement but wanted instead real concessions that would cut into the Ottawa agreements. This might entail double losses for the UK because if the dominions were to lose some of their preferential position in the British market, how were they to be compensated? Unless they were to be persuaded that political advantages were to accrue from an Anglo-American accord that would transcend any material loss, or that the general stimulus that such an agreement would give to the international economy would compensate them for the loss of privileges, the dominions needed the assurance of some tangible concessions. There was no question of the Americans offering any such compensation: the US had no intention of paying twice for any improvement of their position in the British market. Nor was there much scope for Britain to offer the dominions offsetting advantages: most of their exports were admitted duty free, and even if London had wanted to raise preferential margins, treaty obligations blocked such a course. This left Britain with little option but to acquiesce in the relaxation of the preferential margin British goods enjoyed in Empire markets, a move which would give the dominions greater freedom to negotiate offsetting deals with third countries.

There were other problems. US demands were likely to threaten customs receipts, a lucrative source of budgetary revenue. This became a more important consideration as discussions progressed, certainly by 1937 when both the shape of American demands had become clearer, with their emphasis on such revenue raisers as tobacco and timber, and when the rearmament programme was starting to impose strains on government finance.

In summary, the economic case for negotiation with the United States appeared very thin. An agreement would probably widen the balance of payments deficit, already causing considerable anxiety by 1936, reduce customs revenue, and involve paying twice for any concessions in the American market. And these, moreover, looked to be modest. In principle, at least, Britain would only be able to negotiate on items for which it was the main supplier, and tariffs were likely to remain at uncomfortably high levels. All this in a market which absorbed a little over 6 per cent of UK exports, a figure dwarfed by the dominion markets from which Britain was going to accept a retreat.

Talks start

From the British government's viewpoint, the case against talks was strong. Nonetheless they started, albeit tentatively, on an exploratory basis. Informal talks reached the stage where in September 1936 the British Commercial Counsellor in Washington, H. O. Chalkley, agreed with American officials to exchange a list of requests by 16 November.[47] This was to be the first part of three official stages required of negotiations by the US Reciprocal Trade Agreements Act of 1934, that of 'conversations'. These were to last a year until on 18 November 1937 both governments announced that negotiations were contemplated, the second stage in the process.

Two forces were at work to induce British participation. One was undoubtedly the pressure generated by Hull. Not content with haranguing Lindsay and other visitors, he kept up the momentum by sending memoranda and making representations through the US Ambassador in London, R. W. Bingham.[48] At first Hull sought a general declaration of support for his policies of international trade liberalisation. But when, after some prevarication in London, this was duly made, Hull considered the declaration inadequate both in tone and substance. To the irritation of Whitehall, he insisted it should be followed up by tangible action. On the basis of the surviving documents it is difficult to imagine that much would have happened if the initiative had been left to London. Even then Hull's remonstrations might have led to nothing more than a rising tide of resentment in Whitehall if the deteriorating European situation had not created a second set of forces that pushed the British government towards *rapprochement* with the United States.

Lindsay had noted in February 1936 that American trade officials were starting to change their advocacy of the American programme: whereas previously they had argued that economic nationalism retarded recovery while US policy promoted it, they now emphasised the contrasting effects of these policies on world peace.[49] This was symptomatic of growing anxiety about the international situation. As tensions rose in Europe, in particular, improved relations with the USA became ever more vital for Britain. When British officials first met to consider the Anglo-American conversations, by then underway, the Board of Trade's W. B. Brown opened the discussions by saying that the Board 'did not attach any great commercial importance to an agreement with the United States'.[50] He was

---

[47] Drummond and Hillmer, *Negotiating Freer Trade*, 42.
[48] *Ibid.*, 41–2, and Rowland, *Commercial Conflict*, 199–209.
[49] BT 11/591, Lindsay to Eden, 5 Feb. 1936.
[50] BT 11/796, USA minutes (UK) 1/36 UK–USA Commercial Negotiations, 3 Dec. 1936.

countered by Frank Ashton Gwatkin, who said that the Foreign Office 'would look upon an agreement with the United States as of major importance from the political point of view'. To lend weight to the Foreign Office case, Lindsay, prompted by Eden, produced an influential review of Anglo-American relations.[51] Asked for suggestions of how the good will of the American government and public opinion might be maintained in the event of a major crisis in Europe, Lindsay's recommendations were clear: America was generally unapproachable on major political issues, the ambassador asserted, and was particularly so at the present moment. But the economic approach was open, and moreover, if the initiative came from the US it was imperative not to reject it. Furthermore:

in the event of a major crisis in Europe, the factor which will most impede any measures which the American Government might take in favour of Great Britain will be the Middle West, and it is just the Middle West, the centre of the agricultural community, which will be directly and favourably affected by the conclusion of a commercial treaty with the United Kingdom, improving or facilitating the export of agricultural produce from the United States to Great Britain. It might even be a deciding factor in the attitude which America would take. I respectfully, but forcibly submit to you, Sir, that an American hand is being proffered to us, and it is full of gifts...I earnestly hope that it will be grasped.

Essentially the same message had been given to Eden by one of Roosevelt's emissaries, Norman Davies, who had stated that while a political settlement was unlikely, the United States might be persuaded to involve itself in Europe through an economic agreement: 'One could get away with murder under the name of economic appeasement in the United States today', and the administration was particularly anxious for a trade agreement with Britain.[52]

Concessions sought by the United States

If the lofty aims of economic appeasement were to be achieved, Hull's trade agreements programme had to survive, and since its chances of doing so were greater if farmers' support could be won, concessions were needed for the fruit growers, hog raisers and other groups. Although the structure of UK imports from the USA was diverse, primary products featured prominently in the list, as Table 10.1 indicates.

The list of US requests handed to Chalkley was described by the Americans as containing their 'minimum essential demands'.[53] It in-

[51] CAB 27/620, TAC (36) 37, Memorandum by Eden, 7 Apr. 1937, enclosing despatch by Lindsay, 22 Mar. 1937.
[52] Quoted by Drummond and Hillmer, *Negotiating Freer Trade*, 34.
[53] *Ibid.*, 43 and Kottman, *Reciprocity*, 142–3.

Table 10.1. *UK retained imports from the USA, 1929, 1931, 1933 and 1936* (£000s)

	1929	1931	1933	1936
Apples	3,623	3,731	1,373	1,360
Preserved fruit	4,518	3,852	2,970	3,457
Lard	6,691	4,767	4,288	1,566
Wheat and flour	13,305	3,835	63	71
Ham	4,333	2,315	1,957	1,496
Tobacco, unmanufactured	14,393	7,855	7,713	13,743
Raw cotton and linens	36,899	9,884	18,023	17,041
Wood, sawn, hard	4,616	2,726	1,968	2,369
Machinery parts	8,524	6,997	3,051	7,753
Metals, non-ferrous	10,927	3,741	631	530
Petroleum spirit	11,345	5,581	2,379	2,229
Lubricating oil	3,555	2,821	2,259	2,027
Road vehicles	5,972	1,612	563	2,957
Total	183,977	97,620	71,155	87,114

Source: Annual Statement of Trade of the United Kingdom, 1931 and 1936.

corporated a range of products covered by the Ottawa agreements, including rice, fresh apples, grapefruit and pears, a variety of preserved fruits, honey, tobacco, raisins, planed softwoods of Douglas fir or Southern pine and patent leather.

Ominously, the United States promised a further set of requests to come. This highlighted differences in bargaining approaches between the US and UK teams: while the British worked to maximise concessions on a set list of requests, the American technique was, if blocked on one commodity, to substitute new demands. Thus, nearly two years later, as the negotiations ground towards a conclusion, the American requests creating the greatest difficulty included those for lard, hams and various industrial products, not one of which had featured on the original list.

Chalkley's initial response was to question the wisdom of a 'must' list, to stress the difficulties in the way of concessions wanted by the Americans and to suggest that what he envisaged was an agreement in which the principal features would be the freezing of duties at current levels and, where it already existed, the guarantee of continued free entry.

It soon became clear, however, that while this approach had paid handsomely for Britain in past negotiations with the countries of Northern Europe, trade bargaining with the USA was to be on a very different basis.

When the Trade and Agriculture Committee (TAC) of the Cabinet met in April 1937 they had before them both Whitehall's assessment of the likely concessions that could be made to American demands, and also Lindsay's despatch recommending that the hand be grasped.[54] The recommendations of the departments held little prospect of a generous response. It was politically impossible to reduce the rice preference just at the moment when the main beneficiary, Burma, was starting its 'separate career under British auspices'. But something might be done on apples, for the United States attached special importance to a lowering of the duty on apples from 4s 6d to 2s 3d per cwt throughout the year; here it was recommended that the UK approach the dominions with a proposal to lower the duty to 3s 6d, although recognising that the reduction might have to be limited to that part of the year when northern hemisphere supplies were being marketed. Compromises might be made by offering limited duty reductions on honey and selected fruits, but not on the 'close settlement' products such as dried prunes, apricots or raisins being produced by the ex-soldier settlers of Australia, a group which included British migrants and which had featured so prominently in the ambitious Empire Settlement schemes of the 1920s. Nor did a concession on tobacco look likely. Under the Ottawa arrangements Britain had guaranteed a 2s per lb preference on Empire supplies that was to last for ten years in order to provide a firm basis for the development of the industry. This Whitehall considered immutable, the Southern Rhodesians being particularly attached to the preference. There was a well-entrenched taste in Britain for Virginia tobacco, so that the volume of US sales had held up well during the depression, and by 1936 was well above pre-slump levels. The British refusal to secure a reduction in the tobacco preference was to continue to cause trouble in the negotiations. Another source of difficulty which persisted was over the American demand for duty free entry for sawn softwood of Douglas fir or Southern pine. The US supplied less than 3 per cent of sawn softwood imports in 1936, and Douglas fir was for practical purposes indistinguishable from Baltic pine. Even if Canada agreed, the UK would have either to abolish the duty on all such imports, a valuable source of revenue, or court difficulties with the North European suppliers, at a time when trade treaties were due for renewal. Southern pine, however, a US speciality, was distinct, so demands could probably be met.

The strongest reservations about the American demands were expressed by W. S. Morrison, the Minister of Agriculture, who emphasised both the political nature of the agreement sought by the Americans, and the attack on the Ottawa agreements. Discussing Cordell Hull's attempt to make a breach in the imperial preference system, Chamberlain asserted that while Hull must not be allowed to have his way, no UK statesman would dream

---

[54] CAB 27/619, TAC (36) 11th meeting 12 Apr. 1937 and CAB 27/620 TAC (36) 35, 36, 37.

of saying the Ottawa agreements were immutable. Warmed by the prospects of American concessions, the terms of which, according to Chamberlain, were 'far better than he had previously believed to be within the range of possibility', the Trade and Agriculture Committee decided that it would discuss the proposed responses to the American requests with the dominions. This involved risking an economic element being added to the Imperial Conference planned for the summer of 1937, a prospect that many in Whitehall, with memories of the 1932 Ottawa Conference, had dreaded. They hoped the discussions could be held bilaterally, and a united dominions front avoided.

The United States replied that the British responses provided too narrow a basis for worthwhile negotiations. In early June, fearing that their offers had been too meagre, the State Department decided to 'bait the hook with real concessions in order to influence the Imperial Conference now underway in London', Francis Sayre reported to Roosevelt.[55] The following day, 4 June, Sayre and Hawkins met Chalkely to offer improved terms.

Runciman had addressed the Imperial Conference on 27 May, stating that with negotiations underway, the Ottawa agreements would need modifying. In a memorandum to the delegates, the Foreign Secretary emphasised the political advantages of an Anglo-American accord, asserting that in Europe the appearance of solidarity between Britain and the United States was already 'having its effect on curbing the dictators and in keeping up the spirits of the Central European Powers', and suggesting that in the Far East good Anglo-American relations were an essential check on Japan. Chamberlain, speaking days before succeeding Baldwin as Prime Minister, stressed the political as well as the economic advantages of a trade pact.[56] The public response of the dominion representatives were helpful. C. A. Dunning of Canada, J. A. Lyons of Australia and N. C. Havenga of South Africa all stressed the difficulties that fixed margins of preference placed in the way of their efforts to negotiate trade treaties outside the imperial framework. Zafullah Khan of India also spoke of the need for multilateral trade, with only Walter Nash of New Zealand, pressing strongly for a bilateral agreement with Britain, being unsympathetic.

Dominion support in principle was one thing, acting on it was another. By the time the conference ended the Ottawa agreements remained intact. The dominions proved unwilling to accept arguments that the general expansion of international trade would compensate them for unilateral concessions. The Southern Rhodesians were adamant in refusing to accept

[55] Sayre to Roosevelt, 3 June 1937, quoted by Rowland, *Commercial Conflict*, 265.
[56] CAB 27/620 TAC (36) 47.

a reduced preference on tobacco: it would have alienated the politically dominant agricultural settlers, 70 per cent of whose tobacco production was sold in the UK.[57] The South Africans had been expected to prove recalcitrant, but had reportedly changed their attitudes after being reminded that the South African economy was dependent on American gold policy.[58] The Australians, with an election pending, were so nervous that Prime Minister Lyons refused to go near the Board of Trade, and had even turned down an invitation to visit Roosevelt on his journey back to Australia lest he be suspected of talking about trade concessions. Nothing could be expected from there until after November. It was the Canadians, likely to have to make the greatest concessions of the dominions for an Anglo-American pact to succeed, who were most emphatic in their need for simultaneous and linked discussions with the USA.

The price Britain had to pay for commonwealth co-operation was to acquiesce in forgoing some of the privileges its exporters enjoyed in their markets. In conversations with Canadian representatives, Overton put it this way:

the logical counterpart of any concessions by Canada to facilitate an agreement with the U.S.A. would be for the United Kingdom Government to give very sympathetic consideration to any cases arising in Canadian negotiations with foreign countries where bound margins under the United Kingdom–Canadian agreement were found to be an obstacle.[59]

Oddly enough the Canadians appear to have forgotten the promise, a failure that was to lead to misunderstandings in the next months between Washington, Ottawa and London.

Between June and November 1937 contacts were maintained between the three capitals. The State Department, not least because of opposition from farmers, wanted to hold direct discussions with Canada only after the completion of the Anglo-American accord, but suddenly, and for no obvious reason, changed its mind, Francis Sayre informing the Canadians on 13 October that simultaneous negotiations would be held.[60]

The negotiations

On 18 November the UK and the USA, with little apparent enthusiasm on either side about each other's trade offers, nonetheless announced that they were prepared to 'contemplate' negotiations. Another milestone on the

---

[57] *Ibid.*
[58] Carl Kreider, *The Anglo-American Trade Agreement: A study of British and American commercial policies, 1934–1939* (Princeton, 1943), citing *The Times*, 6 July, 1937.
[59] CAB 27/620 TAC (36) 47, Appendix F, note of meeting 1 June 1937. This is discussed by Drummond and Hillmer, *Negotiating Freer Trade*, 78–81.
[60] Drummond and Hillmer, *Negotiating Freer Trade*, 89.

Table 10.2. *UK principal exports of domestic produce to USA, 1929, 1931, 1933 and 1936*

	1929	1931	1933	1936
Spirits	—	—	146	5,323
Raw wood and waste, etc.	2,995	556	1,001	2,175
Apparel and footwear	1,860	693	578	867
Cotton goods	2,831	806	781	942
Leather	2,696	576	826	772
Non-ferrous metals	3,848	647	4,395	1,797
Linen goods	3,609	2,409	2,342	2,411
Wool tissues	3,361	716	766	1,284
Total	45,558	18,246	19,137	27,626

Source: Annual Statement of the Trade of the United Kingdom, 1931 and 1936.

tortuous path to negotiations was passed when on 7 January 1938 the US government formally announced its 'intention to negotiate'.[61]

Final touches were being put to the briefings for UK delegates.[62] British sales to the United States, particularly before the depression and American tariffs took their toll, were dominated by textiles. Table 10.2 shows the major export commodities. Instructions to the delegates stressed the great importance placed on obtaining substantial reductions in the duties on woollens, cottons, linens and other textile manufactures. Greatest optimism was felt over linens, which despite very little production in the USA faced a tariff of approximately 35 per cent. Some reductions in the high duties on the finer grades of woollens were anticipated, but little was expected on the cheaper cloths. While in London it was thought it would be difficult to obtain reductions in excess of 20 to 30 per cent on cotton, even this would be of 'material interest to Lancashire'. Beyond those, concessions were to cover 'a very wide variety of articles, the value of the trade affected being comparatively small in each case but considerable in the aggregate'. Guarantees of free entry for curios and works of art, and for tea and undressed leather, the latter important re-exports, were also wanted. The delegates were also instructed to seek the consolidation of certain duties which the United States had reduced in treaties with other countries. The item that worried the Board of Trade was the 50 per cent reduction in the duty on whisky which had featured in the Canada–United States pact of 1935. The Canadians, by 1938, had virtually exhausted their stocks of matured whisky and were thought to be less interested in

---

[61] Kreider, *Anglo-American Trade Agreement*.
[62] BT 11/918, Note for UK delegates, nd but Jan. 1938.

maintaining the lower rate of duty. Ironically, the repeal of prohibition together with the duty reduction of 1935, a unilateral gesture by the United States that was anticipated to benefit sales of Scotch, did more for British exports to the USA in the 1930s than the collective and arduous labours of British negotiators over the four years from 1934 to the conclusion of the pact in November 1938.

At least the negotiators were spared having to discuss American grievances about proposed British legislation on films.[63] Fearing that the domestic British industry would be swamped by the Hollywood output, the 1927 Cinematograph Films Act had established restrictions on American films with provision for a stipulated ratio of British made films having to be shown. This had not prevented remittances to the US increasing in the 1930s, and to some extent the intentions of the Act had been defeated by the introduction of 'quota quickies', short, low-budget British films designed to fill the quota requirements. With the legislation due to expire in 1938, the Moyne Committee had reported in November 1936 with recommendations to tighten up the legislation. Hollywood, already suffering from reduced exports to Continental Europe, mobilised help from Washington to stem the protectionist tide. Hull saw the film matter as a touchstone of British seriousness about trade liberalisation, and stipulated that unless the British made concessions, the chances of a trade agreement would be poor. Oliver Stanley, arguing that the issue was a cultural one, that people should be able to see the life and manners of their own country, managed to exclude the film industry from the negotiations. He had to give some ground to American wishes, but it was one thing less to occupy the negotiations in Washington. They were to be fraught enough anyway.

Although the British delegation arrived in Washington late in February, negotiations did not begin until April 1938. The delay was in large part the consequence of American procedures laid down by the Reciprocal Trades legislation. Two key elements in the process were the meetings of the Committee on Reciprocity Information, which did not finish its hearings until late in March, and the Public Hearings which began on 4 April. The announcement the previous November that negotiations were contemplated had already brought a wave of representations from US interests likely to be affected. These now received public scrutiny.

When finally the US list of proposed concessions was handed to the British team on 26 April 1938, it was found to have shrunk considerably since the previous June. Then the US had promised to consider tariff

---

[63] Sarah Street, 'The Hays Office and the defence of the British market in the 1930s', *Historical Journal of Film, Radio and Television*, 5 (1985), 37–55.

reductions of 40 per cent or more on nearly $20 million worth of 1935 imports; they now offered similar reductions on only $13 million of the larger 1936 imports from the UK.[64] Some of the offers on the key textile commodities – Overton had said in February that Britain's 'essentials' list could really be reduced to textile items – were modest indeed. To make matters worse, not only were the Americans offering less, they were demanding more. Commodities which had not featured on the first 'must' list, such as flour, lard and hams, now appeared as key items. Industrial products, including potentially troublesome items such as cars, tractors, machine tools and typewriters, also appeared, and old demands resurfaced, notably those for tobacco and softwood timber.[65] Lindsay obtained an interview with Hull that proved fruitless. The UK team speculated on this American change of heart, attributing it to a worsening political situation within the US and to the sharpness of the slump that had set in late in 1937:[66] between May 1937 and June 1938 industrial output fell 30 per cent and employment by 2 million, one of the most precipitate declines in American history. A third factor in the tougher US stance was thought to be the tactical one of tightening up their bargaining position. As one weary negotiator, J. A. Stirling, plaintively wrote:

England now seems further away than ever... it seems more than ever impossible to foresee when we shall get home but personally I have given up any hope now of leaving before the end of July. When we do get back I hope that the C.R.&T. [Commercial Relations and Treaties] Department will be closed down for a full six weeks.[67]

By July, however, after some tough discussions, the situation brightened. American offers improved sufficiently for Stanley to circulate a memorandum on 16 July to the Trade and Agriculture Committee of the Cabinet.[68] The US representatives were 'at last showing themselves more reasonable both in their demands on us and in the extent of the concessions they are prepared to offer in return', although there were some difficult issues to be negotiated. He wanted permission to settle on the basis of the paper circulated: this he would regard as an agreement 'which can be justified on strictly commercial grounds and at the same time as a really substantial contribution to economic appeasement'.

US offers are tabulated in Table 10.3, and a comparison made with the British assessment of the American offer of 26 April. The US also offered to bind existing duties on $32 millions worth of imports (including whisky sales of $27 millions in 1936), and to guarantee continued free entry for $48

[64] Rowland, *Commercial Conflict*, 314.   [65] *Ibid.*, 316.
[66] Drummond and Hillmer, *Negotiating Freer Trade*, 112–13.
[67] Stirling to R. M. Nowell, 21 June 1938, BT 11/934.
[68] CAB 27/621, TAC (36), 53, 16 July 1938.

Table 10.3. *UK assessment of US offers of April and July 1938*

Reductions of:	Value of imports in 1936 ($m)	
	July	April
40% +	17	13
30–40%	17	10·3
20–30%	14	11·6
Less than 20%	7	17·3
Total	55	52·2

Source: CAB 27/621, TAC (36) 53, 16 July 1938.

millions of imports. Together, these concessions covered $135 millions out of a total of $199 millions of British trade. So far as the reductions were concerned, the offers on textiles, at the forefront of the concessions wanted by Britain, were mostly thought satisfactory, particularly on cotton piece goods and linens. Stanley thought there were still problems, notably over American demands for tobacco and timber, but the general tone of the document was bullish, as was the note sent to the British delegation in Washington which said there were 'now only 5 or 6 agricultural items outstanding and apart from these we were in sight of an agreement'.[69]

Stanley had misjudged. No, it was not merely five or six products that were at stake, came the message from Hull, but over half the items on which the USA was seeking concessions, including many industrial items. So much for the assumption that America was swapping industrial concessions for improved access for primary product exports. Probably just as ominous was the news that the Congressional elections due in November were no longer regarded as setting a time limit for the negotiations. The Americans, Overton reported, intended to go on pegging away until they were given satisfaction on their requests.[70]

Therefore, when the Committee met on 21 July, Stanley's assessment of the negotiations was very different from his memorandum of five days earlier. The telegram from the delegation had 'thrown everything into the melting pot'.[71] The Committee debated the pros and cons of continuing to seek an agreement, and the extent of the concessions that had to be made.

The major problems centred on lumber, hams, lard, apples, rice, flour, tobacco, anthracite coal and a number of industrial products, notably cars, tracklaying tractors and typewriters.[72] Canada, holding simultaneous

[69] Rowland, *Commercial Conflict*, 323.   [70] *Ibid.*
[71] CAB 27/620, TAC (36), 16th meeting, 21 July 1938.   [72] *Ibid.*

discussions with the USA, was the country most affected by apple preferences, the flour duty and American insistence that Britain should give up its preference on anthracite coal imports to Canada. A seasonal duty reduction on apples affected the Canadians but not the Australians, and at Canada's suggestion the wheat duty was abolished. This the Americans gladly accepted, but went on to suggest that the flour duty should also be abolished. Both dominion suppliers and the UK milling industry were opposed, and, citing fear of Continental European dumping, the British negotiators refused to give way.[73]

Canadian interests were also involved in one of the most complex issues of the negotiations. The Americans wanted free access to the British market for their Douglas fir and Southern pine.[74] Ottawa was willing to waive rights to a preference if in return the US would relax restrictions on imports of Canadian lumber. But there were problems from the British end. Douglas fir, however genetically distinct, proved all too interchangeable in usage with Baltic softwoods, so, in the view of Whitehall, concessions to the United States would contravene the mfn rights of the Baltic states which supplied approximately 90 per cent of UK imports. Revenue losses from any substantial cut in timber duties would have been high. American efforts were concentrated on ways of circumventing mfn constraints, and, having been rebuffed on their claims to botanical distinctiveness, they eventually hit on a proposal that differentiated by length and width of timber, Douglas fir being taller and wider than Baltic timber. Despite administrative problems for Customs, and some potential loss of revenue, this was accepted by Britain subject to Congress removing discrimination against Canadian lumber. As mentioned earlier, Southern pine was much less of a problem because it had uses distinct from Baltic supplies, and could thus be given free entry without contravening the treaty rights of the North Europeans. The clauses on Douglas fir, however, represented naked evasion of the mfn principle.

Northern European countries were affected also by US demands for an enlarged ham quota which was met by negotiating with Poland and Denmark for modification of their treaty entitlements, a process, it was pointed out to the State Department, that cost Britain goodwill with the countries concerned.[75]

The difficulties about timber and pig products emphasise how wide were Britain's treaty enmeshments. The Americans were bent on undermining the economic empire. In fact, the complex web of Britain's treaty obligations extended well beyond the bounds of formal empire, so that US

---

[73] Drummond and Hillmer, *Negotiating Freer Trade*, 132–6.
[74] *Ibid.*, for a clear discussion of the issue.
[75] CAB 27/621, TAC (36) 56, Note by Stanley, 10 Oct. 1938.

demands encroached on virtually every trade pact that Britain had made since 1933. There was nothing inconsistent in this with the United States avowed liberalising mission, but time and again the details of the negotiations revealed the Americans as involved above all in a drive to expand their exports. Where this might be inhibited by benefits being bestowed on other competitors as well, the Americans were perfectly capable of conniving in bending the rules.

The British response to other American requests also underlines just how little the aims of economic appeasement and trade liberalisation imbued the negotiations. Whitehall resisted American pressure for stabilising the duty on all cars over 20 horsepower, arguing that German competition was intensifying, and although concentrated in the range below 20 hp, it could easily switch to larger models in future: they cited a 24 hp Opel, in fact made by General Motors, that was being developed.[76] The Americans had to make do with the binding of the $33\frac{1}{3}$ per cent duty on cars of 25 hp and above. Similarly, although duties were reduced on standard typewriters and some portables, other sorts were excluded because Germany looked likely to reap the main benefit.

British agricultural protectionism was a further obstacle to a far-reaching agreement. The negotiations nearly foundered on Whitehall's refusal to grant the Americans a cut in the duty on lard which, if Stanley's calculations were right, would have cost the pig farmer about $1\frac{1}{2}$d per animal. There were, it is true, Exchequer considerations to take into account, but the principal problem was the Ministry of Agriculture's argument that the viability of the industry would be undermined by duty reductions.

These issues were discussed by the TAC on 21 July. The Committee decided it must refer to the full Cabinet the decision whether to make further concessions, and, if these were still unacceptable to the United States, whether to end the negotiations. At the Cabinet meeting a week later the Chancellor of the Exchequer broke the impasse over the lard duty by offering to extend a subsidy to pig producers. More concessions were suggested, and if it was necessary the Cabinet would meet again during the recess. Meanwhile the Cabinet decided to leave on record the importance they attached, from a political and international point of view, to concluding a trade agreement with the United States.[77]

In fact the Cabinet did meet during the recess when on 30 August it discussed the Sudeten crisis. Although the possibility of speeding up the conclusion of a trade agreement was debated, nothing was done.[78]

[76] *Ibid.*, TAC (36) 53, Memorandum by Stanley, 16 July 1938, and CAB 27/619 TAC (36), 16th meeting, 21 July 1938 and 17th meeting, 13 Oct. 1938.
[77] CAB 23/94 CAB 36 (38) 28 July 1938.   [78] Rowland, *Commercial Conflict*, 340–1.

In early October the USA put forward another set of demands. It was widely interpreted as an ultimatum, although when taxed with this, Francis Sayre denied it, asserting there was no such thing among friends.[79] Stanley argued that since his last note to the TAC:

the balance of the agreement had shifted to the United States by means of additional timber concessions, a lowering of the rice duty from 1d to 2/3d. per lb. (a move much resented by Burma, India, Australia and by the U.K. millers), larger quotas on hams and a reduction of duty on track laying tractors from $33\frac{1}{3}$ to 25 per cent. Not content with these additional concessions the Americans have now produced their consolidated list of final demands.[80]

Hull required the UK to guarantee maintenance of free entry for maize, to abolish the three-year limit on the ham quota, bind the 10 per cent duty on wheat flour and reduce the duty on softwood plywood from 10 to five per cent. In addition he wanted new concessions on a range of manufactured products, including typewriters, stockings and light electric motors. Furthermore, Hull wanted Britain to give assurances about reducing the tobacco preference when imperial obligations expired in 1942, one year beyond the expiry of the proposed Anglo-American agreement. Stanley pointed out to the committee the difficulties of convincing the public that such an agreement was fair: there was already an enormous disparity in the trade balance between the two countries, he argued, and there would still be a substantial gap between the tariff rates of the two countries with US duties still in the region of 30 to 40 per cent or more while the general level of UK duties would be in the region of 10 to 15 per cent. Since 'we can neither wait for ever or pay a price out of all proportion to the benefits we are to receive', the time had come, political considerations notwithstanding, to 'make our position quite plain and insist on a definite decision by the United States Government to conclude the Agreement or to break off negotiations'. The committee decided to recommend accepting US requests on maize and lard, and to devise some formula for tobacco.[81] Despite Foreign Office requests, the rest were refused, and it was left to the Cabinet to decide whether the negotiations should be broken off if the offer proved unacceptable to the Americans. There was pressure for a strong stand, notably by Stanley but also by the Chancellor, and former Foreign Secretary, Simon, who observed that it 'was impossible to say that the treaty, as it now stood, was one which on balance would be approved by the commercial community'.[82] Yet even at this stage it was Chamberlain,

[79] Drummond and Hillmer, *Negotiating Freer Trade*, 137.
[80] CAB 27/621 TAC (36) 56, Note by Stanley, 10 Oct. 1938.
[81] CAB 27/619 TAC (36) 17th meeting, 13 Oct. 1938.
[82] CAB 23/96 CAB 49 (38), 19 Oct. 1938.

perhaps ironically in view of his earlier reputation as anti-American, who stood out for further Cabinet consultation if necessary.

In the event, Hull grudgingly recommended the agreement to Roosevelt, subject to a few drafting modifications, particularly over the complex timber clauses. As he informed Joseph Kennedy, the new ambassador in London, 'the present offers represent the ultimate limit to which the British are prepared to go without reopening our proposed concessions to the United Kingdom'.[83]

Conclusions

That the immediate economic impact of the treaty was small was only partly because it operated for so short a time before the outbreak of the European war. Effective from January 1939, the agreement ran for barely eight months before war started, and even during these eight months international trade was dominated by stockpiling in preparation for war. But it was a limited and unspectacular treaty, produced by difficult and protracted negotiations.

That the negotiations should have proven so fractious is not difficult to explain. One problem was the difference in negotiating tactics. The British procedure was to maximise the concessions from an unchanging list of requests. By contrast, the American practice, if blocked on one request, was to substitute another entirely fresh demand. Personality may well have contributed to the difficulties. The Canada–US discussions had been smooth, perhaps in part because of closer personal rapport, possibly helped by shared North American interests: Jack Hickerson, heading the US team, would sometimes slip off with his Canadian counterpart Norman Robertson to watch a game of baseball when the Washington Senators were playing at their home field. As Robertson wrote, striking according to his biographer an uncharacteristic note, 'our direct negotiations with the Americans are the least of our worries right now. We can cope with them but not with God's Englishman and the inescapable moral ascendancy over us lesser breeds.'[84]

The economic backdrop to the negotiations was also distinctly unhelpful. The very sharp recession of 1937–8 was particularly severe in the USA, which anyway by most indicators had not recovered from the traumas of the earlier depression. Sterling's depreciation from the middle of 1938 increased American doubts about the value of the concessions they were getting. But the UK side felt they were benefiting little from the

[83] Drummond and Hillmer, *Negotiating Freer Trade*, 141.

[84] Robertson to Pearson, July (?) 1938, quoted by J. L. Granatstein, *A Man of Influence: Norman Robertson and Canadian Statecraft, 1928–1968* (Ottawa, 1981).

negotiations: American tariff barriers, even when reduced by the maximum 50 per cent, generally remained high, and liberalisation on this scale would do nothing to rectify the enormous American trade surplus with Britain. For their part the Americans found the UK unyielding. Demands were frustrated by the web of obligations that Britain had incurred in the previous six years of treaty making. That as much progress was made was due in large part to the willingness of the Canadians to give up privileges in the British market, notably for wheat, timber and apples. True, over and above their role as honest brokers, the Canadians hoped to see in response easier access for their exports south of the border, but it would have been virtually impossible to have secured an Anglo-American accord without Canadian compliance.

For its part the UK was prepared to see some whittling away of preferences for its exports in the dominion markets. At least it was willing to do so in principle, but less happy when it came to specific instances when Britain could be found hanging on tenaciously: anthracite in the Canadian market was a case in point.

Yet British domestic protection remained virtually unbreached. Carl Kreider's study, published in 1943, made this clear.[85] Agricultural concessions had spearheaded American demands, and while some inroads into the Ottawa system had been made, little was achieved at the expense of British farmers. Even though duties on apples and pears were reduced, they were still equivalent to roughly 15 per cent, and there was the added buffer of transatlantic freight rates. The earnings of wheat growers were buoyed up by subsidies, and bacon producers were safeguarded by a Treasury guarantee under the Bacon Industry Act. The same legislation could have been extended if the removal of the duty on lard threatened the income of the pig farmers. Whitehall had refused to lower tariffs on malting barley. By the late 1930s a system of Exchequer financed subsidies had evolved to protect agriculture, and the modest concessions made to the Americans were mainly at the expense of the Treasury rather than the British farmer.

The major American exports of machine tools, iron and steel and of cars gained practically nothing. No guarantees were secured for machine tool exports, many of which were subject to Board of Trade discretionary licences for tariff free import. Although the existing tariff on cars of 25 hp and more was conventionalised, this was more than negated by a sharp rise in road tax licence fees in the Finance Act of 1939 that particularly penalised larger engined vehicles.[86] Although concessions were made on less important items, they were generally on products not manufactured on

[85] Kreider, *Anglo-American Trade Agreement*, chs. 6, 7.   [86] *Ibid.*, 133.

any scale in the UK, and, moreover, frequently involved tariff reclassification so as to restrict the advantage to US exporters and to prevent other countries benefiting.

Policy at the end of the 1930s

On the face of things, the United States had been one agent in the pursuit of more liberal international economic policies, and the Anglo-American accord has been interpreted in these terms. United States influence had been discernible in the pledge forming part of the Tripartite Monetary Agreement of September 1936 to seek the relaxation and eventual abolition of quotas and exchange controls. In addition to American action there was the initiative of Paul Van Zeeland, the Belgian Prime Minister, to discuss with other European governments the possibility of multilateral economic cooperation. These pressures for trade liberalisation did influence the discussion of government policy in Britain: the December 1936 memorandum of Leith-Ross on the balance of payments, in recommending against further obstacles being placed on imports, was clearly influenced by the need for international action to be taken to revive European trade, and the Board of Trade, in rejecting the taking of clearing powers, cited the attitude of the American Secretary of State.[87]

Yet it is doubtful whether these pressures for trade liberalisation were ever the critical factor in policy decisions, and certainly not to the extent of inspiring any grand initiative in the dismantling of trade barriers. When considering its reaction to the Tripartite declaration, the government was not willing to enlarge or abolish agricultural quotas or do anything to imperil the existing iron and steel duty quotas, nor relax the anti-Japanese restrictions in the colonies: instead, the government saw Britain's contribution to the general effort to liberalise trade as being limited to currency cooperation with other countries and refraining from introducing new protectionist barriers.[88] The Board of Trade had opposed clearings in 1934 with very much the same arguments it was using in 1936–7. The same line of reasoning lay behind Whitehall's opposition to the Nash proposals for a customs union with New Zealand, although reinforced in this case by the danger to imperial relations of using overt discrimination in favour of one dominion. The opposition of levy-subsidies and the move towards Exchequer-financed agricultural subsidies was inspired less by principles of

---

[87] CAB 24/265 CP 339 (36), 18 Dec. 1936, p. 12 on the balance of payments. On Hull, W. B. Brown to Ashton Gwatkin, 2 Feb. 1937, BT 11/785, 'It is contrary to our declared policy to endeavour to insist on direct bilateral balancing, and, as you know, it is contrary to the declared policy of the United States whose Secretary of State is at present such an eager observer of the least deviation by us from his policy.'

[88] T 188/146, Foreign Office Print, 6 Nov. 1936.

liberal international trading policy than by the real threat that the consequential treaty revision would be damaging to British exports. What little initiative there was within Whitehall towards trade liberalisation came from the Foreign Office and was aimed at easing international tensions. Elsewhere, although lip service was paid to the desirability of restoring multilateral trade, virtually nothing was actually done to bring this about. There was considerable weight of official opinion against further tariff increases, not only on grounds of diplomacy but because of their impact on costs.[89] Yet Britain was reluctant to initiate any unilateral reductions, not least because it might mean having to disarm from lower tariff levels in the event of any future multilateral negotiations. If there had been greater outside pressure placed on government by backbenchers, or by economic interest groups in the United Kingdom, then alternative policies may have been given more active consideration. Inevitably tariff reductions would have been met by opposition from affected groups – and the government's experience with dairy farmers after the abandonment of the levy-subsidy principle in 1937 was a clear reminder of the hazards involved. Meanwhile the FBI was pressing for a three-tier tariff to give it bargaining leverage in its international cartel negotiations. As for multilateral schemes, there was scepticism about their chances, and as late as 1938 a government committee stated that bilateralism had worked as a method of trade liberalisation whilst multilateralism had not.[90] Where any such scheme threatened British trade, as in the proposed Oslo Convention, a low-tariff scheme for Northern Europe, the UK government opposed it, citing mfn rights and also that regionalism in trade was anathema to Cordell Hull.[91]

British protection stood virtually intact at the end of 1938. The growing menace of Germany had led to consideration of more liberal measures. It had intensified Hull's campaign as well as making British policy makers more than usually solicitous of American goodwill. It had also stimulated some debate in Whitehall about the economic appeasement of Germany. But the eventual outcome of these responses was decidedly illiberal: the relaxation of the trade agreements had been grudging and modest, as represented in the Anglo-American treaty, while German economic appeasement had finally manifested itself in the form of abortive cartel discussions between industrialists.

[89] E.g. memorandum by F. Phillips (undated), T 177/38, cited by Eyers, 'Overseas trade policy', 244.
[90] BT 11/845, 'Report of the Interdepartmental Committee on M. van Zeeland's Report', 25 June 1938.
[91] FO 371/21081, memorandum, 9 Mar. 1937.

11 Some general conclusions

The trade agreements were a by-product of Britain's adoption of protection in 1931–2. The prime motive for tariffs was the protection of British industry in its home market, and for that reason the success or failure, wisdom or folly of the policy must be assessed mainly in terms of its dominant objective.[1] An indication of the secondary role of the trade agreements in the government's economic strategy was the small size of the Commercial Relations and Treaties Department of the Board of Trade. This limited the number of trade negotiations that could be conducted at any one time, and was criticised not only within Whitehall by the Foreign Office, but was the subject of some quiet and partly successful campaigning by the Manchester Chamber of Commerce.[2]

Neutralising the impact of international deflation

Yet the overall effects of protection cannot be assessed purely in terms of its impact on domestic production, employment and incomes through reducing imports. One of the long-standing arguments against tariffs is that they are likely to encourage retaliation against exports. By giving a further twist to the protectionist spiral, by encouraging 'beggar-my-neighbour' policies, any benefits that protection brings through the

[1] H. W. Richardson, *Economic Recovery in Britain, 1932–1939* (1967); F. Capie, 'The British tariff and industrial protection in the 1930s', *Economic History Review*, 2nd. ser., 31 (1978), 399–409: J. Foreman-Peck, 'The British tariff and industrial protection in the 1930s: an alternative model', *Economic History Review*, 2nd ser., 34 (1981), 132–9; T. J. Hatton, 'Perspectives on the economic recovery of the 1930s', *Royal Bank of Scotland Review*, 158 (1988) and 'The recovery of the 1930s and economic policy in Britain', in R. G. Gregory and N. G. Butlin, *Recovery from the Depression: Australia and the world economy in the 1930s* (Cambridge, 1988); M. Kitson and S. Solomou, *Protectionism and Economic Revival: The British inter-war economy* (Cambridge, 1990); M. Kitson, S. Solomou and M. Weale, 'Effective protection and economic recovery in the United Kingdom during the 1930s', *Economic History Review*, 44 (1991) and F. Capie, 'Effective protection and economic recovery', in *ibid.*

[2] FO 371/17319, minute by R. L. Craigie, 27 July 1933, and Marguerite Dupree, *Lancashire and Whitehall: The Diary of Sir Raymond Streat*, I, *1931–39* (Manchester, 1987), 313–14 and 448–51.

curtailment of imports will be countermanded by loss of exports. In the case of Britain in the 1930s the dangers were all the greater because of its central position in the international economy. Not only was there the danger of direct retaliation, but closure of the British market was liable to damage the delicate fabric of the system of multilateral settlement. Deprived of sterling, other countries would have their access to foodstuffs and raw materials restricted. Autarky would be given a powerful stimulus, and British exports would suffer in third markets.

The impact of UK action on the world multilateral payments system is hard to assess. A higher proportion of world trade came to be settled bilaterally during the 1930s, and the British trade agreements system was part and parcel of that process.[3] From the middle of the decade there was vociferous complaint, especially from Germany, that access to raw materials was being denied. Because this was bound up with Germany's demands for colonial restitution, it is probable that the case was exaggerated anyway, but rearmament and attempted self-sufficiency had a great deal of responsibility for Germany's foreign exchange shortage. This is not to deny that Britain's protectionism contributed to the problems of the international economy during the decade before the war, but it is worth recording that the British current account was in deficit for a number of years and therefore could not overall have deprived countries of sterling or threatened their reserves. The enormous accumulation of gold by France and the USA in the late 1920s was of substantially greater damage to the functioning of the international system. So far as British action was concerned it seems probable that the devaluation of sterling had a far more devastating impact on the international economy than the adoption of protection. The response of the major industrial countries gave further impetus to deflationary forces. Both Germany and France, faced by a choice between devaluation and domestic deflation, responded by raising taxes, cutting government expenditure and erecting further barriers to international trade. In the United States, commodity prices, imports and industrial production declined faster after the devaluation of sterling than before.[4] The way countries reacted to the abandonment of gold and the subsequent depreciation of sterling led to a dramatic deterioration in the international economy in late 1931 and early 1932. The response to Britain's inauguration of protection was almost certainly less damaging to international trade. The point is, however, that the trade agreements, together with devaluation, provided an opportunity to salvage something

[3] League of Nations, *The Network of World Trade* (Geneva, 1942), 89–95.
[4] W. A. Lewis, *Economic Survey 1919–1939* (1949), 91–2, 98; H. W. Arndt, *The Economic Lessons of the Nineteen-Thirties* (1944), 100, 101; C. P. Kindleberger, *The World in Depression 1929–1939* (1973), 162–79.

for British exports from the wreckage of the international economy. The UK could use its bargaining leverage to extract concessions for its exports.

The scope for bilateralism

A multilateral solution to the trade problems of the depression was never seriously considered by Whitehall. The greatest opportunity for any initiative would have been the World Economic Conference held in London during June and July 1933. But the major trade agreements had already been signed by then, and British preparatory work for the conference reveals a determination both to hold on to the benefits estimated to accrue from these treaties, and to continue making new ones. Although the British government agreed to participate in a tariff truce (a very feeble one), this was more to humour Cordell Hull than out of any sense of conviction. Even if it had been possible to reach some sort of accord over currency stabilisation, it is difficult to believe that any significant liberalisation of trade would have been possible. Would the French, committed to keeping the franc on the gold standard, have risked relaxing import restrictions? Was Hitler's Germany likely to have been genuinely interested in a greater role for the market? The outstanding obstacle to trade liberalisation was the insistence of the industrial countries on maintaining their protection, and Britain was no exception to this. British industry was adamantly opposed to any diminution of the protection gained in 1932 – its antagonism to the very modest tariff concessions on industrial products in the agreements with Germany, Sweden and Norway is clear evidence of this. Not only was a multilateral agreement therefore ruled out, but by the same token the range of countries with which bilateral treaties could be made was also restricted. As Ashton Gwatkin observed, commenting on the indefinite postponement of trade talks with industrial countries: 'The power of our tariff policy to reduce foreign tariffs is clearly very limited.'[5] In effect, Britain was able to negotiate only with primary producers. The paramountcy of domestic protection circumscribed the possibilities of trade agreements.

The range of countries with which Britain could negotiate was therefore relatively modest. Yet, as was discussed in chapter 4, Britain did possess considerable bargaining leverage with the primary producers. The depression had accentuated its near-monopsonist position in the international markets for beef, lamb, bacon and butter, and it was also an important buyer of wheat and timber. On the other hand, countries not supplying these products were less open to pressure from the UK, and once the trade agreements at Ottawa and with north European countries had

[5] FO 371/17319, minute, 26 July, 1933.

been signed, there were few other candidates for trade treaties (see Appendix B). Nonetheless, Britain was able to capitalise on the willingness of the suppliers of meat and dairy products to offer advantages in their markets in return for guarantees on their exports to Britain. The UK's leverage was further enhanced by the trade deficit it ran with most of these suppliers. Britain's large import market could therefore be harnessed in trade negotiations aimed at minimising the harm to its own exports caused by the dislocation of the international economy and by the adoption of protection.

Limitations on leverage

While in some respects Britain was well-endowed with bargaining leverage, there were powerful factors which stood in the way of really successful agreements. The most fundamental obstacle lay in the economic problems of many of the agreement countries. The collapse of primary prices and the cessation of international lending impoverished many of the very countries with which trade treaties were negotiated. The dramatic fall in food and raw material prices probably played a major part in the domestic recovery of the British economy in the 1930s, although this view is not without its critics.[6] The resurgence of housebuilding and the 'new' industries during the pre-war decade, partly based on the rising real incomes of the employed, was secured at the expense of Britain's overseas suppliers. It would therefore be unrealistic to expect the UK to have engineered a second stimulus to recovery through a growth in exports to those very same countries which were in effect subsidising its consumers. The ox could not be skinned twice. Low incomes and exchange problems in many of the agreement countries were thus a formidable barrier to securing a major expansion of British exports.

The lesser difficulties were discussed in earlier chapters. It is useful to distinguish between the dominion and the foreign treaties, although both had common features. Britain and the self-governing dominions had been brought together at Ottawa because of the depression. So although the dominions were being offered preferential access to the British market, and were able in return to give explicit preferences to British products, the depression made dominion governments reluctant to concede much to UK exports. Balance of payments difficulties and revenue needs militated against too generous a treatment of UK products. Appalling poverty in the

---

[6] M. Beenstock, F. Capie and B. Griffiths in Bank of England, *The UK Economic Recovery in the 1930s* (Panel Paper No. 23), and M. Beenstock and P. Warburton, 'Wages and unemployment in interwar Britain', *Explorations in Economic History*, 23 (1986) and 'The market for labor in interwar Britain', *Explorations in Economic History*, 28 (1991).

rural areas made dominion governments all the more determined to preserve secondary industry and employment. The main opportunities for UK exports therefore lay in trade diversion. The problem here was that except in Canada the British share of imports was already high and the scope for further advance correspondingly restricted. A major deterioration in Britain's trade balances with the dominions had to be accepted if they were to service debts, and, again with the exception of Canada, they were to rebuild their sterling balances.[7] Moreover, Britain was inhibited from using all its bargaining power by the need to preserve imperial unity and some semblance of goodwill. But any weaknesses from Britain's failure to deploy its bargaining power to maximum advantage, or to offer the dominions adequate concessions, were of minor importance compared with the overriding constraints imposed by the depression and by the high market share it already possessed.

When it came to negotiations with Northern Europe and Argentina, some of the same considerations applied. Notably this was so of the balance of payments, revenue needs and the protection of secondary industry. But there were significant differences. While the dominions were offered privileged access to the British market, foreign suppliers were discriminated against. The greatest problem they faced was competition from the Empire, but although at Ottawa the Minister of Agriculture, Gilmour, had been continually thwarted in his attempts to protect British agriculture, his successor, Elliot, was able to put up more effective resistance in London during the foreign negotiations. On the other hand, Britain was not hampered by considerations of imperial unity, and except in Argentina did not have heavy investments to preserve. In that the UK's share in the import markets of its foreign suppliers was much lower than in most of the dominions, there was far greater potential for worthwhile trade agreements. The great difficulty was in finding ways of realising this potential. The Scandinavians in particular were low tariff countries. In the absence of explicit preferences, ruled out by the decision to adhere at least notionally to the mfn clauses, there was a danger that the benefits of tariff concessions would accrue as much to Britain's competitors as to itself. Accordingly, the tariff demands made on the Scandinavians were extremely modest. Purchase agreements were one way of circumventing the restrictions of mfn articles, but in the cases of Norway and Sweden were made only for coal. The best opportunities for trade diversion occurred when countries operated exchange control or import licensing systems. The trade agreement with Denmark proved fruitful largely because of import licensing. Ironically, Britain had obtained no guarantees about its use in

---

[7] P. J. Cain, 'Free trade, protection and the sterling area in the 1930s', Discussion Paper, Institute of Commonwealth Studies, 2 March 1989.

the treaty negotiated; this was a serious tactical error, although not in the event a particularly costly one because the UK possessed sufficient leverage to secure reasonable allocations of licences during most years of the agreement. Exchange controls and import rationing were effective instruments for achieving trade diversion in the Baltic countries, although these markets were too small to bring much assistance to UK exports as a whole.

In Argentina the operation of exchange rationing also provided a mechanism for advancing British exports at the expense of rivals. The Argentine tariff was higher than that of the Scandinavian countries, and the negotiations did achieve some reduction, although not great enough to reduce it to pre-depression levels. Apart from the severe impact of the depression in Argentina, the chief obstacle to substantial trade gains was the need to unblock frozen assets and to secure payment of dividends, interest and other remittances. To that extent the requirements of the rentier stood in the way of higher exports. It was not so much that British investments in Argentina were a hostage as that they were given priority over trade.

Agricultural protection and the trade agreements

The paramountcy of industrial protection limited the range of countries with which Britain could make trade agreements. The form of agricultural protection was crucial to the prospects of Britain's economic recovery and might also have affected the possibilities of signing good trade treaties with the primary producers.

The collapse of primary prices from 1929 threatened British farmers and was one strand in the protectionist campaign. Yet the fall in food and raw material prices, by contributing to rising real incomes for the employed, was probably of central importance to UK economic recovery in the 1930s. A policy of insulating British domestic agriculture by raising substantially the price of imported food could have stifled the revival of the economy. As it was, the devaluation of sterling should have raised import prices, but was largely nullified by the currency depreciation of most of Britain's suppliers. The small size of the agricultural sector (it employed only 6·4 per cent of the workforce in 1931) meant that it was easier to avoid a highly protectionist farm policy. Farmers had less political muscle than their counterparts in Continental Europe, and their comparatively small number made it possible at least to alleviate their problems without imposing heavy burdens on the rest of the community.

Such a relatively costless outcome was by no means certain in 1932–3. More restrictive policies would not only have jeopardised expansion of the domestic economy but might have threatened treaty-making prospects as well. At Ottawa, as was argued in chapter 3, the demands of British agriculture placed no serious restraint on the ability of the UK ministerial team to conclude trade agreements.[8] Ministers were inhibited in meeting dominion demands more by consideration of their impact on the cost of living or on foreign suppliers than on UK agricultural output. But when the time came to negotiate with the Scandinavians and Argentina, not only had the agricultural crisis deepened but the Minister of Agriculture was presenting his case more effectively, and it played a prominent part in the discussions.

Nonetheless it is doubtful whether agricultural protection really diminished the value of the agreements to Britain. Imperial trade diversion did hurt foreign competitors, but it was only in the case of bacon and egg production that UK agriculture seriously threatened total imports from Northern Europe. Moreover, it was not the attractiveness of the offers that Britain could make to its trade partners that was the crucial determinant of the outcome of the negotiations, but the capacity to threaten or blackmail them. Denmark was the principal victim of imperial preference and protection, but yielded probably the most valuable of the agreements.

Therefore British agricultural policy, although both complicating the trade negotiations, especially with foreign suppliers, and dictating the actual terms of the agreements, did not seriously reduce Britain's bargaining leverage. More important was the likely effect of agricultural protection on UK economic recovery as a whole. Here the fondness of the Ministry of Agriculture for quota restrictions on imports could have raised the price of food to British consumers and slowed the pace of recovery. This should not be exaggerated because it was not until mid-1932 that the Ministry started to press for such measures, and by then the fall in import prices had already made a major contribution to rising real incomes. But that quotas could raise prices was shown by the effect of the bacon scheme, and the widespread application of such measures would almost certainly have restrained the continued revival of the British economy. That they were not generally adopted was in large measure a consequence of the terms and operation of the various trade treaties. Either the stipulations of the pacts prevented Britain from applying quotas, or the experience of attempting to operate quotas was shown to be too costly to consumers and to relations with the supplying countries. From early 1935 any major expansion of UK agricultural output had been ruled out, but farmers had still to be protected. As an alternative to quotas, levy-subsidies were given serious consideration. At least the British consumer would not have borne the burden, but overseas suppliers would have done so instead. They used

[8] For a similar view, see A. F. Cooper, *British Agricultural Policy, 1912–1936: a study in Conservative politics* (Manchester and New York, 1989), ch. 8.

their treaty rights, as was shown in chapter 8, to delay the introduction of levy-subsidies, and also made clear their hostility. London, considering the maintenance of the trade agreements as essential, paid the price for this in abandoning levy-subsidies. So faced with apparently incompatible objectives – the need to assist British farmers conflicting with the needs to keep living costs low, to preserve valuable exports markets and to facilitate debt servicing – Whitehall was driven to Exchequer-financed subsidies. The ultimate form of agricultural protection was thus shaped by the agreements. They helped ensure that low price policies prevailed, that consumption was encouraged, and that British farmers were maintained in a way that inflicted minimum damage to overseas suppliers.

The trade agreements, exports and United Kingdom economic recovery

Britain was able to use its bargaining leverage to secure an overall expansion in the volume of its exports to the trade agreement countries. There was a marked divergence in the experience of UK trade to Northern Europe on the one hand and that to the dominions and Argentina on the other. The main factors determining the outcome were analysed in chapter 9. At the risk of over-simplification, these may be summarised briefly.

Success in Scandinavia was in large part because of the buoyancy of these countries' import markets, especially those of Sweden and Finland. This in turn was a reflection of the way in which the prominent role of housebuilding in the UK recovery created opportunities for suppliers of timber products. By 1937 both Finland and Sweden were selling more to Britain than in 1929, even when expressed in current values, and both had substantially increased their share of British imports. However, it was not merely the comparative resilience of North European markets that accounted for a growth of exports, but the possibilities of trade diversion. In all of Northern Europe the UK was successful in securing a switch of imports in its favour. The huge cutback of imports into Germany made countries more willing to divert their purchases in Britain, and thus made it a beneficiary of German action. There were two major determinants governing the degree to which Britain was able to increase its *share* of imports. The first was the relative dependence of countries on the British market: the extent to which countries relied on the UK market was a far more important influence on the benefits they gave to British exports than the generosity or otherwise of UK treatment of their produce. But, secondly, it also helped greatly if countries possessed systems of import licensing or exchange control and could thus evade the restrictions imposed by the mfn clauses. Either countries had surpassed their pre-depression import levels by 1937 (Sweden, Finland and Norway), or they used systems of exchange/import allocation (Denmark, the Baltic states and Poland).

British exports achieved a major advance in their share of the Argentine market between 1929 and 1935. Argentina's high dependence on sales to the UK and its operation of exchange control were important factors accounting for this, but the overall results for British trade were disappointing. By 1936–8 exports were still a third below their values of 1928–30. Argentina was badly hit by the depression, and the collapse of purchasing power together with foreign exchange shortages depressed its aggregate imports. However, it is hard to believe that without the need to unblock frozen balances in Argentina and to allow currency for debt servicing, Britain could not have driven a harder deal on exchange, thus securing more for its exports.

The Ottawa agreements, except for that with Canada, produced surprisingly little in the way of enduring trade diversion for the UK: until 1933 or 1934 the British share of imports was bolstered by favourable structural shifts, by enhanced competitive strength, and by the terms of the treaties, but the scope for massive and sustained trade diversion was limited because Britain already possessed a high import share at the beginning of the decade. Canada was an exception to this, but here the increased share in imports was completely swamped by the collapse of Canadian export earnings and purchasing power. South Africa proved to be the best dominion market for Britain, but the gains made here by the late 1930s owed everything to South African prosperity and nothing to trade diversion.

By 1936–8, British domestic exports to the trade agreement countries stood at £187 million, £10 million below the average for 1928–30. Since export prices had fallen by about 12 per cent during these years, export volume was higher than at the end of the 1920s. But was this helpful to the recovery of the 1930s? Most commentators have emphasised domestic factors, attributing little to the external account and certainly not to exports. Unanimity on this, however, has still left plenty of scope for controversy about the mechanism of recovery, particularly about the contribution of cheap money and, more recently, about the effects of real wage changes. Monetary policy, especially low interest rates, has been seen as a major cause of the housebuilding boom of the 1930s and as helpful to the revival of investment in general.[9] But this explanation has found little favour with the 'old optimists', who dismiss government policy as being unimportant and instead emphasise natural economic forces as sparking

[9] S. Howson, *Domestic Monetary Management in Britain, 1932–1938* (Cambridge, 1975); N. Dimsdale, 'British monetary policy and the exchange rate 1920–1930', *Oxford Economic Papers* (1981).

and then sustaining recovery: technical and organisational changes in the new industries worked on the supply-side while rising real wage rates stimulated demand.[10] This line of argument has not only been sceptically received by writers who have difficulty in attributing any special role to the new industries,[11] but has also been stood on its head by those who insist that far from stimulating output, the rise in real product wages between 1929 and 1931 induced a contraction in output and employment, while the subsequent slowing of real wage increases and then their decline initiated an expansion of output and employment.[12] There are problems with this latter view, not least because real wages exhibited a fairly steady rise to 1933, and by the time they declined, barely perceptibly, in 1934, recovery had probably been underway for eighteen months or more.

Where there is agreement in these explanations, however, is in according a secondary role to the external sector. For those who emphasise the positive part played by the rise in real wages, one of the keys to revival was the collapse in food and raw material prices; Britain in effect climbed out of the depression on the backs of the primary producers. For the advocates of cheap money, on the other hand, the contribution of the external sector was the way in which devaluation released government policy from the straitjacket imposed by the need to defend an overvalued pound sterling, so that once the gold standard had been abandoned and the Exchange Equalisation Account and protection were providing an element of stability to the currency, the path was open to the introduction of cheap money.

More recently external policy has been given greater prominence by those who assign an important role to protection in boosting industrial production and gross national product.[13] Perhaps understandably, though, exports have continued to be dismissed as a cause of economic recovery. After all, by 1937 they accounted for a smaller share of gnp than before the depression, and most accounts have focused on housebuilding and the

---

[10] The classic statement of this view is by Richardson, *Economic recovery in Britain.*

[11] N. Buxton, 'The role of the "new" industries in Britain during the 1930s: a reinterpretation', *Business History Review*, 49 (1975); G. von Tunzlemann, 'Structural change and leading sectors in British manufacturing, 1907–68', in C. P. Kindleberger and G. di Tella (eds.), *Economics in the Long View: essays in honour of W. W. Rostow*, III, 1982; S. Broadberry, 'Unemployment in interwar Britain: a disequilibrium approach', *Oxford Economic Papers*, 35 (1983) and B. Alford, 'New industries for old? British industries between the wars', in R. Floud and D. McCloskey, *The Economic History of Britain*, II, *1860–1970s* (Cambridge, 1981).

[12] See note no. 6. and, for a critique, N. Dimsdale, 'Employment and real wages in the interwar period', *National Institute of Economic Research* 110 (1984) and Hatton, 'Perspectives on the economic recovery'.

[13] Foreman-Peck, 'The British tariff and industrial protection in the 1930s; Hatton, 'Perspectives on the economic recovery' and 'The recovery of the 1930s'; Kitson and Solomou, *Protectionism and economic revival.*

expansion of the new industries which were far less dependent on overseas markets than the nineteenth-century staples. Even more tellingly, export volume by 1937 was actually lower than it had been in 1929. By extension, therefore, the trade agreements could not have played a major direct and positive part in economic recovery. This, however, is to undervalue their contribution. Between 1931 and 1932 there was a dramatic fall in manufactured imports into Britain and the share of domestic output in total sales increased sharply. What the trade agreements were able to do was to hold the ring, to neutralise or offset at least in part the adverse repercussions of protection and the gold standard abandonment as other countries retaliated or deflated. And this they did surprisingly well. British exports began to revive as early as 1932. The timing was crucial, for at this stage the only sources of growth in gnp came from the external account. The reason British exports recovered as early as this was the increasing share that the UK was able to achieve in the import markets of its customers, especially among the trade agreement countries. Thus the trade pacts, together with the devaluation of sterling and favourable structural movements in the patterns of demand for its products, enabled the UK to increase its share of world exports in the early 1930s. For Britain the trade agreements diminished the deflationary forces generated by the international depression, and together with protection, eased the balance of payments difficulties of the UK. What pressures might have been placed on government policy in the absence of protection and trade bargaining must be conjectural: possibly a worse deficit on the balance of payments could have been addressed through a depreciation of sterling, but lower revenues caused by reduced economic activity and smaller customs receipts would have pushed a government wedded to balanced budgets towards an even more contractionary fiscal stance than it in fact pursued. The major advantages from the treaties had been gained by 1935. From then until late 1937 the retreat Britain suffered in market shares was more than compensated for by the expansion of world trade, while at home rearmament was causing a reluctant government to operate, by default, an expansionary budget.[14]

Imperial and regional integration

Britain drew relatively closer to the Empire and to the countries of Northern Europe, especially in the early 1930s. By 1936–8 the agreement countries took nearly 40 per cent of UK exports as against less than 30 per cent in 1928–30. For all these countries except South Africa, Britain was

[14] R. Middleton, *Towards the Managed Economy* (1985) and M. Thomas, 'Rearmament and economic recovery in the late 1930s', *Economic History Review*, 2nd ser., 36 (1983).

supplying a greater proportion of their imports by 1937 than in 1929. They also, as a group, supplied a relatively larger part of UK import needs, and all had come to depend more heavily on the British market as an outlet for their exports. The tendency of the dominions to rely less on the UK, very apparent in the 1920s, was reversed at least until the mid-1930s. The closer integration between Britain and its main suppliers of primary products gives some confirmation to the views of Gilpin, Krasner and Skidelsky of how a great economic power will behave once it has lost its global primacy.[15] Not that Britain's behaviour was unique. France and Holland also drew closer to their Empires during the 1930s. But in the British case the scale of trade involved was much greater, and the extent of the process extended beyond formal empire. Furthermore, Britain now became the centre of a currency group. With the fall of the gold standard the nascent sterling area was enlarged and formalised, and it was no coincidence that it was roughly coterminous with the trade agreement countries. Canada, the major exception, had at one time toyed with the idea of linking with sterling, and had received encouragement from UK financial interests.[16] London, anxious to enlarge membership, attempted to draw China into the network, and the Bank of England consciously worked towards cementing sterling area relationships, particularly through currency stability.[17] The linking of these countries to sterling arose out of their close trading links with Britain, although Britain may have had to accept some export losses so that member states could build up their reserves.[18] By 1935 Ashton Gwatkin could write of the Baltic area that: 'It provides an almost homogenous region of special commercial and financial relations, a kind of unacknowledged economic empire, of which London is the metropolis. In this sense the commercial agreements may be regarded as corollaries to the inter-Imperial agreements of Ottawa.'[19] No doubt there was some exaggeration in this view, especially since Germany was included in the definition of the Baltic area, but UK influence in the region had grown.

[15] R. Gilpin, *American Power and the Multinationals: the political economy of foreign investment* (New York, 1975), 66.; R. J. Skidelsky, 'Retreat from leadership: the evolution of British economic foreign policy, 1870–1939' in B. M. Rowland (ed.), *Balance of Power or Hegemony? the interwar monetary system* (New York, 1976), 164, and S. D. Krasner, 'State power and the structure of international trade', *World Politics*, 28 (1976), 317–47.

[16] I. M. Drummond, *The Floating Pound and the Sterling Area 1931–1939* (Cambridge, 1981), 64–71 and R. A. Dayer, *Finance and Empire: Sir Charles Addis, 1861–1945* (1988), 247–9.

[17] Dayer, *Finance and Empire*, esp. 288–303 and A. Trotter, *Britain and East Asia 1933–1937* (Cambridge, 1975).

[18] F. V. Meyer, *Britain, the Sterling Area and Europe* (1952), who also suggests that, until 1938, the accumulation of sterling by the RSA (Rest of the Sterling Area) may have pushed up the exchange rate, presumably at a further cost to British exports.

[19] FO 371/19439, 'Report on trade relations and economic conditions in the Baltic area, September 1935', F. Ashton Gwatkin, 12 Sept. 1935.

Sweden in particular turned from Germany to the UK, although British prestige had waned somewhat by later in the decade. In great measure Britain was able to exert influence in Northern Europe because of Germany. German domestic policies under Hitler were viewed with widespread repugnance in Scandinavia; German isolationism created opportunities for British trade, and caused a vacuum which Britain filled. In Argentina the depression led to intensified metropolitan pressure, although in the view of one historian of the Anglo-Argentine connection the Roca–Runciman treaty temporarily stabilised rather than consolidated or cemented the commercial linkages between the two countries.[20] By stimulating forces hostile to the *Concordancia* and Britain, it eventually undermined the relationship.

While British influence in Northern Europe grew, and economic ties were strengthened in the early 1930s with the agreement countries as a whole, it must be emphasised that the pursuit of closer integration had never been a dominant motive in the adoption of protection. It is true that it was an important theme in the advocacy of influential campaigners such as Amery and Beaverbrook and that by the 1930s a wide spectrum of both industrial and financial interests were united in their demands for protection combined with imperial consolidation. Certainly protection enormously enhanced the leverage Britain could employ in securing privileged access to the markets of its suppliers. But this was essentially an opportunity that arose from the achievement of the prime objective, the protection of British manufacturing industry in its own home market. Hence Britain never pursued the construction of preferential trading blocs with real commitment or vigour, and policy throughout the 1930s was marked by compromise. The debate about the mfn clause was a touchstone of the administration's attitude. Backbench Conservative and industrial pressure for cancellation of mfn treaties and for the introduction of a three-tier tariff structure was deflected by government. Most senior Board of Trade officials were deeply uneasy about such a derogation from the principles of multilateralism. In addition, Runciman, in a key position as President of the Board of Trade, retained a lingering attachment to the free trade beliefs of his past. The same attitudes were apparent in the discussion of clearing powers. If these had been taken they would have given the UK more effective leverage in securing advantages for British trade. But although Whitehall had honoured mfn clauses in the breach, it abjured the more powerful instruments of bilateralism.

Nor, unsurprisingly, did the agreement countries appear to see participation in a system where they would act as primary producing satellites to

[20] E. F. Early, 'The Roca–Runciman Treaty and its significance for Argentina, 1933–41' (Ph.D. thesis, University of London, 1981), 369.

the UK as offering an attractive long-term prospect. The Scandinavians kept their distance as far as possible, and import-substitution continued. Britain might frustrate but could not prevent it. The dominions, especially Australia, appeared worried about the limited absorptive capacity of the British market and were often furious at the reluctance of London to exclude foreign suppliers from it. They sought new markets for their primary products, and to continue the development of their secondary industries. And in Britain, some of those who perhaps had been unrealistically optimistic about Ottawa were coming belatedly to recognise that secondary industries in the dominions had not only come to stay, but were essential for their future prosperity. Chamberlain, in 1936, said they

have reached an important turning point in their history ... in recent years they had begun to realise that their markets for agricultural products were limited. It must be brought home to them that their most important market, namely the United Kingdom, could no longer absorb their expanding production, and in years to come would take a diminishing rather than an increasing share of their production. In these circumstances, if the Dominions in future were to be able to find employment for an increasing population, they must develop their secondary industries.[21]

There were other signs that the closer ties established between Britain and the agreement countries in the early 1930s were beginning to fragment on the eve of war. In most countries the UK was unable to maintain the market share it had staked out for itself prior to around 1935. Rising incomes caused structural movements in demand unfavourable to British products. Competition became fiercer, particularly in 1938. In these conditions the UK lacked weapons, such as clearing powers, which might have been used to stem such an erosion of its position. In a period of re-expansion, the trade agreements were not capable of counteracting the economic forces that undermined Britain's grip on its primary suppliers. They were too weak an instrument for maintaining an enduring economic interdependence.

Policy in the late 1930s

By the late 1930s policy was at an impasse. Faced with growing competition in the markets of the agreement countries, and concerned about the threat to the balance of payments posed by rearmament, the main response of

[21] CAB 27/619 TAC (36), 4th meeting, 21 May 1936. The Privy Seal, reporting on a visit he made to Australia in 1938, stated that the development of secondary industry in Australia should receive every encouragement from Britain (CAB 24/276 CP 96 (38)). This appears to have become so much the accepted wisdom that the Secretary to the Department of Overseas Trade warned the Cabinet against expressing the view too strongly to the Australians (CAB 24/276 CP 107 (38)).

Whitehall was to seek a market-sharing agreement with Germany. This not only proved fruitless, but was probably also wrong because the diagnosis was incorrect. As indicated in chapter 9, competition in the markets of the agreement countries came from several sources, and even if British and German industrialists had been able to reach an accord, it would only have dealt with part of the problem. An informal trade 'ratio' was agreed with Denmark, but otherwise clearing agreements were generally ruled out by Whitehall (see Appendix B for exceptions). If Britain was going to use such weapons, almost certainly they would have been better employed earlier in the decade when the UK's bargaining leverage was stronger.

This highlights the compromises that marked British overseas economic policy between 1932 and the Second World War. While unquestionably protective, particularly towards industry, and therefore playing a part in the general world-wide extension of illiberal trading practice, Britain held back from the fullest exploitation of its position. Yet there is little evidence of a return to economic liberalism by the end of the decade. For if Britain spurned the path to greater protection, the alternatives of multilateral or unilateral tariff reductions were also rejected. This was a realistic judgement. Lowering of industrial protection would have been strongly opposed by British industry, and it is difficult to believe that it would have been met by any serious reciprocation. Moreover, the interested departments held that the trade agreements were working well, and Runciman had refused to countenance their dismantlement. Not that they were ever assessed rigorously, but by 1937–8 the Board of Trade and the Foreign Office wanted their continuation with the absolute minimum of any adjustment that might be forced by British agricultural policy.

The *rapprochement* with the United States in 1938 did not signal disillusion with bilateralism. The Americans had been bitterly critical of the Ottawa agreements and were keen to use what leverage they possessed to undermine the system. That was part of the American motive in seeking a trade agreement with Britain. Britain's acquiescence in this was neither informed by any acceptance of the failure of bilateralism nor were the meetings infused by any spirit of economic liberalism. When the British delegation was drawn reluctantly across the Atlantic to the negotiating rooms of Washington, political necessity impelled its journey. The fact that the talks took place, however, was a portent of the way in which the Americans were to use their growing power in an attempt to recreate a more liberal and open world economic regime after the war, and to undermine the regional and imperial system Britain had built in the 1930s.

Appendix A. United Kingdom: payments, clearings, etc. agreements in force 1931–1938

Country	Subject	Date of signature
Argentina	Trade and Commerce: Convention	1. v. 33
	Supplementary Agreement	26. x. 33
	Agreement	1. xii. 36
Brazil	Commercial Payments: Agreement	27. iii. 35
Germany	Commercial Relations: Exchange of Notes	13. iv. 33
	Transfer Moritorium: Papers	15/20. vi. 34
	Transfer Agreement	4. vii. 34
	Commercial Payments: Exchange Agreement	10. viii. 34
	Payments Agreement	1. xi. 34
	Payments (Amendment) Agreement	1. vii. 38
	Transfer Agreement	1. vii. 38
	Transfer Agreement: Supplementary Agreement	13. viii. 38
Hungary	Payments Agreement	1. ii. 36
Italy	Imports from the United Kingdom into Italy: Provisional Agreement	18. iii. 35
	Trade and Payments: Exchanges of Notes	27. iv. 35
	Clearing Office: Order	10. vii. 36
	Commercial Agreement	6. xi. 36
	Commercial Exchanges and Payments: Agreement	6. xi. 36
	Clearing Office Amendment: Order	11. xi. 36
	Commercial Exchanges and Payments: Exchange of notes	24. xii. 37
	Commercial Agreement	18. iii. 38
	Commercial Exchanges and Payments: Agreement	18. iii. 38
	Clearing Office Amendment: Order	28. iii. 38
Romania	Payments Agreement	8. ii. 35
	Payments Agreement	3. vii. 35
	Commercial Payments: Agreement	2. v. 36
	Payments (Supplementary) Agreement	28. v. 36
	Clearing Office: Order	28. v. 36
	Payments (Supplementary) Agreement	5. xii. 36
	Clearing Office Amendment: Order	17. xii. 36

Appendix A. (*cont.*)

Country	Subject	Date of signature
	Payments (Supplementary) Agreement	27. v. 36
	Payments Technical (Amendment) Agreement	27. v. 36
	Clearing Office Amendment: Order	1. vi. 37
	Payments (Amendment) Agreement: Exchange of Notes	12. xi. 37
	Payments (Supplementary) Agreement	25. ii. 38
	Clearing Office Amendment: Order	28. iii. 38
	Payments (Supplementary) Agreement	11. vi. 38
	Commercial Payments: Agreement	2. ix. 38
	Clearing Office Amendment: Order	9. ix. 38
	Modification of Annex to Agreement of 2. ix. 38	23. xii. 38
Soviet Union	Temporary Commercial Agreement	16. ii. 34
	Export Credits Guarantee Department: Agreement	28. vii. 36
Spain	Payments Agreement	6. i. 36
	Clearing Office: Order	9. i. 36
	Payments (Amendment) Agreement	6. vi. 36
	Clearing Office Amendment: Order	8. vi. 36
	Clearing Office Amendment No. 2: Order	17. xii. 36
Turkey	Trade and Payments: Agreement	4. vi. 35
	Trade and Clearing: Agreement	2. ix. 36
	Clearing Office: Order	8. ix. 36
	Clearing Office No. 2: Order	27. xi. 36
	Guarantee Agreement	27. v. 38
	Trade and Clearing: Agreement	27. v. 38
	Armaments Credit: Agreement	27. v. 38
	Clearing Office Amendment: Order	15. vi. 38
Uruguay	Trade and Payments: Agreement	26. vi. 35
Yugoslavia	Trade and Payments: Agreement	27. xi. 36

Source: National Institute of Economic and Social Research, *Trade Regulations and Commercial Policy of the United Kingdom* (Cambridge, 1943).

Appendix B: Miscellaneous trade and payments agreements

The United Kingdom made, and attempted to make, a number of other trade and payments agreements. There were two unsuccessful efforts to seek full trade agreements on the model of the North European and Argentine treaties: in the case of Spain nothing was achieved, while with Peru only a limited agreement resulted. The other treaties were essentially defensive measures to redress discrimination against British products or to unfreeze blocked payments.

The limitations on Britain's bargaining power were amply demonstrated in a series of frustrating negotiations with Peru, Spain and Turkey.

Peru

The Foreign Office, anxious to counter the United States trade drive in Latin America, had provided the main pressure within Whitehall for negotiations with Peru. The Board of Trade had been sceptical of achieving much because Britain lacked the power to hurt Peruvian export interests.[1] On the other hand, Japanese textiles had been making inroads into the market and the Board did see some chances of bolstering Lancashire's position. The final outcome, after long and difficult negotiations, was not especially fruitful for the United Kingdom. Some reductions in the tariff rates, raised by Peru during the course of discussions, were secured, and private purchasing arrangements were concluded between British exporters and Peruvian cotton, wool and sugar interests. Benevolent treatment of UK investments in Peru was promised by the government, and, in a confidential note, the Peruvian administration made undertakings, albeit weak ones, to encourage government departments and agencies to give opportunities for British exporters to tender for contracts.

[1] BT 11/379, minute by A. E. Overton, 7 Oct. 1935.

Spain

Trade negotiations with Spain were another exercise in frustration, and illustrate clearly some of the restrictions on UK bargaining leverage. The current account of the balance of payments was strongly adverse to Britain, and the UK was able also to threaten imports of Spanish oranges and potatoes.[2] Moreover, because of increased Spanish protection and losses suffered by the UK coal trade to Spain as well as pressures from the local British business community, there were plenty of incentives to negotiate an agreement. But several factors hampered success. Spain's international balance of payments was in growing deficit by 1935, not least because the surplus Spain enjoyed with the UK was narrowing. This limited the capacity of the Madrid government to boost imports from the UK even if it had wanted to do so. There was not only a general distaste in Whitehall for clearing powers, but Spain had threatened that if they were imposed, Spain itself would use clearings with those dominions, notably India, with which it had trade deficits.[3] This joined the Dominions Office with the Treasury in opposing such measures advocated only by the Mines Department and the Department of Overseas Trade. Nor were other sanctions which might be applied necessarily painless to the UK itself. Restrictions on Spanish oranges, which were cheap, would hurt the poorer consumers, and the Spaniards would be likely to retaliate by further restricting imports of UK coal. Negotiations, which had begun in April 1935, yielded little, and in the face of Spanish obduracy and British reluctance to take either strong measures or even conciliatory ones such as granting loans, were adjourned and never reopened.[4]

Turkey

Trade discussions with Peru and Spain had been trade expansionary in intent, and thus followed the pattern of the 1933-4 agreements with the Scandinavian and Baltic countries. Those with Turkey were in response to Turkish discrimination against UK trade, and in that sense were defensive. Britain had a balance of *trade* surplus with relatively few countries. Turkey was one of them, and the difficulties of retaliating against such countries when they took action against the UK was made apparent when in 1933 quotas were imposed on British products in an endeavour to achieve a 70:100 ratio in Turkey's favour. Britain ruled out retaliation because the

[2] FO 371/21228, memorandum, 22 Mar. 1937.
[3] FO 371/19738, memorandum, Nov. 1935.
[4] FO 371/21228, memorandum, 22 Mar. 1937.

Turkish government was thought certain to take counter-action which would have meant the virtual destruction of the UK export trade and serious harm to British interests in Turkey. Arbitration was rejected because it was likely to be too protracted. The third option, that of negotiations, was therefore reluctantly pursued.[5] During the extended discussions that followed, the Turks further tightened restrictions on imports from the United Kingdom. There was considerable pressure on London from the British interests involved, including those who had been prohibited from tendering for contracts because of the absence of an Anglo-Turkish 'balancing' agreement. Eventually the UK was forced to sign a new Trade and Payments agreement in which the principle of a 70:100 trade ratio was conceded by London, together with some tariff concessions to Turkey. Apart from some relaxation of discriminatory quotas and release of goods from Turkish customs, very little was obtained in return.[6]

France

The Anglo-French trade agreement of June 1934 was another attempt at remedying discriminatory action against British exports. Economic relations between the two countries had been fractious for some years before the depression: French exports had been peculiarly badly exposed to Britain's nascent tariff protectionism in the 1920s, but it had been the introduction of sanitary restrictions on imports of French cherries and potatoes that had really soured relations.[7] With the onset of the depression conditions had deteriorated further until in January 1934 a limited trade war started. In that month the French government, which was already applying a wide range of quotas, reduced each country's 100 per cent entitlement of its base-line share of imports to one of 25 per cent with the intention of using the balance for bargaining with supplying countries. A similar device was applied to selected coal imports, although in this case the bargaining element was only 10 per cent as against 75 per cent for other products. These measures adversely affected many British exports, but particularly textiles. What made them especially obnoxious to Britain was the element of discrimination involved: once the French had made agreements with other countries, notably Belgium and the USA, which gave them higher import quotas than those enjoyed by the UK, Britain

[5] BT 11/269, memorandum, Mar. 1934.
[6] FO 371/19629, memorandum, 21 Sept. 1935.
[7] R. W. D. Boyce, 'Insects and international relations: Canada, France, and British agricultural "Sanitary" Restrictions between the wars', *International History Review*, 9 (1987).

decided to retaliate. Surcharges of 20 per cent were made on imports of French silk and artificial silk.

Negotiations were held in March 1934. The major French objective was the cancellation of the 20 per cent surcharge, but they were also anxious to prevent further duty increases on silk which were being considered by IDAC, and wanted relaxation of the sanitary restrictions on French potatoes and various other horticultural products. The March negotiations failed, largely because of British unwillingness to give guarantees about silk duties.[8] Further arduous discussions eventually produced an agreement. Britain gained restoration of full quota allocations on most products, together with a secret undertaking that guaranteed minimum absolute limits for its exports.[9] The French withdrew a threat to include unregulated coal imports (mainly of coal for bunkering and of metallurgical coal) in their quota schemes, and also modified arrangements in the administration of quotas. In return the UK cancelled the silk surcharges and overhauled the protection of the silk industry, basically by reducing duties on raw material imports and excise taxes, substituting this for large-scale increases in duties on the manufactured imports.[10] Further very minor duty reductions were made, including, for example, those on imports of French asparagus during March and the first half of April, and of snowdrops during December and January. Guarantees were also given that existing duties on sparkling wine, brandy and a few other luxury products would not be increased. Sanitary restrictions on imports of certain French fruit and vegetable supplies were also relaxed though not abolished.[11]

An integral part of the agreement – indeed the French would have dropped their coal concessions if it lapsed – was an understanding between French coal importers and UK colliery owners that 26,000 tons of French pitwood would be imported each month in exchange for 40,000 tons of coal. The Mines Department calculated that by averting French action 877,000 tons of UK coal exports were saved – but this represented the avoidance of further losses rather than any increase in sales.[12]

Soviet Union

Trade relations with the Soviet Union followed their own distinct pattern and are not capable of being classified with those of other countries. The Temporary Commercial Agreement of 1930 led to a substantial increase in

[8] BT 11/272, memorandum by W. Runciman, Mar. 1934.
[9] FO 371/18470, memorandum, 3 Dec. 1934.
[10] CAB 24/249 CP 165 (34), memorandum by Runciman, 18 June 1934. The cost to the Exchequer was estimated at £2 million.   [11] Ibid.
[12] FO 371/18470, notes by Mines Department, nd.

British exports to the Soviet Union at the same time that imports from Russia were falling.[13] However, it was denounced by London in October 1932 as a direct consequence of the Ottawa agreements following continued complaints by Canadian timber interests about Russian dumping of wood products. A new agreement was made in February 1934 which not only renewed reciprocal mfn treatment (with specified exceptions) but aimed at reducing the substantial Russian trade surplus with the UK ultimately with the intention of achieving an approximate balance in payments. Payments ratios were established, starting at 1·7 to 1 in Russia's favour for the year 1934, gradually closing 1·2 to 1 by 1937 and 1·1 to 1 in later years. In fact UK domestic exports fell slightly between 1934 and 1937, the major benefit accruing to the entrepôt trade with an enormous expansion in re-exports of raw materials.[14] Partly in order to boost British exports of manufactures, especially of capital goods, an Exports Guarantee was made to the Soviet Union in an agreement in July 1936.[15]

Payments agreements

A large number of payments agreements were made (see Appendix A) aimed at saving UK trade from clearings, exchange restrictions and quotas and also at liquidating frozen debts.

For instance *Romania*, plagued by foreign exchange shortages, had ceased to provide sterling for the payment of debts. Arrears quickly mounted, and Britain finally signed an agreement in February 1935 which allowed the Romanian government to restrict imports of UK goods to 55 per cent of Romanian exports to the UK during the previous quarter, some of the balance being used to liquidate the outstanding debts.[16] An agreement was also signed with *Brazil* whereby the Brazilian government agreed to provide exchange for 40 per cent of certain commercial debts and to provide an annuity to service newly created 4 per cent stock representing the balance of unpaid debts.[17] Broadly similar arrangements were made with *Uruguay*, but in this case understandings on British trade and other interests were also reached; 30 per cent of frozen debts owing to UK traders and residents were to be paid in cash, and the balance was to be covered by the issue of $3\frac{1}{2}$ per cent 5-year sterling bonds. While exchange was to be available for the purchase of British goods, if Uruguay was forced to control imports, every endeavour was to be made not to restrict imports of coal from the UK. Coal imports were to be free and the

---

[13] National Institute of Economic and Social Research, *Trade Regulations and Commercial Policy of the United Kingdom* (Cambridge, 1943), 180–1.
[14] FO 371/21228, memorandum, 22 Mar. 1937.   [15] *Ibid.*
[16] FO 371/19629, memorandum, 21 Sept. 1935.   [17] *Ibid.*

Uruguayan government undertook to accord benevolent treatment to British enterprises.[18]

Whitehall had strongly resisted the use of compulsory clearings. Reluctance to resort to these instruments had hampered negotiations with *Italy* for a full agreement in 1935 after British trade had been severely hit by import restrictions.[19] The agreement with Romania also broke down, largely because the Romanian government failed to make sterling available either for current trade or for outstanding debts. Similarly difficulties arose with Turkey following an agreement in 1935 whereby only Turkish importers were obliged to place currency in a Central Bank account. British importers, on the other hand, were only *requested* to deposit sterling at the Bank of England, and, partly because of the resulting seepage, arrears in Turkey accumulated rapidly.[20] Although the trade negotiations with Spain had proved abortive, increasing payments difficulties and debts at last convinced Whitehall that compulsory clearing powers should be used, and, for the first time, these were embodied in the payments agreement concluded with Spain on 6 January 1936.[21] This was a new departure in Britain's commercial policy, and taken with great reluctance partly through fear of Spanish retaliation, but also because of the impetus it was feared might be given generally to bilateralism. But once introduced, clearing powers were used again with other recalcitrant governments. The mounting problems with Romania and Turkey led to compulsory clearing agreements being made in May and September 1936 respectively, and unilateral clearings were also imposed on Italy in July 1936 in an attempt to wrest back debts following the ending of sanctions. The other agreements signed, such as those with Hungary and Yugoslavia, followed the pattern of the earlier treaty made with Romania, and were designed to provide a proportion of sterling earnings for payments of imports from the UK and for liquidation of debts.

This summary of Britain's other trade and payments agreements gives some indication of the restricted scope of Britain's trade bargaining powers once the major treaties with the dominions, Argentina and Northern Europe had been made. Until the Anglo-American treaty of 1938, no full agreement was made with a major industrial power. Negotiations with Peru and Spain proved largely fruitless, and, for the rest, British action was limited to defensive measures designed to minimise the damage inflicted on exports by discriminatory trade controls, or to secure payment of debts.

---

[18] *Ibid.*   [19] FO 371/21228, memorandum, 22 Mar. 1937.   [20] *Ibid.*
[21] FO 371/19738, memorandum, Nov. 1935 and FO 371/21228, memorandum, 22 Mar. 1937.

Appendix C *Imports into Britain from foreign agreement countries (£000s and percentages)*

	1929	%	1930	%	1931	%	1932	%	1933	%
Finland	14,945	1·2	12,634	1·2	11,630	1·4	11,733	1·7	12,767	1·9
Estonia	2,497	0·2	1,992	0·2	1,908	0·2	1,260	0·2	1,217	0·2
Latvia	5,467	0·4	4,747	0·5	2,928	0·3	2,683	0·4	2,641	0·4
Lithuania	587	0·04	791	0·08	1,488	0·2	1,882	0·3	1,967	0·3
Sweden	25,709	2·1	22,581	2·2	17,342	2·0	13,424	1·9	15,938	2·4
Norway	14,149	1·2	11,967	1·2	8,630	1·0	8,283	1·2	6,961	1·0
Denmark	56,178	4·6	54,118	5·2	46,696	5·4	40,570	5·8	35,428	5·3
Poland	6,908	0·6	7,949	0·8	8,612	1·0	6,184	1·0	6,551	1·0
Total North Europe	126,440	10·3	116,779	11·2	99,234	11·5	86,021	12·2	83,470	12·3
Argentina	82,447	6·8	56,666	5·4	52,744	6·1	50,885	7·3	41,687	6·2
Total Above	208,887	17·1	173,445	16·6	151,978	17·6	136,906	19·5	125,157	18·5
Total Foreign	861,923	70·6	739,946	70·9	613,836	71·3	453,533	64·7	425,879	63·1
Total	1,220,765		1,043,975		861,253		701,670		675,016	

	1934	%	1935	%	1936	%	1937	%	1938	%
Finland	15,215	2·1	14,915	2·0	18,145	2·1	22,437	2·2	19,275	2·1
Estonia	1,996	0·3	1,825	0·2	1,934	0·2	2,254	0·2	2,067	0·2
Latvia	2,715	0·4	2,920	0·4	3,412	0·4	5,339	0·5	4,595	0·5
Lithuania	1,856	0·3	2,338	0·3	2,991	0·4	3,275	0·3	3,086	0·3
Sweden	17,926	2·5	17,010	2·3	20,629	2·4	26,191	2·6	24,542	2·7
Norway	8,359	1·1	8,213	1·1	8,940	1·1	11,574	1·1	11,020	1·2
Denmark	32,885	4·5	32,038	4·2	33,234	3·9	36,570	3·6	37,868	4·1
Poland	7,438	1·0	7,281	1·0	9,856	1·2	10,834	1·1	9,533	1·0
Total North Europe	88,390	12·1	86,540	11·5	99,141	11·7	118,474	11·5	111,986	12·2
Argentina	47,030	6·4	43,967	5·8	45,060	5·3	59,836	5·8	38,471	4·2
Total above	135,420	18·5	130,507	17·3	144,201	17·0	178,310	17·3	150,457	16·4
Total Foreign	460,129	62·9	471,482	62·4	515,390	60·8	622,600	60·6	547,977	59·6
Total	731,414		756,041		847,752		1,027,824		919,509	

Source: UK *Annual Statement of Trade* (various years).

330

Appendix D *Total exports from Britain to foreign agreement countries and four dominions £000s.*

	1929	1930	1931	1932	1933	1934	1935	1936	1937	1938
Finland	3,893	2,844	1,773	2,505	3,102	3,999	4,617	4,579	6,360	5,850
Estonia	700	513	263	420	458	635	902	937	1,581	1,169
Latvia	1,631	1,247	622	635	1,190	1,395	1,262	1,371	1,839	1,811
Lithuania	394	398	307	409	690	1,100	1,601	1,739	1,963	2,225
Sweden	11,704	10,936	8,463	7,553	7,849	9,876	10,542	11,297	13,973	12,828
Norway	10,327	13,273	7,860	6,141	5,814	6,546	7,006	7,399	9,315	7,831
Denmark	11,498	10,990	9,213	10,351	12,274	14,087	14,536	15,586	17,569	16,367
Poland	5,284	4,181	2,577	2,670	3,846	4,263	5,102	6,571	7,627	7,476
Total North Europe	45,431	44,382	31,078	30,684	35,233	41,901	45,568	49,479	60,227	55,557
Argentina	29,677	25,676	15,055	10,863	13,287	14,904	15,601	15,540	20,392	19,715
Total Above	75,108	70,058	46,133	41,547	48,510	56,805	61,169	65,019	80,619	75,272
South Africa	34,110	27,702	22,930	18,625	23,970	30,846	34,256	38,214	42,194	40,129
Australia	56,340	33,069	15,153	20,612	22,077	26,958	30,038	32,979	38,275	38,944
New Zealand	22,186	18,629	11,731	10,646	9,805	11,698	13,632	17,645	20,553	19,497
Canada	37,511	31,246	22,151	17,386	18,555	21,115	22,560	24,327	28,810	23,568
Four dominions	150,147	110,646	71,965	67,269	74,407	90,617	100,486	113,165	129,832	122,138
Total Exports	839,051	657,591	454,489	416,045	416,990	447,229	481,137	501,374	596,525	532,280

Source: UK *Annual Statement of Trade* (various years).

Appendix E. Imports of selected commodities in UK, 1931, 1937, showing percentage from Empire sources

			1931			1937	
			£000s	% of total imports	% Empire supplies	£000s	% Empire supplies
1	Grain & milling	A	57,307	12·4	35·0	82,342	47·5
		B	20,063			39,152	
2	Meat & poultry	A	93,706	20·3	22·9	87,059	40·4
		B	21,473			35,136	
3	Butter, cheese & eggs	A	72,012	15·6	45·5	69,352	50·3
		B	32,732			34,880	
4	Fruit, fresh & dried	A	37,875	8·2	29·0	24,652	61·8
		B	10,997			15,236	
5	Sugar	A	14,813	3·2	42·9	20,349	70·5
		B	6,356			14,356	
6	Tea	A	29,620	6·4	86·7	29,663	91·7
		B	25,675			27,205	
7	Alcoholic beverages	A	11,879	2·6	50·5	11,748	43·6
		B	5,998			5,122	
8	Tobacco	A	11,376	2·5	16·6	18,007	15·7
		B	1,883			2,819	
9	Ores & concentrates etc.	A	9,566	2·1	30·7	31,801	36·3
		B	2,941			11,550	
10	Wood & timber & manufactures thereof	A	46,067	10·0	6·5	84,464	16·4
		B	3,002			13,863	
11	Paper & newsprint	A	4,137	0·9	70·2	4,092	74·7
		B	2,903			3,058	

Appendix E. (*cont.*)

			1931			1937	
			£000s	% of total imports	% Empire supplies	£000s	% Empire supplies
12	Seeds & nuts for expressing oil therefrom	A	11,466	2·5	38·5	17,500	70·6
		B	4,416			12,354	
13	Petroleum crude & refined	A	28,997	6·3	3·7	47,799	5·5
		B	1,079			2,648	
14	Hides, skins etc	A	11,696	2·5	53·0	25,169	40·2
		B	6,203			10,116	
15	Leather & manufactures	A	16,681	3·6	21·8	9,740	71·8
		B	3,630			6,991	
16	Rubber	A	4,496	1·0	77·5	12,248	80·7
		B	3,483			9,888	
Total		A	461,694			575,985	
		B	152,834 = 33·1%			244,374 = 42·4%	

Row A = total imports of the commodity
Row B = imports from Empire of commodity
Source: Parliamentary Papers, *Statistical Abstract for the British Empire, 1929–1938*
(Cmd, 6140).

Bibliography

PRIMARY SOURCES

A ARCHIVES

Public Record Office, London

Cabinet Office
  CAB 23 Cabinet Minutes
  CAB 24 Cabinet Memoranda
  CAB 27 Cabinet Committee Minutes and Memoranda
  CAB 32 Imperial Economic Conferences
  CAB 58 Economic Advisory Council
  Prime Minister's Office
  PREMIER 1 Correspondence and Papers
Treasury
  T 160 Finance Files
  T 172 Chancellor of the Exchequer's Office
  T 177 Phillips Papers
  T 188 Leith-Ross Papers
Foreign Office
  FO 371 Political
Dominions Office
  DO 35 Dominions: Original Correspondence
Board of Trade
  BT 11 Commercial Department: Correspondence and Papers
  BT 59 Department of Overseas Trade: Development Council
Ministry of Power
  POWE 16 Coal Division: Correspondence and Papers
Ministry of Agriculture, Fisheries and Food
  MAF 40 Trade Relations and International Affairs
Public Record Office
  PRO 30 James Ramsay MacDonald Papers

National Archives of Canada, Ottawa
  Department of Finance Records
  Department of Trade and Commerce Records
  Bennett Papers

Other

Sir Charles Addis Papers (School of Oriental and African Studies, University of London)

Arthur Neville Chamberlain Papers (University of Birmingham Library)

Sir Patrick Joseph Henry Hannon Papers (House of Lords Record Office)

1st Baron Norman of St Clere (Montagu Norman) diary (Bank of England)

1st Viscount Runciman Papers (University of Newcastle Library)

Bank of England

Baring Brothers & Co. Ltd

Bradford Chamber of Commerce (West Yorkshire Archives Department, Bradford)

British Engineers' Association (Modern Records Centre, University of Warwick Library)

Conservative Research Department (Bodleian Library, Oxford)

Cycle and Motor Cycle Association (Modern Records Centre, University of Warwick Library)

Empire Industries Association (House of Lords Record Office and Modern Records Centre, University of Warwick Library)

Lloyds Bank Archives (Lloyds Bank Head Office, London)

Federation of British Industries (Modern Records Centre, University of Warwick Library)

Manchester Chamber of Commerce (Manchester Public Library)

B STATE PUBLIC DOCUMENTS

Denmark

Danmarks Statistik. *Statistisk Aarbog*, Copenhagen, 1929–38
Danmarks Statistik. *Danmark Handel*, Copenhagen, 1929–38

Estonia

Riigi Statistika Kesburoo. *Valiskaubandus*, Tallinn, 1929–38

Finland

Tilaastollinen Paatoimiston. *Suomen Tilastollinen Vuosikirja*, Helsinki 1929–38

Latvia

Valsta Statistika Parvalde. *Latvijan Statistiskā Gada Grāmaja*

Norway

Det Statistike Centralbyrá. *Norges Handel*, Oslo, 1929–39
Det Statistike Centralbyrá. *Statistisk Årbok*, Oslo, 1930, 1936–7

Sweden

Statistiska Centralbyrán. *Statistisk Årsbok för Sverige* Stockholm, 1930–9

United Kingdom

Committee on Industry and Trade. *Survey of Overseas Markets*, London, 1925
Committee on Industry and Trade. *Survey of Metal Industries*, London, 1928
Committee on Industry and Trade. *Survey of Textile Industries* 1928
Department of Employment and Productivity. *British Labour Statistics: Historical Abstract, 1886–1968*, London, 1971
Department of Overseas Trade. *Report on Canada 1933–4*, London, 1934
Department of Overseas Trade. *Report on Economic Conditions in Denmark*, London, 1930–38 (titles vary)
Department of Overseas Trade. *Economic Conditions in Finland*. London, 1931, 1933, 1935, 1938 (titles vary)
Department of Overseas Trade. *Economic and Trade Conditions in Latvia*. London, 1932, 1934, 1935, 1938 (titles vary)
Department of Overseas Trade. *Economic Conditions in Lithuania*. London, 1931, 1935
Department of Overseas Trade. *Economic Conditions in Norway*. London, 1932, 1936, 1938
Department of Overseas Trade. *Economic Conditions in Poland*. London, 1934–1938
Department of Overseas Trade. *Economic Conditions in Sweden*. London, 1932, 1935, 1937, 1939
Imperial Economic Committee. *Dairy Produce Supplies*. London, 1933–1938
Imperial Economic Committee. *Cattle and Beef Survey: A Survey of Production and Trade in British Empire and Foreign Countries*. London, 1934
Imperial Economic Committee. *Meat. A Summary of Figures of Production and Trade Relating to Beef, Mutton, Lamb, Sheep, Bacon, Ham, Port, Cattle, Canned Meat*. London, 1935, 1936
Imperial Economic Committee. *Mutton and Lamb Survey. A Summary of Production and Trade in the Empire and Foreign Countries*. London, 1935
Imperial Economic Committee. *A Survey of the Trade in Electrical Machinery and Apparatus*. London, 1936
Imperial Economic Committee. *A Survey of Trade in Motor Vehicles*. London, 1936
Parliament. *Parliamentary Debates* (Commons). London, 1930, 1932, 1933
Parliament. *Parliamentary Papers. Statistical Abstract for the British Empire, 1929–1938*. London, 1939

United States of America

Department of Commerce. *Survey of Current Business*. Washington, DC August 1982

NEWSPAPERS AND PERIODICALS

Bankers Magazine
Daily Express
The Economist
Manchester Guardian

Manchester Guardian Commercial and Financial Review
The Times

THESES

Alhadeff, P. 'Finance and the economic management of the Argentine government in the 1930s', D. Phil. Thesis, University of Oxford (1983).

Asteris, M. 'Britain and the European coal trade 1919–1939', M. Soc. Sc. Thesis, University of Birmingham (1971).

Beckerman, W. 'Some aspects of monopoly and monopsony in international trade as illustrated by Anglo-Danish trade, 1921–38', Ph. D. Thesis, University of Cambridge (1952).

Capie, F. H. 'The British market for livestock products, 1920–1939', Ph. D. Thesis University of London (1973).

Cooper, A. F. 'The transformation of agricultural policy, 1912–1936: a study of Conservative politics', D. Phil. Thesis, University of Oxford (1979).

Early, E. F. 'The Roca-Runciman Treaty and its significance for Argentina, 1933–41', Ph. D. Thesis, University of London (1981).

Evans, K. 'The development of the overseas trade of the British Empire with particular reference to the period 1870–1939', M. A. Thesis, University of Manchester (1956).

Eyers, J. S. 'Government direction of Britain's overseas trade policy, 1932–37', D. Phil. Thesis, University of Oxford (1977).

Gravil, R. 'The Anglo-Argentine connection: trading relations, 1900–1939', Ph. D. Thesis, CNAA (1974).

Janeway, W. H. 'The economic policy of the second Labour government, 1929–31', Ph. D. Thesis, University of Cambridge (1971).

McCulloch, T. 'Anglo-American economic diplomacy and the European crisis, 1933–1939', D. Phil. Thesis, University of Oxford (1978).

Seymour, S. 'Anglo-Danish relations and Germany: 1933–45', Ph. D. Thesis, University of London (1979).

SECONDARY SOURCES: BOOKS AND ARTICLES

Abbott, G. C. 'A Re-examination of the 1929 Colonial Development Act', *Economic History Review*, 2nd ser., 24 (1971).

Abel, D. *A History of British Tariffs, 1923–1942* (1945).

Ahvenainen, J. 'The competitive position of the Finnish paper industry in the inter-war years', *Scandinavian Economic History Review*, 22 (1974).

Albert, B. and A. Graves (eds.). *The World Sugar Economy in War and Depression, 1914–40* (1988).

Aldcroft, D. H. *The Inter-War Economy: Britain, 1919–1939* (1970).

Aldcroft, D. H. (ed). *The Development of British Industry and Foreign Competition, 1875–1914* (1968).

Aldcroft, D. H. and H. W. Richardson. *The British Economy 1870–1939* (1969).

Alford, B. *Depression and Recovery? British Economic Growth 1918–1939* (1972).

'New industries for old? British industries between the wars', in *The Economic History of Britain since 1700*, II, *1860–1970s*, ed. R. Floud and D. McCloskey (Cambridge, 1981).

Allen, G. C. *A Short Economic History of Japan*, 3rd edn (1972).

Amery, L. S. *My Political Life*, III, *The Unforgiving Years 1929–1940* (1955).

Andersen, P. M. *Danish Exchange Policy, 1919–1939* (Copenhagen, 1942).

Arndt, H. W. *The Economic Lessons of the Nineteen Thirties* (1944).

Astor, Viscount and B. S. Rowntree. *British Agriculture. The Principles of Future Policy* (1938).

Atkin, J. 'Official regulation of British overseas investment 1914–1931', *Economic History Review*, 2nd ser., 23 (1970).

Bairoch, P. 'Europe's gross national product: 1800–1975', *Journal of European Economic History*, 5 (1976).

Barnes, J. and D. Nicholson (eds.) *The Empire at Bay. The Leo Amery Diaries 1929–45* (1988).

Bassett, R. *1931, Political Crisis* (1958).

Beenstock, M. and P. Warburton, 'The market for labor in interwar Britain', *Explorations in Economic History*, 28 (1991).

'Wages and unemployment in interwar Britain', *Explorations in Economic History*, 23 (1986).

Beer, S. H. *Modern British Politics* (1980).

Benham, F. *Great Britain Under Protection* (New York, 1941).

Beveridge, W. H. (ed.). *Tariffs, The Case Examined* (1931, 2nd edn, 1932).

Boyce, R. W. D. *British Capitalism at the Crossroads 1919–1932. A study in politics, economics and international relations* (Cambridge, 1987).

'Insects and international relations: Canada, France and British agricultural "sanitary" restrictions between the wars', *International History Review*, 9 (1987).

Brebner, J. B. *North Atlantic Triangle: The Interplay of Canada, The United States and Great Britain* (New York, 1945).

Brett, E. A. *Colonialism and Underdevelopment in East Africa: The Politics of Economic Change 1919–1939* (1973).

Broadberry, S. N. 'The North European Depression of the 1920s', *Scandinavian Economic History Review*, 32 (1984).

'Unemployment in interwar Britain: a disequilibrium approach', *Oxford Economic Papers*, 35 (1983).

Brunner, K. (ed.). *The Great Depression Revisited* (Boston, 1981).

Bullock, A. *The Life and Times of Ernest Bevin*, I, *Trade Union Leader, 1881–1940* (1960).

Burley, K. *British Shipping and Australia 1920–39* (1968).

Burn, D. *The Economic History of Steelmaking 1867–1939: A Study in Competition* (Cambridge, 1940).

Burnham, T. and Hoskins, G. *Iron and Steel in Britain 1870–1930* (1943).

Burton, H. 'The trade diversion episode of the 'thirties', *Australian Outlook*, 22 (1968).

Butlin, N. G. *Australian Domestic Product, Investment and Foreign Borrowing 1861–1938/9* (Cambridge, 1962).

Buxton, N. 'The role of the "new" industries in Britain during the 1930s: a reinterpretation', *Business History Review*, 49 (1975).

Cain, N. and S. Glynn. 'Imperial relations under strain: The British–Australian debt contretemps of 1933', *Australian Economic History Review*, 25 (1985).

Cain, P. J. 'Free trade, protection and the sterling area in the 1930s', Discussion Paper, Institute of Commonwealth Studies (1989).

Cain, P. J. and A. G. Hopkins. 'Gentlemanly capitalism and British expansion overseas, 11: new imperialism, 1850–1945', *Economic History Review*, 2nd ser., 40 (1987).

Cairncross, A. *Home and Foreign Investment 1870–1913* (Cambridge, 1953).

Cairncross, A. and B. Eichengreen. *Sterling in Decline: the devaluations of 1931, 1949, and 1967* (Oxford, 1983).

Capie, F. 'The British tariff and industrial protection in the 1930s', *Economic History Review*, 2nd ser., 31 (1978).

Depression and Protectionism: Britain Between the Wars (1983).

'Effective protection and economic recovery', *Economic History Review*, 44 (1991).

'The pressure for tariff protection in Britain, 1917–31', *Journal of European Economic History*, 9, (1980).

Cassel, G. *The Crisis in the World's Monetary System* (Oxford, 1932).

Chatterji, B. 'Business and politics in the 1930s: Lancashire and the making of the Indo-British Trade Agreement, 1939', *Modern Asian Studies*, 15 (1981).

Clarke, S. V. O. *Central Bank Co-operation 1924–31* (New York, 1967).

The Reconstruction of the International Monetary System: The Attempts of 1922 and 1933 (Princeton, 1973).

Clay, H. *Lord Norman* (1957).

Cooper, A. F. *British Agricultural Policy, 1912–1936. A study in Conservative politics* (Manchester, 1989).

Copland, D. P. and James, C. V. (eds.). *Australian Trade Policy – A Book of Documents 1932–1937* (Sydney, 1937).

Cottrell, P. L. *British Overseas Investment in the Nineteenth Century* (1975).

Cox, R. W. *Production, Power and World Order: social forces in the making of history* (New York, 1987).

Cumpston, I. M. *Lord Bruce of Melbourne* (Melbourne, 1989).

Dales, J. H. *The Protective Tariff in Canada's Development* (Toronto, 1966).

Davenport-Hines, R. P. T. *Dudley Docker. The Life and Times of a Trade Warrior* (Cambridge, 1984).

Dayer, R. A. *Finance and Empire: Sir Charles Addis, 1861–1945* (1988).

de Cecco, M. *Money and Empire: The International Gold Standard, 1890–1914* (Oxford, 1974).

Dewey, C. 'The end of the imperialism of free trade: the eclipse of the Lancashire lobby and the concession of fiscal autonomy to India', in *The Imperial Impact: Studies in the Economic History of Africa and India* ed. C. Dewey and A. G. Hopkins (1978).

Diaz Alejandro, C. F. *Essays on the Economic History of the Argentine Republic* (New Haven, 1970).

Dilks, D. *Three Visitors to Canada: Baldwin, Chamberlain and Churchill* (1985).

Dimsdale, N. H. 'British monetary policy and the exchange rate, 1920–1938', *Oxford Economic Papers* (1981), also published in *The Money Supply and the Exchange Rate*, ed. W. A. Eltis and P. J. N. Sinclair (Oxford, 1981).

'Employment and real wages in the interwar period, *National Institute of Economic Research*, 110 (1984).

Drummond, I. M. *British Economic Policy and the Empire, 1919–1939* (1972).
  The Floating Pound and the Sterling Area, 1931–1939 (Cambridge, 1981).
  Imperial Economic Policy, 1917–1939: Studies in expansion and protection (1974).
Drummond, I. M. and N. Hillmer. *Negotiating Freer Trade: The United Kingdom, the United States, Canada and the Trade Agreements of 1938* (Waterloo, Ontario, 1989).
Duncan, R. 'The Australian beef export trade and the origins of the Australian Meat Board', *The Australian Journal of Politics and History*, 5 (1959).
  'The Australian export trade with the United Kingdom in refrigerated beef, 1880–1940', *Business Archives and History*, 2 (1962).
Dupree, M. (ed.). *Lancashire and Whitehall. The Diary of Sir Raymond Streat*, 2 vols. (Manchester, 1987).
Edwards, C. *Bruce of Melbourne* (1965).
Egerer, G. 'Protection and imperial preference in Britain: the case of wheat 1925–1960', *Canadian Journal of Economic and Political Science*, 31 (1965).
Eichengreen, B. J. *Sterling and the Tariff 1929–32*. Princeton Studies in International Finance, no. 48, 1981.
Elbaum, B. and W. Lazonick (eds.). *The Decline of the British Economy* (Oxford, 1986).
Eldridge, C. (ed.). *From Rebellion to Patriation: Canada and Britain in the nineteenth and twentieth centuries* (Lampeter, 1989).
Eltis, W. A. and P. J. N. Sinclair (eds.). *The Money Supply and the Exchange Rate* (Oxford, 1981).
English, H. E. *The Role of International Trade in Canadian Economic Development since the 1920s* (Microfilm) California, 1957.
Fairlie, S. 'The nineteenth century Corn Laws reconsidered', *Economic History Review*, 2nd ser., 18 (1965).
Farquharson, J. E. *The Plough and the Swastika: The NSDAP and agriculture in Germany 1928–45* (1976).
Feiling, K. G. *The Life of Neville Chamberlain* (1946).
Feinstein, C. H. *National Income, Expenditure and Output of the United Kingdom, 1855–1965* (Cambridge, 1972).
Feis, H. *1933: Characters in Crisis* (Boston, 1966).
  Europe, The World's Banker, 1870–1914 (New Haven, 1930).
Ferns, H. S. *Argentina* (1969).
Ford, A. G. *The Gold Standard 1880–1914: Britain and Argentina* (Oxford, 1962).
Foreman-Peck, J. 'The British tariff and industrial protection in the 1930s: an alternative model', *Economic History Review*, 2nd ser., 34 (1981).
Freidel, F. *Franklin D. Roosevelt: Launching the New Deal* (Boston, 1973).
Gardner, L. C. *Economic Aspects of New Deal Diplomacy* (Madison, 1964).
Garside, W. R. *British Unemployment, 1919–1939: a study in public policy* (Cambridge, 1990).
  'The north-eastern coalfield and the export trade, 1919–1939', *Durham University Journal*, 83 (1969).
Gilbert, M. *Winston S. Churchill*, V, *1922–39* (1976).
Gilpin, R. *American Power and the Multinationals: the political economy of foreign investment* (New York, 1975).

The Political Economy of International Relations (Princeton, 1987).

Goodwin, Jr. P. B. 'Anglo-Argentine commercial relations: a private sector view 1922–43', *Hispanic American Historical Review*, 61 (1981).

Gould, J. D. *Economic Growth and History: survey and analysis* (London, 1972).

Granatstein, J. L. *A Man of Influence: Norman Robertson and Canadian statecraft, 1928–1968* (Ottawa, 1981).

Gravil, R. *The Anglo-Argentine Connection, 1900–1939* (Colorado, 1985).

Gravil R. and T. Rooth. 'A time of acute dependence: Argentina in the 1930s', *Journal of European Economic History*, 7 (1978).

Gregory, R. G. and N. G. Butlin (eds.). *Recovery from the Depression: Australia and the world economy in the 1930s* (Cambridge, 1988).

Gupta, P. S. *Imperialism and the British Labour Movement, 1914–1964* (1975).

Habakkuk, H. J. *American and British Technology in the Nineteenth Century: the search for labour saving inventions* (Cambridge, 1962).

Hall, A. R. (ed.). *The Export of Capital from Britain, 1870–1914* (1968).

Hall, N. F. 'Trade diversion – an Australian interlude', *Economica*, n.s., 5 (1938).

Hancock, K. J. 'The reduction of employment as a problem of public policy 1920–29', *Economic History Review*, 2nd ser., 15 (1962).

Hancock, W. K. *Survey of British Commonwealth Affairs*, II, *Problems of Economic Policy 1918–1939*, pt. 1 (Oxford, 1942).

Hannah, L. 'Managerial innovation and the rise of the large-scale company in interwar Britain', *Economic History Review*, 2nd ser., 27 (1974).

Harberger, A. C. 'Some evidence on the international price mechanism', *Journal of Political Economy*, 65 (1957).

Harris, J. *William Beveridge: a biography* (Oxford, 1977).

Hatton, T. J. 'Perspectives on the economic recovery of the 1930s', *Royal Bank of Scotland Review*, 158 (1988).

'The recovery of the 1930s and economic policy in Britain', in *Recovery from the Depression: Australia and the world economy in the 1930s* (ed.) R. G. Gregory and N. G. Butlin (Cambridge, 1988).

Hiden, J. *The Baltic States and Weimar Ostpolitik* (Cambridge, 1987).

Hinkkanen-Lievonen, Merja-Liisa. 'Britain as Germany's commercial rival in the Baltic states 1919–1939' in *From Competition to Rivalry: the Anglo-German Relationship with countries at the European Periphery, 1919–1939*, ed. Marie-Luise Recker (Stuttgart, 1986).

British Trade and Enterprise in the Baltic States, 1919–1925 (Helsinki, 1984).

'Exploited by Britain? The problems of British financial presence in the Baltic states after the First World War', *Journal of Baltic Studies*, 14 (1983).

Hirschman, A. O. *National Power and the Structure of Foreign Trade* (Berkeley and Los Angeles, 1945).

Hobsbawm, E. J. *Industry and Empire* (1968).

Holland, R. F. *Britain and the Commonwealth Alliance 1918–1939* (1981).

'The Federation of British Industries and the international economy 1929–39', *Economic History Review*, 2nd ser., 34 (1981).

Houghton, D. H. and Dagut, J. *Source Material on the South African Economy 1860–1970*, III (Cape Town, 1973).

Howson, S. *Domestic Monetary Management in Britain, 1919–1938* (Cambridge, 1975).

'The origins of dear money 1919–20', *Economic History Review*, 2nd ser., 27 (1974).

Sterling's Managed Float: the operations of the exchange equalisation account, 1932–39 Princeton Studies in International Finance, 46, 1980.

Howson, S. and D. Winch. *The Economic Advisory Council, 1930–1939* (Cambridge, 1975).

Hubbard, G. E. *Eastern Industrialisation and its Effect on the West* (1935).

Hughes, H. *The Australian Iron and Steel Industry, 1848–1962* (Melbourne, 1964).

Hull, C. *The Memoirs of Cordell Hull*, I (1948).

Imlah, J. A. H. *Economic Elements in the Pax Britannica: Studies in British foreign trade in the nineteenth century* (Cambridge, 1958).

International Institute of Agriculture. *World Trade in Agricultural Products, its Growth, its Crisis and the New Trade Policies* (Rome, 1940).

Jebb, H. M. G. *The Memoirs of Lord Gladwyn* (1972).

Johnson, D. G. 'The nature of the supply function for agricultural products', *American Economic Review* 40 (1950).

Kahn, A. E. *Great Britain in the World Economy* (New York, 1946).

Kaiser, D. E. *Economic Diplomacy and the Origins of the Second World War. Germany, Britain, France and Eastern Europe, 1930–1939* (Princeton, 1980).

Kelly, Ruth. 'Foreign trade of Argentina and Australia, 1930 to 1960', *United Nations, Economic Bulletin for Latin America*, 10 (March 1965, no. 1 and October, 1965, no. 2).

Kennedy, W. P. *Industrial Structure, Capital Markets and the Origins of British Economic Decline* (Cambridge, 1987).

Keynes, J. M. *The Economic Consequences of the Peace* (1919).

Essays in Persuasion (1933; reprinted 1951).

Kindleberger, C. P. 'Competitive currency depreciation between Denmark and New Zealand', *Harvard Business Review*, 12 (1934).

The Terms of Trade: a European case study (Cambridge, Mass., 1956).

The World in Depression, 1929–1939 (1973).

Kirby, M. W. *The Decline of British Power Since 1870* (1981).

Kitson, M. and S. Solomou. *Protectionism and Economic Revival: the British interwar economy* (Cambridge, 1990).

Kitson, M., S. Solomou and M. Weale. 'Effective protection and economic recovery in the United Kingdom during the 1930s', *Economic History Review*, 44 (1991).

Kottman, R. M. *Reciprocity and the North Atlantic Triangle, 1932–1938* (Ithaca, 1968).

Krasner, Stephen D. 'State power and the structure of international trade', *World Politics*, 28 (1976).

Kreider, C. *The Anglo-American Trade Agreement: a study of British and American commercial policies, 1934–1939* (Princeton, 1943).

Lake, D. A. *Power, Protection and Free Trade. International sources of U.S. commercial strategy, 1887–1939* (1988).

Landau, Z. and J. Tomaszewski. *The Polish Economy in the Twentieth Century* (Beckenham, 1985).

League of Nations. *Europe's Trade* (Geneva, 1941).

International Currency Experience: Lessons of the inter-war period (Geneva, 1944).

International Trade Statistics. 1930–1939 (Geneva, various years).

Network of World Trade (Geneva, 1942).

Review of World Trade, 1934, 1938 (Geneva, 1935, 1939).

Statistical Yearbook 1938/9 (Geneva, 1940).

Lester, R. A. 'The gold parity depression in Norway and Denmark, 1925–1928', *Journal of Political Economy* 45 (1937).

Liepmann, H. *Tariff Levels and the Economic Unity of Europe* (1938).

MacDonald, C. A. 'Economic appeasement and the German "Moderates" 1937–1939', *Past and Present*, 56 (1972).

MacDougall, D. and R. Hutt. 'Imperial preference: a quantitative analysis', *Economic Journal*, 64 (1954).

MacGibbon, D. A. *The Canadian Grain Trade 1931–51* (Toronto, 1952).

Macleod, Iain. *Neville Chamberlain* (1961).

Maddison, A. 'Growth and fluctuations in the world economy 1870–1960', *Banca Nazionale del Lavoro Quarterly Review*, 15 (1962).

Maier, C. S. 'Between Taylorism and technocracy: European ideologies and the vision of industrial productivity in the 1920s', *Contemporary History*, 5 (1970).

Maizels, A. *Industrial Growth and World Trade* (Cambridge, 1963), new edn, *Growth and Trade* (1970).

Malenbaum, W. *The World Wheat Economy, 1885–1939* (Cambridge, Mass., 1951).

Marquand, D. *Ramsay MacDonald* (1977).

Marrison, A. J. 'Businessmen, industries and tariff reform in Great Britain, 1903–1930', *Business History*, 25 (1983).

Matthews, R. C. O., C. H. Feinstein, and J. C. Odling-Smee. *British Economic Growth 1856–1973* (Oxford, 1982).

Megaw, M. R. 'Australia and the Anglo-American Trade Agreement of 1938', *Journal of Imperial and Commonwealth History*, 3 (1975).

Melchett, Lord. *Imperial Economic Unity* (1930).

Meredith, D. 'The British government and colonial economic policy, 1919–39', *Economic History Review*, 2nd ser., 28 (1975).

Meyer, F. V. *Britain, the Sterling Area and Europe* (Cambridge, 1952).

International Trade Policy (1978).

Meynell, Dame Alix. *Public Servant, Private Woman: an autobiography* (1988).

Middlemas, K. and Barnes, J. *Baldwin, A Biography* (1969).

Middleton, R. 'The constant employment budget balance and British budgetary policy, 1929–39', *Economic History Review*, 2nd ser., 34 (1981).

Towards the Managed Economy (1985).

Mitchell, B. R. and Deane, P. *Abstract of British Historical Statistics* (Cambridge, 1962).

Moggridge, D. E. *British Monetary Policy 1924–31: The Norman conquest of $4·86* (Cambridge, 1972).

Nakamura, T. 'The Japanese economy in the interwar period: a brief summary', *Japan and the World Depression: Then and Now* ed. R. Dore and R. Sinha (New York, 1987).

National Institute of Economic and Social Research. *Trade Regulations and Commercial Policy of the United Kingdom* (Cambridge, 1943).

Nicholson, D. F. *Australia's Trade Relations* (Melbourne, 1955).

O'Rourke, K. 'Burn everything but their coal: the Anglo-Irish economic war of the 1930s', *Journal of Economic History* 51 (1991).

Political and Economic Planning. *Report on International Trade* (1937).

Pollard, S. 'Capital exports, 1870–1914: harmful or beneficial?', *Economic History Review*, 2nd ser., 37 (1985).

Pressnell, L. S. '1925: The burden of sterling', *Economic History Review*, 2nd ser., 31 (1978).

Prichard, M. F. Lloyd. *An Economic History of New Zealand to 1939* (Auckland, 1970).

Ramsden, John. *A History of the Conservative Party: the age of Balfour and Baldwin 1902–1940* (1978).

Randall, Laura. *An Economic History of Argentina in the Twentieth Century* (New York, 1978).

Ratcliffe, B. M. (ed.). *Great Britain and Her World, 1750–1914. Essays in honour of W. O. Henderson* (Manchester, 1975).

Raumolin, J. 'Natural resources exploitation and problems of staple-based industrialisation in Finland and Canada', *Fenna*, 163: 2 (1985).

Redford, Arthur. *Manchester Merchants and Foreign trade*, II, *1850–1939* (Manchester, 1956).

Redmond, J. 'An indicator of the effective exchange rate of the pound in the nineteen-thirties', *Economic History Review*, 2nd. ser., 33 (1980).

Reitsma, A. J. *Trade Protection in Australia* (Leiden, 1960).

Reuber, G. L. *Britain's Export Trade with Canada* (Toronto, 1960).

Richardson, H. W. *Economic Recovery in Britain, 1932–1939* (1967).

'Overcommitment in Britain before 1930', *Oxford Economic Papers*, 17 (1965).

Richardson, J. H. *British Economic Foreign Policy* (1936).

Robertson, Alex J. 'Lancashire and the rise of Japan, 1910–1937', in *International Competition and Strategic Response in the Textile Industries since 1870*, ed. Mary B. Rose, (1991).

Robertson, D. H. 'The future of international trade', *Economic Journal*, 48 (1938).

Rock, David P. (ed.). *Argentina in the Twentieth Century* (1975).

Rooth, T. 'Britain and Canada between two wars: the economic dimension', in *From Rebellion to Patriation: Canada and Britain in the nineteenth and twentieth centuries*, ed. C. C. Eldridge (Lampeter, 1989).

'Imperial preference and Anglo-Canadian trade relations in the 1930s – the end of an illusion?', *British Journal of Canadian Studies*, 1 (1986).

'Limits of leverage: the Anglo-Danish Trade Agreement of 1933', *Economic History Review*, 2nd ser., 37 (1984).

'Trade agreements and the evolution of British agricultural policy in the 1930s', *Agricultural History Review*, 33 (1985).

'Trade and trade bargaining: Anglo-Scandinavian economic relations in the 1930s', *Scandinavian Economic History Review*, 34 (1986).

Rose, N. *Vansittart, Study of a diplomat* (1978).

Rowland, B. M. (ed.). *Balance of Power or Hegemony: the interwar monetary system* (New York, 1976).

Royal Institute of International Affairs. *The Baltic States. A Survey of the Political and Economic Structure and Foreign Relations of Estonia, Latvia and Lithuania* (1938).

The Problem of International Investment (1937).

The Scandinavian States and Finland (1951).

Russell, Ronald S. *Imperial Preference: its development and effects* (1947).

Safarian, A. E. *The Canadian Economy in the Great Depression* (Toronto, 1970).

Salmon, P. 'Polish-British competition in the coal markets of Northern Europe, 1927–1934', *Studia Historiae Oeconomicae*, 16 (1983).

Sandberg, L. G. *Lancashire in Decline: a study in entrepreneurship, technology and international trade* (Columbus, 1974).

Saul, S. B. *The Myth of the Great Depression* (1969).

Studies in British Overseas Trade, 1870–1914 (Liverpool, 1960).

Saville, J. 'Review article: The development of British industry and foreign competition 1875–1914', *Business History*, 12 (1970).

'Some retarding factors in the British economy before 1914', *Yorkshire Bulletin of Economic and Social Research*, 13 (1961).

Saxonhouse, G. R. 'Productivity change and labour absorption in Japanese cotton spinning, 1891–1935', *Quarterly Journal of Economics*, 91 (1977).

Saxonhouse, G. R. and G. Wright. 'New evidence on the stubborn English mule and the cotton industry, 1878–1920', *Economic History Review*, 2nd ser., 37 (1984).

Sayers, R. S. *The Bank of England 1891–1944*, II (Cambridge, 1976).

Schatz, George. 'The Anglo-American Trade Agreement and Cordell Hull's search for peace, 1936–1938', *The Journal of American History*, 57 (1970).

Schedvin, C. B. *Australia and the Great Depression* (Sydney, 1970).

Schlesinger, A. M. *The Age of Roosevelt* (Boston, 1959).

Schlote, W. *British Overseas Trade from 1700 to the 1930s*, translated by W. O. Henderson and W. H. Chaloner (Oxford, 1952).

Schmidt, G. *The Politics and Economics of Appeasement. British foreign policy in the 1930s* (Leamington Spa, 1987).

Scott, M. Fg. *A Study of United Kingdom Imports* (Cambridge, 1963).

Shimizu, Hiroshi. *Anglo-Japanese Trade Rivalry in the Middle East in the Inter-War Period* (1986).

Sinclair, Keith. *A History of New Zealand* (1969).

Skidelsky, Robert. *Politicians and the Slump: The Labour Government of 1929–1931* (1967).

Smith, Peter H. *Politics and Beef in Argentina: patterns of conflict and change* (1969).

Snowden, Philip. *An Autobiography*, II, *1919–34* (1934).

Street, S. 'The Hays Office and the defence of the British market in the 1930s', *Historical Journal of Film, Radio and Television*, 5 (1985).

Svennilson, I. *Growth and Stagnation in the European Economy*, United Nations Economic Commission for Europe (Geneva, 1954).

Taylor, J. *The Economic Development of Poland, 1919–1950* (Ithaca, 1950, reprinted Connecticut, 1970).

Teichova, A. *An Economic Background to Munich: international business and Czechoslovakia 1918–1938* (Cambridge, 1974).

Thomas, B. *Migration and Economic Growth: a study of Great Britain and the Atlantic Economy* (2nd edn Cambridge, 1973).

Thomas, M. 'Rearmament and economic recovery in the late 1930s', *Economic History Review* 2nd ser., 36 (1983).

Thompson, J. H. and A. Seager. *Canada 1922–1939: decades of discord* (Toronto, 1985).

Thomsen, B. N. and B. Thomas. *Anglo-Danish Trade 1661–1963: a historical survey* (Aarhus, 1963).

Tolliday, S. *Business, Banking and Politics: the case of British steel, 1918–1939* (Cambridge, Mass., 1987).

Tomlinson, B. R. 'Britain and the Indian currency crisis, 1930–32', *Economic History Review*, 2nd ser., 32 (1979).

Tomlinson, Jim. *Problems of British Economic Policy, 1870–1945* (1981).

Trotter, A. *Britain and East Asia 1933–1937* (Cambridge, 1975).

Tsokhas, K. *Markets, Money and Empire. The political economy of the Australian wool industry* (Melbourne, 1990).

Tsutomi, Ouchi. 'Agricultural depression and Japanese villages', *The Developing Economies*, 5 (1967).

Turner, B. S. *Free Trade and Protection* (1971).

Tyszynski, H. 'World trade in manufactured commodities, 1899–1950', *Manchester School of Economic and Social Studies*, 19 (1951).

Vaizey, John. *The History of British Steel* (1974).

von Tunzlemann, G. 'Structural change and leading sectors in British manufacturing, 1907–68', in *Economics in the Long View: Essays in honour of W. W. Rostow* (ed.) C. P. Kindleberger and G. di Tella (1982).

Warriner, D. *Economics of Peasant Farming* (Oxford, 1939, London 1964).

Waswo, A. 'Origins of tenant unrest', in *Japan in Crisis: Essays on Taisho democracy*, ed. B. S. Silberman and H. D. Harootunian (Princeton 1974).

Webber, A. 'Cereals production and policy, 1921–39: the background to the International Trade Agreements Policy of the 1930s', The City University, Centre for Banking and International Finance, Discussion Papers Series, no. 59.

Whetham, E. H. *The Agrarian History of England and Wales*, VIII (Cambridge, 1978).

Wicker, Elmus R. 'Federal Reserve monetary policy 1922–33: a re-interpretation', *Journal of Political Economy*, (1965).

Wilkins, M. *The Maturing of Multinational Enterprise: American business abroad from 1914 to 1970* (1974).

Wilson, C. F. *A Century of Canadian Grain: government policy to 1951* (Saskatoon, 1978).

Winch, D. *Economics and Policy, A Historical Study* (1972).

'The Keynesian revolution in Sweden', *Journal of Political Economy*, 74 (1966).

Yates, P. L. *Forty Years of Foreign Trade* (1955).

Zelder, R. E. 'Estimates of elasticities of demand for exports of the United Kingdom and the United States, 1921–1938', *Manchester School of Economic and Social Studies*, 26 (1958).

Index

347